INDIGENOUS COSMOLECTICS

CRITICAL INDIGENEITIES

J. Kēhaulani Kauanui and Jean M. O'Brien,
series editors

SERIES ADVISORY BOARD

Chris Anderson, University of Alberta

Irene Watson, University of South Australia

Emilio del Valle Escalante,
University of North Carolina at Chapel Hill

Kim TallBear, University of Texas at Austin

Critical Indigeneities publishes pathbreaking scholarly books that center Indigeneity as a category of critical analysis, understand Indigenous sovereignty as ongoing and historically grounded, and attend to diverse forms of Indigenous cultural and political agency and expression. The series builds on the conceptual rigor, methodological innovation, and deep relevance that characterize the best work in the growing field of critical Indigenous studies.

 # Indigenous Cosmolectics

Kab'awil and the Making of
Maya and Zapotec Literatures

GLORIA ELIZABETH CHACÓN

THE UNIVERSITY OF NORTH CAROLINA PRESS
CHAPEL HILL

© 2018 The University of North Carolina Press
All rights reserved
Manufactured in the United States of America

Designed by April Leidig
Set in Minion by Copperline Book Services, Inc.

The University of North Carolina Press has been a member of the Green Press Initiative since 2003.

Cover illustrations: background, Adobe Stock image © Andril Pokaz; foreground, based on a photograph of a Mayan flint that some scholars identify with kab'awil. The flint was found in a burial behind one of the longest hieroglyph texts in Copan, a Mayan ceremonial center in Honduras.

Library of Congress Cataloging-in-Publication Data
Names: Chacón, Gloria Elizabeth, author.
Title: Indigenous cosmolectics : kab'awil and the making of Maya and Zapotec literatures / Gloria Elizabeth Chacón.
Other titles: Critical indigeneities.
Description: Chapel Hill : The University of North Carolina Press, [2018] | Series: Critical indigeneities | Includes bibliographical references and index.
Identifiers: LCCN 2018004677 | ISBN 9781469636757 (cloth : alk. paper) | ISBN 9781469636795 (pbk : alk. paper) | ISBN 9781469636825 (ebook)
Subjects: LCSH: Maya literature—History and criticism. | Zapotec literature—History and criticism. | Mexican literature—Indian authors—History and criticism. | Central American literature—Indian authors—History and criticism.
Classification: LCC PM3968 .C43 2018 | DDC 897/.42709—dc23
LC record available at https://lccn.loc.gov/2018004677

Portions of the introduction and chapter 5 appeared earlier in somewhat different form in Gloria Chacón, "Contested Histories: Indigenista Literature and the Rise of Contemporary Indigenous Literatures," in *The Routledge History of Latin American Culture*, ed. Carlos Salomon (New York: Routledge, 2017). Portions of chapter 3 are based on Gloria Chacón, "Cultivating Nichimal K'op (Poetry) from the Heart: Indigenous Women of Chiapas," in "K'óoben: Subjetividades indígenas en la literatura latinoamericana: Antiguas paradojas y nuevos enfoques," special issue, *Revista Canadiense de Estudios Hispánicos* 39, no. 1 (2004): 165–80; and Gloria Chacón, "Cuerpo y poesía: Transgresiones culturales en el trabajo de mujeres mayas," in *Poéticas y políticas de género: Ensayos sobre imaginarios, literaturas y medios en Centroamérica*, ed. Monica Albizúrez Gil and Alexandra Ortiz Wallner (Berlin: Tranvía, Walter Frey, 2013), 269–83.

To my son, Nawal,
amor que brotó
de mi corazón

CONTENTS

ix Preface: "Bilanguaging" Indigenous Texts

1 Introduction: Sculpting Cosmolectics

25 Chapter One. Literacy and Power in Mesoamerica

45 Chapter Two. The Formation of the Contemporary Mesoamerican Author

69 Chapter Three. Indigenous Women, Poetry, and the Double Gaze

103 Chapter Four. Contemporary Maya Women's Theater

125 Chapter Five. The Novel in Zapotec and Maya Lands

153 Epilogue: Inverting the Gaze from California

159 Acknowledgments

161 Notes

197 Bibliography

237 Index

PREFACE: "BILANGUAGING" INDIGENOUS TEXTS

Every time you speak an indigenous language, you resist. To speak an indigenous language, in the present circumstances, is to inhabit a cognitive territory that has not yet been conquered, at least not all of it. (Cada vez que hablas una lengua indígena, resistes. Hablar una lengua indígena, en las circunstancias presentes, es habitar un territorio cognitivo que todavía no ha sido conquistado, al menos no del todo.)—Yásnaya Elena Aguilar Gil (Mixe 2015)

THE INDIGENOUS EXPERIENCE with bilingual productions diverges considerably from twentieth century philosophical theories on the subject of translation. The task of *auto-traducción* or self-translation, an indispensable undertaking for many Maya and Zapotec writers and other art practitioners, correlates, in part, to the political status indigenous languages hold within nation-states. Indigenous writers are compelled to translate onto the dominant Spanish language, to authorize themselves in other cultural venues, but also to make their works accessible to a wider audience. Although not every cultural product is published or articulated in an indigenous language, the questions of translation and language are exceedingly relevant in discussions of indigeneity and literature. History has not been kind to translators in Latin America, trying them as either traitors or mediators (i.e., La Malinche or a cultural informant). In either role, the translator continues to represent a highly polemical and controversial figure, shrouded in ambiguity. Pertaining to the bilingual productions of indigenous textualities, simultaneous translations often veer from standard adaptive intentions to conclude as alternatives to an original text, making authors fret that the spirit of their pieces is lost in translation.[1] While, according to Walter Benjamin, translation is "a mode [in which] one must go back to the original, for that contains the law governing the translation: its translatability," self-translating involves a laborious navigation of the linguistic intricacies between two versions.[2] The process also enables writers to cast what I call "a double gaze," a method that must account for two particular linguistic and diverse cultural codes. The term *pulsadores* (*pik'ch 'ich'*), for example, refers to elders who can read and interpret an individual's blood and diagnose disease. This is also a challenge when translating from Spanish to the indigenous language. Hence, translation is relentlessly struggling against the tensions of history. This incessant movement from the borderless land of an old and yet continuously evolving language to the more restrictive parameters of another offers unparalleled opportunities for the writers to articulate an indigenous ontology. An ordinary greeting such as *Bix a wanii*? (How are you?), requires embedding cultural precepts in the translation from the Maya Yukatek to Spanish. That is because the question literally asks, "How do you hear today?" The issue is ultimately about the sensory awareness of being, bringing the senses in a double gaze that reaches out to the world, drawing from within.

Another fundamental way this process differs, to return to Benjamin's work, is the proposal that "translation comes later than the original" and that "important works of world literature never find their chosen translators at the time of their origin, their translation marks their stage of continued life," as it has little bearing on the process of self-translation.[3] It also diverges from bilingualism in Latino literatures, where Spanish is interspersed or peppered in English-language texts. The process of translation empowers the writers to fully exploit the potential strengths and complexities of language. Of course, not all indigenous practitioners write or publish in their respective indigenous languages. This reality inevitably leads to another serious set of questions. What is the function of Spanish? What happens when the indigenous writer expresses himself or herself solely in Spanish? Do linguistic traces remain? I think so. Nonetheless, the issues that emerge from the process bilingual indigenous writers undergo require considerable contemplation.

Between 2003 and 2010, I attended various workshops in Chiapas and in Mexico City, where the participants were captivated by these concerns. In 2004, Waldemar Noh Tzec, a Maya Yukatek poet and teacher, led one of the organized workshops in Chiapas. He began by insisting that indigenous writers should familiarize themselves with the linguistic sensibilities that traverse their respective indigenous languages. Noh Tzec emphasized that "[indigenous writers] need to defend the uniqueness of [their] languages," but he also noted the importance of the Spanish language.[4] He advised participants to explore the rich poetic legacy of indigenous languages and use Western tools to produce the aesthetic effect sought after. Noh Tzec reviewed poetic terms like metaphors, alliteration, and similes. He cautioned us to differentiate between metaphors that sounded innovative and evolving in their Spanish translation but that were stagnant in the indigenous language. In Noh Tzec's estimation, the process invites indigenous writers to innovate indigenous languages as well. Shortly thereafter, a fascinating discussion ensued about the rich metaphorical content in the Maya languages: a term like *yat kok* for example, could mean "flame" or "penis," depending on the context.

Other significant interventions included those by José Antonio Matamoros Reyes, a Ladino writer, who shared his experiences by conducting creative writing workshops with Tsotsil and Tseltal writers.[5] He anthologized the pieces created through this process in *Sbel sjol yo'nton ik'/ Memoria del viento*. The writers involved in this project, who were also present at the workshop, discussed the challenges they faced in creating sonnets and other forms in Tsotsil by writing them first in Spanish and then undertaking the challenge to replicate the same rhythm in the indigenous language. Matamoros Reyes writes: "the problem was . . . of rigor in the translation: as if the characteristics of poetry in other Mayan languages just barely opened the field."[6] Reversing the process — creating first in Spanish, then translating into the indigenous languages — added another dimension to the poetic landscape of indigenous languages. The participants asserted that this type of experimental work is needed to exploit their languages' poetic distinctiveness.

Several years later, in 2010, the National Council for Culture and Art or Conaculta (Consejo Nacional para la Cultura y las Artes) organized the first Mayan and Zapotec literary gathering. The Mazatec writer Juan Gregorio Regino, the first indigenous writer to work for this prestigious institution, organized the event. Though the meeting was strictly for the writers, a few of us observers had the privilege to attend the various sessions. The general thrust of the meeting was to think about these literatures as constituting two distinct literary traditions. Some of the most prominent Maya and Zapotec writers discussed their creative processes. Irma Santiago Pineda (Zapotec) described how the rhythmic patterns of the poem and its translation move in parallel trajectories that stay faithful to their original course. Sharing her process, Natalia Toledo (Zapotec) admits to utilizing various methods, including drawing words as well as writing simultaneously in both languages.

Offering a very different perspective, Javier Castellanos Martínez (Zapotec) argued that indigenous literature should not be reduced to language.[7] He is focused on the title of a poetry anthology, *Volcán de pétalos* (Volcano of petals), published in 1996 by the Zapotec writer Mario Molina, to demonstrate his point. "It is also not enough just to translate," Castellanos said, "because anything can be translated. One can search for a similar meaning in another language, but immediately one notices that something is wrong, for example, in the phrase *Volcano of Petals*."[8] Castellanos focused on the complexity of translation, which addresses a lexicon via other disciplines that have not been integrated in indigenous languages.

> This phrase (volcano of petals) reminds us of a volcano that erupts and — instead of spewing lava, smoke, and ash — spews not flowers but petals, which is undoubtedly a beautiful image. In my region there are no volcanoes, which are only known in textbooks or on TV, and when people speak in Zapotec, they say "volcan" without the accent [in the standard Spanish *volcán*] and, for what volcanoes expel, say, *dxichen*, that it shits, that it wastes. Further, in this region the parts of a flower in all its components have not been linguistically broken down, as in Spanish, so the translation would be: *volcan dxichen yej* (a volcano that shits flowers) but the indigenous writer manages to make this translation from *Ya' byalhje xtak yej*, which means "the mountain from which flower petals emerged," which is a pretty expression, but it is not what people say in Spanish or Zapotec — what he says is not what is translated into Spanish.[9]

This type of translation inadequacy is not due to incompetence in the Spanish language; rather, it underlines the difficulties facing indigenous languages as writers translate and make their works legible in Spanish.

In his contribution to the debate, the Maya writer Jorge Cocom Pech synthesized the pressure on indigenous writers for translation. I speak of pressure since indigenous writers are expected to translate their work into Spanish in order to be recognized as authors. Cocom Pech proposes that "a writer in an indigenous language, or in any language, who self-translates, should have four skills: proficiency in their mother tongue; proficiency in the language to which they will translate the original text, the terminal language; competence in the methodology of translation; and, derived from this, competence in literary, lyrical, narrative, or dramatic writing; and no more. Essay writing is a different matter."[10] His list demonstrates that the indigenous writer has to assume multiple functions not required of nonindigenous writers.

I base the majority of my literary analysis on the self-translated Spanish versions, or those published exclusively in Spanish, but I do consider some knowledge of the indigenous languages in which the work is presented to be pertinent, even critical, to the study of this literature. For me, that has entailed formally and informally studying Maya K'iche', Maya Tsotsil, and Yukatek Maya. That said, my language experience with Zapotec has been limited to listening to the poets read and speak about their process of creating and translating their literary works. Needless to say, my study of Maya and Zapotec literatures has immensely benefited from my linguistic knowledge and, more so, from having cultivated friendships with the various writers and other "cultural agents."[11] The production of Maya and Zapotec literatures assumes a politicized position in the preservation of these languages. Translation adds another constructive dimension to the writers' roles as organic intellectuals. In Guatemala, the linguistic academic group Oxlajuuj Keej Maya' Ajtz'iib' (OKMA), or the Thirteen Deer Maya Writers, asserts in its publication that literature is a crucial component in the cultivation of Maya languages: "To write novels, poems, news, or posters in Mayan languages is a way of assuring the survival of the languages."[12]

By delving into this context about translation, I underscore the dynamics involved in examining much of what has been produced by contemporary Maya and Zapotec writers and other indigenous intellectuals in Mesoamerica. The complex questions generated by indigenous language production cut across literary studies, Latin American studies, and indigenous studies, but also to the discipline of translation studies — a field that Lawrence Venuti concedes tends to focus almost exclusively on international languages such as English.[13] How and why did these indigenous artistic movements emerge? What does this corpus say about indigeneity, epistemology, gender, and autonomy and politics in Mesoamerica? What is the relationship between what I propose as an indigenous cosmolectics manifested by *kab'awil* (translated as the "double gaze") and ontology in relationship to literary and other artistic productions? The rest of this book sets out to answer these questions and tells the story of the emergence of indigenous cultural producers, who rose from a symbiotic relationship between "glyphing" the cosmos to writing everyday reality in Mesoamerica.

INDIGENOUS COSMOLECTICS

INTRODUCTION

Sculpting Cosmolectics

Ser indígena es poseer un universo y nunca renunciar a él.
(To be indigenous is to possess a universe and refuse to give it up.)
—Natalia Toledo Paz (Zapotec poet, 2002)

Estar inmerso en una lengua y cultura que nos permite ver al mundo con otros ojos, nos impulsa a resistir y re-existir, ahí radica el resurgimiento. (To be immersed in another language and culture allows us to see the world with different eyes, it propels us to resist and re-exist, therein lies the resurgence.)—Isaac Esau Carrillo Can (Maya poet, 2013)

Al cabo de cinco siglos de discriminación social, alienación cultural, explotación económica y opresión política, con orgullo indígena, evoquemos nuestro glorioso pasado y reafirmemos nuestra vocación de lucha por conservar y desarrollar nuestra propia identidad desde nuestro quehacer literario. (After five centuries of social discrimination, cultural alienation, economic exploitation and political oppression, with indigenous pride, we evoke our glorious past and reaffirm our vocation of struggle to conserve and develop our identity through our literary work.)—Dagoberto Huanosto Cerano (Purépecha writer, 1992)

THE NUMEROUS PROTESTS by indigenous peoples in the Americas against celebrations of the Columbian quincentenary in the 1990s coincided with my early political, cultural, and intellectual development. The Five-College Consortium, in the Pioneer Valley of western Massachusetts, where my higher education trajectory began, freed up spaces for indigenous intellectuals from various parts of the continent to share their histories of resistance to the obstinate conditions of colonization.[1] These experiences established the groundwork for my critical thinking about history, writing, and indigeneity, including questions concerning culture and epistemology. These issues would continue to inspire the academic interests that motivated the writing of this book.

In 2003, I volunteered and engaged in research at the Mexico City–based National Indigenous Writers Association (Escritores en Lenguas Indígenas, Asociación Civil, ELIAC). I immediately realized that the endeavors of indigenous writers rarely ended with the publication of books. Their duties included teaching, speaking at local schools, and organizing events, as well as readings in indigenous communities and other venues, among various other responsibilities. The day the Canadian embassy called to invite the organization to an international writers conference we also learned that the General Society of Writers in Mexico (Sociedad General de Escritores de México, SOGEM) and PEN International Mexico were hosting the conference. These prestigious national literary entities had not considered the Indigenous Writers Association significant enough to participate. Homero Aridjis, an internationally renowned Mexican writer, presided over both establishments at the time.[2] Disregarding the Indigenous Writers Association confirmed its peripheral status in what the literary critic Pascale Casanova calls the "Republic of Letters." Casanova asserts that there "exists a literature-world, a literary universe relatively independent of the everyday world and its political divisions, whose boundaries and operational laws are not reducible to those of ordinary political space. Exerted within this international literary space are relations of force and a violence peculiar to them.... [This domination should not be] confused with the forms of political domination, even though it may in many respects be dependent upon them."[3] Aridjis's omission spoke volumes about the elitism contemporary indigenous authors and other artists feel compelled to challenge as they navigate the Republic of Letters. He had not anticipated that the Canadian embassy—at the appeal of indigenous writers from Canada—would invite the Indigenous Writers Association to the international gathering. Poetic justice or not, it motivated the Indigenous Writers Association's then-president, Maya writer Jorge Cocom Pech, to publicly confront Aridjis about the exclusion during the lavish gathering in Mexico City's *ayuntamiento* (city hall)—an event attended by many official government representatives, including presidential candidate Manuel López Obrador. The incident brought an immediate response from international intellectuals and writers at the conference (which had linguistic diversity at its central theme): the PEN members voted to seek the participation of indigenous writers from Latin America at every future congress, regardless of the country hosting the meeting.

Another international event that reflected the political aura literature has assumed for indigenous peoples was the 2004 refusal of Maya K'iche' poet Humberto Ak'abal to accept Guatemala's Miguel Ángel Asturias National

Literary Prize. Ak'abal announced that he would decline the award, named after one of Latin America's most canonical writers, due to the racism permeating Asturias's early writing. Ak'abal cited Asturias's senior thesis (1923), which claims that "Indians" are an inherently inferior race and an obstacle to the nation's social progress. The thesis was honored by the University of San Carlos and its School of Law, reflecting the dominant society's racist attitudes toward indigenous peoples in the 1920s.[4] Ak'abal's action inspired the winner of the next year's prize, Rodrigo Rey Rosa, a Ladino, to donate his monetary award to efforts to foment literary publications in languages other than Spanish.[5] The funds helped establish the B'atz' Literary Prize to support indigenous language publications. Pablo García and Miguel Ángel Oxlaj Cúmez were the first recipients of this prize in 2007 with their books *B'ixonik tzij kech juk'ulaj kaminaqib'/Canto palabra de una pareja de muertos* and *Ru taqkil ri Sarima'/La misión del Sarimá*, respectively. Both events represent a critical shift for the indigenous writers in the Republic of Letters. In fact, not long ago, eminent Latin American critics expressed skepticism over whether indigenous literature even existed. Latin America's foundational literary critic, Ángel Rama, once remarked, "Introductions or preambles to literary histories devoted to indigenous literatures make me uncomfortable. I have always found this form of organization a bit mythical, because it is a pipe dream; and I wonder if we are not obeying a kind of dominant chronology: they were here before and obviously had produced literature, let's place them before at the outset and be done with the problem. Historically, what happened was a completely different thing: indigenous literatures are a product of European culture using existing materials."[6] How did this change happen? In great part, activism across the hemisphere created new possibilities that directly affected the literary realm.

The 1970s were a watershed decade for a spirited local and international activism centered on indigenous collective rights. The highly successful Barbados meetings (I and II, held in 1971 and 1977, respectively), organized by various religious leaders, were instrumental in the development of many indigenous peoples' organizations and political agendas. In the decade that followed, protests erupted throughout the hemisphere and drew loud expressions of outrage at the planned quincentenary festivities by several countries around the world. These organized responses of "500 years of resistance" amplified the voice and revealed the objectives of indigenous nations. Activists proudly referred to this period as "the second independence," alluding to the *longue durée* of linguistic segregation and cultural exclusion imposed on indigenous peoples by nineteenth-century hegemonic national projects. The fecund 1990s witnessed the rise of the powerful voices of Rigoberta Menchú and the Zapatista revolutionaries in Chiapas. These two pivotal occurrences further emboldened indigenous activism, generating unparalleled international solidarity and fueling indigenous nations' desire to carve their own stories in writing. Despite a steady decline in the study of the humanities, the rise of the indigenous writer in Mesoamerica renews the promise for creating social change through personal and collective literary perspectives.[7] Indigenous literary and artistic expressions have become distinct signs of difference from national, canonical literatures.

While the cultural agents whose works are featured in this book are generally understudied, their standing is quickly evolving. Their works differ from colonial indigenous texts, which have been widely analyzed across numerous disciplines.[8] Fewer works exploring contemporary indigenous literatures, those produced after the 1980s, have been published in English or Spanish.[9] *Indigenous Cosmolectics* offers a distinct periodization, and a comparative analysis of Maya and Zapotec literatures, in addition to introducing kab'awil, an indigenous theoretical concept originating in the early classical period that has evolved across time to read and theorize literature published mainly in the twenty-first century.[10] In 2006, I theorized kab'awil as a philosophy and logic applicable to Maya writing that embodied past and present temporal modes that dissolved contradictions.[11] In this book, I expand kab'awil's philosophy to Zapotec literary works, which represent another important corpus in Mesoamerican literatures to demonstrate its relevancy to other indigenous literary practices. The book underscores that unlike the historical violent encounters that fashioned colonial indigenous texts (the second phase of indigenous literatures), the production and circulation of late twentieth- and early twenty-first-century indigenous literature (the third phase) in Mexico and Guatemala emerge under different conditions and circumstances.

Beyond National Literatures

The presumption that national literatures are a segment of a wider European Spanish-language tradition leaves out indigenous literatures that reference other linguistic universes. Marcelino Menéndez y Pelayo, the author of the first history of Spanish American literature, asserts that it was the honor of the classical languages (like Spanish) to colonize and bring civilization to backward places, characterizing poetry written in any of the indigenous languages as "primitive" and with "false" literary value, unworthy of inclusion in his anthology.[12] In 1959, the critic Salvador de Madariaga noted that "the Indians have nothing in common; neither language, tradition, physique, or customs, folklore or anything. If there is unity from Argentina to Chile to Mexico and Guatemala, this unity is Hispanic; without Hispanic [culture], there is no unity."[13] Today's unprecedented number of indigenous writers in Mesoamerica challenges these assumptions by claiming a literary tradition of their own, a tradition that is expressed in Maya and Zapotec languages, along with Spanish translations, or, in some cases, exclusively in Spanish. Following Dipesh Chakrabarty (2008), Arturo Arias observes that by publishing in the official Spanish language, indigenous authors provincialize its status.[14]

I use *Latin* America, as opposed to *Spanish* or *Hispanic* America throughout the manuscript, to concede that indigenous writers publish in a variety of languages, including French, Spanish, Portuguese, and English.[15] Walter Mignolo proposes that the idea of Latin America emerged in the nineteenth century and has two distinct genealogies: (1) imperial and colonial conflicts and (2) use by Spanish Creole intellectuals and politicians against the Anglo-Saxon world in the Americas.[16] Aims McGuinness explains that the precise origins of the term remain muddled.[17] Indeed, McGuinness argues it may have been created in France by Latin American intellectuals, pointing to this pan-Latin geographical category as distinct from the conventional assignation of the continent as an extension of the Latin nations of Europe.[18] All of these nomenclatures leave out other tongues spoken in Latin America, including indigenous languages, Arabic, Asian languages, Creole, and Afro-indigenous languages like Garifuna (a mixture of West African, Arawak, and European languages).[19] The emergence of Abya Yala as an indigenous renaming and repossessing of the continent frames an important moment, to which this book contributes in spirit, but the book essentially dialogues with a body of knowledge and literatures that are currently understood as Latin American.

Mesoamerica

Literature produced in multiple indigenous languages has left an indelible mark throughout the Americas in the last fifty years. In fact, many indigenous literary festivals and congresses have been hemispheric from the very beginning. This book concentrates on the study of the Maya and the Zapotec literatures anchored in the Mesoamerican region. This regional designation encompasses an area reaching from central Mexico south through Central America. These territories share a cultural legacy that includes, among other things, the use of writing scripts, calendars, domesticated animals, key plants, and a vigesimal counting system.[20] I trace the contours of a Maya and Zapotec intellectual genealogy to a past when the formal borders of nation-states had yet to be drawn. The charted course of this book contests modern-day borders, redrawing the maps of official linguistic and ethnic demarcations.

During the First Maya and Zapotec Literary Congress, held in Mexico City in 2010, writers stressed the need to think through these literatures comparatively—albeit within the parameters of the Mexican nation-state. My work partially responds to this demand and simultaneously scrutinizes these two distinct literatures for two other reasons. First, I do so because the Maya and Zapotec people developed sophisticated ideographic and phonetic writing systems long before the armada of the Spanish colonizers arrived on their shores—and that fact becomes an important knowledge and power reference in public proclamations.[21] Second, the Maya and Zapotec represent the most prolific writing communities today among the various indigenous peoples in Mesoamerica. The Maya authors I examine are separated by imposing nation-state limits, but they transcend these artificial boundaries through collective poetry readings and writing festivals, which have brought them together since the 1990s. The chapters that follow center on Maya writers from Guatemala and Mexico as well as Zapotec writers from Juchitán and the Sierra Norte in Oaxaca, Mexico. Members of the Maya nations discussed in this book include Humberto Ak'abal, Gaspar Pedro González, Calixta Gabriel Xiquín, Maya Cú Choc, Rosa María Chávez, and the theater troupe Ajchowen as well as Jorge Cocom Pech, Briceida Cuevas Cob, Marisol Ceh Moo, Ana Patricia Martínez Huchim, Enriqueta Lunez Pérez, Angelina Díaz Ruiz, and the theater group Fortaleza de la Mujer Maya (Strength of the Maya Woman, or FOMMA). The Zapotec intellectuals examined are mainly from Juchitán. Irma Pineda Santiago, Macario Matus, Víctor de la Cruz, and Natalia Toledo Paz have strong ties to Juchitán, while the novelist, Javier Castellanos Martínez, is from the Sierra Norte. I underscore the differences between the Juchitán and Sierra writers because the Zapotec languages spoken in the two regions are not mutually intelligible. Besides assuming a politics of language and knowledge, indigenous writers are "situated," in the way that the historian Claudia Zapata differentiates, between elitist intellectuals who distance themselves from society, hiding their position of enunciation, and indigenous intellectuals who are grounded in a particular history of the continent.[22] A periodization of Maya and Zapotec literature as a third phase locates Mesoamerica within larger debates about knowledge and power, and in conversation with coloniality and decoloniality scholarships, in and outside of Latin America.[23] This geographical construct compels a rethinking of national historiographies, suggesting new relations between Mesoamerica, Latin America, and Abya Yala.[24]

The autonomies each chapter explores reflect different hues on the literary canvas, stretching from the domain of language, knowledge systems, and politics to questions of gender and the body. These cultural agents recognize the roots and the bonds that unite them to larger and ancient community configurations. Correspondingly, the book moves from macro- to micro-Mesoamerican indigenous literary histories. Maya writing represents the most robust body of literature as it transcends nation-states, followed by an equally imaginative Zapotec literature.

The book begins by debunking three popular premises about indigenous aesthetic practices that continue to appear in Latin American discussions of literature. The first is the naturalized assumption that indigenous peoples lacked a comprehensive writing system until the introduction of the alphabet by the Spanish in the sixteenth century — a key revision for the decolonization of knowledge in Mesoamerica.[25] Not knowing Mesoamerican writing scripts is a disciplinary issue. As Dennis Tedlock observes in *2000 Years of Mayan Literature*, "The time has come to take a further step and proclaim that literature existed in the Americas before Europeans got here — not only oral literature but visible literature."[26] Second, I work from the premise that twentieth- and twenty-first-century Maya and Zapotec literatures resist the sharp distinction between orality and literacy, modernity and tradition, Western and non-Western. These partitions risk missing the interconnectedness between ancient scripts, performance, provenance, narratives, and their blending with contemporary literature through what I call a Mesoamerican cosmolectics, which, as I detail below, foregrounds their insistence on a different universe and a singular way of experiencing the world. Third, the book demonstrates that the far-reaching chronology evoked in this body of literature challenges the assumption that aesthetic expressions in formal literary genres originate outside Mesoamerica. A focus on genre unravels the premise of Carlos Montemayor, who, after assembling several volumes on contemporary indigenous writings, concludes, "In fact, from an indigenous perspective there is no clear demarcation between what a literary tale [is] and medical, religious, or historical information."[27] Contemporary indigenous writers not only distinguish between formal genres, but they also add to a literary archive by including pre-Columbian forms such as *difrassismo*, the conjuring up of two images to invoke a third meaning; or *libana*, a Zapotec marriage petition learned by memory and passed down by males. Genres like poetry, theater, and story have always been part of indigenous communities' cultural archive, but named in other linguistic codes. Although a bilingual novel does not appear until the 1990s, the Zapotec poet and anthropologist Víctor de la Cruz reports that the Zapotec term for novel was already present in the colonial Zapotec dictionary, compiled in 1578 by Friar Juan de Córdova. The Crown's prohibition against importing novels to its colonies, enacted in 1531 and 1543, directly correlated to the colonizer's fear that if "Indians" read works of fiction, they might subsequently assume the *Bible*'s teachings to be yet another fabrication (as I discuss in chapter 5).[28] Despite the Crown's interdiction against novels in the colonies, the Zapotec term for the genre preceded the first novel's publication in the Spanish Americas of *El periquillo sarniento* (*The Mangy Parrot*) by José Joaquín Fernández de Lizardi (1816), which indicates that the form may not have been unfamiliar to the Zapotecs. Contemporary Maya and Zapotec literatures produced at the end of the twentieth century and in the early twenty-first century complicate dated assumptions about literary forms. Indeed, in the twenty-first century, Zapotec novelist Javier Castellanos Martínez likens oral narratives that take days to be narrated to modern fiction, calling them oral novels.

The leading discussions in the following chapters do not offer a teleological analysis of Maya and Zapotec literatures that shift from the oral tradition to written expression, because these practices coalesce, diverge, and coexist. Instead, I underscore how the production of literature in formal genres becomes an important space for decolonization that differs from other forms, like myths or fables.[29] Expressed differently, the use of certain discursive structures indicates a cultural and political shift in indigenous cultural productions that contest the notion of orality as exclusively indigenous, establish a new relationship to the function of authorship, advance projects of autonomy, and articulate new relationships with the past and present.[30] Following Caroline Levine's work, my book acknowledges that forms are "as valuable to understanding social political institutions as [they are] to reading literature. Forms are at work everywhere."[31] The content of contemporary indigenous literatures may share numerous traits with the oral tradition, but genres offer important political, social, and historical dimensions that are not always discernible in the oral tradition.[32] Contemporary Maya and Zapotec writers transgress the literary world-system, naturalized as originating in Western Europe and moving across its peripheries, as some critics would have it in their theorization of the novel.[33] Indigenous writers know that the institution of literature endorses and validates power, as the Latin American critic Horacio Legrás points out in a different context.[34] Maya and Zapotec writers are starting to participate in well-established venues like the

International Book Fair (Feria Internacional del Libro) in Guatemala and its counterpart in Guadalajara, Mexico, often sharing panels with prominent national and international writers. Their growing presence in these settings allows them to articulate a literature that demands intellectual autonomy in the same way that Native American scholars Jace Weaver, Craig Womack, and Robert Warrior articulate in *American Indian Literary Nationalism*. Autonomy, as I demonstrate through examples from Maya and Zapotec literatures, plays out differently across various con/texts. With this in mind, I highlight the recent theorization by indigenous women of their bodies as geopolitical territory and of their works as an important contribution to the notion of autonomy from a feminist perspective—a trope or leitmotif that transpires in much of the literature by Maya and Zapotec women poets. While indigenous poets speak on a number of issues and themes, I underscore the association between indigenous women and territory because it responds to an unconventional understanding of the body as shaped by historical process, not merely by a biological evolution.[35] The current assertion that there will be no decolonization while patriarchy remains entrenched in social customs and conventions permeates the literature.[36]

Through an Indigenous Historiography

The adoption of pluricultural, intercultural, multicultural, and plurilingual discourses by nation-states in Latin America has bolstered indigenous intellectuals and writers' claims to cultural difference. The terms of this political development have frequently come under intense scrutiny and criticism, but in its first iterations it contested homogeneity and monolingualism.[37] Rather than reading this production as symptomatic of neoliberal policies and globalization, I examine the conceptual, political, and imaginative spaces presented. Indeed, at the beginning of the twentieth century, decades before nation-states turned to multiculturalism, the first generation of Zapotec intellectuals, including Rosendo Pineda, Adolfo C. Gurrión, Enrique Liekens Cerqueda, Jeremías López Chiñas, Pancho Nácar, Nazario Chacón Pineda, and Andrés Henestrosa, had begun to publish poetry in community-driven local newspapers.[38] Many of these poets published bilingual editions, writing Zapotec phonetically, as a standardized alphabet had yet to be established. The foundational Zapotec critic and poet Víctor de la Cruz asserts that this literature was the first written contemporary indigenous literature in Mexico.[39] Cruz explicitly periodizes as Zapotec literature those texts exclusively published in the Latin alphabet, after the consolidation of the nation-state. This early twentieth-century literature prefigures the number of social movements that led to the establishment of the Coalición Obrera, Campesina, Estudiantil del Istmo (Coalition of Workers, Peasants, and Students of the Isthmus, or COCEI). The founding of literary and political journals like *Neza* in 1930, *Neza Cubi* in 1960, and *Guchachi' Reza* in 1990 illustrates the growing cultural and political importance of writing in Zapotec, particularly in the isthmus of Oaxaca.[40] Appropriating the Latin alphabet to write in indigenous languages increased their political breadth, as such writing became an important medium for the affirmation of cultural identity and the preservation of heritage.

In the Maya context of the Yucatán Peninsula and Chiapas, oral literature was the dominant mode of expression in the early part of the twentieth century. Writing workshops led by the well-known novelist Carlos Montemayor strengthened the production of Maya literatures in both regions.[41] Cristina Leirana Alcocer, a professor and writer at the Autonomous University of Yucatán, has closely followed and classified three main tendencies in the formation and objectives of the different groups that constituted the bedrock of the Maya Peninsula literary movement in the 1980s. In her analysis, the first group of writers leaned toward a connection to the past, the second trend produced didactic literature, and the third focused on the aesthetic forms of the Maya language.[42] Alcocer aptly points out that each group's objectives relate to its genre preference. Those writers affiliated with Culturas Populares (Popular Cultures, a government institution overseeing art and culture in different parts of Mexico) like Ismael May May and Feliciano Sánchez Chan preferred to compile the oral tradition. Those like Briceida Cuevas Cob and Waldemar Noh Tzec, associated with the group Génali or Yaajal K'in, tended to excel in modern poetry. The third group of writers, according to Alcocer, consists mainly of teachers associated with the organization Maya'on, which tends to focus on children's literature, an underserved field in Maya-language materials.

In Chiapas, the 1980s saw the founding members of the La Unidad de Escritores Maya-Zoques (Unity of Maya-Zoque Writers, or UNEMAZ), Sna Jtz'ibajom (House of the Writer), and FOMMA, as well as the Centro Estatal de Literatura, Artes y Lenguas Indígenas (State Center for Literature, Arts, and Indigenous Languages, or CELALI). Robert M. Laughlin, a well-known anthropologist, was instrumental in the creation of Sna Jtzi'bajom in Chiapas. He also encouraged the preservation of the oral tradition through writing. While some indigenous organizations did not become official until the 1990s, they had previously started informal discussions on issues of language standardization, publications, and circulation. More important, these regional writers' groups would come to collaborate and become part of the Indigenous Writers Association. In 1991, the second National Congress of Literature in Indigenous Languages, held in the city of San Cristóbal de las Casas, concluded with the writers announcing their opposition to any government participation in the quincentenary commemoration of Columbus Day. Notably, they took a stand against the North American Free Trade Agreement and committed to promote the participation of indigenous women, among several other objectives.[43]

In Guatemala, the political mobilization organized by various sectors of society in the 1960s was met with widespread government repression and violence, curtailing to a great degree the written production of indigenous literatures. The massacre of Panzós in 1978 initiated a systemic targeting of indigenous peoples for genocide, thus transforming the production of literature into a subversive act of political transgression, resistance, and survival.[44] The Maya authors who published during the 1960s and 1970s did so predominantly in Spanish. The Kaqchikel literary critic Manuel de Jesús Salazar Tetzagüic, however, identifies a handful of Maya writers in the 1970s who published individual bilingual poems and short narratives in Chimaltenango's local newspapers.[45] Emilio del Valle Escalante identifies Francisco Morales Santos, whose publications date to the early 1960s, as a precursor to the Maya literary renaissance, while Arturo Arias identifies Luis de Lión as playing that role.[46] Morales Santos and de Lión did not identify as Maya but rather employed the more generic term *Indian*. Their work was published exclusively in Spanish. Enrique Sam Colop was the first Maya K'iche' to publish two books of poetry in a bilingual edition in 1978 and 1980.[47] The 1990s saw the emergence of the pan-Maya movement, with a strong focus on language revindication.[48] In Guatemala, the Asociación de Escritores Mayances de Guatemala published the first bilingual issue of its magazine *Chatwalijoq* (translated into Spanish as *Levántate* [*Rise*]) in 1990.[49] This issue included songs, tales, explications of Maya glyphs, and the explanation of Maya calendars.[50] The pan-Maya movement and the peace accords signed in 1996 strengthened and created more national space for the production of literature as well.[51] Alongside the entrance of the Maya into the literary world came a rejection of neoliberal politics and a strong critique of the monolingual and Ladino/mestizo paradigm embedded in official discourse.[52]

Contemporary Maya and Zapotec writers are involved in creating a literary corpus and advancing ways of thinking about literature as more than a set of books to be shelved in libraries or bookstores. While not all contemporary indigenous writers continue to adhere to what I formulate as a Mesoamerican cosmolectics represented by kab'awil, a great majority of the first generation of bilingual writers did, and they employed this "continuity" as an epistemological difference vis-à-vis other literatures. In this context, the leading generation of authors advanced an alternative way of periodizing literature. The authors profiled in the chapters that follow share a desire to imagine and contribute to a contemporary indigenous literature that upends the colonialist association between criollo descendants and knowledge.

Cosmolectics

Kamau Brathwaite, writing against the notion of a dialectics, proposed *tidalectics* to name the relationship between historical process and seascape. Brathwaite rejected *dialectics* due to its implicit notion of progression, whereas for him, tidalectics captured a back-and-forth Caribbean ontology.[53] Following Brathwaite, I propose *cosmolectics* for Mesoamerica, tying together the fundamental role that the cosmos and history, sacred writing and poetry, nature and spirituality as well as glyphs and memory play in articulating Maya and Zapotec ontologies. Although the term *cosmos* is etymologically Greek, meaning "order," it is an accepted translation in English and Spanish to name an arrangement that includes stars, planets, gods, galaxies, nature, and an indigenous autonomy that reaches beyond land. In this proposition, I follow Cree scholar and artist Karyn Recollet, who argues that indigenous futurities require that we rethink space as more than land territory, to include "star glyphing, celestial mapping, kinstallations."[54] In the Mesoamerican context, the very self-naming of the indigenous nation reflects this cosmolectics. The Zapotec self-name is *Binnigula'sa'* or *Binnizá*, meaning Cloud People.[55] The Zapotec poet Natalia Toledo Paz likes to state that she "speaks cloud." The Mixtec are *Ñúu Savi / Na Savi* or Rain People, inspiring titles such as "Nocturnal Rain/ Lluvia nocturna" by Mixtec poet Carlos España. *Maya* has various meanings, but many nations under this umbrella term acknowledge nature. *K'iche'* literally translates as "place of trees," *Kaqchikel* means "red authority tree," and *Ch'orti'* means "people who speak milpa." The Zapotec conceive of everything as having *pée* (spirit, breath). The poet Mario Molina Cruz asserts that the roots of all Zapotec poetry from the Sierra Norte can be found in the gratitude given to the god of productivity, Bada'o Bzan, "who later transformed to song, music, and dance, giving origin to oral expression distant from the sacred, dedicated to women, time, and nature."[56] While the production of literature attempts to vertically order the world/word in indigenous communities as much as in the political arena, the focus has been on the horizontal notion of land. As the

UNEMAZ board asserts in its statement, "Through pencil and paper we began to defend our tongues, our roots, our wisdom, jp'ijiltik, jch'uleltik, our grandparents said, guided by the splendor of Father Sun and Mother Moon, we walk the four corners of Osil Balamil, the universe."[57]

Cosmolectics, then, refutes the academic tendency to differentiate cosmogony from epistemology.[58] Adhering to this cosmolectics allows writers to challenge the idea that "the 16th-century collapse of the Amerindian world left the colonized subjects without the possibility of producing critical thinking."[59] A Mesoamerican cosmolectics transgresses disciplinary boundaries between philosophy and poetry. Finally, cosmolectics counters the sociological imagination that indigenous (thesis) and European roots (antithesis) produce a mestizo synthesis, or, in José Vasconcelos's work, the culmination in the cosmic race where Indians and blacks eventually disappear. Mesoamerican cosmolectics involves not just thesis, antithesis, and synthesis but also a fourth element known in Mesoamerican philosophy as *kab'awil*, a vision that duplicates.[60] Maya and Zapotec cultural producers offer an intricate tapestry of their world/word designs. These tessellates are informed not only by land, community, and language but also by the moon, stars, sun, and other "kinstallations."

Theorizing Kab'awil

The book underscores kab'awil as a foundational cosmolectics, fixed in pre-Columbian writing and grounded on the direct and retrograde movement of planets. There is evidence that kab'awil represents the planet Jupiter in retrograde on the Dresden Codex.[61] From its emergence in the preclassic to the postclassic and its references in colonial texts, kab'awil has undergone alterations in its denotation, connotation, and representation — and yet it is always in conversation with the cosmos and society. Its contemporary deployment in the twentieth and twenty-first centuries also commands distinct but similar vertical and horizontal movements. Ethnohistorian Sergio Mendizábal recognizes kab'awil as a Mesoamerican civilization concept.[62] One of its salient features is that it differs from the binary system that dominated in the sixth century BCE. Hanneke Canters and Grace M. Jantzen argue that Western philosophy "has operated with a rigid binary system of logic ever since its inception in Ancient Greece. Indeed, . . . binary logic is arguably its starting point and framework."[63] Both scholars scrutinize the Pythagorean table of opposites, developed in the sixth century BCE, to illustrate the early articulation of a binary system that in their analysis has had everlasting effects in philosophy, from G. W. F. Hegel to Maurice Merleau-Ponty. They underline that the Pythagorean table sets in motion a chain of meanings that attributes positive and negative characteristics to men and women, day and night, and so on. Canters and Jantzen discover that this line of thinking was supported by figures like Parmenides, the thinker of the fifth century BCE, who declared a "rigid division between the realm of sensory experience and the realm of thought, a division that has plagued Western Philosophy, to the disadvantage of women."[64] They conclude that the origins of Western logic did not allow for gray areas.[65] Of course, this binary system has been challenged by feminist, deconstructionist, and postcolonial theorists. But my point is that kab'awil's development is at least contemporaneous with this logic. Furthermore, it offers what Carlos Lenkersdorf, in the context of Maya Tojolabales, terms an "intersubjective" indigenous philosophy where social relations are based on a duplicity of "I's" and "we's" in the same utterance.[66] In theorizing kab'awil, my work adds to other intellectual projects seeking to decolonize knowledge in the continent.[67]

Kab'awil surfaces in preclassic Maya glyphs with a smoking mirror glyph (T617a), and an ax for a foot, which sometimes stands for obsidian or lightning.[68] In classic and terminal classic Maya representations, kab'awil's foot is substituted by a serpent usually thought to be *itzamná*. Postclassic, the serpent foot representation continues, but with a new variation that includes bird wings, beaks, and claws.[69] In other archeological records, kab'awil is referenced as the god of divination, a Maya Prometheus as it were, or simply as "God K." Maya kings often added the glyphs for kab'awil alongside their names to denote a sacred genealogy, whether they ruled in Tikal (Guatemala), Palenque (Mexico), or Copán (Honduras), as well as to emphasize a connection to their sacred genealogy, literally adding "god-like lord" through kab'awil.[70] In other representations, kab'awil is associated with maize and other vegetation symbols. In ceramic art, kab'awil can be read iconographically as a metaphor for corn. In many *incensarios* (vessels for burning incense) found in Palenque, "k'awiil" functioned to integrate "two opposite and complementary halves of a larger idea."[71] Sculpted as scepters held by important rulers, it represented their ascension to authority or the passing down of authority.[72]

The Catholic conversion of the Maya population in the sixteenth century prompted other shifts for *kab'awil*. For starters, its glyphic representation transformed into an alphabetic *kawiil*, *cab'awil*, or *kauuil*. In the *Books of Chilam Balam*, it appears spelled as *kauil*, *ku kauil*, or *kawil itzamná*. Ethnohistorian Ruud van Akkeren dates the change to the debate that ensued between the Franciscan and Dominican orders about the use of *kab'awil* to name the Christian god in the seventeenth century. The Dominican friars thought *kab'awil* was the most apt term since the Maya used it to refer to their own deities. The Franciscans, however, considered that even though the term referred to deities, Maya representations of god were effigies of stone and wood, and therefore, idols — things of the devil — and thus *kab'awil* became negative and suppressed from being used — at least in the public domain. Needless to say, the Franciscans won. Friar Ximénez translates *cabauil* as "ídolo" for twenty-nine pages and renders it in Castilian as "cabawil" once.[73] Kab'awil makes an appearance in other colonial texts as well: *El ritual de los bacabes*, Friar Diego de Landa's *Relación*, and the sacred *Popol Vuh*. Yet, despite the *Popol Vuh*'s international renown and translation into numerous languages, the concept's import gets glossed over.

In the twentieth century, kab'awil reenergizes previous debates on its meaning. In 1979, Adrián Inés Chávez, one of the first modern Maya K'iche' writers to revisit the sixteenth-century text, linguistically and culturally translated *kab'awil* in his version of the *Pop Wuj (Popol Vuh)*.[74] Chávez recovers the cosmolectics and defines *kab'awil* as "two visions at the same time, to see in the darkness and in lightness, to see close and far, a "doble mirada / double gaze."[75] In the 1990s, the Maya K'iche' linguist Enrique Sam Colop translated *kab'awil* as simply an icon. He argued against the historical confusion that the Maya misinterpreted the Spaniards as kab'awil or gods.[76] My take on this issue is that *kab'awil* was and continues to be a polysemous term — thus the different uses. The Spanish colonizers constructed a self-aggrandizing tale in which the indigenous populations mistook them for deities. The invading Spaniards told of similar anecdotes about the Aztec and Taino.[77] This fib may have influenced Sam Colop's contention that *kab'awil* refers to icon and not god. However, he maintains the notion of duality in his translation of the *Popol Vuh*, translating the concept as "heart of sky, heart of earth," but the term in the K'iche' language version is *kab'awil*: *ka* (the numeral two) and *wil* (to see).

Although its derivation is traceable to the preclassic Maya civilization writing tradition, kab'awil or the double-headed eagle held singular significance for the K'iche' Maya, since they were known as the "sons of the eagle, sons of the dawn" before they settled in Utatlán around 1200 AD.[78] The eagle represented a ritual symbol given to them by the ancestor Balam Akap. Incidentally, the eagle was also the symbol of the Austro-Hungarian Empire. After the Spanish defeated the fierce Nijaib K'iche', they awarded them an eagle as their insignia. The image was a frontispiece of the Buenabaj pictorials in Santiago Momostenango between 1550 and 1560.[79] The K'iche' differentiated between the symbol of the Austro-Hungarian Empire and the *k'ot*, the double-headed pre-Columbian image in their textiles. Europeans may not have noticed, but their version became the *Glavicote* or the underworld bird Xecotocovach.[80] Margot Blum Schevill's research on Guatemalan textiles produced over eighty years singles out the double-headed eagle design, mainly in *tzutes* (woven cloth headdress), worn by important and revered people in the community or spiritual leaders, whereas the Austro-Hungarian eagle was reserved for textiles sold to tourists.[81] She observes that in the Kaqchikel community of San Juan Sacatepéquez, those of noble rank wore the double-headed eagle in textiles. The insignia continued to represent the great god who had two faces, "one to look forward and the other to look backward, the one looking for good, the other for evil, a variation of the Janus-head."[82] She concludes that *k'ot* and represent the dualism and conflict between Maya and European beliefs.[83]

More than representing this conflict, kab'awil's transformation from its glyphic etchings in stone and its painted replicas in codices to its present significance suggests a relationship with the cosmos that goes back to the preclassic era and a resistance to the experience of coloniality in Mesoamerica. In its late twentieth- and twenty-first-century deployment, kab'awil straddles spiritual practice, politics, gender, aesthetics, philosophy, and social experience. In a more overtly political fashion, it becomes a methodology for the empowerment of young women in education.[84] The double gaze transforms into a systematized and holistic methodology in a pilot school program, taking as a given the connection between kab'awil and gender because it is made visible in the double-headed eagle woven in K'iche' and Mam huipiles.[85] Damián Upún Sipac returns to kab'awil (god) as the universe that exhibits through duality, writing that it "is everything, time, space, and movement."[86] To paraphrase the Maya Achi sociologist José Roberto Morales Sic, kab'awil has a center that makes it possible to process and connect multiple dimensions.[87] He characterizes this philosophy as a unitary dimension, an inclusive vision. He interprets it as "a theory of knowledge that is recognized as an inclusive logic because kab'awil is a symbol developed by the Maya ancestors to gain a better appreciation and understanding of multiple contexts in the unit of time in which it dwells."[88] Most notably, as Edgar Matul and Daniel Cabrera assert, "Kab'awil moves us beyond dualisms or opposites that impede access to a totality."[89] This double gaze does not adhere to a Cartesian split of mind/body.

In other connections to genre, the Nobel Peace Prize laureate Rigoberta Menchú offers a similar example when she accentuates it as a social experience: "'*kawilo saqil hab'e*' means . . . don't just look at your path, for you must also see your steps and direction transparently... not just the physical path... but also the path of destiny."[90] Juana Batzibal Tujal, a Kaqchikel intellectual, day keeper, and activist, contends that kab'awil embodies a Maya philosophy:[91] "We can say that in almost all of our people's traditional dress, our philosophy is represented by the Kab'awil, or Double Gaze, who sees day and night, who sees the past and sees the future."[92] Kab'awil is deeply connected to gender and genre, not only because women continue to weave the double-headed eagle but also because they see it as a reminder of a different type of writing. She overlooks any contradictions between a modern book/textile and alphabetic/ideographic writing. Batzibal Tujal remarks, "These textiles equal a type of Maya alphabet, that is why it is said that we dress in books written thousands of years ago."[93] Batzibal Tujal also argues for an ancestral continuity through the reproduction of textiles because the grandmothers "have taught us to write our logic in an aesthetic manner."[94] Hence, the concept functions to mediate temporal, writing, and knowledge systems. In the Mam-Maya language, the term *kawb'il* describes a narrative that represents advice offered by the elders to a younger generation; Rainer Hostnig and Luis Vásquez Vicente thus call attention to the limiting scope of Western classifications of genres when applied to Maya literary narrative strategies.[95] Women writers and other cultural agents display it to assume an autonomy outside of *usos y costumbres* or customary law.[96] Kab'awil becomes productive in thinking about gender and genre across Mesoamerican geography, because through it women maintain a critical gaze to sexist practices under the guise of tradition.

Reclaiming a Negated Past

My initial interest in kab'awil as a Mesoamerican cosmolectics was due to its temporal dimension. Nation-states in Latin America have established a distance between pre-Columbian civilizations like the Maya and Zapotec by fixing them in the past and disconnecting that past from the living indigenous peoples they continue to attempt to assimilate. It is not an accident that all archeological sites are considered the patrimony of the nation-state, and that indigenous peoples have to petition to revere their ancestors. The indigenous past has been systematically subjected to erasure and suppression. It has been appropriated and packaged as a commodity by nation-states through official institutions. This distancing forecloses projects of autonomy. Reclaiming hieroglyphic writing in the present as a power and knowledge genealogy and underscoring its remembrance in the praxis of an indigenous imaginary exemplifies a *doble mirada*, or double gaze. My discussion and periodization of Maya and Zapotec literature represents a decolonizing move, one grounded in an indigenous epistemology.[97] Kab'awil, as a Mesoamerican cosmolectics, advances the project of indigenous autonomy in the present based on its preclassic and postclassic legacies.

In the twentieth and twenty-first centuries, writers adopt alphabetic literacy under a different ideological goal. Maya Yukatek writer Jorge Cocom Pech's ironic remark recapitulates this appropriation: "To Spain, I return its cross because with it they subjugated our people; the sword, because with it they destroyed our communities. But there is something I will not return to Spain: *El Quijote*. Thanks to *El Quijote* and the Spanish language, I can write my mother tongue."[98] In this remark, the writing system is arbitrary; the Maya language continues in a different semiotic system. Writers uphold a tradition that challenges critics' periodization of this literature as new in public discourses.[99] It connects to indigeneity as *survivance*, to use Gerald Vizenor's term, and serves contemporary writers as a mechanism to resist the trappings of assimilation and to establish other genealogies of knowledge.

Kab'awilian Strategies

I name "kab'awilian strategies" those maneuvers that invert or help indigenous cultural producers imagine possibilities outside the matrix of coloniality and its ordering of things. Indigenous writers invert the linear and evolutionary notion of orality to literacy. In the words of María Sabina, a Mazatec healer, "I learned wisdom from the book. Later . . . the book no longer appeared because its contents were already safeguarded in my memory."[100] Sabina is a significant example because her prayers demonstrate how entrenched the idea of books is in Mesoamerica. Indigenous poets and other intellectuals read her prayers as poetry, and they serve as an intertextual text. Feliciano Sánchez Chan deploys a kab'awilian strategy when he asserts that the motivation behind writing a book is to return the story to the oral realm since books get shelved, but stories are utilized in the community.[101] Writing, memory, and orality are interrelated concepts that do not have an evolutionary order in these kab'awilian maneuvers. In an admittedly different context but also exhibiting a kab'awilian strategy are the women who inform Ámbar Past's *Incantations: Songs, Spells, and Images by Mayan Women*. Past explains: "The Tzotzil authors of this anthology claim their spells and songs were given to them by the ancestors, the First Fathermothers, who keep the Great Book in which all words are written down."¹⁰² She cites Pasakwala Kómes as having "learned her conjurations by dreaming the Book."¹⁰³ Past concludes that "it is clear the First Fathermothers were writers, and it is rumored that some of their books — that no one can read anymore — lie hidden in old chests in Chamula. Each year they are taken out with great reverence, perfumed with incense and wrapped up again in embroidered cloths. Some say the books inside the chests have begun to talk. Women who learn the words are said to have writing in their hearts."¹⁰⁴ Other important scholars argue that books are an integral component of processions, safeguarded from foreigners, thereby maintaining the pre-Columbian notion of writing as sacred.¹⁰⁵

Interpretive Tool

By applying kab'awil or the double gaze to literary exegesis, my work analyzes how the late twentieth- and early twenty-first-century meaning appears through the characters or issues raised in contemporary indigenous literature. W. E. B. Du Bois's "double consciousness" functions in a similar way. "Double consciousness" attempts to theorize the internal racial and social conflict African Americans experience in a U.S. American context. Likewise, Maya and Zapotec writers and other intellectuals are cognizant of how the dominant society sees them as well as how they see themselves. In Gaspar Pedro González's novel *La otra cara*, the main protagonist manifests kab'awil as a double gaze living under coloniality after violently learning that his official name in Spanish must be Pedro Miguel and not Luin: "This had been the starting point — as he would later recall — to begin a double personality, double attitude, double name, double behavior: one form before his people and the other before the Ladinos."¹⁰⁶ This social ontology is even more acute at school where assimilation was enforced, as Luin remembers: "Those were two worlds, two experiences and two concepts of oneself: the school and the family. When I began to get used to the joy of home on weekends, I had to get rid of this and put it aside on Monday and go back to a false personality and artificial manners in school."¹⁰⁷ The K'iche' feminist Alma López, in a discussion of Maya tradition, asserts that she "would also recover the double vision, or the idea of the cabawil, the one who can look forward and back, to one side and the other, and see the black and white, all at the same time. To recover this referent, as applied to women, implies knowing one's self with all the sad and terrible things that are part of my reality as a woman and to reconstruct myself with all the good things I have. It means to recognize that there are women different from me, that there are ladinas [not indigenous] and indigenous women, that there are black, urban and campesina women."[108] For López, kab'awil is a lived experience, one that does not become a symbolic gesture.

The younger generation of writers has more liberty in the subjects they select to write about, but the first generation faced societies that saw them as homogenous "Indian" subjects, racialized in opposition to a Western subject. Indigenous writers had to engage the "eyewitness" testimonies of researchers living in indigenous communities who "know" them. Patrolled by an unspoken code of conduct, policed by insiders and outsiders, contemporary Mesoamerican indigenous writers cross an uncertain line that spans the past and present, tradition and innovation, oral and written. They accomplish this by adhering to a cosmolectics embodied in their kab'awilian literary stances. Precisely because kab'awil is multiple and one at the same time, it allows me to deploy it at different levels. The chapters that follow illustrate that kab'awil can be read as a "double gaze," operating in Maya and Zapotec productions, thematized or fictionalized through the main characters. The double gaze allows a critique of assimilationist projects, nation-state history, sexism within indigenous communities, and progressive political parties. It has moved from its association with power and kings in pre-Columbian times, to the sacred and the profane during the colonial period, to a methodology for equality in the twentieth and twenty-first centuries. Like double consciousness, border thinking, interstitial spaces, and *nepantla* among other theoretical concepts that name in-betweenness, kab'awil facilitates multiple negotiations. However, kab'awil offers us a glimpse of pre-Columbian philosophy and current indigenous epistemes to better understand resistance, a force that permeates the conceptual, spiritual, political, and social realms. Kab'awil can extend toward analyzing other nonindigenous literatures that engage with the past and present, oral and written, traditional and modern, but due to its Mesoamerican glyphic writing genesis, my focus is on how it works through Maya and Zapotec literatures.

Chapter 1 explores Maya and Zapotec systems of communication as well as contradictory colonial representations regarding writing in Mesoamerica. The first chapter examines kab'awilian instances that become visible in the appropriation of the alphabet to safeguard and transpose indigenous knowledge in the sixteenth century. I propose that regardless of the system of writing employed, power and writing were already intertwined in Mesoamerica. The second section of the chapter points out that despite the foundational and critical contributions of theorists in the 1990s, who emphasized the effects of a European colonization of indigenous orality, these critics end up naturalizing orality as more authentically indigenous than writing. The colonization of orality exposes a polarity that may have characterized the encounter but that also limits what Serge Gruzinski has termed indigenous people's "passion for writing."[109] The third section discusses poems by Gaspar Pedro González, Macario Matus, Víctor de la Cruz, and other foundational authors who enacted kab'awil in establishing a strong foundation for a millenarian Mesoamerican literary tradition.

Chapter 2 draws attention to the discursive formation of the indigenous author intraregionally, arguing that kab'awil facilitates a transgression of the dominant society's modern/traditional, individual/collective, and religious/secular binaries, which inform debates over indigenous identities. It registers the movement of organic intellectuals whose publications reveal the distance between testimonial and collaborative compilations, on the one hand, and authorial subjects who respond to an immediate social experience, on the other. Here, I discuss the notion of the author to examine its divergences and similarities from a contemporary Mesoamerican authorship and how kab'awil reveals the ideological maneuvers these writers engage with as they maintain a double gaze to the past and present. I postulate that the works of Humberto Ak'abal (Guatemala), Nicolás Huet Bautista (Chiapas, Mexico), Jorge Cocom Pech (Campeche, Mexico), and Ana Patricia Martínez Huchim (Yucatán, Mexico) grapple with key tensions surrounding the past and present, modernization and tradition, spirituality and secularism. All of these anthologies were published in the twenty-first century and hold structural tensions that speak to the way indigenous writers have transformed the notion of the traditional storyteller through kab'awilian strategies.

Chapter 3 examines the notion of "gender complementarity" reframing it through kab'awil — not as a natural state of gender affairs — but as a paradigm that can be achieved. The chapter discusses kab'awil's transparency in contemporary indigenous poetry as it contests the unequal power relations between men and women by producing a double gaze. Contemporary indigenous women poets use the body and its eroticism to subvert cultural arguments about women's proper behavior in their communities. I bring to the forefront feminists who speak to the condition of being indigenous, poor, and women. I divide my analysis of the poetry into two main segments. In the first, the discussion features Maya and Zapotec women's poetry in Mexico, highlighting Irma Pineda Santiago, Natalia Toledo Paz, Briceida Cuevas Cob, and María Enriqueta Lunez Pérez as well as Angelina Díaz Ruiz. The second section focuses on Maya women's poetry in Guatemala, foregrounding the work of Maya Cú Choc, Rosa

María Chávez, and Calixta Gabriel Xiquín. I conclude by discussing the contradictions embodied by indigenous women who happen to occupy the lowest economic and social echelons in society, and the indigenous women poets who have also become central in the indigenous literary movement. Because these poets link eroticism to sexual autonomy, the chapter centers on the way women link their bodies to territory and its history, especially in Guatemala.

Chapter 3 offers a regional and national comparison of the first Maya women's theater troupes from Chiapas, Mexico, and Sololá, Guatemala, respectively. The theater companies transgress male/female hierarchies of power through kab'awil. I explore the plays *Una mujer desesperada* (A desperate woman) and *Migración*, by FOMMA, and *Ixkik*, the first play by Ajchowen (Monkey). FOMMA's plays underscore the complexity of gender and autonomy in Chiapas and the need for women to develop a strong sense of independence within and beyond their communities. Ajchowen's *Ixkik* offers a contemporary interpretation of the sacred sixteenth-century text the *Popol Vuh*. The play reinterprets women's roles in the future of Maya people. Both women's theater groups intersect in their concern with gender, tradition, and the futurity of indigenous peoples. While literary criticism has surfaced about FOMMA, a theater troupe that has been around since the late 1980s, Ajchowen's recent work has yet to be critically engaged in English or Spanish.

Chapter 5 examines the first novel published by a Maya woman, *X-Teya, U puksi'ik'al ko'olel / Teya, un corazón de mujer* (Teya, heart of a woman), and the first published Zapotec novel, *Wila che be ze lhao / Cantares de los vientos primerizos* (Songs of the first winds), as a rejection of first and second world-system alignments. This final chapter argues that the novelists transgress the political landscapes sketched by political ideologies, beginning a contemplation and imagining of what autonomy involves. I propose that the authors reject the nationalist liberal emphasis of integration as well as Marxist discourses as answers to the so-poorly termed "Indian problem." The chapter evaluates the role of *indigenista* literature and its divergence from indigenous literatures. Even though the novel as a genre has traditionally been assumed as European in its source, indigenous writers have adapted it as another storytelling form requiring a "longer breath."[110]

Indigenous Cosmolectics ends with an epilogue that contemplates writing this book from Luiseño land, specifically a park created in Oceanside, California, where I now live, on ancestral lands of the San Luis Rey Band of Indians. I meditate on Mesoamerican literature as a new sign of Latin America's transition from officially Spanish-speaking and mestizo to recognizing and affirming its multilingual and intercultural distinction. Literature becomes an important and transformative act for indigenous peoples and an open-ended site for articulating and exercising cultural difference and autonomy. The work of contemporary writers redirects our understanding of how indigenous identity and everyday practices are affirmed and contested across temporal, spatial, and linguistic grounds. I argue that the power of contemporary indigenous literature lies in its kab'awilian expression, a double optic that allows cultural producers to disembody binaries commonly associated with indigeneity: present/past, modernity/tradition, and writing/orality. Undoing these binaries enables indigenous writers and other intellectuals to theorize their own subjectivities and activate a set of kab'awilian epistemologies that has been neglected. In other words, this undoing does not deny the material and cultural influences in the work of contemporary indigenous writers, or disregard any individual's mixed heritage; rather, it affirms an intellectual legacy that has been systematically denied to indigenous peoples in Latin America. Literature is the site of ideological struggle. These texts offer the complexities behind decolonization and autonomy in all of their intersections. Kab'awil as ontology moves indigenous cultural agents closer to a Mesoamerican (Abya Yalan) future based on more equitable relations.

CHAPTER ONE

Literacy and Power in Mesoamerica

Our culture comes from Europe and we can't help it.
Besides, why avoid it?—Ernesto Sábato (2007)

Pure abstraction, metaphysics per se, will not take
root in America.—Juan Bautista Alberdi (2007)

Without colonialism from Europe, there would not exist this
corpus of cultural productions, written down in alphabetic
script in various languages.—Rolena Adorno (1996)

ON THE HEELS OF Spain's colonial intrusion, images of the uncivilized "Indian" and the noble savage circulated throughout Europe. Thomas King asserts that the first image, that of the wild Indian, emerged from colonial accounts while the second, that of the noble savage, emanated from an incipient nation-formation discourse.[1] In 1493, Columbus's accounts portraying the Taino nation were immediately translated and broadly disseminated. Eleven editions of his first letter were printed, including a paraphrase of its contents in Italian verse.[2] Other testimonies followed. Among the most prominent, published years after, was Francisco López de Gómara's *Historia general de las Indias* (1553) — translated into French, Italian, and Nahuatl (one of the major indigenous languages spoken in central Mexico).[3] Across the Atlantic Ocean, these early texts left indelible imprints of indigenous nations as lacking true writing.[4]

While these associations came to dominate the popular imagination, leading to the erroneous belief that literature and writing were virtually absent from indigenous nations, other, lesser known accounts contradicted these writings.[5] These differing narratives demonstrate that whereas certain stories became naturalized to support the Europeans' colonizing project, others that did not fit their prejudices went unnoticed. These lesser-known documents reveal that invaders did not comprehend the vast and different indigenous literary practices. In the twentieth and twenty-first centuries, contemporary Maya and Zapotec writers strategically enact kab'awil, or a double gaze to the past in the present, to reclaim a pre-Columbian written legacy that has been historically denied. They use these documents as evidence that their ancestors' own writing systems were displaced by the Latin alphabet introduced by the Spanish missionaries.[6]

The missionaries who penned their impressions of the Mesoamerican region, particularly those focused on the Maya and Zapotec nations, expressed surprise at the existence of writing. In the sixteenth century, Friar Alonso Ponce wrote regarding the Maya that "the Natives of Yucatán are, among all the inhabitants of New Spain, especially deserving of praise for three things: First, that before the Spanish came they made use of characters and letters, with which they wrote out their histories . . . in books made of bark of a certain tree. These . . . resembled a bound book. . . . These letters and characters were understood only by the priests of the idols. . . . Afterward, some of our friars learned to understand and read them, and even wrote them."[7] Indeed, the Europeans struggled to comprehend the multilayers and "cumbersome figures" of the Mesoamerican script structures they encountered. Friar Francisco de Landa's attempt to "translate" Maya glyphs in the Latin alphabet illustrates the misunderstandings that ensued following the Spanish incursion into Mesoamerica: "I will give here an A, B, C, of their letters, since their ponderousness does not allow anything more; for they use one character for all the aspirations of their letters."[8] The friar erroneously assumed that each glyph could correspond to a Latin letter. De Landa continued, "These people also made use of certain characters or letters, with which they wrote in their books their ancient matters and their science. . . . We found a large number of books in these characters and, as they contained nothing in which there were not to be seen superstition and lies of the devil, we burned them all, which they regretted to an amazing degree, and which caused them much affliction."[9] The colonialist violence against indigenous knowledge evinced in the response of the Maya offers a hint of the high regard in which writing and history were held.[10] Similarly, in the Zapotec region, Friar Juan de Córdova recorded many terms related to writing, such as *tolábaya* (reading out loud), *ticha, lana* (a letter when it is pronounced), *líchi quichi* (a library), and *quíchi cáayee* (a written book), among many others.[11] The Dominican Francisco de Burgoa also remarked that in Oaxaca "there are so many follies in their [Zapotec] stories and paintings, of which the devil [must have] persuaded them, that it is indecent [to] mention them. . . . As their language was so metaphorical, like that of the Palestinians, [whatever] they wanted to [they could] persuade, [they] always spoke in parables, and their historians wrote out in characters what they said."[12] Spanish missionaries drew analogies to their own understanding of writing, books, and literature in the Mesoamerican region even as they tried to supplant them with their own writing system and beliefs.

Considerable work on the general understanding of calendars, mathematics, astronomy, and notations, all of which offered partial insight into Mesoamerican writing, did not take place until the late nineteenth century, which brought the insights of various aficionados of Maya writing.[13] Scholars who have studied the various notation conventions in the Mesoamerican region have traditionally categorized them into hieroglyphic and pictographic scripts, with Maya and Zapotec writing falling under the former, and Mixtec and Nahuatl under the latter.[14] These forms of expression and techniques of communication, which combined logographs and syllabic components, are now regarded as being more complex than the Latin alphabet.[15] In their function as systems of information exchange, they shared similar objectives: to immortalize the names of rulers, to record histories, and to establish intimate bonds to the gods. While some critics consider Zapotec writing to be the most ancient — and the Oaxaca Valley to be its site of origin — others see glyphic writing in the region as having emerged simultaneously across indigenous contexts and languages.[16] Understanding Zapotec and Maya glyphs requires a visual and conceptual reorienting of left-to-right reading. Javier Urcid observes that in reading Zapotec linear texts, one could move from "top to bottom, from bottom to top, and from left to right, from right to left, or even the latter two combined in the case of inscriptions 'split' along a central axis."[17] Zapotec glyph studies are not as robust or as established as the Maya, mainly because of the scarcity of available texts, which are mainly found in the ceremonial center Monte Albán. Maya writing constitutes a combination of logographs and signs (phonetic ones, usually representing open vowels), and syllabic components (i.e., consonant and vowel, ba, be, bi, bo, bu).[18] These are grouped in blocks of vertical columns and could be read from top down within the pair. Out of the 800 glyphs that constitute Maya writing, only 300 have thus far been deciphered.[19] Perhaps the main distinction between Zapotec and Maya writing (aside from the obvious linguistic difference) is that Zapotec glyphs evolved from ideographic and phonetic components to exclusively ideographic ones — probably due to the linguistic diversity in Oaxaca.

Codices represent another key piece in rethinking power/knowledge genealogies, but these too were not easily accessible to scholars or the general public interested in Mesoamerican history. Many did not circulate until the twentieth century because they were in the hands of private collectors. María Sten observes in *Codices of Mexico* that forty of the most important indigenous codices are still found abroad.[20] Four Maya codices survived de Landa's infamous fires. A librarian purchased the Dresden Codex in 1739, while the Paris Codex surfaced in a French library in 1859. In 1866, a descendant of Hernán Cortés made public the Madrid Codex—his heirloom. In 1979, Michael Coe published the Grolier, which had been found in a cave in Chiapas in 1965. All these codices, with the exception of the Grolier (whose original remains in Mexico), are archived in the European cities after which they are named. Despite the work of archeologists and epigraphers, throughout the nineteenth and early twentieth centuries, most Western European countries perceived the Latin alphabet to be the system that best represented language and enabled the recording of history. Scholars, from Isaac Taylor (1889), to Bloomfield Leonard (1933), to David Diringer (1962), to John DeFrancis (1989), held on to the idea that writing represented spoken language, and that people without an alphabet lacked the tools to produce accounts of their past deeds, thus leaving them without writing and history.[21] Indeed, before the 1960s, scholars espoused the notion that pre-Columbian cultures did not develop true writing.[22]

Despite the evidence, not all scholars in the twentieth century agreed that literacy existed in the pre-Columbian Mesoamerica. Foundational scholars like Eric Thompson (1971), Juan de Villagutierre Soto-Mayor (1983), Cecil Brown (1991), and Alfred Tozzer (1941) saw writing in Mesoamerica as a privilege accessed exclusively by a priestly class. Joyce Marcus, one of the most prominent archaeologists of Mesoamerica, also adheres to this traditional way of thinking about literacy, following Diringer's definition of writing as the graphic counterpart of speech, "the fixing of spoken language in a permanent form."[23] Marcus dismisses the notion that Maya and Zapotec societies were literate; instead, she argues literacy was maintained in the hands of a few elite male scribes (as writing was for the most part conducted by men) — at least in the extant archeological record.[24] Her distinction between literacy and "craft literacy" — meaning only a selected class cultivated writing — illustrates conventional understandings of literacy as widespread outside Mesoamerica and ostensibly a right enjoyed by many only in the twentieth century.[25] Literacy in precontact Western Europe was also restricted. Indeed, indigenous and European practices of literacy during the Middle Ages (fifth–fifteenth century) were not broadly different. Literacy during the sixteenth century was not widespread in the kingdoms that would become Spain and England, for instance. Indeed, as the editors in *La planificación lingüística en países multilingües de Abya Yala* remind us, "We cannot forget, that, in the case of Spanish, for example, writing norms were still oscillating throughout the sixteenth century and that they became fixed only in the first third of the eighteenth century."[26] Not only was there great linguistic variation in these areas but the act of writing was also restricted to elite circles in both cultures. Keeping this comparison in mind, it is not impossible to assume that power and writing were allied in Spanish, Maya, and Zapotec societies.

The pre-Columbian bond between writing and power gave birth to a large number of texts, produced by indigenous writers in the Latin alphabet, following the conquest.[27] During the colonial period, scribes experienced a kab'awilian ontology as they witnessed the substitution of their writing tradition for the one introduced by Spaniards. Anthropologist María de los Ángeles Romero Frizzi, in *2000 años de escritura zapoteca*, describes this in other terms: "It is possible to think that the employment of the new writing form by indigenous [individuals] had a practical motivation, to defend what was theirs before the new authority.... If writing and power had been associated with one another, it is probable that this same manner of acting would influence their utilization of the new form of recording."[28] Romero Frizzi contends that the Zapotec culture, in its attempt to appropriate the Spaniards' writing, simplified a rather complex system of writing and transmission, and moved away from their own writing to the sphere of orality. The rapid assimilation and utilization of alphabetic writing by indigenous scribes in Mesoamerica contests many erroneous colonialist assumptions, primarily, the largely discredited evolutionary view that the lack of an alphabet consequently leads to a deficit in cognitive development — thus challenging the presumed intellectual dearth in indigenous nations.[29] In effect, among the most insidious outcomes of the initial confrontation between the Mesoamerican populations and the Spanish invaders is that the conquistadores' methodical dismemberment of an existing indigenous writing system associated with indigenous political power precipitated the alienation of Maya and Zapotec societies from their own scripts. An obstinate remembrance of a Mesoamerican cosmolectics postcontact and postindependence fueled the desire of indigenous scribes to safeguard important historical events of their civilization and to preserve their histories through writing. In this chapter, the cosmolectics represented by kab'awil is the gaze turned toward a nonalphabetic script, embedding it in colonial texts. Continuing this kab'awilian strategy, indigenous poets in the twentieth and twenty-first centuries also return to these colonial texts to assert a different genealogy. Indeed, it is during the colonial period that kab'awil transliterated from its glyphic representation to an alphabetic one.

Kab'awil or the Double Gaze in Indigenous Colonial Writing

Almost all texts that survive in alphabetic script written by indigenous writers during the colonial period maintain consistent references to kab'awil and other glyphs, sustaining a double gaze to their past during the colonial period. Texts like the *Popol Vuh*, *The Books of Chilam Balam*, and *Los cantares de Dzitbalché*, among a variety of others, clearly indicate that they originated in a complex grammar dependent on an array of oral performances and language representations. Maya texts from the colonial period, primarily from the Yucatán Peninsula in Mexico and the highlands of Guatemala, formulate this clearly and explicitly, and offer insight into the goals of the scribes. Victoria Bricker calls attention to the subtle ways hieroglyph writing conventions appear in *The Books of Chilam Balam*.[30] *The Books of Chilam Balam* collectively include history, astrology, predictions, poetry, and incantations, among other subjects. References to the twins, the central characters of the *Popol Vuh*, and other cosmological elements are all present in calendar glyphs, stelae, vases, and lintels. In the Zapotec region, much of the production visible in ceremonial centers continued in the oral tradition and other genres such as the *libanas* or sermons and *títulos primordiales* (land titles). María de los Ángeles Romero and Michel Oudijk analyze the Oaxacan *títulos* as a Mesoamerican genre with pre-Hispanic origins in the practice of writing sacred geneaologies.[31] Scribes preserved, contested, and made ancestral land claims.

Scribal use of glyphic conventions while adopting the Latin alphabet indicated a paradigmatic kab'awilian strategy. Dated to the sixteenth century, the *Popol Vuh* did not circulate until the late nineteenth century, and much like the explorers' letters, it was first published in Europe. Although an account of the K'iche' nation, the text predates current nation-state borders and continues to exert its influence on the rest of the Mesoamerican world. In fact, other versions of the twins' story abound in the oral tradition of the Zapotec nation in Oaxaca. In the *Popol Vuh*, the narrators lament that the original book of council is no longer accessible. The first protagonists of the story are the twin brothers who were later transformed into monkeys by Ixbalamque and Hunahpu, the patrons of the arts and writing. Ixbalamque and Hunahpu are present in ancient lintels, the Tzolk'in/Cholq'ij (the ceremonial Maya calendar), as well as in hieroglyphics. Hence, one can discern that the contents of the *Popol Vuh* (or *Pop Wuj* in contemporary Maya usage) have pre-Columbian sources. The opening and the end of the narration highlight their use of alphabetic writing as a strategic instrument in transposing, transmitting, and preserving knowledge. Writing in alphabetic script or hieroglyphics served a historical and cultural function in pre- and post-Columbian Mesoamerica. Postcontact, many sixteenth-century indigenous colonial texts offered competing versions of the Spanish *crónicas*. I will cite extensively from the beginning and end of Dennis Tedlock's English translation: "This is the beginning of the ancient word, here in this place called

Quiché. Here we shall inscribe, we shall implant the Ancient Word.... There is the original book and ancient writing, but the one who reads and assesses it has a hidden identity. It takes a long performance and account to complete the lightning of all the sky-earth."[32] Further toward the end of the text, the translation reads, "This is enough about the being of Quiché, given that there is no longer a place to see it. There is the original book and ancient writing owned by the lords, now lost, but even so, everything has been completed here concerning Quiché, which is now named Santa Cruz."[33] The narrators acknowledge that they are indeed writing the *Popol Vuh* subsequent to the colonial encounter. They clearly indicate that they seek to pass down knowledge prior to the epistemological rupture represented by colonialism: "We shall bring it out because there is no longer a place to see it, a Council Book."[34] The instrument used for writing is different from what their ancestors deployed, but a sense of urgency drives the authors to write in this new system for preservation. In other words, the alphabetic writing system is an arbitrary semiotic system as the text is in K'iche'. This echoes Eric Havelock's premise in *Origins of Western Literacy* when he reminds us that "the spoken tongue and the sign system used to represent it are theoretically independent of each other."[35]

In a similar fashion, the narrators of *The Books of Chilam Balam* (from the Yucatán Peninsula) maintain that it is their responsibility to protect and preserve Maya knowledge. One of the distinctive features of these texts is their uniform appearance. *The Books of Chilam Balam* are usually named after the town in which they were safeguarded. From these books, two leading assumptions can be drawn about the role played by writing in postcontact Maya society. Foremost of these is its continuity in a new semiotic system, in which it served a similar social function as in the pre-Columbian world when important historical events were recorded. For example, in the *Chilam Balam*, the arrival of the foreigners into Maya land is recorded as "11 Ahau had not yet been fully counted [11.17.0.0.0: 1539–59], when the Spaniards arrived, rash men. From the east they came when they arrived for the first time here to this our land of Maya men, in the year 1513. 9 Ahau [11.18.0.0.0: 1559–79]. Christianity began; baptism was verified. Within this same katun [twenty years] arrived the first Bishop, by the name of Toral. Hanging also ceased."[36] Scribes continued an important cultural and social function throughout the colonial period and thereafter. These records used both Maya and Algebraic numbers, demonstrating that the long count and short count calendars were and continue to be employed.

El ritual de los bacabes (The ritual of the bacabs) and *Los cantares de Dzitbalché* (The songs of Dzitbalché) did not circulate until the twentieth century. *El ritual de los bacabes* stands out for its medical, ritualistic, magical, sacred, and poetic sense. "Ix Hun Pedz Kin / Deadly Goddess," one of the incantations to cure a frenzy, names the goddess of writing as its source.[37] One of the verses reveals this sacred aspect:

> Who is her mother?
> One must say that it is *Ix Hun You Ta*, "Well-aimed Lance."
> *Ix Hun You Ton*, "Well-aimed Member,"
> *Ix Hun Tah Dzib*, "Goddess of Sacred Writing,"
> "Goddess of Glyphs."[38]

Itzamná, the god of writing, along with the four sacred inks, is invoked as the text continues:

> from there [*Sac Bat*, "White-Monkey"] he got the red ink,
> the white ink,
> the black ink,
> the yellow ink.[39]

Writing takes on a poetic and sacred quality. Reference to a "babbling stone" possibly alludes to the lintels or stelae used to deliver texts in oral performances. The Mesoamerican writing system is referenced through the use of the alphabet.

Los cantares de Dzitbalché, offers a unique compilation of spiritual, love, and ritual poems or songs. Alfredo Barrera Vásquez, translator of *Los cantares*, describes the collection as "constituting the only example known today of a codex of this type of literature in all of the Maya area."[40] The manuscript *Los cantares* also includes one of the only poems extant about sacrifice and its cosmological significance. In "X-Kolom-Che" the text alludes to human sacrifice by assuaging and encouraging the warrior. This poem reads like a transliteration of the many murals, or a stelae's depiction of sacrifice.[41] The first part of the poem develops through a detailed description of the environment, alluding to the central plazas of ceremonial centers and their use of stone:

> In the middle of the plaza
> is a man
> tied to the shaft of a column
> made of stone
> thoroughly painted
> with beautiful
> indigo. Many *Balché* flowers have been placed

to perfume him
there in the palms of his hands, on
his feet, and on his body as well.[42]

The poem includes the tradition of using blue paint for ceremonial purposes. The reference to flowers of the *balché* tree is interesting here because their use was prohibited by the Spaniards.[43] The Maya boiled the tree's bark and mixed it with corn (among other ingredients) to make a fermented drink. In the second part, the language is lyrical and tautological:

Sweeten your spirits, beautiful
man; you will
see the face of your Father
up high. There will be no
return here on
earth under the plumage
of the small Hummingbird or
under the skin
... of the beautiful Stag.
of the Jaguar, of the small female *Mérula* or small male *Pají*.
Give yourself courage and think
only of your Father; no
do not fear; it is not
wrong what will be done to you.[44]

Pre-Columbian writing served to commemorate and celebrate the births, deaths, and successes of certain leaders. Postcontact texts in alphabetic script functioned against erasure while preserving historical, mythical, and sacred memory. Notwithstanding the taboo and prohibition surrounding acts of sacrifice due to their cosmological links, this poem strives to preserve its memory.

Independence from Spain represented not a cultural, epistemic, or linguistic break from colonial models but rather the inauguration of a mercantile and exploitative liberal model founded on colonial precepts that intended to absorb and assimilate indigenous nations. This fact has guided contemporary indigenous writers in making cultural and literary claims on this continent prior to the foundation of nation-states. Such decolonizing moves impel us to rethink the foundations of knowledge in Mesoamerica as well as the idea of one nation, one language — narratives that largely explain why Maya and Zapotec alphabetic writing decreased dramatically after the consolidation of nation-states.

Indigenous intellectuals rejected and mobilized against pernicious and stereotypical discourses about illiteracy, backwardness, and poverty throughout the twentieth century. They saw in the museumification of indigenous civilizations in the twentieth century through the erection, in 1964, of the monumental Museo Nacional de Antropología, where sacred objects from various regions in Mexico are centralized and symbolically nationalized, another political attempt to shred the historical testament that binds indigenous nations to their civilizations. Modernizing discourses, in effect, tried to cut indigenous people's historical and cultural ties to their textual legacy by promoting nationalism.

Considering the rich glyphic pre-Columbian and alphabetic postcontact legacy as well as the fact that, for the first 100 years after contact, the first printing presses imported to the continent published exclusively in indigenous languages, what accounts for the persistent stereotype of indigenous illiteracy?[45] The reasons may lie in that the epistemes such as *kab'awil* have remained unknown not only to the society at large but also various fields of study, and is only now being openly discussed by indigenous communities. The field of Latin American literary studies rarely refers to Maya and Zapotec glyphs because these require some fluency in indigenous languages and systems of knowledge that are anchored temporally before nation-state formation and differ from Spain's culture and literary tradition. This lapse may also be due to a tacit consensus among Latin American literary critics who labor under the assumption that the Latin alphabet has been the only technology used in Mesoamerica, disregarding the history of pre-Columbian writing and the intimate function of indigenous ontologies in relationship to writing. A hierarchy of writing as alphabetic — institutionalized in the aftermath of the Spanish conquest — assigned a lesser value to the scripts used in indigenous collectivities in Mesoamerica (as too cumbersome, the devil's work, etc.). Writing in the sixteenth century, José de Acosta believed that "their figures and characters were not as adequate as those of our own writing and letters, this meant that they could not make the words conform exactly but could only express the essential part of ideas."[46] Understanding glyphs has remained outside the purview of literature. Literary critic Roberto González Echevarría, for example, in a foundational text on the history of Latin American literature published in 1996, asserts, "There was poetry, of course, in the New World before the arrival of the Europeans, much of it very difficult to account for because of the lack of writing among most pre-Columbian civilizations."[47]

After 1821, *letrados* turned to Columbus's letters as their intellectual legacy because these were rendered in a writing system they recognized as legitimate.

"Literature" in Latin America, by and large, was not conceived or rooted in any remote relationship to hieroglyphs or codices but seen as growing from the literature-making machinery enabled by the Spanish introduction of the Latin alphabet.[48] The *letrados* wielded two complex discursive processes in the late nineteenth and twentieth centuries. In the first instance, nineteenth-century intellectuals nationalized the Spanish *crónicas* (chronicles) as the origins of Latin American literature and history.[49] In the second maneuver, intellectuals nationalized those indigenous texts penned in Latin letters after the colonial invasion. But, whether historians or other critics posit that the story of Latin America's literary production begins in 1493 with Columbus's "Letter Announcing the Conquest," or with the *Popol Vuh*, the ultimate conclusion is that the Latin alphabet made indigenous texts possible, as evidenced in Rolena Adorno's assertion in the third epigraph to this chapter. Furthermore, as the editors of one of the first Maya literature anthologies plainly note, "as long as we cannot read their codices and inscriptions, these [texts] will form part of an archaeological heritage instead of a literary heritage."[50] Walter Mignolo theorizes the connection between the coloniality of power and literature by recalling that literature and history are institutionalized, translated, and validated because they are in alphabetic writing.[51] Mignolo admonishes that we cannot forget that aspects of colonial literature and culture "were fully-fledged instruments of colonization."[52] Writing in ceremonial centers, ceramics, and textiles, among other mediums, remained largely obscure to literary critics, who simply didn't see it as writing.

Literary and Cultural Debates, Part 1

The debates laboring to separate orality and literacy range from Jean-Jacques Rousseau's assertion that people without the alphabet are uncivilized barbarians to Jack Goody's assessment that not everyone can read the stars.[53] These premises have been incessantly contested but linger across various disciplines. In literacy studies, James Collins and Richard K. Blot adduce that the "field has often presumed dichotomies such as literate versus illiterate, written versus spoken, educated versus uneducated and modern versus traditional."[54] Within literacy studies, two major camps that have left a mark in other fields emerge: one constituted by figures such as Walter Ong, Ian Watt, and Jack Goody, who advance that lack of an alphabet in oral cultures translates to an absence of abstract thought found in cultures with writing.[55] The second school, represented by scholars like Ruth Finnegan, Brian Street, James Paul Gee, and

Shelley Heath, challenges these positions, shaping what has been called new literacy studies.[56] Shifting the field to "situated literacies" or multiple literacies in the 1980s, these discussions point to the intricate link between the alphabet and civilization, on the one hand, and the rise of colonialism and print culture, on the other.[57] The so-called conquest of the world by the Latin alphabet represents an erroneous view of cultural processes as well as a convenient dismissal of other systems of writing (i.e., Hebrew, Chinese, Japanese, Arabic).[58] In *The Origins of Writing*, Wayne Senner notes that the use of an alphabet does not translate into democratic societies, as the most underdeveloped countries employ alphabetic writing while one of the most advanced, Japan, uses a non-alphabetic writing system.[59] Despite changes in the field of literacy studies in the 1980s, the opposition between literacy and orality has not disappeared from common parlance in Mesoamerica, which has critical implications for indigenous literatures and Latin American studies, as I discuss in the next section.[60]

Orality and the Violence of Writing

Within Latin American literary studies, the connection between writing and colonialism in the Americas has been provocatively discussed by many critics who underline the role of the *Requerimiento* and its epistemic violence as well as the role of the Spanish grammarian Antonio de Nebrija in the importation of Western writing in the Americas.[61] Their work argues that the most traumatic element of the "conquest" was not the burden of a new political apparatus but rather the imposition of alphabetic writing and its discourse of power.[62] Ergo, the colonizer's assault on a putative pristine orality becomes central to the discussion of indigenous epistemologies, unwittingly reifying the indigenous subject in the realm of orality, which as I have shown was neither exclusive to indigenous peoples at the time nor the only mode of communication. Orality in these studies figures as the antithesis of writing. It is regarded as the space in which the subaltern takes refuge from the Western world, and it is located outside the national or Western canons. These arguments rely heavily on binary suppositions: orality/writing, conquered/conquistador, codice/book, and glyphs/alphabet. There is no doubt that orality represents an important vehicle of indigenous cultural practices and political postures, but, as I have shown, its exclusiveness to indigenous narrative practices is arbitrary. Scholars cannot discount the fact that literacy was not widespread across European contexts in the fifteenth and sixteenth centuries. Many "explorers" did not write in standard Spanish, nor were they always capable of writing and reading the Castilian tongue they imposed in the Americas.

Ángel Rama's *La ciudad letrada* has been paradigmatic in thinking through the orality/literacy debate in Latin America. The text has been dutifully criticized for leaving out nonalphabetic practices and knowledges, as well as for categorizing indigenous texts using the alphabet as transculturated and not indigenous, but his work transparently and forcefully depicts the imbrication of knowledge and elites in Latin America.[63] *La ciudad letrada* offers key insights into the formation process of religious and intellectual elites in the colonial period. Rama's focus is on the foundations of the first universities, the role of the Jesuits, alphabetic writing and standard Spanish, as well as how political and cultural power transferred from religious hands to those of a privileged few in the nineteenth and early twentieth century. He thoroughly researched how the *letrados* documented and collected oral traditions for the production of official national cultures and literatures from the 1880s to the 1920s.[64] In these compilations, the point of view is from the lettered city, whereas the indigenous "other" functions as a useful object that enables the articulation of a national identity distinct from that of other nations. This move to "fix" oral traditions does not represent a break from the coloniality of power reigning over knowledge production. What's more, Rama stresses, it demonstrates the triumph of the lettered national project over oral traditions.[65] Oral expressions were tethered—and in some respects continue to be—near the margins of academic scholarship as folklore. Tensions between alleged folkloric and more "cosmopolitan" literary productions has divided Latin America's most important writers, reaching its peak during the heated debates between the cosmopolitan Argentine writer Julio Cortázar and the *indigenista* Peruvian writer José María Arguedas—arguments so visceral that some believe they were responsible for Arguedas's suicide.[66] Indigenous oral myths and folklore made Latin American literature distinct from European literary trends, but they have never occupied the same literary or social status. For the most part, early Latin American literary historiographies assume, as Antonio Cornejo Polar points out, that indigenous literature ended with the imposition of a Spanish colonial system.[67]

The will to develop and affirm a national and continental identity, on the one hand, and the need to name the reality of linguistic and cultural confluences, on the other, led to various paradigms that purported to capture processes that could lead to national or regional unity. From the early twentieth century to the 1980s, this inspired Latin America writers and other intellectuals to propose a number of social, cultural, anthropological, and literary theories that aimed for national cohesion, steeped in metaphors of racial mixture. These paradigms excise internal difference, consolidate national and regional identity, and continue to uphold Spanish as the only option for indigenous communities.[68] Similar to the function of what literary critic Doris Sommer (1991) termed as *Foundational Fictions*, these theories attempted to stimulate continental unity and identity despite internal linguistic and ethnic pluralism. Of course, as I have already mentioned, these discourses have been contested by many critics, including such disparate figures as Antonio Cornejo Polar, John Beverley, and Analisa Taylor.[69] Mexican philosopher José Vasconcelos's ideas about *mestizaje* and the formation of a fifth race gained currency in the 1920s, when Mexico — and by extension Latin America — aimed to forge a national identity distinct from European and U.S. models.[70] Rama's theory of *transculturación narrativa* emerged at the same time that social discontent escalated in the 1970s.[71] Cornejo Polar's theory of heterogeneity to characterize Latin American literatures and Néstor García Canclini's celebratory use of hybridity to account for the transformation of traditional practices added new dimensions to this discussion, but they, too, ultimately failed to engage directly with indigenous claims to intellectual autonomy and self-determination.[72] While the latter theories address questions of indigeneity in more sophisticated ways, the works of Cornejo Polar and García Canclini depoliticize indigenous cultural productions. Cornejo Polar does not account for other reordering of borders based on language and indigenous nations like the Quechua/Kichua or the new borders proposed by Mapuche intellectuals between Argentina and Chile. García Canclini's use of hybridity retains the positivist racial connotations implied in the term's etymology.[73]

Scholars working on twentieth- and twenty-first-century indigenous literatures published in the last twenty years have enriched the debates on indigenous orality and literacy.[74] Carlos Montemayor complicates this construct by underscoring its complex interrelationship in indigenous literatures, as well as its Western and non-Western sources. In *Arte y trama en el cuento indígena* (Art and plot in the indigenous short story), Montemayor notes, "The origins of the oral tradition of indigenous people are not 'primitive': they are at least the Spanish written and oral tradition as well as the written and oral tradition of the pre-Hispanic civilization."[75] This perspective demonstrates that there are multiple layers to what is perceived as "indigenous orality." In other words, orality does not function exclusively as an act of speech, one that reiterates an unchanging story across time and space. Micaela Morales López, in her study of indigenous literature in Chiapas, *Raíces de la ceiba: Literatura indígena de Chiapas*, perceptively observes, "The concept of orality is a construct elaborated from within a written culture."[76] Quoting Raúl Dorra, Morales López continues, "One can only speak of orality from a letter-centric position."[77] In recent studies, the critic Luz María Lepe Lira theorizes indigenous literatures as border literature but maintains the orality/literacy dichotomy. In the United States, Paul Worley focuses on the importance of oral literature and the work being done by cultural producers to accord it a value equal to writing for the Yukatek Maya. Other scholars, including Emilio del Valle Escalante and Arturo Arias, argue that indigenous literatures are also part of intellectual autonomous projects.[78]

Maya and Zapotec literatures reflect the local and the global contexts that indigenous writers are engaged in as they challenge precepts about orality and literacy, literature, and national identity. Indigenous literary production runs parallel to Latin American intellectuals' longing for a unified Latin American subject. Indigenous claims to regional autonomy, even in the literary terrain, resuscitate deep-seated fears about the state's failure to "nationalize" Indians. The project of homogeneous nation-states under the guise of cultural and biological mixture is propagated at the expense of indigenous autonomy. As Kichua literary critic Armando Muyulema clearly points out, "At the cultural level (García Canclini, 1989) and in the area of Latin American literary studies (Rama, 1980 and Cornejo Polar, 1978), cultural and linguistic heterogeneity is set up as a formula that will give way to hybridity as the desired synthesis in the formation of culture and literature."[79] Muyulema continues, "Notwithstanding, even in this perspective, a yearning for unity can be perceived, a yearning that carries the implicit assimilation of one by the other; of the Europeanized criollo culture as the paradigm whose constitution indigenous cultures will only cosmetically add to, at best."[80] Gayatri Chakravorty Spivak's foundational question, "Can the subaltern speak?" must be redirected, for the pressing inquiry in this context is "Can the subaltern write?" The answer is a sonorous affirmative in multiple languages and their regional varieties.[81]

Cosmolectics and An(other) Literary Legacy

Contemporary indigenous writers, artists, and other intellectuals politicize the various attempts by nation-states in Mesoamerica to eradicate indigenous languages and cultures. Enrique Sam Colop (a foundational K'iche' poet and critic) returns to the nation-state's decree of 1824, summarizing its goal as to "extinguish the language of the first indigenous [people]."[82] The inchoate literary movement of the 1980s, most widely represented in Mexico, forced writers to reflect on their relationship to pre-Columbian systems of writing and the oral tradition, thus enacting kab'awil. The Tseltal writer Josías López Gómez writes that "when indigenous peoples came under the power of culture and language from Europe, they lost their own art of writing and were subjected to another kind of art that no longer had anything to do with their own worldview."[83] The K'iche' poet Humberto Ak'abal states that the appropriation of the alphabet to create and diffuse literature represents a central undertaking: "Given the loss of our forms of writing, we must [out of] necessity adopt the Spanish alphabet and force it to give our languages written forms."[84] These two interrelated knowledge systems inspired writers to assert a cosmolectics, reinforcing kab'awil as a double gaze to the past and present. Mixe linguist and public intellectual Yásnaya Elena Aguilar Gil writes that "long ago, we also wrote our language. There were other signs, not the ones we use now. But that script was eventually lost. When non-Mixes arrived here, they brought with them their spellings and forms of writing that we now use. When we write our language, those are the signs, forms and writing we use."[85] Twentieth- and twenty-first-century Zapotec and Maya literature challenge traditional ways of thinking about writing as mimesis or even "speech acts." Maya K'iche' Enrique Sam Colop argues that "the origins of the Maya writing system can be placed between 100–600 BCE, and the production of books at least from 300 CE. Thus, writing and books did not first come to this continent in the sixteenth century with the European invasion, nor is it the case that Maya people stopped reading and writing after colonization."[86] Indigenous visions challenge the monolithic ideas circulated in the sixteenth century about Indians' agraphic nature. Sam Colop emphasizes the expansive notion of writing-as-communication by reiterating that "the ancient Maya wrote (carved or painted) on jade, bones, stone monuments, stucco tablets, murals, ceramic vessels, and on bark paper."[87] Similarly, Víctor D. Montejo, Maya Popti' professor emeritus at the University of California, Davis, underscores that "the Mayan writer has been present since the first date (3114 BCE) was inscribed on the Mayan calendar, on the 'stones that speak,' or stelae, during the preclassic, classic, and postclassic Maya periods."[88] He continues, "We can take pride in having a literary tradition that goes back several millennia, enabling us to know at least part of the history and the spirituality of the Maya in ancient times."[89]

As contemporary Maya and Zapotec writers and other intellectuals gained audiences and more publishing territory, they affirmed intertextuality with previous texts originating in the ceremonial centers or those produced postcontact as well as the oral tradition. Montejo evokes *The Books of Chilam Balam* in his *Oxlanh B'aqtun: Recordando al sacerdote jaguar,* claiming them as part of a Maya heritage that knows no borders (*The Books of Chilam Balam* are attributed to the Maya in Mexico). Through a kab'awil cosmolectics, writers contest and reconfigure the traditional Latin American literary and cultural model that positions them outside the production of literature. In a similar vein, the Zapotec scholar and poet Víctor de la Cruz asserts, "In pre-Hispanic times the Binnigula'sa' [literally "People from the Clouds," or Zapotec people] created a writing system to represent their language . . . some in stone tablets or integrated into buildings and other loose sculptures, stelae developed by the scribes of the time."[90] He proudly writes that ceremonial centers like Monte Albán and Mitla are proof of the Zapotec's great intellectual achievement.[91] The lack of pre-Hispanic literary documentation for the Zapotec, from his perspective, is attributable to the destruction by the Spaniards of documents written in cloth, deerskin, or stone. He identifies, however, the importance of those genres guarded in the memory of individuals such as music and sermons. In de la Cruz's poem, "¿Quiénes somos, cuál es nuestro nombre?" (Who are we, what is our name?) words are sculpted in stone by the ancestors.

> the word sculpted by our grandparents
> on the stones,
> sung at night,
> while they danced,
>
> used to decorate their homes, in their sanctuaries,
> in their royal palaces?
> Those who brought a second language
> came to kill us along with our word, came to trample on the people
>   as if we were worms
> fallen from a tree, thrown on the ground. Who are we? What is our
>   name?[92]

The first stanza summons the ancestors who sculpted writing on the rocks, while in the second stanza de la Cruz offers a powerful indictment of the imposition of the Spanish language as a foreign element. The questions that conclude the stanza force Zapotec readers not to identify themselves with the Spaniards who came to kill but to remember by turning their gaze to the ancient Zapotec, or Cloud People, again reverting to a cosmolectics that moves vertically and horizontally in remembrance of the ancestors.

Another foundational Zapotec writer, Macario Matus, in his poem "Binni Záa / Los zapotecas," performs a similar symbolic re-turn. Matus makes use of the zoomorphic characteristics found in ceremonial calendars and places like Monte Albán as the genesis of the Zapotec. In the poem he links the sacred and Zapotec origins, another example of a cosmolectics move.

> Everything was darkness
> when the Zapotec were born.
> They sprang from the old trees,
> like the ceiba,
> born from the belly of the beasts,
> like the tiger, the lizard.
>
> When the great light launched
> By the high sun fell,
> our great father,
> They interwove their hands
> with otters,
> who are our Mothers, too.
> The Zapotec were saved
> by floating on water
> like large turtles.
> They were inundated in water
> Like hollow serpents,
> carrying their children on the nipples.[93]

That first stanza counters the biblical book of Genesis. Matus invokes the animal representations that abound in Mesoamerican ceremonial centers and calendars as the Zapotec's creation story. Similar to other Mesoamerican nations, the concept of animal doubles or *nahuales* is presented with force. Indeed, the imagery of serpents traditionally represents rain and references the idea of the Binnigula'sa'/Binnizá as People from the Cloud. Irma Pineda Santiago gracefully writes of this in her poem "Laanu/Nosotros" (Us):[94]

> Us,
> Our word will continue being song
> We are the offspring of trees
> That will shade our path
> We are the offspring of stones
> That will not allow forgetting

In this short poem, she references the oral tradition (song), nature (trees), and hieroglyphic writing (stones). The reiterated theme is that of continuity and the Zapotec legacy as a source of identity and strength.

In Guatemala, Q'anjob'al writer Gaspar Pedro González, another key figure in organizing hemispheric literary conferences in the early 1990s, consciously builds this millenarian trope in his novels and poetry. His poem "Stz'ib'" culminates this kab'awilian move gracefully and foregrounds this "double gaze" to the past and present. In the poem, a young Maya writer gradually becomes intoxicated by the omnipresence of glyphs surrounding him. The first line creates an ambiguity between the speaker and the subject of the poem: "And over the stone, appear the imprints of his hands."[95] The speaker's unexpected discovery in the rocks of an ancient city alludes to a glorious Maya past, coming full circle to face his contemporary identity. One may argue that it is the speaker's immediate presence that makes the prints of the past visible. The reference to "his hands" functions as a literal discovery of his own identity, a reconciliation of his contemporary identity with the past, one that serves as a synecdoche for the whole of Maya culture. The remaining lines employ strong verbs that reflect the perseverance and persistence of Maya writing:

A throng of signs
Sprung amid the glyphs:
Engraved in the ample facades
Rooted in the silent monuments.
Rolled over the steps
Fell from the vaults
Surged from the high and low reliefs,
Exploded like the roars of jaguars
Between the density of green jade;
Like a symphony of drums and *atabales*
Wrapped between musical staffs of *amate*.[96]

The metaphors gradually move from the image of "signs / sprung amid the glyphs" to their explosive jaguar-like roar. González's poem ends with the image of the codices, the sacred books, usually made from the bark of the *amate* tree. His poem documents the underpinnings in this millenarian literary tradition based on the palpability of the ancient Maya cities and codices. González's work reconciles past and present in this literary continuum.

The memory of hieroglyphic texts in the Maya and Zapotec cultures plays an important role in the revision of dominant literary and cultural histories. Jacinto Arias, in *Cuentos y relatos indígenas*, boldly announces, "Our fathers and mothers of antiquity knew how to read and write. They forgot [how] when the Spanish confiscated their writings. That is why we only know how to write our language as if our eyes were closed."[97] Contemporary indigenous writers have not attempted to write in hieroglyphics, yet the cultural referent provides an alternative genealogy to the idea of knowledge/power seen through a European lens. Glyphs are prominent in many of the book and journal covers, representing a significant link to heritage and a pre-Columbian literary tradition.[98] The collective memory of glyphic writing serves to contest the social stigmas attached to the colonialist binaries of literacy/orality, progress/backwardness, and modernity/premodernity. While glyphic writing may have been in decline by the time the Spanish arrived, writers maintain that colonialism severed them from its practice. Contemporary Maya and Zapotec writers and intellectuals participate in efforts to understand and reconnect to glyphic writing while they assert its role in the production of literature.[99]

Conclusion

Maya and Zapotec scribes utilized the new alphabetic writing system since its adoption in the sixteenth century, but the palpability of a literary and cultural movement that challenged and inverted the dominant image of a passive, monolithic Indian soared in the 1990s. Kab'awil allows writers to defy temporality and periodization of Maya and Zapotec literature as new by reclaiming hieroglyphs and the oral tradition, thus engaging a Mesoamerican cosmolectics through the double gaze represented by kab'awil. Mass migration to cities as well as the gradual professionalization of indigenous men and women are macroevents that have directly influenced this change. Maya and Zapotec writers set out to establish a literary tradition of their own, one that predates the Latin alphabet by utilizing it to write in their languages and to offer writing that distinguishes their experience from that of nonindigenous writers. Maya and Zapotec nations occupy a unique position given the legacy of unrivaled hieroglyphic writing systems in the Americas and a rich alphabetic writing tradition. Their entrance into the Republic of Letters challenged the monolingual and mestizo paradigm entrenched in official discourse since independence from Spain. The next chapter examines the short story as a genre that traces the formation of the indigenous author through which writers consciously distance themselves from other mediated genres such as the *testimonio*.

CHAPTER TWO

The Formation of the Contemporary Mesoamerican Author

You cannot destroy me, I move under the empire of words,
of sacred words.... The word nurtures my soul, it gives me
vigor and strength.—Josías López K'ana (Maya writer, 1999)

They say that Zapotec is vanishing
no one will speak it anymore; it has died, they say,
the language of the Zapotec
. . . .
Ay! Zapotec, Zapotec
language that gives me life,
I know that you will die,
the day the sun dies.
—Gabriel López Chiñas (Zapotec poet, 1982)

CHAPTER 1 EXAMINED the contradictory colonialist narratives, regarding indigenous writing systems, literature, and kab'awil, or the intervening double gaze. It discussed how the oral tradition has come to stand in as representative of indigenous authenticity, while ignoring existing pre-Columbian indigenous writing systems. The chapter argued that the academic propensity to split orality from literary texts undermines how scribes in the postcontact period quickly appropriated the alphabet and surreptitiously included glyph conventions in their work. Adherence to indigenous cosmolectics allowed postcontact scribes to embrace an alphabetic writing system without disconnecting from or losing sight of their own glyphic traditions. The contemporary writer's exercise of the double gaze makes it possible for Maya and Zapotec writers to recognize ancient writing practice as an important legacy that contemplates a power/knowledge genealogy in conversation with a cosmolectics.

This chapter underlines the intricacies involved in the development of the indigenous author. It counters the traditional view that defines indigenous literature as a tributary study, predominately seen as fitting more appropriately within the scope of ethnography. Micaela Morales López, and other scholars, situates "traditional" indigenous literature as part of the field of ethnography.[1] "It is therefore important," Morales López argues, "to conduct an analysis related to myth criticism and anthropology in order to clarify whether the texts perform a function in the daily lives of the diverse communities. If the answer is yes, it is important to understand how they are manufactured in the indigenous imaginary."[2] Critics who rely heavily on myth exegesis tend to overemphasize the oral tradition as indigenous authenticity in their analysis of indigenous literatures of Mesoamerica, thus missing the ideological stakes generated by the emergence of indigenous authors and their insertion in the literary world. Albert Braz (2011) forcefully argues that writer/author indeterminacy marks the production of indigenous literature in the Americas due to their collaborative nature. He writes, "The identity of the producers of texts, including Indigenous texts, is simply not as transparent as some critics would have us believe" (8). Braz builds his argument by identifying the indeterminacy of the author(s) in the *Popol Vuh*; *I, Rigoberta Menchú*; and *Cogewea*.[3] The indeterminacy of indigenous authorship reached its climax with the Rigoberta Menchú / Elizabeth Burgos-Debray controversy.[4] In contrast, Paja Faudree positions indigenous authorship as the opposite of universal authorship in general.[5] Faudree proposes that indigenous authors are compelled to ask different questions. Braz's "writer indeterminacy" does not clearly differentiate between ethnography, testimonies, and the diverse body of work produced by indigenous authors in the last decades, whereas Faudree does not engage with the politics of autonomy. Luz María Lepe's *Lluvia y viento, puentes de sonido* (Rain and wind, bridges of sound) (2010), concludes that "the tension [between] orality and writing is produced with great intensity, because the basic strategies of literary composition are products, on the one hand, of traditional forms of orality that the authors live every day in their communities and, on the other hand, of a different type of rationality that gives a primordial place to the word and its sound."[6] She finalizes by adding that the indigenous writer "from the primitive subverts what is cultured.... Writing became an artifact of the Indians [in order] to revive their language and culture."[7] Hers is one of the first books published in Spanish that addresses the relationship between indigenous literature in Mexico and literary theory. Her concluding remarks reinforce sharp divisions between the oral and written, "primitive" and "cultured."

The deployment of binaries to describe the relationship between indigenous writers and Western society disavows the aims of indigenous writers and their lived experiences, as they do not exist in isolation. Indexing contemporary texts in such simplified ways reinscribes them within a racialized hierarchy of knowledge production.[8]

Hierarchies are also present in the *testimonio* genre. Defined as "a bearing witness," the *testimonio* is an oral account of an urgent political matter or series of events that require immediate dissemination and attention recounted to an intellectual/academic, typically an outsider to indigenous communities. The subaltern subject, who claims to represent his or her community, calls attention to an urgent political or social state of affairs. The collaborators involved in the production of the testimonial assumed it to be a "democratic" form that captured authentic voices or reproduced more faithfully the social reality of indigenous peoples.[9] Reducing indigenous narratives to works in which an outsider's intervention is required has tended to ignore local creative endeavors, tagging them as modest extensions of ethnography and testimonial practices.[10] Arturo Arias, Luis E. Cárcamo-Huechante, and Emilio del Valle Escalante state that the authority attained by the *testimonio* in the academy has benefited contemporary indigenous literature.[11] Nonetheless, the academy's fixation with this mediated practice has overshadowed the status of contemporary individual indigenous authors in Latin America.[12] Also at play in these attempts to define the field is a constant negotiation of what is considered indigenous literature in Latin America. Miguel Figueroa Saavedra concedes that many indigenous narrators or "nonauthors" formed successful "literary couples" with renowned anthropologists.[13] This type of collaboration gave birth to a robust ethnographic corpus in the social sciences, serving as a critical reminder of the giant strides made by indigenous writers whose cultural output does not require authentication from scientists.[14] The indigenous author is not confined to an "ethnic" collectivity, as his or her works circulate through international circuits via the Internet, in compact discs, translations, and international festivals in Europe and Latin America. Most indigenous writers who spearheaded literary movements have been translated mainly into Western European and Semitic languages (Humberto Ak'abal into Hebrew and Feliciano Sánchez Chan into Arabic, to name a couple). In this chapter, I demonstrate that the authors' use of cosmolectics, represented through kab'awil, reflects a social, sacred, and aesthetic ontology, experienced by indigenous intellectuals as they grapple with questions that revolve around authorship and oral traditions, spiritual and secular practices, indigenous identity and assimilation.

Jorge Cocom Pech's *Secretos del abuelo/Muk'ult'an in nool* (Grandfather's secrets), Nicolás Huet Bautista's *La última muerte/Ti slajebalxa lajele* (The last death), Humberto Ak'abal's *Grito en la sombra* (Scream in the shadows), and Ana Patricia Martínez Huchim's *U yóol xkaambal jaw xíiw/Contrayerba* (Antidote) resist reduction to notions of orality as authenticity and tradition versus modernity. These writers invigorate storytelling by removing the conventional precepts anchoring indigenous peoples to the dictums of the oral tradition. In the context of Mesoamerica, the heralded disappearance or death of the author creates a vacuum, a space from which the indigenous author emerges. This absence and (re)emergence ultimately strengthen the function of indigenous authorship. The process calls on the central notion of intention and the rapport that exists between the text and its author. In a modern society where the marginalization of indigenous communities persists, the emergence of the indigenous author is fundamental to the creation of intercultural spaces and exchanges that participate in a Mesoamerican cosmolectics.[15] A kab'awilian gaze filters the ideological maneuvers that indigenous writers engage in as they reimagine the invisible constituents of the past and rearrange the frame of the visibility of the present. The age-old craft of storytelling has always been an integral part to indigenous literary practices. That craft's embrace of other forms signals a change in contemporary indigenous subjectivity. This change correlates to the political activism of the 1970s and the role played by public education. Working against the goal of state-sponsored literacy programs to assimilate indigenous communities, many contemporary writers seized on the opportunity to broker for equitable relations between government institutions and their communities. They articulated a cosmolectics (past *and* present, preservation *and* innovation) as an alternative to the pressure of homogenization. The works examined illustrate a movement away from testimonial and collaborative compilations to those of published authors who straddle various registers.[16]

In these short narrative units, the indigenous writers recast the notion of the oral tradition to a process of fictionalizing a contemporary subjectivity by using the affect of an oral tale to narrate a modern life at the beginning of the twenty-first century, without giving up the importance of the cosmolectics that informs their work. This, in effect, fashions a novel, subjective tone of voice in the corpus of indigenous literatures, a voice that is nuanced, distinct, and highly personal. The narrative's structural tensions that emerge in each short text respond to the authors' awareness of their work's reception and their own creative intentions. Indigenous intellectuals' relationships to writing, from the pre-Columbian periods to the present, naturally manifest differently across time and space. In the twenty-first century, the authors' narrative force lies in the double gaze they deploy as they straddle historical literary divides. Before delving into each of the author's texts, the next sections point out general developments in education policies and their impact on the production of indigenous authors.

Education and Assimilation

Education legislation is one of the most important factors affecting the emergence of writers in indigenous languages. A cursory view of Mexico and Guatemala's education policy demonstrates its impact on the production of bilingual literature. During the colonial period, education led to religious conversion. In the nation-formation era culminating in the 1930s, education policy forced linguistic and cultural assimilation. Changes in pedagogical philosophy initiated in the 1940s, mainly in Mexico, worked toward an integrationist policy through less coercive mechanisms.[17] In Guatemala, government schools like the Escuela Normal de Indígenas established in 1920 aimed to assimilate "Indians" for their alleged benefit.[18] The creation of various government institutions advocating for bilingual and intercultural education helped open important spaces for indigenous communities. In effect, the increasing participation of indigenous men and women in the teaching profession nurtured the emergence of indigenous writers.

Mexico established its first boarding school following a model similar to the U.S. one instituted by Captain Richard H. Pratt at the Carlisle Indian School.[19] In 1926, the Casa del Estudiante Indígena (House of the Indigenous Student) opened its doors in Mexico City. Students learned a standard Secretaría de Educación Pública (SEP) curriculum and other skills-based courses, but the Casa did little to address the academic needs of the larger indigenous communities. Responding to this failure, the SEP founded *internados indígenas* (indigenous boarding schools). According to Alexander Dawson's research, eleven boarding schools operated in 1933; five years later, thirty-two provided services.[20] Student enrollment reached 4,000 in these indigenous-only schools in the l960s, while federal schools enrolled around 636,600 indigenous students.[21] Simply put, the idea of racially segregated schools was not as popular in Mexico. Although Mexico's boarding schools followed the militaristic model of the U.S. Indian schools, they differed in their ideological objectives. In Mexico, the few boarding schools strove to cultivate ethnic affiliations as an alternative to coerced assimilation. Indigenous communities were imagined to be crucial to developing and modernizing the nation. Unlike the United States and Canada, Mexico's discourse of mestizaje influenced how the founders related to indigenous peoples—and they believed in education as the solution to the many difficulties the indigenous communities faced.[22] Due to retention failures in Mexico City, other schools were established in specific ethnic communities, which facilitated the learning and transmission of local languages. With the exception of the 1940s, bilingual education was conceived as a critical tool to train and promote indigenous students to become cultural advocates.[23] Literacy instruction in indigenous languages remained sporadic throughout the twentieth century, with increased political leverage once the SEP realized its usefulness in promoting acquisition of Spanish.

In Guatemala, politicized state legislation on the adequacy of indigenous languages for instruction, as well as a succession of twentieth-century political upheavals, have inevitably affected the country's literary output. Jorge Skinner-Klee points out that after Guatemala's independence from Spain in 1821, the Constituent Congress announced the need to eradicate all indigenous languages, claiming they were "so diverse, incomplete, and imperfect [and] not sufficient to enlighten the people."[24] The Escuela Normal de Indígenas, established in 1920, aimed to assimilate "Indians" for their alleged benefit.[25] Adding to the official linguistic discrimination was the legislation enacted by dictator Jorge Ubico to oppress indigenous peoples in Guatemala. In 1934, for example, he passed a vagrancy law forcing peasants owning less than two hectares of land to perform manual labor for a minimum of 100 days per year.[26] Beginning in the 1930s, the Ministry of Education promoted coercive integrationist measures.[27] The Summer Institute of Linguistics joined the Guatemalan Ministry of Education in 1952 and developed the first alphabets for indigenous-language instruction.[28] Other models emerged from the religious boarding schools established under the auspices of Monsignor Mariano Rosell in many poor and rural communities after the 1950s.[29]

The direct input of the Instituto Indigenista de México in education policies led to important benefits to indigenous communities, but the Instituto Indigenista de Guatemala had a less systematic impact. The dictator Ubico blocked all funding for the operation of the Instituto Indigenista Guatemala. Any measures that would positively affect indigenous communities had to wait for the governments of presidents Juan José Arévalo and Jacobo Árbenz. *Castellanización* was in full force under the direction of monolingual Spanish-speaking teachers, without cultural or linguistic ties to the communities they were appointed to, throughout most of the 1960s. Amendments to the constitution were ratified and a new law enacted, the *Ley orgánica de educación* (Organic Law of Education), in 1965. This new law repositioned education as an instrument of integration.[30] Ratifying Article 9 in the constitution permitted the use of Native languages for instruction for the first time in the history of the nation-state. In 1967, the Ministry of Education trained bilingual instructors. Teacher-training schools like Santiago de Caballeros for indigenous men in Guatemala City, which aimed to "civilize" indigenous communities, ironically formed many of the most vocal, high-profile contemporary pan-Maya intellectuals. Adrián Inés Chávez, for example, one of the first graduates of an all-boys school, developed one of the first K'iche' alphabets. Many of the young men and women who studied in bilingual education schools experienced a social dissonance that led them to deploy numerous kab'awilian strategies. The creation of various government institutions advocating for bilingual and intercultural education created important spaces for indigenous communities in the 1980s. In effect, the increasing participation of indigenous men and women in the teaching profession has had helped foster the emergence of writers as well.

I am not tracing a straight line from cultural opposition to integration necessarily, as plenty of groups that formed believed in assimilation as a way to improve living conditions in indigenous communities, or what, in the Maya context of Guatemala, Emma Delfina Chirix García, following Edgar Esquit, calls *la superación*.[31] This accommodating position can be traced to indigenous social movements in Mexico during the late 1940s. In *The Truth of Others*, Alicja Iwańska isolates the realists and the utopians. Both groups advocated for the integration of indigenous communities. The stance of the indigenous teachers and intellectuals were at least cosmetically assimilationist. Iwańska emphasizes the motto of the Asociación Mexicana de los Profesionales e Intelectuales Indígenas (Mexican Association of Indigenous Professionals and intellectuals): "Let's Mexicanize Indians, not Indianize Mexico!"[32] Ironically, one of its political objectives read, "This [nationalizing process] should be carried out by Native intellectuals who come from an Indian community and understand them."[33] Nonetheless, these political projects had unforeseen consequences in spurring the creation of Native-language newsletters and newspapers.

Presidents Lázaro Cárdenas in Mexico and Juan José Arévalo in Guatemala enacted important changes that contributed to the programs in health, education, and economic prosperity through their respective indigenista institutes. Despite the progressive policies, indigenous communities continued to be socially and economically marginalized. In Mexico, progressive governments sought to integrate indigenous groups since, as Gilda Waldman explains, "the liberal trend, as well as the Marxist one, favored the loss of indigenous ethnic identity."[34] In Guatemala — as Santiago Bastos and Manuela Camus point out — while the so-called progressive revolution in 1944 abolished obligatory work for indigenous communities, it did not consider them as distinct ethnic subjects that did not fit the liberal model.[35] In 1954, the CIA-sponsored coup d'état halted progress in relationship to indigenous people's educational reforms.

Public school teachers, who were recruited through the various state-sponsored assimilationist projects in Guatemala and Mexico, initiated similar literary movements. For example, poets Calixta Gabriel Xiquín and Maya Cú Choc, trained as teachers, were the first Maya women in Guatemala to publish as individual authors. In Mexico, public schoolteachers constituted organizations, like Maya'on on the Yucatán Peninsula, that are well established today. Jorge Cocom Pech trained as a teacher before getting involved in local politics and becoming an independent writer. Others maintained careers as "native informants" to anthropologists or as cultural promoters (under the auspices of cultural and governmental organs such as the Instituto Nacional Indigenista [National Indigenista Institute, or INI] or Culturas Populares) specifically in Mexico. As educators and cultural promoters, they embodied a strand of social kab'awil where recruitment into teaching programs did not have the intended effect of assimilation. State policies seeking to assimilate indigenous men and women via education compelled this generation to seek alternative solutions to their political condition.

Access to education encouraged writers and other intellectuals to value the oral tradition and other ways of knowing the word that were debased by institutions of higher education. Their position was not informed by an ontological determination linking "Indians" to orality but rather resulted from the fact that indigenous peoples have been denied literacy in their own languages. For Maya intellectual Ajb'ee Jiménez Sánchez, the fact "that Maya languages have existed solely orally shows that their underdevelopment in their written form results precisely from the political and social conditions they have been subjected to."[36] In other words, the loss of pre-Columbian systems of writing and a lack of literacy in indigenous languages due to colonization precluded the production of written literature.

Three Literary Modalities

Indigenous writers practice a wide spectrum of literary genres and modalities. Maya Tsotsil writer Antonio López Hernández identifies three practices: the oral tradition, the transcription of the oral tradition, and the "literary revolution" of "individual creations."[37] Tenek writer Nefi Fernández Acosta likewise argues that indigenous literatures can be grouped into three modes: the compilation of the oral tradition, re-creating the oral tradition, and lastly, the creators or those writers who fictionalize in ways closer to modern literary tradition.[38] This distinction is not evolutionary or temporal, as all three modes coexist in practice. However, for the purpose of the sections developed in this chapter, I focus on the third modality, the *creadores*, because this is where kab'awil features most prominently. Through these individual creations, a new body of texts surfaces that moves from the practice of transcribing myths and oral narratives to creating stories that address issues outside the parameters of what has been established as traditional indigenous literature. In this sense, storytelling undergoes a conversion, from the standard short, fable-like narration to fully conventional "literary" short stories. I do not attribute more value to one or the other, as my research is not a teleological undertaking. Rather, I aim in this chapter to historicize an important shift that is taking place and that speaks to these specific writers and their relationships to authorship and the oral tradition. In that process, their work embodies another intellectual project, one that demands not only intellectual autonomy but also a different hermeneutics. They must be understood through their own historical and literary context, where a double gaze marks their movement between institutions and communities, privileging a Mesoamerican cosmolectics.

The Indigenous Author

In their structure, language, and content, Jorge Cocom Pech's *Secretos del abuelo / Mukult'an in nool* (Grandfather's secrets), Nicolás Huet Bautista's *La última muerte* (The last death), Humberto Ak'abal's *Grito en la sombra* (Scream in the shadows), and Ana Patricia Martínez Huchim's *U yóol xkaambal jaw xíiw / Contrayerba* (Antidote) reflect the issues this chapter delineates. Roland Barthes, in his seminal essay "The Death of the Author," posits that "to give a text an Author is to impose a limit on that text."[39] While Barthes's theoretical position is not without controversy, it does offer important insights in rethinking, not just the connection between ethnography and indigenous knowledge but also the struggle for representation. Literary critics and writers are rightfully skeptical in their critique that the notion of the dead author coincides with the emergence of Third World authors, and their beginning to claim a space in the Republic of Letters. Barthes's insights into the birth of the reader may also be useful in reframing the presumed function of the indigenous author, who must create readers and be mindful of their reception. If, as Michel Foucault asserts, the name of an author "performs a certain role with regard to narrative discourse, assuring a classificatory function," the becoming of an indigenous writer authorizes subject making.[40] The demands that weigh on the classification of an indigenous author exemplify this Foucauldian contention. For one, they trigger a number of expectations and semantic associations that the indigenous author endorses or contests. Indigenous writers participate willingly in the formation of a new corpus where certain themes, ideas, and issues come to define indigenous literature.

As cultural artifacts, the stories I discuss allude to the oral tradition, but they are not transcriptions of oral stories. Their content and form diverge from those that characterize the *compiladores* of the oral tradition. In other words, they are not collaborations in the same vein as earlier compilations, and their production is not similar to that of traditional testimonies. Each story in the collections develops a conflict, a plot, and a resolution. I examine one short text from each of these anthologies to demonstrate that they grapple with the fantastic and magical markers of the oral tradition, but that they gesture toward the secular and knowledge as lived experience.[41] While the authors emphasize the blurring of oppositions through kab'awil, the tension created by attempting to meet the demands of their status as "authors," as well as conventional notions of what constitutes indigenous literature, begs further analysis. These stories illustrate a web of complexity that indigenous writers face as they transit from the collective to the individual authorial voice. Walter Benjamin's "The Storyteller" advances the idea that the storyteller disappears with the advent of modernity, when experience has stopped having the same value. In the Mesoamerican context, the storytellers do not disappear; they resist disappearance by assuming the status of authors. Of course, I am not suggesting that all indigenous writers transition from the oral to the written, following a similar path. However, the four texts examined in the next section deploy a kab'awilian strategy as they maintain a double gaze toward the oral and the written, tradition and modernity, without yielding to oppositions or binaries.

A Maya poet, narrator, essayist, and professor of Maya language and Spanish, Jorge Cocom Pech was born in the town of Calkiní, Campeche, on the central western coast of the Yucatán Peninsula. From 2002 to 2005, he was president of the National Indigenous Writers Association (ELIAC). He has published numerous articles and his work has been translated into French, Italian, Serbian, Romanian, and Arabic. He has also received numerous awards, including the 1994 Quintana Roo Prize in Journalism for his narrative *Testimonio de una iniciación: La prueba del aire, la prueba del sueño* (Testimonial of an initiation: The air challenge, the dream challenge), which would later become part of his book *El cazador de auroras* (The hunter of dawns).

Secretos del abuelo, in broad strokes, tells of the grandfather Gregorio, the latter's shamanistic teachings, and the grandson's (presumably the author's) apprenticeship experience. Ana Luisa Izquierdo reads Cocom Pech's book as a testimonial but also as six short essays, while Emilio del Valle Escalante reads it as an autobiographical novel.[42] I read each chapter in this book as an independent narrative unit, since the chapters do not necessarily depend on each other for intelligibility. Cocom Pech tells the reader that Gregorio mandated that his grandson write one day about his teaching. Ironically, the grandfather's desire is for disclosure through writing. Cocom Pech lures the reader with the promise to reveal the grandfather's secrets. Doris Sommer discusses the function of "secrets" in Rigoberta Menchú's *testimonio*.[43] Sommer sees these "secrets" as resistance to the outsider's gaze. Cocom Pech's *Secretos del abuelo*, in contrast, aims to divulge secrets. Cocom Pech tantalizes the reader's expectations of a story about a young man's (presumably the author's) shamanistic apprenticeship with his grandfather.

In *Secretos del abuelo*, the protagonist relates the grandfather's selection of a grandchild to inherit his ancient knowledge. The choice of the narrator as this grandchild supports the veracity of his account. It contrasts works like Carlos Castaneda's *The Teachings of Don Juan*, with its conventional pairing of anthropologist and informant. In effect, the grandfather's choice to pass the baton of storytelling to his chosen writer-grandson attests to the intellectual flexibility and adaptability of indigenous literature, reinforcing the foundations of an inherited cultural and literary tradition — a Mesoamerican cosmolectics. The text includes incantations, the secret language of birds, and the currency of Kukulcán, the ancient plumed serpent god. This short text exemplifies the writers' deployment of cosmolectics by invoking Kukulcán in the twenty-first century on the same plane as the town's church.

From this book, I have selected "El secreto de los pájaros II" to discuss the tensions generated when moving from the collective to the individual author without losing sight of its kab'awil cosmolectics. Throughout *Secretos del abuelo*, Cocom Pech establishes the reader's expectations for a supernatural theme and lyrical language. The very title "El secreto de los pájaros II" deceptively promises the reader more supernatural events, which would logically follow, since the previous chapter "El secreto de los pájaros I" indulges the reader's expectations. But the onomatopoeia that initiates "El secreto de los pájaros II" emanates from not a bird but a train. The author converts the sounds of nature we anticipate to those of a machine, and therefore, to modernization. The contrast between the title and the beginning of the story creates a textual dissonance between the protagonist's immediate experience and the spiritual training inherited from his grandfather. Indeed, the writer spends four of the story's first pages establishing a setting that clashes with the grandfather's context, which the reader has encountered many times in the other chapters (i.e., the transcription of the narrator's grandfather's teachings). The text's four-page description of Uncle Ch'el (a name that in Maya curiously means "light" or "clear" and is used for someone with fair skin), his attire, and accouterments reads as a completely different story from the one promised by the title. The minute descriptions of the uncle's clothing, which the narrator describes in very different terms from those of his grandfather Gregorio, may puzzle the reader, but they mark the narrator's modern subjectivity. "Coming from the city of Campeche," the narrator reminisces, "where he worked as a ticket checker in the United Railways of Yucatán, he would arrive dressed in beige pants and jacket; the jacket, always open, would allow him to parade a white t-shirt—a Pirate brand made in China—he would also wear a dark brown felt hat.... In his right hand he tightly carried a portable radio, which emitted *norteñas* to the rhythm of an accordion."[44] These descriptions offer a restructured and modern version of ordinary, everyday Maya on the peninsula. *Escritura* leads the writer off his original path (i.e., that of fulfilling his grandfather's mandate to he write down his teachings); the language becomes self-referential and not about the grandfather. Tellingly, the uncle's world is saturated with print culture and mass media signifiers, through newspapers and popular magazines: "There was never a shortage of copies of the *Diario de Yucatán* and *Alarma* magazine, which he carried, on the verge of falling [out], in either of his back trouser pockets."[45] The overwhelming prominence of magazines and newspapers, as well as the transnational waves of radio stations from Texas and Cuba contrasts with the writer's introduction, in which Cocom Pech offers a palpable absence of written literature and modern culture, where his grandfather's ancestral knowledge is passed on through the oral tradition and rooted in nature. In the chapter titled "El poder de un grano de maíz," Cocom Pech writes that "in those days, lacking books and illustrated magazines, we strove to bring into our hard heads the images of all those wonders described in the stories."[46] But in "El secreto de los pájaros II" what becomes transparent is that the grandfather's world is not devoid of print or mass culture.

By the fifth page of "El secreto de los pájaros II," a demonstrable change emerges. The grandfather's voice interrupts the narrator's recollection of night sounds. The reader enters a hyperreality. He hears an owl screech, in Mesoamerican culture traditionally an omen announcing illness or death. In the narrator's feverish state, he remembers his grandfather leading him through the jungle, where he sees Kukulcán, the plumed serpent and ancient Maya god. His uncles find him lying unconscious near the orchard. After a few weeks, the narrator eagerly tries to discuss the events with his grandfather, who claims to know nothing of his trip. But, by underscoring the privilege of seeing Kukulcán, the grandfather supports the idea of his grandson as the narrator chosen by an ancestral power.

In the concluding paragraphs, a second shift occurs, as fireworks and rockets interrupt the grandfather's monologue. The narrator's account of the present and noise of the town's church festivities takes over. Uncle Ch'el's subjectivity and the narrator's vision of Kukulcán do not connect well, as the uncle's story is not developed because the grandfather's training takes over the narrative. However, nearing the conclusion, the narrator watches a saint's procession while sitting by the church's entrance. He describes his bemusement at the town mute, who gestures, as if conducting the orchestra himself. The patron saint's festivities become central. The religious chorus, "¡Viva Cristo Rey!," parallels the lyrics of songs emanating from the uncle's radio in the previous pages.[47] Here the vision of the town disintegrates. Again the protagonist/narrator finds himself in the orchard next to his grandfather, who calls on him to conclude the conversation. "I didn't hear his words anymore," the narrator states. "Just the chorus by the door of the church, intermixing with the incessant sounds of the bells."[48] The sounds of bells, drums, and pyrotechnics drown out the grandfather's voice. The repetition of the second religious chorus has double implications, since it practically ends the story. Does it represent the triumph of organized religion over Maya spirituality? Or does it simply mean that the narrator straddles both? This conundrum is illuminated in the story's final section, where Cocom Pech writes, "I have always thought that the fireworks or rockets, serpents of smoke, explode brightly while splitting the immensity of the heavens during the holidays in my town. . . . A town inundated by sounds, like the one made by the arrival of trains."[49] The narrator's inheritance of traditional subjects like Kukulcán and the immediate experience of fireworks as serpents of smoke and trains represent the structural tension in the story. Instead of reading the narrator's experience of pre-Columbian Maya spirituality symbolized by Kukulcán in opposition to his recognition of Catholicism, what we audibly perceive through the chant "Long live Christ!" is a duality of visions incarnated by kab'awil. The narrator's spiritual vision of the past and his acknowledgement of the Catholic religion in the present represents kab'awil or the double gaze. The narrator embodies this ontology, not only by recognizing both religious and secular beliefs but also by understanding his grandfather's generation and his own present life, at once modern and ancient adhering to a cosmolectics by sharing the grandfather's stories. In the end, the Mesoamerican cosmolectics is maintained through the narrative's vertical ordering that moves from the spiritual (represented by Kukulcán) in the realm of dreams to the earthly (represented by the town) and the realm of a concrete reality.

The simultaneity of collective and individual, on the one hand, and supernatural and secular, on the other, is also present in Nicolás Huet Bautista's short story collection *La última muerte / Ti slajebalxa lajele* (The last death) (2001). A Maya Tsotsil anthropologist, writer, and poet from Chiapas, Huet Bautista is head of the Research Department of Literature and Art at the Centro Estatal de Lenguas, Arte y Literatura Indígenas. Huet Bautista describes his passion for writing as emerging from "the anger of knowing that indigenous cultures and languages have been plundered by foreign researchers."[50]

These stories rebuff the expectation of a colorful, quaint indigenous tradition by depicting evil characters. Envy, greed, and murder in indigenous communities are the main themes of this collection. The fictionalization of these themes is new to contemporary indigenous literature in Mesoamerica. These stories, in Huet Bautista's words, aim "to offer a nonromanticized portrait of indigenous communities."[51] The stories take place in his hometown of Huixtán, a Tsotsil-speaking community. The hyperrealistic description of brutal violence constitutes a radical departure from stories transcribed from the oral tradition in the 1980s and 1990s. A *conjuro* or incantation initiates each story, serving as epigraph. In "Tsajal Chuvel," the epigraph reads,

> Flowered priest, flowered man
> may they be consecrated
> may they be venerated
> your thirteen flowers
> your thirteen words.[52]

These incantations belong to the sacred language of the *ilol* (a healer) and suspend the reader's footing in everyday reality, signaling an entrance into another temporality. The three stories unfold through a child's point of view. Most stories begin in the spiritual realm but in the end gesture toward secular conclusions, even when they do not necessarily reject spirituality. I examine the title story, which, unlike the other tales in the collection, has a conclusion so consciously anticlimactic that it required a closer examination.

"La última muerte" features Don Manuel, the narrator's father, and the brutal crime committed against him and his family by Pedro Okil and his men. An incantation foretells the fragile nature of mortals. This sacred language speaks to the ephemeral nature of human existence:

We are leaves
We are grass
We are lianas
We are trees, we just breathe for a little while we just soil
the sacred Mother Earth.[53]

Initiating the story with sacred language signifies a kab'awilian approach, a nod to the oral tradition, and at the same time marks a narrative distance from Huet Bautista's own work. In some respects, this intertextuality functions as a new literary device for the Maya Tsotsil author.

The story opens with a prayer spoken by Don Manuel, who tends to the spiritual needs of a patient. This scene harks back to the ancient belief that words have a healing effect on a person or situation. The setting situates the reader in a Mesoamerican semiotic system, where sparks, birds, and trees function as signs that need decoding. During festivities for the town's patron saint, the narrator, also named Manuel, overhears other men referring to his father as a strong, evil sorcerer. Don Pedro Okil, the actual wicked sorcerer, rallies other men in town to join him in murdering Don Manuel and his family. Supernatural forces frame the plot of the story. The belief in the *nahual*, or animal spirit in Mesoamerican communities, becomes central in the development of the story. The sorcerer tells the other men in town about Don Manuel's fierce and overpowering spirit, emphasizing his domination over other people's *nahuales*. "I've run into him in the mountains," Okil complains, "high in the sky; we have tested our powers but he always beats me, he can transform into wind and lightning, he knows much about paths in space, and always travels to the third layer of clouds."[54] The men blame Don Manuel for all the ills in their town. Pedro Okil and his accomplices decide to murder the family using guns and machetes, killing children and adults alike. Okil's machete slices off part of the narrator's head. Young Manuel is left for dead in a pool of blood with his brain exposed. Family members and neighbors rescue him. His baby brother feeds on the blood of their mother and survives the ordeal but is taken far away by family members and never heard from again. The author's descriptions of the murders are gruesome and shocking: "Old Pedro reached my mother again with a *machetazo*, she fell face down with her young son, covering him with her body as a hen covers her chicks against the cold. . . . I saw how they sliced my mother's body without compassion, pieces of meat flying in different directions, the sharp metal spilling blood everywhere."[55] These hyperreal descriptions counter the representation of a victimized indigenous community. In this story, supernatural battles between powerful spiritual leaders can lead to murder.

Years transpire in the story. The narrator's perspective shifts. Manuel, the surviving child, has become an adult and finds himself in the same patron saint's festivities he had attended with his father before Pedro Okil led the murders of his family. The survivor of the nuclear family recognizes Okil, who has become a decrepit old man. Manuel walks toward him and greets him. When Okil politely asks his name, Manuel proudly states it and says he is the son of the late Don Manuel. Although not explicitly stated, we can infer from Okil's response that he recalls the name because he does not utter a word and instead starts walking away from our protagonist. The narrator does not follow or confront Okil, however. Instead, the narrative emphasizes that Manuel is the heir to the "parents' words and wisdom."[56] Strategically, the end echoes the incantation that initiates the text, except that it is now incorporated into the narrator's words: "For twenty years I have taken up the air in this space, I have sullied Mother Earth, the splendor of the word has strengthened me, I learned from the roar of the wind and the singing of birds that respect for the little gods of the earth is more powerful than revenge."[57] The spirituality Manuel embraces differs from the magical powers attributed to his deceased father, and the "little gods" the respect for whom he draws his own strength I interpret as humankind.[58] The conclusion of the story appears anticlimactic, insofar as the story's hero rejects avenging his parents' murder and his own near-death at the hands of Okil. The wicked sorcerer's crimes remain unpunished. The magical world of shamans and supernatural struggles that begins the story so powerfully is abandoned in favor of a spirituality that respects human rights. The contemporary storyteller reminds the reader of the present, through the secular discourse of respect for humanity over gods or shamans. In doing so, the author emphasizes a human rights discourse for indigenous people and spirituality as recognition of an individual's agency, rather than as a struggle between good and evil. This story thus moves from an oral collectivity to the making of an individual subject. By rejecting vengeance, the author shifts from a language that focuses on the magical to a language that emphasizes life. The kab'awilian gaze in this short story is exemplified in the tension between the secular and the supernatural as well as the collective versus the individual. A Mesoamerican cosmolectics perseveres in the protagonist's proclamation that he is the inheritor of his father's wisdom and sacred language.

Humberto Ak'abal was born in the municipality of Momostenango, in the western highlands of Guatemala. For financial reasons, he stopped attending school at the age of twelve. His poetry has been translated into numerous languages, including French, German, Portuguese, Italian, and Danish, among others. His many awards include the Quetzal de Oro from the Guatemalan Association of Journalists in 1993. In 1998 he won the Premio Continental Canto de América from UNESCO in Mexico, and in 2006 he was the recipient of the 2006 Guggenheim Fellowship. In 2003 he was awarded the Miguel Ángel Asturias National Literary Prize, which he declined.

Ak'abal's introduction to the collection of stories *Grito en la sombra* (Scream in the shadows), about death, agony, travel, and domestic violence, echoes Cocom Pech's grandfather's cultural mandate to preserve and disseminate. While there are very few Maya short story writers in Guatemala, and Ak'abal is best known for his poetry, this collection offers a key contribution to contemporary Maya writing. Unlike the other books I discuss in this section, which are bilingual, all the stories in *Grito en la sombra* are in Spanish. In comparison to the previously discussed texts, *Grito en la sombra* contains the most eclectic themes. Some of the stories spring directly from the oral tradition, relating the existence of *nahuales* (or *nawales*).[59] Others are more innovative in transgressing local parameters to explore international settings like Paris or Vienna. Despite the linguistic choice Ak'abal makes, the text refuses the eager reader's empathy. In the first paragraph of the introduction, he interrupts the text with a parenthetical note to ensure that while the reader may readily identify with the environment and life of the narrator, this is an other milieu. After meticulously describing the surroundings he calls home, Ak'abal clarifies that "what I call a house was a small construction of adobe without stairs, a roof of mud tiles, and only one room that served as kitchen and bedroom."[60]

In the introduction to his short story collection, Ak'abal describes the important role that nature plays in indigenous communities. He evokes a symbolic system that speaks to indigenous cultural views. Similar to Cocom Pech's sense of responsibility to write, Ak'abal underlines his mother's influence in his interest for *la palabra* (the word): "My mother planted in me an interest in the word. This being an attempt to continue my elders' tradition."[61] The Guatemalan highlands as well as various European countries serve as settings for the stories, which are told in the first person, presumably the writer's. He states that when he asks his mother to tell a story, she sighs, smiles, and laments: "The times are not the same as they once were. It no longer makes any sense to tell these things under electric light. Before, it was satisfying, because the light of the ocote [pine torch] was a different light. You see, even the haunting spirits have left. Now it is your turn to create your own stories to tell your children."[62]

The storyteller does not disappear with the emergence of the indigenous author, as the oral tradition continues, but in these texts the storyteller figure transforms by adapting an ancestral affect to modern short stories. In "De lengua en lengua" (From tongue to tongue), the essay that introduces the collection, the mother's recommendation to the narrator clearly draws a relationship between tradition, translation, and creation. These stories do not necessarily speak about the supernatural, although it is certainly present. Most of the stories in *Grito en la sombra* fictionalize a reality absent in folktales or myths from the oral tradition. Ak'abal's stories do not propose an idealized portrayal of the indigenous world. "Grito en la sombra," the title story and the first in the collection, articulates the protagonist's pain as he witnesses his drunken father cruelly beat his mother. The story transgresses a community's taboo about unmasking the fantasy of a gender-complementary relationship between men and women, revealing an unspoken, gendered violence — an issue I discuss in chapter 3 through women's poetry. Many of the stories are dominated by death, or characters on the brink of death.

In the story "Grito en la sombra," death figures as a central metaphor personified by changes in the protagonist. This metaphor applies to the father and mother's physical deterioration, as well as the conversion of the narrator's life from the bewilderment in a child's eyes to the burden of doubt in manhood, to the transformation of identity for the sake of survival. The scene opens with the scream of a child fastened to its mother's back as the father beats her. The story allegorizes the narrator's escape and disassociation with the town and his identity. The protagonist removes his clothes and sees his mother and sister lying on the floor as if they were dead. This provokes a hallucination. He flees the house, running into things, falling but continuing, until he reaches an empty town. "I made two or three turns dragging my desperation. It appeared as though everyone from the town had left to who knows where."[63] The narrator decides to return, because he fears that his father has killed his mother. The town disintegrates before his eyes: "I looked back and saw that the town was disappearing, the houses crashing against each other and sinking."[64] The narrator continues walking toward his house and finally arrives. He describes a warm feeling behind his neck and says, "I may have fallen asleep."[65] The warmth he experiences behind his neck is left undefined. The narrator dreams about his mother. A roaring laughter awakens him. He recognizes his father sitting outside the house, holding the machete. Fear and trauma overpower him; a "warm feeling" engulfs him again. He admits not knowing how long he stayed this way. "When I gained consciousness I was already a man."[66] As in the other anthologies, the lapse of time remains unaccounted for. And yet the reader surmises that the narrator leaves his community. Once he regains consciousness, his transformation into a mature and grown man is complete. The protagonist/narrator questions his aged mother about his father's fate, to which she replies that he passed away many years ago. Before he left, she tells her son, your father asked for your whereabouts. The narrator asks, "What did you say to him?" She responds, "I told him about your voyage."[67] One of the journeys reaches its limit and is eclipsed by another that has just begun. Life and death, past and present, manifest in an ever-confounding embrace. Even though Ak'abal assures the reader that this collection is a challenge to continue building on his ancestors' words, this story clearly conveys an immediate experience of loss, domestic violence, and growing pains. Ak'abal's tribute to his mother's influence in the narrative, again represents an important duality that speaks to the past, and the oral tradition. Although this short story in particular deviates from the traits of the oral tradition, the protagonist returns to his community. In "Grito en la sombra," kab'awil represents a straddling of the rural and the modern, oral tradition and lived reality.

The genre of the short story is gaining traction among indigenous women.[68] Ana Patricia Martínez Huchim's short story collection *U yóol xkaambal jaw xíiw / Contrayerba* (Antidote) offers an exciting departure from her practice of writing down the oral tradition. The twelve texts focus on women. According to Martínez Huchim, the title *Contrayerba* (Counterherb) has various meanings. It can refer to "an antidote for snakebites but also [applies] to all medicinal plants. I had heard the word *counterculture* [used] to [refer to] non-Western cultures — for indigenous communities, I mean. And I liked [the idea of] titling the book using a word that existed in everyday language, that isn't Western medicine but traditional medicine; 'contrayerba' is everything that isn't Western. Then, I did the translation into Maya. The plant is called 'xkaambal jaw,' and it cures snakebites. The book's title literally translates into 'the energy of the xkaambal jaw herb,' but I liked the word *contrayerba* itself more. It's easy to say and remember, but it has a deep meaning."[69] I focus on her collection precisely because she has been at the forefront of preserving the oral tradition and the creation of collaborative compilations with Maya elders.

Martínez Huchim was born in the city of Tizimín, Yucatán, in 1964. She has a degree in anthropology with a specialization in linguistics and literature and a postgraduate degree in ethnohistory from the Autonomous University of

Yucatán. She has won numerous awards including the 2005 Enedino Jiménez National Indigenous Literature Prize for her book *U k'a'ajsajil u ts'u noj K'aax/ Recuerdos del corazón de la montaña* (Memories of the heart of the mountain). Her other texts include narratives of oral tradition such as the storybook *U tsikbalo'ob mejen paalal/ Cuentos de niños* (Children's stories) and *Chen konel/ Es por demás* (It is pointless). In 2002 she founded *K'aaylay* (The song of memory), an electronic journal, which she continues to manage. She wrote her first play in both Maya and Spanish in December 2011 titled *U tsikbalil juntúul Tsíimin tuunich/ El caballo de Piedra* (The story of the stone horse), which was performed in Tizimín. Martínez Huchim has explored many genres and actively promotes the oral tradition through various projects she has initiated.

Unlike the previous collections, which are told mainly from the perspective of male protagonists, Martínez Huchim's characters are all Maya women from the Yucatán Peninsula. *Contrayerba* is her first foray away from the oral tradition, or *recopilación*, an effort to preserve the oral tradition by writing down the stories of the elders. Her collection of short stories is also the first major endeavor by an indigenous intellectual to narrativize a Maya woman's subjective voice. The characters acquire a psychological depth often absent in stories from the oral tradition. The collection begins with a tale that serves as a kind of preamble, significantly titled "Frenesí." It alludes directly to the Maya incantations recorded in the eighteenth-century text *El ritual de los bacabes* and used to treat maladies such as frenzy, lust, and madness.

The short stories offer individual accounts of women left out of the arenas of dominant history and literature. The main characters are liminal figures such as the *yerbatera* (herbalist), the *curandera* (healer), and the prostitute. According to Martínez Huchim, the real-life women who populated her childhood memories inspired these stories. The author dedicates the midwife story to the woman who helped bring her into the world. The names titling the stories reveal their subject and content. The story about the yerbatera relates the story of a woman who heals with herbs and plants. The stories offer windows on women's intimate worlds and their critical role in the community, as well their often tragic lives. They give a human dimension to otherwise nameless and faceless professions. The characters' names hint at their destinies.

I concentrate on the short text, titled "Frenesí," that opens the book and the epilogue by Soledad Cahum Dzib, the narrator whose vision ushers readers in and out of the various stories. Soledad's ability to see the spirits of women who have passed on gives readers a glimpse of these women's deeply personal struggles. Soledad's name means "solitude" in a society that considers a woman who has chosen not to marry, or have children, an anomaly. Soledad's last names are consciously symbolic, since Cahum and Dzib together, according to the author's glossary, translate as "began to write" or "writes with force."[70] In contrast to the traditional storyteller, who depends on a live audience, the author here, embodies solitude as the condition that generates writing, another key distinction. In the story, "Frenesí," we learn that Soledad's only companion is a dog. In the Mesoamerican tradition, the dog occupies an important role as a companion who assists people as they pass from life to death. She removes the dog's *lagañas* (eye discharge) and dabs them onto hers. Soledad hears and sees the older women's life stories that constitute this short story collection. She tries calling on the women, but she feels mute and thus decides to write their stories instead, transforming the traditional storyteller figure. Because she did not have a pen or notebook, Soledad improvises by breaking off a stick from her roof, which is made of hay, to write them. She steeps her makeshift pen in achiote and water. Achiote has different functions. The bright red seeds make their way into Mesoamerican cuisine, but they are also used as natural ink or dye. In the story, Soledad removes her *fustán* (slip), which in typical Yukatek attire shows like a long white gown under a huipil. The white *fustán* becomes the *lienzo* on which she writes the women's stories.[71] Writing on cloth invokes the type of writing tradition of the sixteenth century known as *lienzos*. The use of achiote references the sacred red ink. The author makes the textile/writing connection by describing Soledad's etchings on her clothing.[72] The first piece of writing on the cloth resonates as a type of prayer in its rhythm and form. Soledad asks for permission to write the things she witnesses from her home: "My lord, / I ask that you give me the capacity to write, the things that appear to me, / my Lord."[73]

After several stories focused on the different labor women undertake within the community, a one-page text tells the reader that Soledad realized that her destiny is to use writing to denounce. A frenzy takes over her and she comes to the realization that her death is imminent. The dog understands this, too, and together they begin the ultimate journey. The neighbors find Soledad and her animal companion lying peacefully on the floor. In the epilogue, we learn that Soledad has passed away, leaving her undergarment/cloth filled with the women's written stories. The conclusion brings us full circle to Soledad's predicament as a writer and storyteller, as well as to the theme of this chapter. Tellingly, the women who find the bright red writings on her attire decide to burn her *fustán*: "Let's burn it, if not people will think it's some kind of spell and the priest will not allow her to be buried in the cemetery, but [will bury her] in the mountains, like an animal."[74] Their decision is driven by fear that the priest and others in the community will think the writing is witchcraft. The ending has compelling historical and philosophical implications. The image veers toward the symbolic. It takes the reader back to the sixteenth century and Friar de Landa's incineration of hundreds of books. The conceptual implication may be that even though past written documents (or woven texts in women's garments) have been burned by religious extremists in the past, modern technology grants them immunity through archival technologies like the book itself, thus preserving knowledge for generations to come, in an exemplary kab'awilian move.

The storyteller Soledad is re-created and kept alive, fictionalized, in this short story compilation. Soledad's character has a psychological dimension made possible by Martínez Huchim's poetic re-creation. In other words, her story does not aim to replicate a *testimonio* or pretend to be a true account of Soledad's life. The stories articulate and establish Maya women as subjects in different facets of history and society. Once again, in these short texts kab'awil allows the writers to straddle the oral and the written, the past and the present, the spiritual and the secular. The protagonist, Soledad, adheres to a Mesoamerican cosmolectics, referencing glyphic and alphabetic writing, weaving and painting in the past to demonstrate its connection to the present. In the end, Soledad embodies kab'awil.

Conclusion

Cocom Pech's *Secretos del abuelo*, Huet Bautista's *La última muerte*, Ak'abal's *Grito en la sombra*, and Martínez Huchim's *Contrayerba* exemplify a Mesoamerican cosmolectics through kab'awil. Even though there may be critical overlaps between what may be interpreted as myths, nature, and spiritual practice in indigenous literatures, the formation of the indigenous author demands thinking beyond ethnography and anthropology. These writers want to ensure that they are representing culture as a way of life and seek to exert creative license in their work. Indigenous writers embody kab'awil as they negotiate their insertion into the literary scene and their role in their communities.

These short story collections wrestle with external forces that impose certain themes in their literature — a central issue that manifests in public forums. Inevitably, their status as authors in the larger circuits of mass communication affects their literary output. Mainstream writers tend to see indigenous writers' commitment to cultural (re)vindication as the antithesis of creativity. Indeed, some writers have dismissed indigenous writers as simply reproducing *indigenista* literature or ethnography. Other critics see their commitment to individual creativity as lacking cultural authenticity. Nonetheless, as I have demonstrated in this chapter, the indigenous writers treated here re-create the storyteller through their literary artifacts. They vehemently contest the entrenched historical and cultural opposition of tradition versus innovation, written versus oral expression, modern versus premodern. These issues generate significant tensions in their literary production. In assuming the status of authors, indigenous writers challenge the old power dynamics between the *letrados* as the interlocutors for the indigenous masses and indigenous intelligentsia. Thus they directly contribute to a repositioning of indigenous subjects as agents. Though the contents of tradition change, the idea of passing down from generation to generation is immutable, making the notion of creativity highly malleable. Indigenous authors remain acutely aware of their underprivileged social realities. As I have tried to make clear, their work does not constitute a teleology of a progression from the oral tradition to the written word; rather, their production challenges the widely held assumption that the oral tradition is intrinsically a more authentic indigenous practice. The production of the indigenous author through the short story genre initiates a shift pointing to a literary autonomy that does not have to conform to any outdated separations of orality and literacy. Chapter 3 focuses on women's poetry—a genre perennially associated with orality and indigenous expression. However, I center my study on the use of eroticism, territory, and tradition to demystify the figure of the indigenous woman and the rarefied notion of gender complementary. I unravel the image of the indigenous woman as both the locus of authenticity and the steward of tradition in indigenous political and cultural activism as well as the obsequious female subject associated with social backwardness in dominant discourses.

CHAPTER THREE

Indigenous Women, Poetry, and the Double Gaze

Today's woman has taken letters as the primary tool for her voice to be heard—that same voice previously heard only within her home has been transferred to the current literature... writing allows her work to be appreciated by other people and other communities.... But most of all as strong women who fight hard every day for a place in the world of indigenous letters. Because we have to recognize that it is not always easy to assume the role of creators in societies where women have had a differently defined role in the literary world.
—Irma Pineda Santiago (Zapotec nation, 2008)

With the concept of duality anchoring their daily lives and rituals, equality does not make sense.—Sylvia Marcos (2005)

POETRY STANDS AT THE TOP of the indigenous literary pyramid as the most popular form of expression practiced among Native communities. Historically, it is intimately connected to song, prayer, and various religious rituals. In contrast to Plato's rejection of poetry as an activity that spreads lies, Mesoamerican communities — according to the historical records preserved — venerated their poets, who descended from the noble and priestly class. Representations of speech scrolls or volutes — whether representing song, chants, history, or myths — depict the nobility in many pictorial documents. Women poets were not as prominent in indigenous texts from the colonial period, but in the twenty-first century, they are among the most visible and highly profiled poets in Mesoamerica. This chapter focuses on the essential themes Maya and Zapotec women poets address. The poems I chose for this study valiantly interrogate the prevalent notions of gender and sexuality, which they link to land and political autonomies. Kab'awil cosmolectics appears in the critical posture women poets take in relationship to the past and present, tradition and innovation, as well as sexuality and reproduction.

Gender complementarity is one of the most distinctive paradigms ascribed to indigenous peoples.[1] Numerous critiques since the 1980s have destabilized its validity, rejecting it as a fantasy or a romantic representation of indigenous peoples, whose lived reality is marred by gender violence and an entrenched patriarchal system.[2] Throughout this book, I argue that indigenous productions are informed by a cosmolectics and that kab'awil functions as an important indigenous ontology that is valuable in thinking through gender. By bringing kab'awil to the conversation between gender and poetry, I focus on how kab'awil — as the K'iche' feminist activist Alma López asserts — can be a paradigm to strive for in everyday social relations.[3] That is, it is not a given, but it can be achieved. Kab'awil escapes the reach of patriarchal logic, represented in the poets' engagement with gender and sexuality, capitalism, spirituality, and politics. While the poetry of indigenous women is informed by a variety of themes and personal subject matter, the poets I discuss in this chapter vehemently and unapologetically condemn misogynistic practices. They do so by maintaining a double gaze, looking back to a past that engaged gender relations differently while simultaneously casting a critical eye on the existing power differential in their communities. Informed by a consciousness of being seen by both indigenous men and dominant societies in ways that undermine their humanity, these poets offer another constellation of images. Kab'awil frees these poets to resignify their association with a tradition that in this context, I imply, demands adherence to cultural dictates based on strict gender roles. Here the double gaze performs as a way to indict traditional sexist norms.

This chapter journeys across regions and nation-states to illustrate how women respond to set ideas about "customary law," the body, sexuality, and autonomy. I propose that poets increasingly disassociate themselves from traditional representations of the body as a mass of flesh and look upon it instead as body-as-territory and land in relationship to the cosmos. The K'iche' writer Dorotea Gómez Grijalva argues, for example, that she understands her body in historical not biological terms, now more than ever, as she came to understand that the Guatemalan civil war manifested in different ailments of her body.[4] In the first sections, I examine women poets within the nation-state of Mexico and contextualize the various poetic efforts spearheaded by indigenous women. My discussion focuses on poetry by Irma Pineda Santiago and Natalia Toledo Paz, two of the most prominent and established Zapotec poets from Juchitán, Oaxaca. From there, my study progresses south to the highlands of Chiapas, then journeys east to the Yucatán Peninsula, and finally reaches across the border to Guatemala. Within the Maya region, I introduce the work of Briceida Cuevas Cob, born on the Yucatán Peninsula, and Enriqueta Lunez Pérez, and

Angelina Díaz Ruiz, both Maya Tsotsil poets from Chiapas. I conclude the chapter by examining the work of key Maya women poets in Guatemala and their focus on the body, sexuality, pleasure, and territory. Although the political landscape of Chiapas and Guatemala still bears the scars of war, and all of the poets discussed in this chapter have been affected by regional violence and historical trauma, the intensity and strength of these writers continues unabated.

The relationship of the cosmos to conceptions about gender, the body, and sexuality in indigenous communities is abundantly expressed in pre-Columbian and colonial manuscripts preserved on paper or etched in stone. Of course, in the case of Spanish accounts, we cannot forget that the prejudiced ecclesiastical gaze limits their trustworthiness and the reliability of their details. Despite the shortcomings of their religious filter, however, through those documents we can discern how certain conceptions of the body have changed or continue to evolve among Mesoamericans. Sylvia Marcos writes that in ancient times "corporeality was not only acknowledged but conceived of as intertwined within the circumscribing universe."[5] The historian and philosopher Miguel León-Portilla states that the idea of a divine pair of feminine and masculine characteristics was rooted in Mesoamerican thought.[6] The concept of complementarity (female and male) or, as my argument demonstrates, a kab'awil ontology, was a vital component of Mesoamerican social fabric and reflected a connection to the cosmos. Unveiling and owning women's sexuality is another key theme in contemporary indigenous women's poetry. Some of the poets turn to earlier sources that point to non-Catholic influences. León-Portilla explains that historically "it has been said at times concerning indigenous cultures that there is a lack of erotic themes . . . but, contrary to those who think this way, there are some old texts . . . collected from native lips" that reflect an interesting look at eroticism and sexuality outside Christian conceptions and ideas of sin.[7] These sources inspire poets to challenge Christian precepts imposed on indigenous sexuality. Decolonizing ideas of sin allows poets to relate the body to sexual pleasure, as Kaqchikel intellectual Emma Delfina Chirix García affirms. Past and present conceptions of the body and eroticism coexist in the manifestation of a double gaze in women's poetry.

The poets studied in this chapter confront a highly codified image of the indigenous woman as passive and submissive. While in indigenous discourses her image generates an indomitable sense of origin prior to the geopolitical formations of Mexico and Guatemala, nation-states offer her image as a vestige of a bygone, premodern era and promote it as a tourist attraction. The poets employ kab'awilian maneuvers to critique these static images and protest the deplorable material conditions indigenous women experience. The sociologist Natividad

Gutiérrez Chong, in her analysis of gender, ethnicity, and nationalism, writes that "the contradictions of nationalism, modernity and backwardness, urban and rural, tradition and culture, reappear and intensify when broaching the situation of [indigenous] women."[8] Similarly, in Guatemala, anthropologist Diane Nelson argues that the nation-state, the pan-Maya movement, and North American feminists engaged in solidarity efforts with Third World women all rely on the figure of the Maya woman as a discursive construct, a type of prosthetic, for their own existence.[9] Building on feminist and postcolonial scholars in other regions, Nelson persuasively argues, "efforts to form a 'whole' national body politic [are achieved by] deploying . . . the *mujer maya*."[10] Poetry, then, facilitates women's articulation of empowered indigenous voices.

Feminisms

Adding to this meticulously constructed, convenient image is the attendant traditional anthropology and leftist feminism research that tend to focus on the plight of indigenous women who need rescuing by Westerners from the ill treatment of their male counterparts. Christine Eber's scholarship departs from this approach and argues that indigenous women should not be perceived as completely oppressed within their communities, or envisioned as functioning within "complementary" systems where sexism does not operate.[11] Instead, she argues that individual experiences must inform the ways we understand social movements and women's lives. In a similar trajectory, contextualizing the unprecedented collaboration among women, Mexican anthropologist Rosalva Aída Hernández Castillo asserts that at the beginning of the 1980s, indigenous women were positioned between "ethnocentric feminism and ethnic essentialism." She reflects on how Mexican feminists who chose to work with indigenous women, especially in Chiapas, wrestled with the legacy of a Marxist theoretical premise that they (the feminist intellectuals) could bring indigenous women to consciousness about their oppression as bearers, by definition, of a "false consciousness."[12] A few traditional indigenous women critics add another layer of complexity to the issue by dismissing any feminist critique of indigenous movements as evaluations operating from a Western base of thinking.[13]

Poetic Intersections and Indigenous Feminisms

A cadre of indigenous feminists across Latin America has begun theorizing the predicament indigenous women face. These women speak mainly from the social sciences. Among these indigenous theorists in Chiapas is Georgina Méndez Torres, a sociologist from the Maya Chol community. She calls attention to the reduction of indigeneity to women's clothed body. She carefully synthesizes indigenous women's reality: "Even though we indigenous women begin to be protagonists of our stories, we are required, either by our community or by the nonindigenous society, to be the bearers of indigenous 'authenticity,' articulated through the use of traditional dress, the transmission of indigenous languages, and the managing of the body — elements that act as identity markers that reproduce, in certain contexts, power relations between the genders, and we face the dilemma of how to live changes in our identities without thereby allowing others to question our word."[14] Méndez Torres is cognizant of the burden indigenous women carry as representatives of culture, language, and external markers.

Drawing similar conclusions, the Zapotec feminist Judith Bautista Pérez condemns the "naturalization of social and cultural roles attributed to indigenous women [because it] represents the synthesis of the national project to consolidate the Mexican state. Therefore, being an indigenous woman was and continues to be a fundamental resource for the formation and maintenance of the Mexican state; the consolidation of our subordination is one of several factors that enable the reproduction of the capitalist, patriarchal, and white system."[15]

However, the convenient image of indigenous women as passive and docile does not apply to all of them. Outsiders have generated an image of Zapotec women from Juchitán, Oaxaca, in very different terms from those of the Maya. Politicians, writers, and painters represent Juchitec women as matriarchs; they are willful, independent, and sexually precocious.[16] The Zapotec feminist Bettina Cruz Velázquez asserts that even though indigenous women are adversely affected by racism and patriarchy, the Zapotec women of Juchitán represent an anomaly due to the fundamental financial role they play in the community.[17] "In Juchitán," she writes, "this argument [the idea of a submissive indigenous woman] fails due to women's behavior, demonstrating that the community's philosophy is alive and does not depend on the submission of [one] individual to [another]. Rather, it is a collective life, where the collaboration of each family member accounts for communal harmony. In this way, breaking with the idea that men in Juchitán do not work and that the woman is the sole breadwinner, the economic contributions of both give the family and the village as a whole a different level of life, without neglecting tradition or the system of community organization."[18] Yet the projected image of a strong, independent Zapotec woman who controls local commerce and holds power in her family does not translate into political power in Oaxaca. Given these distinct histories, women's poetic contributions should take into account the conditions from which women write.

While indigenous feminists and other academics have recently begun to contest the monolithic use of the indigenous woman's image in academic circles, indigenous poets have used public forums to speak against these stereotypes since the 1990s. María Luisa Góngora Pacheco, a prose writer, actress, and playwright from the Maya peninsula, deplores the plight of women, as bearers of tradition, who lack access to education and economic opportunity. Góngora Pacheco's is one of the first to publicly decry how the folkloric use of the indigenous woman undercuts her contributions.[19] She asserts that this commercial opportunism overlooks Maya women's creative abilities and obscures their intellectual potential. The act of writing poetry for Góngora Pacheco, then, is inherently political.

Since many indigenous women tend to be monolingual, the transmission of indigenous languages becomes part of the private sphere of the home.[20] Ironically, women embody this responsibility largely because they are perceived as lacking the dominant language, in this case Spanish. Men, in contrast, tend to be bilingual due to their obligatory interactions with Spanish-speaking society.[21] The association of monolingualism with gender is not without merit, as it translates into women not having access to the most basic services in Mexico and Guatemala. Despite the important social strides indigenous peoples have made in Mexico and Guatemala, they still have to contest the popular notion that consigns indigenous languages to dialect status. Men have traditionally undertaken the task of writing grammars and dictionaries to counteract this linguistic subordination. Women deliberately appeal to their male counterparts' sensibility by linking the inferior social status of Native languages (which indigenous men also suffer) to sex subordination. Women's approaches range from candid reproach of sexism to taking a moral high ground. Maya Tojolobal poet María Roselia Jiménez Pérez opts for the latter approach. In her essay "El futuro de la palabra" (The future of the word), she cautiously critiques the absence of women's issues from many of the literary congresses held in the 1990s. She calls for a reflection on women's roles in literary movements aimed at decolonization but abstains from mentioning sexism. "This is not a competition," she notes, "we must not allow this to be a struggle about gender."[22] While her tone is pacifist and accommodating, it appeals to the notion of a symbolic parity or kab'awil cosmolectics. Other women intellectuals turn to the *Popol Vuh*, and its sacred status, to counter the social marginalization of indigenous languages. Actress, writer, playwright, and founding FOMMA member Isabel Juárez Espinosa, in her essay, "La mujer maya como fuente de cultura" (The Maya woman as source of [our] culture), evokes the story of Lady Ixquic and the spirit of Jun Ahpu (both protagonists in the *Popol Vuh*) to authorize an ancestral connection between language and women. She alludes to both the symbolic and material impregnation that occurs when Jun Ahpu's spirit spits on Ixquic's hand. Juárez Espinosa indicates that the saliva symbolizes language, thus allowing her to claim that the ancestors adjudicate it directly to women.[23] Symbolically, then, women's ancestral authority trumps dominant and uninformed claims of the linguistic inferiority of indigenous languages. The double gaze allows them to revisit the past in order to change the present.

Engaging Kab'awil in Poetry

By choosing poetry as a tool, Maya and Zapotec women write themselves into a present history that inverts the stereotypical image of indigenous women as traditional, illiterate, and monolingual. Their committed artistry disrupts the ethnic, linguistic, and social conventions and unsettles gender expectations on a continent where the production of literature has been the privilege of a white, affluent, and typically male group. As Irma Pineda Santiago incisively asserts in the first epigraph framing this chapter, indigenous women's role in the Republic of Letters is not a given. Their verse reflects a deep concern with issues of gender, sex, language, metaphors, and form. They remain highly implicated in a decolonizing political project that invigorates indigenous literatures. Of course, they do not represent a homogenous group. They express themselves in different languages, infusing their poems with diverse experiences grounded in their specific indigenous nations.[24] Some prominent poets belong to Native groups with a reduced number of speakers. In Baja California we find work by the Paipai sisters Juana Inés Reza Albáñez and Delfina Albáñez Arballo. In Chihuahua, the music and verse of Dolores Batista (1963–2004), who fought for the preservation of the Raramuri culture and language. In Jalisco, Angélica Ortiz (Wishárika). These poets have less international recognition, but their production is important precisely because of their effort to write in indigenous languages with fewer speakers than Zapotec, Nahuatl, or Maya. Mikeas Sánchez was for years the only woman to have published in Zoque; she has several publications, international recognition, and has managed to study outside of Mexico. While the Nahuatl language has many speakers, few women have published books of narrative or poetry; their work is found more commonly in magazines or on compact discs. Among them is Yolanda Matías García (Nahua), whose work has appeared in magazines and who has recently published a book. Her poetry is inspired by the idea that contemporary poets should restore the ancient word, that is, return to literary conceits attributed to the "flor y canto" (flower and song). Judith Santopietro (Veracruz, Nahuatl) has been promoting indigenous literature with her Iguanazul project. Her book, *Palabras de agua*, is another important contribution to the creation of poetry by Nahua women.

Despite their differences, the poets challenge and redefine naturalized ideas about how gender operates and is construed in the Maya and Zapotec imaginaries. Women add another complex dimension to the paradox of indigenous peoples within nation-states.[25] Nation-states exalt them as embodying cultural authenticity and blame them for being obstacles to progress in societies that value what Walter Mignolo has termed Occidentalism.[26] In the literary domain, indigenous women poets enjoy national and international recognition of a magnitude that no male indigenous writer in Mexico has reached.[27] This phenomenon is recent. At the beginning of the new millennium, most indigenous women poets were published only in anthologies or magazines and had not attained greater renown with their own books.[28] Most of these poets have roots in the linguistically diverse states of southern Mexico, such as Oaxaca and Chiapas, as well as on the Maya Peninsula.[29]

These poets assume a double gaze toward past symbols and practices as well as toward the present conditions that inform their work. Their poetic voices speak against asymmetrical power relations within and outside their communities. In particular, they condemn oppressive religious and cultural traditions, which are expected to regulate conduct and police social behavior. They exploit their image as healers, mothers, weavers, and lovers — positions that remain closely associated and tightly held within the private sphere — while providing new constellation, often affirming and celebrating Eros. Iconic symbols such as the moon and its association with weaving, or the *nahuales* and Mesoamerican calendar, are among the leitmotifs in the work of almost all these poets, reinforcing a cosmolectics.[30] Some poets have published several books, while others gradually transmit their work through digital technologies.[31]

Zapotec Poets (Juchitán)

In the late nineteenth and early twentieth century, men penned all the poetry written in the Zapotec language. Published mainly in newspapers, this generation experimented with a Zapotec alphabet, as a consensus on its orthographic representation had yet to be reached.[32] Among the contemporary poets, Irma Pineda Santiago and Natalia Toledo Paz are the most established figures. In their work, the double gaze manifests in thinking outside and beyond normative codes of behavior. Their poems address a diversity of themes and have consistently been published in bilingual editions. Both poets have participated in international festivals throughout Latin America, Europe, and North America. Their work has also been translated into other languages.

Irma Pineda Santiago was the first woman elected president of the National Indigenous Writers Association. Because of discrimination against Native-language speakers, some families hesitate to pass on their language to their children. Pineda Santiago's parents spoke to her strictly in Spanish, but, as she recalls, "once outside the home everything burst in Zapotec."[33] Pineda Santiago's oeuvre includes love poems, a celebration of culture, and eroticism. She also writes to denounce the injustices carried out by the state against indigenous peoples. Mexican armed forces kidnapped her father, Víctor Pineda Henestrosa, due to his political activism; his commitment to public education and activism as a COCEI member influenced her passion for poetry.[34]

The following poem captures the defiance attributed to Zapotec language and culture on Juchitán from a woman's perspective. Irma Pineda Santiago's verse alludes to "El zapoteco" by the famous poet Gabriel López Chiñas. His poem "Diidxazá / El zapoteco" contests the menace of language disappearance in the last stanza.

Ay! Zapotec, Zapotec,
language that gives me life,
I know that you will die,
the day the sun dies.[35]

López Chiñas's poem is about cultural and linguistic affirmation. In her untitled poem, Pineda Santiago also speaks about survival and the Zapotec's stubborn reinvention of themselves. While her poem is also about refusing a narrative of language disappearance, it moves beyond language and is replete with references to birth, fertility, and growth.

You will not see me die
There will be a seed
hidden in the bushes of the road
that to this land must return
and it will sow the future
and feed our souls

and our word will be reborn
and you will not see me die
because we will be strong
because we will always be alive
because our song will be eternal
because it will be us and you
and the children of our children
and the trembling of this earth
that will shake the sea
and we will be many hearts
clinging to the essence of the Binnizá[36]
and you will not see me die
you will not see me die
you will not see me die[37]

Her poem represents an understanding of *zapotekeidad* (or what she terms the essence of *binnizá*) as being in the land itself. The resistance is closely linked to women's reproductive power. Her use of words such as "seed," "sow," "earth," and "food" establishes that territory also confers identity, moving away from the linguistic emphasis of López Chiñas in his poem to the politics of land.

The *rapto* or abduction is a controversial theme among Zapotec poets and other intellectuals. In general a *rapto* occurs when a man asks a woman to marry and her family denies the request or when the suitor wants to confirm a woman's virginity before nuptials. The abduction can be with or without the woman's consent. If she is found to be a virgin, the suitor's parents apologize to her family and set a date for the wedding. Proof of female virginity in the form of a blood-stained handkerchief or sheet is required before the wedding. While for some intellectuals, the *rapto* is conceived of as cultural right under *uso y costumbre* (customary law), many women feminists rightfully critique this practice as sexist. Male writers view this practice from a very different perspective. They convey the practice of *rapto* as a romantic one shrouded in a traditional valorization of women's virginity. Xhavizende, a musical group, memorializes this act in a Zapotec/Spanish song written by Luis Martínez Hinojosa, "Rapto de amor" (Love abduction). The act is celebratory and portrayed as an ancient and romantic tradition. In 1930, the foundational Zapotec writer and intellectual Andrés Henestrosa unproblematically defended this type of abduction as part of *juchitecos*' extreme valorization of virginity.[38] In that essay, he justifies this practice as one of time immemorial and observes that women usually agree to the *rapto*. Other poets and intellectuals defend this practice as part of an ancient cultural practice. In March 2002 Oaxaca repealed legislation criminalizing the practice of *rapto*, making it instead a minor infraction.[39] The Zapotec academic Obdulia Ruiz Campbell recalls her mother's and other women relatives' violent experience of the *rapto*. She recalls that the women "received blows to their legs so that they would not resist so much and were later pulled by their boyfriends [to] where they were deflowered."[40]

The Zapotec poet Antonio López Pérez offers an innocent version of the *rapto* in his poem "El rapto / Guendaruxhoñenee gunaa," published in the newspaper *La Jornada*.

> The moon falls on the night
> while the crickets sing
> from the river's clay bank,
> they walk intertwined
> without measuring nocturnal love by hours or spaces.
> From afar is visible
> a hut that smells of earth,
> a firefly next to it
> turns off its light intermittently
> and allows
> night's lovemaking to take its course.
> A mother calls the women in the neighborhood,
> the mescal jolts traditions,
> and fireworks awaken the early morning
> to testify
> to dawn's virginity.[41]

Antonio López Pérez's version of the *rapto* is idyllic and bucolic. The couple walks along the river, the moon is their witness, and the firefly's light moves to the beat of lovemaking. Readers learn the young woman is a virgin because a mother's voice calls for a celebration, and fireworks are set off. Violence is notably absent and dressed in metaphors of nature. Women's perception of this act is lost in López Pérez's rendition. The *rapto* is naturalized, again, as a romantic event in which women willingly participate. This version differs greatly from the way Irma Pineda Santiago and Natalia Toledo Paz write about the custom. The anthropologist Marinella Miano Borruso identifies the practice of demonstrating a woman's virginity as a Mediterranean import.[42] She points out that it is a violation of a woman's intimacy, turning her body into a public trial, which favors the honor of the male's nuclear family.[43]

Pineda Santiago addresses the *rapto* in more complex ways. In an untitled poem from *Doo yoo ne ga' bia'/De la casa del ombligo a las nueve cuartas*,[44] she describes the practice of publicly displaying a maiden's virginity, or lack thereof, after the *rapto* as maintained mainly in Juchitán, Oaxaca.

> They light fireworks
> in the male's home the night of the *rapto*
> people know then
> that a flower bled
> and they celebrate with music and garlands
> over the pain.
> But shame is a large stone
> if instead of fireworks
> at the mouth of a house
> a clay pot is placed
> with a wound that tells the story
> of a woman who could not wait.[45]

The tone of this poem appears matter-of-fact in the first lines, with no emotion in the description of the community's knowledge of the young woman's virginity or lack of it. However, the line "But shame is a large stone" strikes a different tone, capturing the oppressive weight of shame if a woman's virginity is not proved. The last stanza offers an important commentary about gender power differentials. It is the boy's family who lights the fireworks, not the woman's. The opposition between the pain and blood of the maiden's "flower" and the celebration of the community over them create another contrast. Irma Pineda Santiago offers a critique of this custom through the use of irony and the juxtaposition of the woman's pain and the community's celebration. Ruiz Campbell writes that many of her friends acknowledged feeling embarrassment, fear, and pain: "It embarrassed them to know that the families of their boyfriends were waiting and asking if they had had sex, eager to see the 'proof of virginity'" (a sheet or handkerchief stained with blood).[46]

In "Abuela," also in *De la casa del ombligo*, publicly displaying a maiden's blood or virginity is a custom that brings joy and pride to the protagonist.

> A wide-bellied grandmother
> gave birth to ten children
> to cultivate the land.
> With a wreath on her head
> she became drunk with joy
> at the wedding[s] of her daughters

because the blood stain on a white cloth
shouted to the community that they preserved themselves well.[47]

If we consider the order of the poems we can postulate that the acceptance of *rapto* by the grandmother represents the values of another generation. It may also be that the poems represent the only possibilities for women of that generation, and the traditional wedding represents the less morally reprehensible. In the poems, women do not have the power to transgress these conventions. Natalia Toledo Paz, another prominent Zapotec poet, tackles this practice and embraces unfettered sexuality in her poems.

Natalia Toledo Paz has published a handful of books and is a considered a pioneer in bilingual publications. Toledo Paz embraces poetry as freedom. She also assumes the Spanish language as her own.

> I don't believe contemporary indigenous poetry has to give up absolutely anything; everything is a part of your life, everything influences you. As someone said, "Nothing is alien to me," not Greek culture or any other, or [any of the ones] we have read [about], fortunately. As a poet I have tried to read the classics and what is written today. . . . We must seek further; it is the only way to make sure our languages survive. We have to create new traditions, new myths. We cannot be forever re-creating the same myths; while they are wonderful, we also have to find what humanity says now. We are [people] of this time; what is going on socially, politically, culturally influences you; one's eyes are not closed.[48]

She published *Mujeres de sol, mujeres de oro* as a celebration of Zapotec women in 2002. Toledo Paz turns to the topics of virginity, sexuality, and *rapto* by offering a varied poetry that also aims to shock the reader. In "Mutilación" she explores the connection between sexuality, life, and death. In this example, the poem scandalizes readers with its provocative and sexually explicit images. The title, "Mutilación," contrasts with the image of a woman masturbating, since it creates an association with genital mutilation. It also connects the violence of mutilation to the *rapto*, as it controls women's pleasure.

> I masturbate in front of the mirror
> Like Egon Schiele.
> A wharf in my eyes separates me from my image.
> The face of death is in a drop of sweat.
> I exhale the final smile of madness,
> My self-portrait does not exist.[49]

Challenging the expectations of the *rapto*, the image created here is of a subject in control of her sexuality; in this poem, sexuality and pleasure are free of men's hold. The speaker of the poem watches herself achieve a maddening pleasure on her own. Any cultural value conventionally attributed to virginity is absent. The reference to Egon Schiele represents an unpoliced sexuality.[50]

In the poem "Tradición," published in *Olivo negro*, Toledo Paz offers an acerbic critique of the *rapto* as a tradition that publicly shames Zapotec women's sexuality and pleasure. "Tradición" in some respects continues the dialogue that Irma Pineda Santiago begins in her untitled poem, but it differs in its direct indictment of the control of sexuality by tradition.

> There was someone who tasted the must of your skin,
> walked from your head to your feet without opening their eyes
> so as to not uncover the sun's glare.
> There was someone who just pinched the food
> and did not want to drink the *compadres*' chocolate
> and the *pozol* of *mamey* seed.
>
> There was someone who hung a broken pot on your door
> and refused to pay for the party.
> The fools did not know that a fallen flower on the ground
> remains a flower until its death.[51]

The poetic voice alludes to the practice of a suitor hanging a broken pot outside the young woman's home after the *rapto* if a woman's hymen does not bleed, making her dishonor public Everyone in the community thus finds out she is not a virgin. The "fools" are those who still continue this misogynist tradition. At the first Maya-Zapotec literary conference I attended in 2010, Toledo Paz admitted that if she could change any cultural practice, it would be the *rapto*. She discussed the fear that the menace of the *rapto* produced in her as a child and jokingly added, "since I was never a virgin!" The *juchitecas* in academia fault this practice as violent and dishonorable. Ruiz Campbell calls the *rapto* a disgraceful and shameful act.[52]

Irma Pineda Santiago and Natalia Toledo Paz re-create and invert images of the Zapotec woman, countering the exotic otherness that occupied the imagination of twentieth-century painters, photographers, and writers.[53] Poetry affords Pineda Santiago and Toledo Paz the authority to answer and change cultural patterns that seek to police women's bodies and sexuality in their communities. As a custom that aims to control women's sexuality, the *rapto* is subtly critiqued by Pineda Santiago and defiantly challenged by Toledo Paz.

Maya Poets

The rise of Maya activism in the late 1970s, whether delimited by region (Maya Peninsula) and state boundaries (Yucatán/Chiapas) or transgressing the borders of nation-states (Mexico/Guatemala), responded to a set of state-sponsored policies aimed at disciplining unruly languages and cultural practices. The Maya live in southern Mexico, Guatemala, Belize, western Honduras, and eastern El Salvador, but due to unique historical and political processes, Maya cultural activism in Mexico and Guatemala has been the most visible, followed by that in Belize and Honduras. No one has published as an indigenous writer in Honduras or El Salvador,[54] a fact that directly correlates to the lack of educational opportunities, demographic marginality, and systematic cultural disempowerment of indigenous communities in these countries. My use of the term *Maya* describes identity formations across multiple official nation-state lines. By deploying this term, I do not intend to obliterate local particularities; rather, I want to underscore that the Maya's claims to cultural difference from the dominant culture in their respective nation-states rely on a shared space-time (*najt*) that predates current geopolitical demarcations.[55] Maya writers and other intellectuals reaffirmed this collectivity through literary congresses in the 1990s. In effect, this umbrella term describes the twentieth-century Maya more appropriately than their pre-Columbian ancestors because it was only in the mid-twentieth century that these linguistically distinct groups began to imagine themselves as sharing a common cultural and linguistic source that superseded individual local communities, whereas what we understand as the classical Maya civilization can best be characterized as composed of very localized chiefdoms. Before Spanish colonialism, *mayanidad* did not exist in the way it is currently articulated. In other words, as Ruth Moya clarifies: "The *mayanidad* that permeates various indigenous spheres originates in the late 1960s with clear debts to the academic work of academics studying the classical Maya civilization, but based on the interpretation of a present Maya intelligentsia emphasizing a contemporary identity."[56]

The idea of *mayanidad* (or what makes people Maya) varies across the contemporary Maya world. Southern Mexico and Guatemala have experienced the strongest social and political activism. Communities in the Yucatán Peninsula, which includes the states of Yucatán, Quintana Roo, and Campeche, hold on to a strong sense of regionalism that diverges from the glorious Aztec past forged by the Mexican state. Maya groups in Chiapas articulate their sense of particularity through a regional autonomy, especially in Zapatista communities (although not all indigenous communities in Chiapas are Zapatista), but more emphatically through linguistic and town distinctions. Maya activism in Guatemala relies on linguistic, spiritual, and cultural difference as well. Despite the diverse articulations, the discourse evokes a simultaneous local, regional, and transnational sense of collective belonging. The political vitality of these movements bolsters the literary terrain, and it is in this space of imagination and memory that a sense of collectivity is also construed.[57]

In this context, the Mexican state of Chiapas occupies a unique place in the political and cultural imagination. Centuries of land and labor exploitation by capitalist sectors as well as institutionalized racism against indigenous people in this state culminated in the 1994 Zapatista revolt. Instantiated through the charismatic figure of Subcomandante Marcos, the movement provoked an outpouring of solidarity throughout the world and continues to attract international interest.[58] Although women's literary production in Chiapas remains largely understudied, indigenous women have been critical to this movement.[59] Despite the dearth of literary criticism, it represents a powerful expression that invigorates and provides another dimension to this rebellion.[60] In the early 1980s Maya and Zoque members founded informal literary groups predicated on identity and cultural expression such as UNEMAZ, which was officially constituted in the 1990s. But it was in the aftermath of the Zapatista uprising that arts and cultural organizations succeeded in officially promoting literary forms like the short story, poetry, and the novel.[61] The State Center for Literature, Arts, and Indigenous Languages (CELALI) became an official cultural entity after the Zapatista uprising. CELALI's initial funding had direct ties to the 1996 peace accords between the Zapatista Army for National Liberation and the Mexican government. In 1997—with the full financial support of the state government—Tsotsil, Tseltal,[62] Chol, and Zoque cultural producers, who in most cases were self-taught, began to energetically create plays, poetry, and narratives. CELALI, along with other cultural centers, continues to encourage this artistic output through fellowships and literary workshops.[63] Headed by indigenous men and women, the organization sponsors creative writing workshops and literary contests in the Maya and Zoque communities of Chiapas—even though its operating budget has been in a precarious state in recent years.[64]

Indigenous women's limited access to higher education correlates to their reduced number of publications, despite the financial support indigenous language literary publications have received in Chiapas.[65] Other indigenous women have made the stage their primary form of expression, as I discuss in chapter 4.[66] Enriqueta Lunez Pérez, Mikeas Sánchez, Angelina Díaz Ruiz, Juana Karen Peñate, and Ruperta Vázquez exemplify women's poetic voices in Chiapas. Given my space limitations, I focus on poems by Lunez Pérez and Díaz Ruiz.

My analysis of Lunez Pérez's "La jti jbe' svayel kajvaltik / Desperté a Dios" (I awoke God") and Díaz Ruiz's "Riqueza/K'ulejal" (Wealth) demonstrates that their locus of enunciation as indigenous women rooted in their community affects and effects their critique of these historical forces. A bilingual and comparative exegesis of their poetry would be optimal, but due to space constraints I focus on the self-translated versions—noting meaningful differences when necessary between the Tsotsil and Spanish versions.[67] Particularly for these two poets, literary production affords them another way to deflect the gaze on the external markers conventionally read as indigeneity to other ways of seeing and hearing indigenous women. Kab'awil allows the poets to engage with two distinct interpretations of history relevant to indigenous peoples, facilitating the poets' display of a superior moral economy in the sense Kevin Gosner gives the term in explaining the reasons leading to the colonial revolts in the highlands of Chiapas.[68] Religion and capitalism have historically interfered with indigenous peoples' rights to subsistence in Chiapas and exceeded their moral limits, leading to a series of racial conflicts between Mayas and Ladinos during the colonial period.[69] Literary production by indigenous women in Chiapas epitomizes an unequivocal, critical departure from the ways writers and anthropologists imagined, represented, and discussed them across disciplines.[70] The poets counter the passive and abject representation of them that simultaneously hails them as embodiments of authenticity.

Enriqueta Lunez Pérez and Angelina Díaz Ruiz, who live in Chamula, a hamlet about fifteen minutes from San Cristóbal de las Casas, have participated in more discussions on the problematics of producing literature in an indigenous language and Spanish than have any of their female peers. CELALI, along with other institutions, sponsors these conversations through conferences and workshops organized in Chiapas, Mexico City, the Yucatán Peninsula, and Oaxaca, among other places. Other issues explored in these regional and national gatherings include theories of translation, self-translation, aesthetics, *cosmovisión*, modernity, and tradition, as well as oral and written conventions.

In contrast to the Latin dictum *cogito ergo sum*, in Tsotsil culture, one thinks and speaks from the heart. Lunez Pérez, for example, insists that her knowledge, stories, and experiences originate from imprints left in her heart by the ancestors rather than the books she has read. When someone inquires, "How are you?," that person means, "How is your heart?" The heart represents the fountain or repository of knowledge, while the mind filters experiences and stories. While analyzing a sixteenth-century Maya Tsotsil dictionary, the linguist and anthropologist Robert Laughlin found over eighty metaphors that refer to the heart, corroborating this organ's centrality in the Maya Tsotsil culture.[71]

Thus, the heart becomes a poignant and powerful metaphor in much of this poetry, contrasting with the usual mind/body split.

The hermetic, religious, and submissive indigenous woman who lacks literacy (in the alphabetic sense) is inverted in the metaphors of Lunez Pérez and Díaz Ruiz. Lunez Pérez condemns the paternalistic image of the indigenous woman, stating that the indigenous woman's image "is in a glass case where no woman can fend for herself, she is treated as handicapped."[72] Against this idea, the poets create politically active and wise speakers who intervene in capitalist (Díaz's "Riqueza") and religious discourses (Lunez Pérez's "Desperté a Dios"). The poets breathe life into this new image through culturally specific symbols and counter the historical suppression of Maya Tsotsil spirituality, as I discuss in the case of Lunez Pérez. They also indict and sentence those who control the modes of production, as in Díaz Ruiz's poem.

Women played a significant role in contesting religion in the colonial past. The poets assume a double gaze toward the historical rebellions of the highlands in the 1700s and the present political injustices. In *Soldiers of the Virgin*, Gosner identifies Dominica López, María de la Calendaria, María López, and their visions of the Virgin Mary as responsible for spurring indigenous communities to revolt against the orthodox Catholicism imposed on them, spawning multiple racial conflicts between the Maya and Spaniards.[73] Indeed, most racial tensions in colonial Chiapas directly involved a symbolic and material wrestling over religious authority.

Enriqueta Lunez Pérez's first book, *Yi'beltak ch'ulelaletik / Raíces del alma* (Roots of the soul) (2007), evokes these struggles. In the poems I analyze here, she evokes a double gaze using cultural references and symbols that both favor a Maya spirituality and are shrouded in Catholicism. Allusions to celestial bodies, *nahuales*, and nature abound in the collection. Through key objects, colors, and rituals, Lunez Pérez exalts the spiritual elements of her culture. The poem "La jti jbe' svayel kajvaltik/ Desperté a Dios" (I awoke God) intervenes in a religious discourse that dialogues with the last 500 years of history in Chiapas.

> I awoke God
> near midnight
> in exchange for his staying up
> I offered him seven verses, seven absolutions
> I confessed to him
> all of my sins
> and I kissed his forehead.[74]

The image of a young woman daring to awake God delicately inverts the historical power relations between indigenous peoples and the imposition of a Christian deity. Direct access to a higher being unravels the notion that individuals need an intermediary, usually a priest. In juxtaposing her contrite confessions and gestures, as in the line, "I kissed his forehead," the speaker invokes a superior moral economy, conjuring up the image of a mother kissing the forehead of a child. The speaker's maternal gesture makes her more powerful than the image of the God-child she portrays in the first stanza.

The poem's second section brings the reader back to everyday religious practices in Chiapas, in which reciprocity is central.

> I awoke God near midnight
> and the never-ending time
> consumed the seven colors
> the earth drank the sacred pox[75]
> The incense holder slowly turned off
> dove became my flesh.[76]

The image of a ceremony or offering is central in these lines. Reciprocity characterizes religious practices in Maya communities. In other words, the speaker makes an offering to obtain something in return. Lunez Pérez evokes the candles used in ceremonies to exorcise evil or cure sickness; the candles must represent seven colors.[77] The explicit mention of the material objects used in a ceremony or offering also allows Lunez Pérez to shift the reader's attention to a moment of spiritual communion. She concludes the poem with the lines,

> I awoke God
> near midnight
> and little by little time
> transformed my prayer into sublime desire.[78]

The image of a dove becoming her flesh forcefully contrasts with the image of the dove in the Catholic version of the Holy Spirit, which is without flesh. In this way, she cleverly undermines the impact of religious indoctrination, exchanging prayer for "sublime desire." The Maya's concept of time trumps the Christian one. Although both indigenous and Catholic traditions influence the poem, the speaker's maternal relationship to God reinforces a Maya superior moral economy. More important, a ceremony or offering represents the right to reciprocity, one in which the female speaker holds ultimate power. Her movement from the past to the present to the sacred and the profane reflect her kab'awil cosmolectics.

Many poets, especially the generation that spearheaded the indigenous literary movement that culminated in the 1990s, insisted that all writing should be originally written in the Native language. For them, fluency in an indigenous language signaled identity, authenticity, and resistance. Nonetheless, Lunez Pérez concedes that she often writes first in Spanish, then translating into Tsotsil. Lunez Pérez indicates that no one should penalize indigenous peoples for not knowing how to write in their language, as the racist political policies enacted through the educational system precluded a majority from acquiring literacy in Native languages. The absence of bilingual books reflects not only her experience as a young student but also that of most indigenous groups before the 1980s. Poets like her have started to fill this void. Now students have access to bilingual books and can simultaneously learn from the standardization of the language's orthography. In fact, secondary schools in Chiapas require their students to read her book *Tajimol ch'ulelaletik/Juego de nahuales*.[79] Literary production, then, acts as an important decolonizing strategy for young Tsotsiles.

In a video interview conducted by the Tsotsil filmmaker María Dolores Martínez Arias, Lunez Pérez offers advice to her Tsotsil compatriots, urging them (whether they migrate within Mexico or abroad) to not feel embarrassed or forget about their culture. She reminds them that culture represents an inheritance the Maya ancestors bequeathed them. The interview concludes with Lunez Pérez in the domestic sphere, shepherding lambs, along with an untranslated version of the poem "Tajimol ch'ulelaletik/ Juego de nahuales" (Game of energies).[80] In Tsotsil land, some people believe lambs represent God on Earth. Notably, the subject of the poem is the concept of *nahual*, a central philosophical tenet in Mesoamerica that thrives in the oral tradition. Depending on the region, but generally similar in spirit, upon birth the *nahual* embodies an energy or animal protector that accompanies an individual throughout life. In some communities these entities correlate to one of the twenty days sculpted in the sacred calendar, while in others, a *nahual* is an individual who can transform into his or her animal double. In the context of this interview and the deliberate use of the poem, the writer establishes a relationship between lambs and God, again strategically reinforcing that Maya spirituality thrives despite the imposition of Catholicism.

Díaz Ruiz's "Mujeres de mi presente"/ "Ta jk'ak'al tana antsetik" (Women of my present) included in the book *Sbel sjol yo'onton ik'/Memorial del viento*,[81] offers readers a different politicized angle. A cursory view of the themes manifested in her poetry invites the reader to immediately recognize a tangible preoccupation with gender. She invokes a feminist geography through Suyul—an area in Tenejapa recognized as the home of the Virgin Suyul—as her own origin, a referent that affects and influences her engagement with women.[82] Most of her poems speak of the women in her life; others pay homage to the Virgin Suyul. Díaz Ruiz's explicit admiration and praise of her mother's grit allude to a strong bond with women and a sense of solidarity between them. In contrast, the poet bluntly reveals in an interview that despite her father's teaching profession, he opposed the cultivation of her writing and her desire to pursue higher education. The adverse reaction of Díaz Ruiz's father to her writing prompted him to confiscate her notebook, work she never recovered.[83]

In the interview, Díaz Ruiz emphasizes the vital role writing played in her empowerment as an indigenous woman. She states that expressing herself through the written word allowed her to defy her community's gender role expectations as well as the dominant society's stereotypes about the Maya Tsotsil, who are supposed to excel only in physical labor. The first prize she earned in an essay contest titled "Soy indígena y tú?" was a fellowship to enroll in a private university.[84] She proudly asserts that composing the essay allowed her "at 17 [to] demonstrate that I am not what they wanted me to be."[85] While Díaz Ruiz expresses beauty and love in her poetry, her poems also offer acerbic critiques of racism, classism, and sexism.

Díaz Ruiz's anticapitalist and antipatriarchal posture directly confronts the modes of production that force people to migrate in search of jobs. The poem "Riqueza/K'ulejal" (Wealth) is a tour de force, putting on trial the capitalist excess that undermines indigenous peoples' right to subsistence.[86] While the poem does not necessarily make the case for a Marxist solution to the exploitation of indigenous people, the poet concretely illustrates how a capitalist system perpetuates their marginalization. Her position departs from an explicit "historical materialism" or an idealized version of a pre-Columbian communism in the way José Carlos Mariátegui imagined the connection between Marxism and indigenous peoples.[87] Capitalism, personified as masculine in her poem, animates a connection between patriarchy and capital, facilitating the speaker's unyielding desire to annihilate the phallus. The phallus represents the origin of all the social ills that make mothers sick, fathers drunk, and others migrants. Through the poem's violent tone and male personification of a capitalist structure, the speaker proclaims her indigenous critique grounded in a shared moral universe.

I want to know what your sweet suicide is like
To think like yesterday, to kill you
I want to pour your black blood on your shoulders
See crosses in the courtyard of the palace without tears
To see you hanging there with your hands covered in filth.

I want to defeat your stinking wealth
Imagine the rainbow in blue-gray for you
Hate you for my sick mother,
Curse you for my drunken father,
Imprison you for my brother who has emigrated,
You stink like the misfortune that you left me
. . . .
I will be back tomorrow,
See your eyes full of coins,
Your teeth dirty with fine lunches,
Your mind full of barbarities.[88]

"K'ulejal" (Wealth) conveys the speaker's anger, hatred, and a desire for vengeance against the capitalist forces, symbolized by a male subject in the poem, that exploit her community. Informed by her position as poor, indigenous, and a woman, Díaz Ruiz interrogates issues related to health care, rampant alcoholism in the communities, and the transformation of the modes of production for indigenous men. The speaker foresees the system's decay and demise, and makes clear that indigenous people will survive and witness its complete destruction. A distinct moral economy resonates in the line, "I will be back tomorrow." The speaker — and by extension the community — will outlive an unjust system that threatens their right to subsistence.

In other poems, Díaz Ruiz broaches themes related to ritual, the importance of the Virgin Suyul, and the empowerment of women. Her poetry furthers the dialogues beginning to take shape in other disciplines about the ways social structures affect indigenous women differently. Legal expert Rosalba Gómez Gutiérrez of the Tseltal community writes, "As indigenous women we find ourselves in a situation of double or even triple discrimination because of gender, ethnicity, and sometimes also age, in the case of girls."[89] When gender and age intersect, being a girl means living under the tutelage of the men in the family, who will make decisions about her education, reproductive health, and marriage. Parents tend to deny daughters the right to attend school, favoring sons. Others express concern for the safety of their daughters, fearing teachers may sexually assault their girls.[90]

Lunez Pérez's and Díaz Ruiz's experience of the literary illuminates the ways that writing authorizes them to confront the prejudices against them due to their sex, class, and ethnicity, making them pioneers in a cultural practice historically reserved for a privileged few in Chiapas. They also grapple with an elitist literary historiography that has traditionally spoken for indigenous peoples in the highlands. Lunez Pérez and Díaz Ruiz deploy a double gaze toward the past to indict injustices perpetuated by religion and capitalism, two social forces that have historically adversely affected indigenous communities. Catholicism, of course, played a different role in indigenous communities after the 1960s, but the poets reference Catholicism in the colonial past. Their vocation as poets in the town of Chamula transforms the ways others see and hear indigenous women. In their community, young women usually do not have access to high school or college, and many wed before the age of eighteen. More important, Lunez Pérez's and Díaz Ruiz's university education and their return to participate as cultural producers in their town set a revolutionary example for other young women who aspire to pursue writing against all odds.

The Muse of the Maya Peninsula

In the Maya Peninsula, poets, storytellers, playwrights, and novelists have established far-reaching organizations that seek to support and influence the craft of inexperienced writers and foment their production. The poetry of Briceida Cuevas Cob, a member of the first generation of writers from the Peninsula, is characterized by unparalleled elegance and unique rhythm. Cuevas Cob's work first appeared in numerous literary magazines throughout Mexico and was followed by the publication of her first book of poems, *U yok'ol auat pek' ti u kuxtal pek'* / *El quejido del perro en su existencia* (The dog's whimper in its existence) (1985). Cuevas Cob has acquired an important status as a poet by participating in international literary festivals, mainly in South America and Western Europe. Many of her poems in *Je' bix k'in* / *Como el sol* (Like the sun) summon the moon; she poeticizes the persistence of certain beliefs about eclipses, which in Maya cosmology result from the sun eating the moon. In her work, as in that of other Mesoamerican indigenous poets, the moon is an important cultural symbol associated with fertility, childbirth, and weaving.

Ixchel, the moon goddess, is part of an engagement with cosmolectics. Cuevas Cob's critique of gender double standards gains full force in *Je' bix k'in / Como el sol*. The title of this collection suggests gender equality, since in Maya cosmology the sun has male attributes, while the moon has female ones. Cuevas Cob returns to this metaphor in many of her initial poems, moving from the sacred to the profane. In "Mi nombre (My name)," for example, originally published in *La Jícara*, she critiques men's double standards about women who transgress their sexual roles and asks, "Why don't they call the moon a whore? She is used to wagering her body, / used to hiding her shame."[91]

In other poems, Cuevas Cob uses ancient symbols traditionally associated with Maya male warriors but dresses them with a feminine sensibility. In 2003, at the Annual Poetry Festival held in Medellín, Colombia, Cuevas Cob read from her poem "Orígenes II," and this is the version I cite (she read a slightly different version at the Poetry Homage to Carlos Montemayor in 2010). "Orígenes II" offers an interpretation of the well-documented and recognized Maya ball game as representative of fertility, duality, life, and death. This poem has not been published yet. The images and the lexicon that Cuevas Cob uses clearly invoke the old ball game, traditionally interpreted as involving only men, and transform it into a space of birth and maternity, feminizing by her use of analogy. The poem begins with a woman in full labor:

> My mother guards a ball in the net of her womb
> In this game goals do not count, rather it is the injury time
> that trembles on her skin.
> From her breasts trickles the moon venerated body of Xbalamque
> She already has nine warnings
> It is time for the precious rain to explode from her womb
> and expel the ball toward the bellybutton of [her] brown field.[92]

There is an allusion to pregnancy in the poem's first line. In the Spanish version, *amonestaciones* resembles the word *gestaciones*. An *amonestación* in modern soccer is a warning to a player. In this sense, "warnings" (as well as the mention of goals) is an anachronistic term. Cuevas Cob takes liberties with images traditionally associated with the pre-Columbian Maya game for a precise purpose; though it seems out of place, accurate timing is not what matters. What does matter is found in the following verse "the prolongation of time that trembles on her skin." Time, in this particular poem, is equivalent to the Mayan culture and history that is continually reproduced. *Amonestaciones* allows the reader to continue visualizing the ball game images. The reference to Xbalamque, one of the twins who eventually becomes the moon in the *Popol Vuh* underscores again the importance of the feminine since ancient times. Cuevas Cob manages to appropriate the most representative symbols of traditional, ancient roles and gives them new meaning by a maintaining a double gaze, often granting the female protagonist creative power. Her poetry thus speaks to micro- and macrohistories, informed by a kab'awil cosmolectics that allows her to play with pre-Columbian and modern temporalities.

Maya Poets from Guatemala

Maya women poets and other intellectuals in Guatemala speak of the body, its pleasure and pain, but also gesture toward the body-as-territory, recognizing it as a product of history and not biology. Their poetry contributes to a project of autonomy, not just in the intellectual and artistic realms but also in the poets' political relationship to land. A critical analysis of the body and how it figures in their poetry alerts us to a change in its material symbolism and its connection to political issues. The books themselves become cultural artifacts fraught with political and aesthetic meanings. For example, the cover of *La palabra y el sentir de las mujeres mayas de Kaqla*[93] features a striking photograph of the contributors lying in a circle, an image that overflows onto the back cover of the book. The image of women in their traditional dress contrasts with the back cover, where candles appear between the legs of the women. This image is striking precisely because the arrangement of candles evokes symbols of the sacred in Maya ceremony. Here the connection between women, sexuality, and the cosmos is tangible — and goes beyond speech or postmodern feminist linguistic discourses. In their introduction to *Material Feminisms*, feminist critics Stacy Alaimo and Susan Hekman reiterate that the linguistic turn in postmodern feminist theory has required that "one distance oneself as much as possible from the tainted realm of materiality by taking refuge within culture, discourse, and language. An emerging group of feminist theorists of the body are arguing, however, that we need a way to talk about the materiality of the body as itself an active, sometimes recalcitrant force. Women have bodies; these bodies have pain as well as pleasure."[94] These poems thus represent the realities of living with racism and the imposition of a culture of sin, in the sense Emma Delfina Chirix García suggests, but also establish conceptions of the body and universe that survive from pre-Columbian times.[95]

The presumed textual silence of women poets correlates to the way writers have narrated the Guatemalan nation. The implicit connection between the novelistic genre and the nation marginalized cultural productions by indigenous peoples until the 1980s. Poetry and other literary forms continued to be produced in indigenous communities even though these productions have not always been written. Aida Toledo and Anabela Acevedo, in *Para conjurar el sueño*, assert that Guatemalan poets in general have been relegated to silence, but that for women "this ignorance is joined by the weight that often means to belong to a tradition that imposes a strict set of behaviors and consciously or unconsciously requires them to respond to particular models."[96] Moral and religious institutions, heteronormativity, and patriarchy are social forces that impose or colonize the female body. The poets who have transgressed these rules in Guatemala since the 1970s have been usually middle-class, nonindigenous women like Margarita Carrera, Luz Méndez de la Vega, and Ana María Rodas.[97] Women continue working on the margins of literary historiography, a condition even more acute for indigenous women poets, since they are isolated not only as women but also as members of liminal indigenous communities that the nation-state attempted to systematically eradicate during the 1980s. The economic realities of indigenous communities have prioritized the education of boys for different reasons. Historically, men have dealt with the Spanish-speaking society, while women have stayed at home. In other instances, families fear for the safety of the daughters who are exposed to sexual abuse in schools.

Emma Delfina Chirix García, Aura Cumes, and Amanda Pop Bol are pioneering studies about the body and affect in their communities.[98] Their analysis, especially within social studies, speaks from the viewpoint of gender and indigenous intersectional theory.[99] Women begin to deepen their reflection of specific problems faced in patriarchal and racist societies. Chirix García, in her essay "Los cuerpos y las mujeres kaqchikeles," argues that in the Kaqchikel community, "one way to understand the human being is through a trilogy that interrelates body, mind, and spirit.... This indigenous worldview perceives the body as living."[100] In her works, she demystifies the validity of a paradigm like complementarity and the lived reality experienced by many indigenous women.

Bodies in Celestial and Land Configurations

Traditionally, the human body has functioned as a barometer through which we learn about the world, what we see, what we hear, what we touch. The anthropologist Mary Douglas suggests that "the body is a surface on which are written the rules, the hierarchies, and even the metaphysical obligations of a culture," making the female body a microcosm of ancient and modern traditions.[101] The body is related to the way one understands the world; for example, the body serves as the basis of order in calendars, social roles, and the universe in Mesoamerica. The Tzolk'in (Cholq'ij), or sacred 260-day calendar, symbolizes human gestation, and each day is associated with different parts of the body. The human body, especially the fingers and toes, constitute the pillars of Maya mathematics. In Maya poetry written by men, certain parts like the ear, heart, and eyes abound. Popti' poet Santos Alfredo García Domingo refers to the heart in twenty of his poems, nine times in *Artesano de palabras* and eleven times in *Raíces de esperanza*.[102] In poetry written by women, references to the breasts, legs, and vagina abound. The body, sex, and gender manifest differently depending on the enunciating subject. Hence critics such as Alfredo López Austin and José Carlos Aguado Vázquez point out that the body cannot exist outside of society; it is a product of society.[103] Pre-Columbian, colonial, and modern ideas about the body influence its representation in the literature.

A Maya women's literary corpus has been in the making since the first publications by Calixta Gabriel Xiquín (1978)[104] to the more recent poetic works by Maya Cú Choc (1996)[105] and Rosa Chávez (2005).[106] Other Maya poets like Adela Delgado Pop, Dorotea Gómez, and Elena Nij have been anthologized, but they have yet to publish a complete book.[107] Calixta Gabriel Xiquín was born in 1956 in Chimaltenango, Guatemala. In 1981, she sought refuge in the United States when her three brothers were assassinated and disappeared. The need to mourn and heal spiritually inspired her to return to Guatemala in 1988. Her first book, *Hueso de la tierra*, was published in 1996.[108] The book had a very low print run and was treated like a cultural artifact designed for special collections due to its high price and artistry. Her poetry is not the result of literary workshops but the product of a need to denounce the injustices against indigenous peoples during the war. Maya Cú Choc, of Q'eqchi' origin, began her career as a poet with a section published in the anthology *Novsimos* in 1997.[109] She has dabbled in theater, music, radio, social activism, and poetry workshops. Cú Choc considers herself an urban Indian, marked by her parents' decision not to teach her the language. Likewise, Rosa Chávez represents a younger generation. She was born in Guatemala City in 1980 to a K'iche' father and a Kaqchikel mother. She has also experimented in theater and music. Chávez has participated in international poetry festivals and meetings in Colombia, Mexico, Europe, and the United States.

In their poems, the body functions as an icon of traditional knowledge but also as a basis and tool for breaking sexual and ethnic stereotypes. Three ways of representing the body are highlighted in their poetry. Through some of these poems, I argue, the poets prompt the reader to see the body as a cultural expression tied to an indigenous cosmology. In others, the female body is read as indigenous and poor, thus subject to violence, as in the poems by Calixta Gabriel Xiquín and Rosa Chávez. In other poems, the body and eroticism are used as cultural and social transgressions. Ironically, poetry by indigenous women has received more attention abroad than domestically in Guatemala. Most of the work by Maya women is unknown in Guatemala because Ladino society has not accorded them the cultural status their work deserves; additionally, some of their books circulate primarily — and with great difficulty — only within a smaller number of academic settings in the United States.

Emma Delfina Chirix García, in her critical essay "Los cuerpos y las mujeres kaqchikeles," emphasizes that in her language a range of signs, symbols, and feelings exist to conceive of the body. She argues that "one way to understand human beings is through a triad that interrelates body, mind and spirit. These three elements form a oneness and if fragmented cause an imbalance in the life of the person. This indigenous worldview perceives the body as a living being, with energies and feelings and needs ... [but] *very little is said about the desires of the body*" (my emphasis).[110] Interestingly, poets reject the taboos associated with sexuality and bodily functions within indigenous communities. Some of the poets relate the body to representative colors of Maya cosmology — even though some conservative Mayas could interpret this move as disrespectful. Rosa María Chávez, in the poem "Cíclica," makes an explicit reference to menstruation, invoking the color red and its many connotations:

> I write with red
> red is my condition;
> [as a] blessing or misfortune
> this color paints my canvas
> captured in each moon
> ....
> female and clandestine
> overflows pleasure.[111]

The color red is central to Maya ceremony and is associated with the sunrise, life, and the sacred heart of heaven. The connection between menstruation and sacred ceremony may be interpreted as sacrilegious. Red also connotes a leftist ideological position when Chávez writes "red is my condition." Her usage of the word *lienzo* in Spanish is also strategic because it refers to both a sanitary napkin and paintings drawn on cotton cloth during the pre-Columbian and colonial period to establish genealogies. Finally, red represents one of the two sacred inks in Mesoamerican knowledge.

Calixta Gabriel Xiquín first published poems under the pseudonym Caly Domitila Canek in newspapers and anthologies. Her first poems denounced the situation she lived through during the war, when her brothers were murdered. The references to two indigenous historical figures in her pseudonym mark a continental resistance and solidarity.[112] Gabriel Xiquín presents the body without any eroticism; instead it is vulnerable to the genocidal forces assailing her community. Subject to military violence, the body in her poems cannot experience pleasure. The body's disposability during Guatemala's civil war forces her to focus on the body's spiritual dimension, as in the following lines from *Weaving Events in Time / Tejiendo los sucesos en el tiempo*:

> In the hands of a woman,
> poetry twinkles, twinkles,
> and her soul creates hope
> with her hands the colors,
> red, yellow, blue, green, and black.
> With these colors she weaves the poetry of anguish,
> of pain, of agony, and
> of hope.[113]

The reference to the five colors of corn directly connects her poetry to the creation of humanity. No doubt Calixta Gabriel Xiquín's poetry production was curtailed by violence — she buried thousands of poems when she fled her home.[114] After her return to Guatemala, she searched for her manuscripts to no avail. The loss of her poetry reflects a systematic violence against cultural memory. This loss makes it more challenging to note any development in her representation of the body and the female subjects in her work.

Gabriel Xiquín represents a female body subjected to violent forces inside and outside the community. She suffered the experience of exile in the United States after the army murdered three of her brothers. The poems represent the body as always covered in a huipil and skirt. The cover of her book *Tejiendo los sucesos en el tiempo / Weaving Events in Time* represents women in conventional images but also alludes to writing/weaving as a practice inherited from the goddess Ixchel. On her book cover, the poet sits in front of a loom. Perhaps, since she is the oldest of the three poets discussed in this section, her vision of the body seems more traditional; still, she subtly critiques the lack of options for indigenous women outside motherhood and their relegation to sexual reproduction. For example, the poem "Mujer," published under the pseudonym Caly Domitila Canek, interrogates women's roles — even if the persona appears "quiet, analytical." Gabriel Xiquín inserts a slight implication of defiance when she writes,

> Woman,
> your profession woman
> your mission mother
> . . . .
> Woman
> good worker
> Mental,
> Physical and spiritual
> Her dignity raped.
> . . . .
> Woman
> you do not go to school because you have many children.[115]

In another poem, "Mujer campesina," the woman's hands stand out since they are "coarse from the hard work on the farms and in the countryside."[116] In Gabriel Xiquín's poems, desire, love, and eroticism are impossibilities, and instead decry injustice with immediacy.

Chirix García, who belongs to the same linguistic community, writes that, in general, in Comalapa, Chimaltenango, women discussing issues of sexuality produces nervous laughter. In her estimation this means the subject produces pleasure among women and men.[117] She elaborates that "there is a significant wealth of words in Kaqchikel for speaking about the body linked to sexuality, which proves that this topic elicits much interest."[118] Genitalia are translated into slang for animal parts. Chirix García offers several phrases that refer to the sexual act defined by the environment of the areas where they live, for example, "job' pa awan" (let's go the maize field), "jo' chu wa xan" (let's go to the wall), or "tasipaj jub'a chuwa" (give me a bit).[119] Her findings reveal that eroticism and sexuality are also informed by the flora and fauna in the communities.

Maya Cú Choc, a Q'eqchi' poet, speaks compellingly of the body. She forcefully inverts the static image of the indigenous woman into a fluid subject. In "¡Pobrecita yo . . . !," a poem included in her third book, *Recorrido*, Cú Choc reflects on a feminine body that desires and reproduces life.[120] She departs from the traditional belief that confines a woman's body to the role of vessel for sexual reproduction. Cú Choc claims the body's right to pleasure and affect. In sharp and bluntly erotic strokes she disrupts the desexualized, customary impression of the mother figure. Her poetry emphasizes that while social norms separate eroticism and motherhood as opposing subjectivities, these divisions negate the reality and materiality of the female body. Her poems transgress the social taboo surrounding talk of sex and bodily pleasure. In one of her poems, she brings together oppositional images about mothers moving between pleasure and pain through the image of a nursing mother and the pleasure breasts inspire:

> poor vagina of mine
> you experienced only one delivery
> in your life
>
> condemned vagina
> you also knew joy
> tenderness and richness
> from burning hands
> and because of them
> you will be convicted
>
> oh, my breasts
> poor breasts
> because they only
> breastfed one baby
> these, will also be convicted
> for not resisting pleasure
> from hands
> and tongues
> full of frenzy[121]

The first stanza depicts the female body as the traditional cradle of life. In the second stanza, in contrast, the sexual organ is presented as receiving and offering bodily gratification. The voice depicts breasts as having both a maternal and a sensual function, closely connecting pleasure and play. Speaking about bodily pleasure runs counter to the social and cultural ideas about indigenous peoples of the highlands. The critic Arturo Arias states that the highland peoples are represented and imagined as asexual: "although the phenomenon may be associated with Catholic ideological traits, the dominant image has been that the Maya, since they are from the mountain villages, are not erotic, unlike the [people] from the coastal towns."[122]

If Maya Cú Choc's poetry breaks with the image of rural indigenous women as submissive and sexless, the poems of Rosa María Chávez represent the body as performance. Her first books captivate not only with her rebellious poetry against a conservative society, but also with the images on their covers. The covers include the image of a naked woman, no doubt Chávez. As noted by literary critic Anabella Acevedo, the photo places Chávez in a position of transparency as well as vulnerability.[123] She has nothing to hide. It challenges the reader to see the indigenous body in the flesh and not as a folkloric icon. For Guatemalan Maya women in particular, this is a cultural transgression in conservative Maya and Ladino society. In referring to the female body, these poems from *Casa solitaria* (Desolate house)[124] defy expectations of modesty:

Solitary woman
of sealed visions
scarred in the soul
and in the womb
you clench your teeth
and your vulva
clenching in your fists
wild melancholies
proudly feminine

celebrating your freedom
screaming to the world that chaotic joy
hidden and protected
in your maternal role
ancestral receptacle of silence.[125]

Chávez celebrates the female body. She breaks with the cultural tradition of not talking about sex organs. Chávez proclaims her feminine pride, one that has been hidden and protected by tradition. In other poems from her book *Piedra/Ab'aj* (Stone)[126] references to the body and its connection to the Maya world abound. Ancient ideas about the body continue and coexist in contemporary poetry. For example, in the next poem, "Nací de comadrona" (Born by a midwife), Chávez associates the number nine with femininity and the idea of the underworld, or *tiku bolom* (the nine layers of the underworld). Burying a person's navel continues as an important practice that symbolizes the material connection of land among Mesoamerican indigenous communities.

On the ninth day
after my birth
grandpa went to the mountains
my navel in his backpack
dry as a husk
hung it on an avocado tree
from there comes
the strength of my spirit
and the safety of my steps.[127]

In Chávez's poetry, the body serves as the forum where social and cultural taboos implode. Relating to the body in this way is unheard of in the villages of the highlands and would embarrass most older women. Explicitly naming sexual organs would be considered inappropriate. This poem's frank use of body parts to convey the difficult lives of sex workers may be offensive to others.

Burn dry vagina
clitoris defeated
foamy saliva
moans calculated per minute
lubricating the blame
scrape the absent body
burn swollen clitoris
piece of no one
burn, bruise, this solitude so dry.[128]

The speaker alludes to a colonized conception of the sexual organs as well as sexual violence against abject bodies in the city. If speaking explicitly of the body breaks with the established norm of proper conduct, what is at issue for indigenous women is not only contravening dominant social interdictions but also the expectation of women's modesty within indigenous communities. Toledo and Acevedo conclude that "poetry created by women in the twentieth century will not abandon engaging with the erotic and recognition of the body, the need to find a way to manifest their voices in a poetic space that belongs to them, to defect in some form [from] the space or spaces ceded to them by the patriarchal system that would marginalize [women] in discussing sexual issues, to discuss political situations in which [women] had no involvement, or [would] engage in courtly and romantic subjects, without confronting in writing a language stripped of the feminine."[129] Indigenous women's poetry offers a complex engagement with ancient and contemporary notions of corporeality. Chirix García concludes with important implications for an ethnic-gender analysis of the body: "The human body that is now mentioned in the Maya languages is interrelated with nature and the cosmos, but has not been associated with [']territory,['] because it involves seeing the body as a political body and the territory as a woman's body."[130] Other indigenous women feminists like Lorena Cabnal (Maya Xinca) are direct and clear in their political position as indigenous women: "It is based on the defense of the body-earth territory. Women's bodies are a part of the territory they inhabit, and the violence that women's bodies suffer is transmitted from generation to generation as a legacy through women's cognitive and corporeal memories."[131] Linking the female body to territory from an affective, indigenous, feminist perspective is already a transformative gesture in this poetry, which builds on the work of Maya sociologists, anthropologists, activists, and psychologists.

Conclusion

I have demonstrated that indigenous women poets share key social, political, and cultural concerns about language and survival with other indigenous writers and poets in Mesoamerica. Specifically, indigenous women's poetry speaks against gendered structures of power within and beyond their communities. Women's efforts to confront prejudice against their gender and ethnicity, as well as their insertion into a cultural practice invariably reserved for a privileged few, makes them literary pioneers. They open spaces through poetry and pave avenues for new generations of indigenous women to assume a role in the Republic of Letters. Their poetry also addresses cultural practices that oppress women: they liberate the body from social expectations by using eroticism, claim important spaces in the political imagination, and speak to an autonomy grounded in the body-as-territory formed by history not biology. Their representation of the body is also informed by past and present cultural conceptions related to nature and spirituality invoking the double gaze or a kab'awil cosmolectics. It is likewise informed by a need to transform the social and material conditions they live through, transgressing key taboos. If for most of the twentieth century indigenous women have been subjected to object positions in regional and national literatures, today they chart new territories through their own writings — on their own terms — imbuing with metaphors the silent spaces of Mesoamerica's history.

CHAPTER FOUR

Contemporary Maya Women's Theater

When Indigeneity emerged as a legal and juridical category during the Cold War era, Indigenous cultural performance and display became essential to its articulation, even its substantiation. Indigeneity is no one's primary identity; yet ... individuals and groups across the globe fashion themselves as Indigenous through performance and performative acts in intercultural spaces.
—Laura Graham and H. Glenn Penny (2014)

The womanly virtues of immobility, invisibility, and silence hardly lend themselves to work in the theater; indeed, opportunities for indigenous women in Chiapas even to see theater are practically nonexistent.
—Tamara Underiner (2004)

The primary magical-religious purpose of this type of theater is to influence the supernatural forces of the great cosmos. It is, in other words, a magic-religious formula that acquires its strength through repetition. This is a characteristic of indigenous art in all its forms, just as all forms of indigenous art are channeled to this very end; The activation of cosmic forces for the benefit of man.
—N. Cayuqui Estage (1994)

CHAPTER 3 FOCUSED ON the artistic approach of indigenous women in challenging the politics that deploy their images as symbolic embodiments of authenticity and difference, in both nation-state and male-dominated indigenous discourses. As we saw, "gender complementarity" is an archetype that has been broadly employed across academic disciplines to portray an idealized, radical indigenous difference that does not correspond to prevailing indigenous reality. While various scholars have questioned the notion of "gender complementary" as an idealization, the concept itself has not been entirely rejected by indigenous women. Many reclaim it as an achievable paradigm, pointing to a symbolic parity in the cosmos and one that is paradigmatically captured in spiritual practices.[1] I argued in chapter 3 that women vigorously exercise their poetic voices to contest lingering sexist attitudes and persistent discriminatory customs — particularly those practiced under the rubric of customary law or *usos y costumbres*.[2] The lyrical use of the body and its complex underlying themes of eroticism and sexuality, while participating in the defense of indigenous women's sexual and economic autonomy, is integral to larger territorial claims.

Throughout this book, I have underlined the importance of writing as a distinctive creative tool of creation, communication, and inquiry for Maya and Zapotec peoples before the European incursion, during the subsequent colonization of their lands, and throughout the nation-formation phase. In this chapter, I turn to indigenous theater formations and performances — practices that escape the constrictions of what Ángel Rama once theorized as the "lettered city" to name the intricate relationships binding colonial power to literacy, urban space, and domination. The practitioners involved in indigenous theater and performance do not depend on particular endorsements from official institutions to bring their productions to the stage, nor do they always have formal training as professional actors. Unlike the other literary genres this book analyzes, theater arts induce an immediate response from an audience. In the twentieth and twenty-first centuries, spectators become a strategic component of political expression in indigenous theater and performance.

While Diana Taylor and Sarah J. Townsend make the argument that *performance*, as opposed to *theater*, represents "a broader concept that includes practices such as ritual and dance," I use the terms interchangeably, as do the actresses featured in this chapter when they describe their work.[3] Their ventures uncouple elite assumptions behind theater production and propose that indigenous dramatic forms demand to be analyzed and discussed in conversation with other notions of theater, even if their provenance is decidedly different. I do differentiate the plays and performances from ritual practices in intent and delivery. Ritual acts are not necessarily performed for public consumption, nor do they pursue a political agenda in the same vein as FOMMA and Ajchowen do in their drama. I make the distinction because rituals can be part of the mise-en-scène, without it necessarily being an end in itself. In other words, ritual aspects can make their appearance, and are staged, but only to stimulate and move the stories forward. While Jean Graham-Jones notes that "cultural production continues to be theoretically polarized as either dictated from above or percolating from below," my aim in this chapter is to show the intersections and connections Maya women's theater troupes exploit to imagine other futures as they enact kab'awil toward gender, economic, or national relations.[4] Kab'awil, as a double gaze, allows women to envision other autonomies, whether these imply self-sufficiency or better gender relations. It becomes palpable in the performances through the simultaneous embodiment of various temporalities, the allusion to ancient historical periods in the present.

During my stay in Mexico (2003–4) researching indigenous literatures, I met the founders of Fortaleza de la Mujer Maya (Strength of the Maya Woman, or FOMMA) as well as the members of Sna Jtz'ibajom and learned about issues both groups faced as nonprofit organizations based in San Cristóbal de las Casas, a colonial city ruled by Ladino elites. Almost a decade later, I traveled to Sololá, Guatemala, to learn about the work being done by Ajchowen (the company's Maya name translates as "monkey," an animal recognized as the patron of the arts and writing as well as one of the first set of twins in the *Popol Vuh*). Their works directly engage with the intersections between gender inequality and autonomy, self-sufficiency and neocapitalist forces. The work of FOMMA and Ajchowen assumes kab'awil as a political posture in the sense of "revisioning, reassembling, and reworking of social reality."[5]

Theater and History

In my study of theater's puzzling origin story, I came to appreciate its similarities to and differences from indigenous theater. The origins of theater and performance are historically uncertain because scripts only became a prevailing technology relatively recently; the first written forms are traceable to a manuscript prepared for King Juba II of Mauretania (ca. 50 BCE–23 CE), titled *Theatriké historia*, whose contents have been lost.[6] As the literary critic R. W. Vince tells us, all references to this manuscript come from secondhand Greek and Latin accounts.[7] Joseph R. Roach writes that this origin of loss speaks to the "perceived contradiction of writing the history of so notoriously transient a form."[8] A critic's engagement with the history of pre-Columbian theater faces a similar predicament. Despite this murky and controversial history, however, most critics support the idea that theater is a form of "one of the most ancient of Western institutions."[9] Parallel to the historiography of other genres like the novel (a subject I take on in chapter 5), most current studies of theater as an art form continue to be constrained and conditioned by positivist, developmental notions. Roach argues that this positivist ideology marks theater historians who "tell a story of progress from the origins of theater in the sympathetic magic of 'primitive peoples' before the beginning of history to the Pisgah sights of European modernism at its end."[10] I propose that theater and performance have emerged across distinct cultures and geographies simultaneously, or rather organically and as needed, not following any a priori or teleological form. In the lands we now term the Americas, theater and performance have been documented as existing prior to the importation of plays to convert indigenous peoples to Christianity in the sixteenth century, thus supporting my take on a polygenesis of these art forms.[11]

The Multiple Origins of Indigenous Theater

Indigenous and Spanish chroniclers offer written evidence of theater and performance as integral components of pre-Columbian societies' cultural activities. These chronicles describe theatrical and performative practices that included music, dance, and various religious rituals. Diego de Landa, in his sixteenth-century *An Account of the Things of Yucatán*, mentions the "stone theaters" in Chichén Itzá that were used to showcase political farces and comedies.[12] Miguel León-Portilla notes that Hernán Cortés, the conquistador who commanded the military forces that brought about the political defeat of the Aztec people, offers one of the few descriptions of pre-Columbian theater in his third letter to the Spanish court.[13] Carlos Montemayor, Donald Frischmann, Dennis Tedlock, and Tamara Underiner cross-reference pre-Columbian notions of theater/performance that coincide with current definitions of what stands as theater.[14]

In addition to indigenous organic theatrical and performative practices, Spanish friars impacted indigenous theater by using it as a less coercive tool to convert indigenous populations to Christianity, as far back as the sixteenth century. Indeed, the well-known friar Pedro de Gante proposed using theater for conversion based on his observations of indigenous peoples' inclination for dance, song, and ritual.[15] In other colonial documents, particularly those produced in the latter part of the seventeenth century by religious officials, the colonizer's rationale for using theater related to a politics of language, since many indigenous people remained monolingual in their native languages. The friars assumed that the "Indians" would eagerly learn the gospels' teachings and grasp their meaning easier and faster if they "saw" the Bible's most important precepts dramatized. Fernando Horcasitas identifies two official documents from the years 1650 and 1698 (which in his estimation came rather historically late, since theater had been implemented by friars from at least 1535) that justified the use of theater to evangelize.[16] Historically, therefore, the plays documented in indigenous languages during the colonial period were practically all religious in content. The critic María Sten notes that, in fact, "it can be said without exaggeration that theater was for spiritual colonization what horses and gunpowder were for military conquest."[17] Needless to say, even in the aftermath of colonization, theater, ritual, and performance served indigenous communities as venues for decrying and denouncing oppressive conditions and commenting on social relations.

Precursors

Due to political and economic constraints as well as the ephemeral nature of the forms used prior to the formation of modern nation-states in the Americas, written plays by indigenous peoples are absent from the historical record for most of the nineteenth and early twentieth centuries. Although the written does not account for other performative practices such as dance, song, and ritual, we can glean their presence from other nonwritten sources. A few were written and published in the nineteenth century. Both *Macho Ratón* (in the Mesoamerican context)[18] and *Tragedia del fin de Atahualpa / Atau Wállpaj p'uchukakuyninpa wankan* (in the Andean context)[19] satirize coloniality. The *Rabinal Achí* (Man of Rabinal), originally known as the *Xajoj Tun* (Dance of the trumpet), is one of the oldest plays with pre-Columbian content in the Americas and remains significant in the lives of contemporary Maya people in Guatemala. The play's kab'awilian qualities include glyphic conventions, oral histories, and other items of material culture.

Dennis Tedlock, in his extensive and detailed research on the play, underscores the invaluableness of an existing script of the *Rabinal Achí*, as traditionally pre-Columbian actors performed by memory. In his study, Tedlock postulates that various scripts may have been produced in the nineteenth century, but the first person to write the play down, in 1850, was Bartolo Sis of Rabinal, who allegedly copied it from an earlier manuscript.[20] Étienne Brasseur de Bourbourg wrote down the second version in the nineteenth century after arriving in Rabinal as a parish priest, but not by directly copying Bartolo Sis's script.[21] Instead, Sis read it out loud to Bourbourg, who transcribed it.[22] *Rabinal Achí* parallels many colonial plays introduced by Europeans, but its distinct elements point to a Maya history that antecedes Spanish colonialism.

Indeed, according to Tedlock, the events that the *Rabinal Achí* dramatizes date to the fourteenth and fifteenth centuries. Tedlock argues that the symbols worn by the warriors evoke a power struggle from the Classic period. This conclusion leads him to trace the images of execution via decapitation as a recurring leitmotif abundant throughout lintels, vases, and reliefs in the Maya world. The play reproduces a conflict between the Man of Rabinal and Kawek of the Forest People from the rival K'iche' nation. The Man of Rabinal captures another warrior, who at the end is decapitated. Tedlock argues against the conventional reading that this play is about human sacrifice. Instead, he demonstrates that the act was a politically motivated execution. Tellingly, it continues to be produced every January 25 in the highlands of Guatemala. Reenacting the performance functions as an embodiment of a history that predates the nation-state. It also serves as a key intertextual referent in contemporary productions, particularly those staged by the Sotz'il Group in Sololá, Guatemala.

Performative acts and dances that emerge during the colonial period may have been based on earlier written texts and oral stories. This palimpsest is a typical kab'awilian straddling of the past and present, resisting cultural loss. Embodied memory has also been subjected to scrutiny. Tedlock reminds us that many theater productions alluding to a pre-Columbian history were banned throughout the sixteenth and seventeenth centuries in Guatemala and Mexico.[23] He cites the proscriptions of dramatic performances in 1593 and in 1624, followed by another in 1625, which coincided with the centenary of the Spanish conquest of the Quiche' kingdom.[24]

During the seventeenth century in Mexico (1631), religious authorities banned a similar drama, claiming Indians were producing a narrative about human sacrifice. Tedlock advances that the various injunctions against these performances or plays throughout the seventeenth and eighteenth centuries were in reality attempts by officials to repress any memory of pre-Columbian life—and any practice of human sacrifice, which they suspected continued despite Christian conversion.[25]

Colonial vetoes of these types of dramatic performances for their potentially subversive influence have left their imprint on nation-states; in the 1980s, the genocidal war in Guatemala curtailed performances of the *Rabinal Achí* in the highlands, where public gatherings were viewed with suspicion, as political instruments to galvanize peoples against the state. Examples of repurposing these colonialist ventures can be found throughout the Americas, particularly in relationship to the imposition of religion. Adam Versenyi and Max Harris remind us "when indigenous performers acted and danced the Spanish religious texts, the resulting performances generated meanings that exceeded the intentions of the latter."[26] Indigenous peoples utilized Catholicism to conceal their own religious and spiritual practices in inventive ways throughout the colonial period.[27]

Early Twentieth Century

While a lack of documentation reflects the ephemeral nature of theater art and performance in indigenous communities in the early part of the twentieth century, the state's use of theater and puppetry to disseminate its ideology and its politics of modernization has been well documented, predominantly in Mexico. The National Indigenista Institute (INI) carried out cultural missions in which theater was envisioned and deployed as an instrument to advance policies of the nation-state. These "cultural missions" created more than 200 theaters and staged over 500 presentations between 1942 and 1946.[28] Rosario Castellanos, one of Chiapas's foremost writers, used a combination of theater and puppetry in the highlands to carry out the work of the Indigenista Institute, for which she worked in the 1950s. Chiapas has the distinction of having served as the first testing ground for the Indigenista Institute, and it is in fact in the highlands where the INI first opened its doors. Castellanos created Teatro Petul, whose dolls — Xun and Petul — were used to inculcate behaviors of model and desirable Mexican citizens. Castellanos described the more Ladinoized puppet Petul as "always being open to the tiding being brought to him by his white or mestizo friends, thanks to whose interventions the play's climax always led to a triumph of intelligence over superstition, of progress over tradition, of civilization over barbarism."[29] Despite the criticisms of the INI, after the 1960s, Stephen Lewis writes, it implemented education, health, and economic programs that without doubt benefited indigenous communities.[30] This institutional legacy, regardless of its assimilationist goals, came to serve another purpose for indigenous activists — the kab'awilian strategy employed here functions to redress the colonial impulse lurking in these initiatives.

Drawing on these kab'awilian or double-gaze strategies, indigenous communities have long used theater and performance to preserve historical memory and cultural practices, and as a pulpit from which to denounce deplorable socioeconomic conditions. Today indigenous performers likewise use their knowledge of community and nation-state politics to infuse their theater with an urgent critique of current economic and political marginalization, particularly of women and children.

Contemporary indigenous women's theater departs from the plays of previous historical periods, as the playwrights produce stories that reflect current events and modern-day life. In the state of Chiapas, Montemayor and Frischmann note another important indigenous theater group that is less known, Chiiltak,[31] which worked mainly out of Ocosingo. Underiner recounts the work of the Laboratorio de Teatro Campesino Indígena, established in Tabasco in the 1980s, in providing a space for peasant and indigenous communities.[32] Although this theater organization aimed to stage classical plays for the edification of indigenous communities, in 1989 it produced a very successful Maya Chontal drama, *La tragedia del jaguar* (The jaguar's trajedy), written collectively under the leadership of Auldárico Hernández Gerónimo, a Maya writer from Tabasco. In the dedication, Hernández Gerónimo writes that he asked the elders for permission to stage the play because they are the real narrators of the story due to the sacred ceremonies guarded by the Chontales.[33]

In Guatemala, a few indigenous theater groups organically formed in the 1970s. The Kaqchikel critic Manuel Jesús Salazar Tetzagüic, in *Rupach'uxik kina'oj qati't qamama' / Características de la literatura maya kaqchikel*, observes that the legacy of colonial religious plays is evident throughout Guatemala.[34] He explains that dramatic dances dating back to the colonial period, such as the *Baile de la conquista* (Dance of conquest), continue to be staged in Spanish by Kaqchikeles every year. He identifies *Los intermediarios* (The intermediaries), a play that accompanies the yearly coronation of the queen of Tecpan, as contemporary theater. Based on his research, particularly examining local newspapers in Chimaltenango, Salazar Tetzagüic concludes that contemporary poetry and theater, in contrast with other forms of narratives, questioned the unsettling grip of the political status quo and offered new interpretations of history. But the work of Sotz'il Group (House of the Bats) and Ajchowen (Monkey) has transcended local levels.

Theater troupes composed exclusively of indigenous women are rare in Mexico and Guatemala. This has led women involved in co-ed theater groups to establish different theater collectivities. Their vision of women empowering women continues to be necessary and serves as the driving force behind their creative work. The plays advance a political agenda focused on the need for horizontal relationships in indigenous communities where indigeneity is not subordinate to gender or vice versa. In the context of the Andes, Marisol de la Cadena, in "Las mujeres son más indias" (Women are more Indian), demonstrates how racial hierarchies wherein indigenous men have been historically feminized naturalize their oppression of domestic partners for being indigenous and women.[35] FOMMA and Ajchowen share a focus on the empowerment of women and reinforce the key role indigenous women can play in conceptual and material decolonization.

Building on Judith Weiss's distinction between "national theater" and the "New Popular Theater," I categorize FOMMA and Ajchowen's plays as new popular theater.³⁶ Conflating indigenous nations with the popular classes neutralizes real differences, as indigenous groups face discrimination in ways that cannot be reduced to economic levels, but the acts and plays share with popular theater a direct confrontation of Ladino hegemony as well as a critique of capitalism in Chiapas and Guatemala.³⁷ In that sense, they depart from the goals of national theater, "which aims to present 'universal' themes devoid of political content."³⁸ Critics Diana Taylor in *Theatre of Crisis* (1991) and John Wesley Shillington in *Grappling with Atrocity* (2002) identify theater produced after the 1970s in Latin America as departing from political crisis because these productions had moved beyond the initial shock of dictatorship, civil war, and human rights violations to direct action. Indigenous theater offers the nation an opportunity to see its other face, one ignored in national theater productions.

The role of theater in indigenous communities as a protest venue has acquired greater urgency at the turn of the twentieth century. Donald Frischmann, in the Maya context of Mexico, notes that drama has become "an increasingly popular means by which contemporary Maya artists consciously work to 'recover reality' for themselves and their communities."³⁹ Similarly, Tamara Underiner finds that ethnic labels such as *Mayan* and *indigenous theater* "mark a moment of cultural reclamation and proclamation and in effect allow these troupes to use nonindigenous theater styles and techniques to become 'More Mayan' or at least more visible as such."⁴⁰ Rather than reinscribing indigenous identity, FOMMA and Ajchowen's plays or performances collectively point to new ways of assuming Mayanness as women. By highlighting other ways of being Maya that contest national and masculine as well as outdated ideas about identities, these plays forge a new space for indigenous women deeply immersed in autonomous intellectual projects that struggle for horizontal relationships at the community and national levels.

Grounding FOMMA

As I have noted, the INI's theater legacy strongly resonated among Mayas whose parents had participated in or experienced its education brigades. Several young men who had served as informants to anthropologists initiated the founding of Sna Jtz'ibajom in San Cristóbal de las Casas.⁴¹ Tamara Underiner points out that theatrical activity in Chiapas was revived partly thanks to one of the members of Sna Jtz'ibajom (Maya for "House of the Writer"), whose father had been puppet master for Rosario Castellanos's marionette theater show.⁴² Once Sna Jtz'ibajom became established, some of the members formed Lo'il

Maxil as a group exclusively in charge of producing plays.[43] Only two of the original founders of the group were women. Manuel Pérez Hernández recalls that Isabel Juárez Espinosa was the only woman who dared to act in front of a large audience surrounded exclusively by male actors. A few years later, Juárez Espinosa (Tseltal) and Petrona de la Cruz Cruz (Tsotsil) parted ways with Sna Jtz'ibajom due to the prevalent sexist attitudes they encountered in the group. They established Fortaleza de la Mujer Maya (FOMMA) to cater to indigenous women and children, especially those who had been excluded from their communities for religious or political reasons and who had settled in the outskirts of the colonial city of San Cristóbal.

Among the community theater groups and cultural revitalization organizations, FOMMA distinguishes itself by being an all Maya women's theater troupe. The playwrights received significant critical attention, and the two plays examined here were translated into English. FOMMA performed these plays throughout Latin America and the United States. The women in the organization have received some training from established artists in the United States. They have forged strategic alliances with New York University's Hemispheric Institute. Teresa Marrero, in her essay "Eso Sí Pasa Aquí: Indigenous Women Performing Revolutions in Maya Chiapas," examines how the political performances of both FOMMA and the Zapatistas speak to the gender demands that became central to indigenous politics in Chiapas.[44] While the group proclaims a "politically neutral" stance in relationship to Zapatismo, this does not make it less political. Indeed, as Marrero continues, both FOMMA and the Zapatistas are reconfiguring the conditions for indigenous women.[45] No indigenous writer in Chiapas has publicly stated any affiliation to Zapatismo. I see this professed political neutrality as a way for writers to shield themselves from reprisals by the state, since many indigenous writers and other artists work in San Cristóbal de las Casas, and open affiliation makes them vulnerable. While FOMMA's plays semiotically link land, women, and autonomy, they also revisit and revise certain traditions, as Marrero notes the Zapatistas do in their camps.[46] This contemporary perspective includes a critical look at misogynist practices that are perpetuated as tradition.[47] The "double gaze" activated in the plays allows FOMMA to engage with city and countryside, land and body, men and women, past and present.

I focus on two of FOMMA's most renowned performances, *Migración* (Migration)[48] and *Una mujer desesperada* (A desperate woman).[49] These were the first plays to be written by indigenous women and among the earliest productions to highlight the particular ways that violence affects women in Tsotsil and Tseltal communities. *Una mujer desesperada* and *Migración* dramatize the structural problems within families and their communities. *Una mujer desesperada* made headlines for accentuating the issue of gender. Petrona de la Cruz Cruz wrote this semiautobiographical play while still a member of Sna Jtz'ibajom, which at the time focused on literacy projects and the writing down of the oral tradition. Sna Jtz'ibajom resisted producing *Una mujer desesperada*, denying that the kind of abuse the play exposes takes place in indigenous communities. At the time, Sna Jtz'ibajom was focused on reclaiming the legacy of classical Maya civilization in the context of the quincentenary commemorations planned around the world. The male members of Sna Jtz'ibajom feared that *Una mujer desesperada* cast indigenous men and thus the communities as a whole in a negative light. They even dismissed its oppressive setting as a figment of the artist's imagination. Petrona de la Cruz Cruz insisted that the play reflected her personal experiences in the community. Other interpersonal entanglements heightened gender tensions for both organizations.

Some critics have analyzed the plays through Victor Turner's theory of social drama,[50] but my focus is specifically on the claims the plays make in the kab'awilian quest of the all-women companies for equal footing with men as the starting point for real social change in indigenous communities — a theme echoed in other works — as in the novel by Marisol Ceh Moo I will discuss in chapter 5.[51] In other words, women produce cultural narratives that call for a transformation in the relationship dynamics between men and women before emancipation can take place at the geopolitical level. In another kab'awilian turn, *Una mujer desesperada* and *Migración* cast a critical gaze on the city to advocate for the economic self-sufficiency of indigenous people on their ancestral lands as the pathway to indigenous autonomy.

FOMMA's Plays

These plays prefigure the critical role that gender will play in the articulation of Zapatismo in Chiapas as well as the heightened political role of indigenous women in the twenty-first century, emblematized by the recent proposal to put Nahua activist María de Jesús Patricio Martínez on the ballot as an independent for the 2018 presidential election. She is the first indigenous woman in the nation's history to attempt to become a presidential candidate.[52] *Una mujer desesperada* involves various characters, but the most central to the plot of this play are a mother named María, her three daughters, their father, and her second husband. The play provides a scathing critique of the subordinated status of women in indigenous communities, and in particular the disempowerment of widows and young unmarried women, illustrating the narrow choices and limited venues they have for economic and political autonomy. According to interviews with Petrona de la Cruz Cruz, the play is loosely based on her own experiences.

The story develops around three key incidents that reflect the only possible paths available to women in that community. The first occurs at the beginning of the story, when, Juan, María's husband, comes home drunk and verbally then physically assaults her. Juan's inebriation is such that when Rosita, the next-door neighbor, pushes him away from María, he falls, hits his head, and dies. Minutes later, Rosita's husband, José, arrives on the scene. He admonishes his wife, but he is not abusive in the same way Juan was. The kab'awilian view of two couples becomes another practical strategy. Rosita and José's relationship offers a different model, or another position from which to view relations between men and women, ones not based on abuse. María, the recent widow, cannot economically support herself and her offspring. In desperation, one of the oldest daughters, Carmen, accepts a job as a nanny and housekeeper in the city, presumably in San Cristóbal de las Casas.

On Carmen's first day of work in the city, a cab driver accidentally hits her while she crosses the street, an injury that ultimately kills her. Neither the taxi driver nor his employer accepts any responsibility. They instead fault Carmen for carelessness. This unexpected development in the family's drama serves as a critique of the decision to leave one's community for a job — even if women do so in response to dire economic circumstances. Going to the city as nannies and housekeepers becomes a foreclosed option. The play warns women about the dangers of the city and ultimately about their symbolic cultural death. Of course, indigenous communities adapt to and survive internal migration to cities or other countries, but the play's message is remarkable in that no external solutions pursued by the women lead to better outcomes for them, thus emphasizing the importance of economic self-sufficiency within indigenous communities.[53]

In act I, scene 2, María decides to accept another man's romantic advances and his marriage proposal because being a widow carries a stigma in the community and she cannot support a household on her own. Economic dependency contributes to her decision. Here, the theme of autonomy is reintroduced. The suitor first comes onstage as a caring, conscientious, and polite character, but once she consents to marriage, the mask falls, his sweet demeanor vanishes, and a violent, alcoholic monster emerges. Antonio's need to control and abuse extends to María's second-oldest stepdaughter, Teresa. His attempts to police her sexuality, ultimately seeing her as an object he deserves to control and sexually possess. The turning point in the play occurs when Antonio tries to prevent his stepdaughter from attending a religious mass, using first verbal then physical violence. He admonishes Teresa, suggesting that people will gossip about her virtue and that this will reflect poorly on his family name. María intervenes to protect her daughter, brandishing a weapon. A struggle ensues, the husband wrestles the machete from her, and the audience witnesses a sudden slaughter.

In the surreal violence that follows, Antonio attempts to rape the surviving daughter while the mother's body lies in a pool of blood. Teresa overcomes her fears, seizes her aggressor's rifle, and ends his life. She flees, but in the end she must face the legal consequences of the murder — a hopeless and overwhelming predicament that leads her to suicide. The play concludes by suggesting that freedom from this insidious cycle of violence lies just beyond the dark horizon. A sliver of optimism for the future seems to be available to the surviving, youngest daughter, Lupita. She will be raised by the neighbors, Rosita and José, who represent the possibility of a more equitable relationship. Lupita would be the only one from her family to escape the cycle of violence and have a chance at a better life within the community. The play illustrates the conditions of women's suffering without offering an easy solution to the daily violence perpetrated against them. The message seems clear, though: unless men and women, through mutual respect and equality, revolutionize the foundations on which gender relations are built, the tragic loss of life will continue. This posture resonates with the work of Aymara feminist Julieta Paredes, who calls for a decolonization of gender and advocates that indigenous women recognize that indigenous patriarchy existed prior to colonialism.[54] The play's political plot makes it clear that the solutions to economic hardship, racism, and an archaic patriarchal hierarchy lie not in abandoning the community for domestic work, such as indigenous women often perform in the city, but rather in the collective economic self-sufficiency and horizontal relationships that disrupt patriarchy. *Una mujer desesperada* challenges women to confront their historic responsibility in fighting for their rights to seek justice along ethnic and sexual lines. Tamara Underiner, Marrero, and other critics see the dramatized stories as testifying to hopelessness, but I see the abject poverty and despair permeating the play as a warning to both sexes that a profound evolution in attitudes based on respect in relationships is fundamental to the future of autonomy.[55]

FOMMA's second foundational play, *Migración*, is likewise loosely based on Isabel Juárez Espinosa's experience. Juárez Espinosa published *Migración* along with other short skits and tales from the oral tradition in 1994. While it similarly engages with themes related to gender relations, it also conveys a direct warning against migration. The play relates the trials and tribulations of an indigenous family recruited by a friend to leave their village for work and a better life in the city. Didactic in nature, the play warns of the pitfalls and precariousness of migration and cautions against the political and ancestral dispossession brought about by selling indigenous lands.

The story revolves around two indigenous families. One has lived in the city for years, while the second sells their land and migrates to the city motivated by the promise of work. After the family in the village decides to sell its land and move to the city, an indigenous foreman named Mario, who had promised them the job, rescinds the offer, citing the company's decision to downsize. Thus the play argues that leaving behind traditions and customs is folly, resulting in forced conformity to an alien environment in which the families will be silent, deterritorialized subjects. Of course, indigenous migration to big cities does not necessarily equal social death, but within the context of the play it signifies material loss. It poignantly conveys the message that selling ancestral lands uproots the children and subjects them to future economic uncertainty, signaling a break with their heritage. In this sense, the play advocates self-sufficiency through working the land. Significant, too, is the fact that it is the wife, Catalina, who expresses attachment to the land. Her reticence to leave it tied to the land reinforces the theme of women's autonomy. It contests the predominant notion that the city offers a solution to economic distress. More important, the play demonstrates that migration disrupts indigenous peoples' sense of community and reciprocity. Outside the community, indigenous migrants will fall prey to a voracious capitalist system.

In 2014, FOMMA celebrated its twenty-fifth anniversary. Although women have gained more political influence since these plays were first produced, both plays remain relevant. Issues of gender, immigration, and political autonomy continue to be prominent in their most recent theatrical performance: *Buscando nuevos caminos* (Searching for new paths). The next sections focus on Ajchowen, the first Maya women's theater group in Guatemala, and their articulation of gender and political autonomy.

Theater and Performance in Guatemala

While Guatemala is the cradle of the only pre-Columbian play in the Americas to be performed every year, Martin Banham's *The Cambridge Guide to Theater* asserts that no plays of true dramatic value were produced there during the nineteenth century.⁵⁶ In the early twentieth century, local theater tended to focus on classical plays and comedies as well as *costumbrista*-style works.⁵⁷ Civil unrest adversely affected the production of theater, particularly during the Jorge Ubico dictatorship (1931–44), a period during which any overt or covert criticism aimed at the dictatorship was punishable by death. Shillington, in *Grappling with Atrocity*, writes that theater after the 1990s acknowledges the trauma of war but moves toward reconciliation.⁵⁸ While Shillington does not deal with indigenous theater, he suggests that more than likely it exists parallel to Ladino/mestizo theater. His premise is that theater in Guatemala has undergone multiple types of suppression and resurgence since the Ubico dictatorship.

Plays by indigenous women have been less prominent but are steadily emerging throughout Guatemala. The well-known Maya poet Rosa Chávez began her cultural work in a theater collective, Caja Lúdica. In the twenty-first century, El Laboratorio Escénico produced plays in Chuj and Mam. Indigenous theater has also gained momentum among the Maya in Guatemala through the Sotz'il Jay Cultural Center and other creative initiatives. Working through the center, the group Ajchowen is the first theater group established by Maya women that has performed beyond national borders. The performers belong to the Kaqchikel and Mam linguistic communities. Before discussing their play, I situate them within the important work of the Sotz'il Jay Cultural Center and discuss how kab'awil is put into praxis in its play *Ixkik*.

Grupo Sotz'il

In 2000, Leonardo Lisandro Guarcax González (Maya Kaqchikel) founded the Sotz'il Grupo. A teacher, spiritual guide, and writer, Guarcax offered artistic presentations that transcended national borders, making Maya art and performance visible in Central America, Europe, and the United States. In 2010, the shocking news of his murder circulated widely. Unidentified men kidnapped Guarcax as he walked to one of the schools where he was a teacher and headmaster. He had become yet another victim of the senseless violence erupting in Guatemala despite the peace accords signed in 1996. Strikingly, Guarcax is the third member in his family to be slain. The other relatives were equally active in the recuperation and conservation of Maya arts as well as vocal proponents of a public education based on indigenous cultures. Signs of torture marked his body, and in this context, the violence permeating civil society appears to target indigenous artists and activists, a troubling echo of the 1980s genocidal acts of war committed by the government.

The investigation into this crime might have met the same outcome as countless other unresolved assassinations, but in response to international pressure the authorities announced the arrest of the alleged kidnappers, who were sentenced to lengthy prison terms in 2012. National newspapers described the suspects as belonging to a local ring of kidnappers, most of them carrying Maya last names and none affiliated with any government-sponsored militia. While the motives driving Guarcax's slaying may remain opaque and dismissed as part of the post–civil war sea of violence engulfing Guatemala, his widow, Clara Alicia Sen, the leading actress in Ajchowen, maintains that he was murdered as a result of his cultural activism.[59]

Guarcax's legacy thrives through the Sotz'il Jay Cultural Center as well as in the recent constitution of Ajchowen, the first all-women's Maya theater group with an international stature, which is affiliated with the center. The four members of the group share family bonds. Clara Alicia Sen, Guarcax's widow, has taken on a leadership position within the center and the women's group. Located amid robust cornfields, the Cultural Center continues to accomplish its mission. Since its official founding in 2007, it has attained a national and international reputation due to its commitment to producing art informed by ancestral knowledge, and inspired by pre-Columbian sources recorded in the Dresden and Madrid codices, among others.[60]

During the summer of 2014, I traveled to Sololá, Guatemala, to meet with the founding members of Ajchowen. I interviewed the actresses and learned more about their work as well as their relationship to the Sotz'il Jay Cultural Center. The four women — Clara Alicia Sen, Mercedes García, Inés Mucún, and Lila González — energetically explained the process that had brought them together. Initially, only a couple of women were actively involved — even though the cultural center attempted to incorporate young women by offering different arts and craft classes. Regular attendance proved difficult for them given social codes that limit women's activities outside the home or that restrict their movements to family-approved spaces. Subsequent workshops attracted a higher number of young women. According to Clara Alicia, more than a dozen participants attended the first workshops. Clara Alicia, Mercedes, Inés, and Lila prevailed against the odds. The primary obstacle preventing young women from attending rehearsals was family disapproval of their interacting with men unfamiliar to their families. Indeed, many of the young ladies were pressured to sever ties to the cultural center. The young women who persevered and stayed decided to become Ajchowen. The decision was important, too, because the group's name honored Guarcax's last play of the same title.

Ajchowen debuted with a collective creation titled *Ixkik*. The play has not been published or translated, but it has been presented outside of Guatemala. They performed the play at the University of California, San Diego, in 2014 at my invitation, and in 2017 they participated in Colombia's theater festival with a new production, *Ximonik*. Not all of the original members continued acting, according to Lila, because of marriage and motherhood, in Inés's case, and work commitments, in Lila's case. Manuel Barrillas Crispín, the artistic director, says the women were encouraged to explore numerous forms of expression based on ancestral traditions. The name of the group references the Maya patron of the arts — the monkey.

In this context, I propose that the theater troupe puts kab'awil into practice as an ontology through which the group carves out for itself a new conceptual, cultural, political, and social stage in Guatemala. Here I am evoking Diana Taylor and Sarah J. Townsend's definition of *stage* "as both the platform on which actors perform as well as a phase, period position, which links a particular artistic practice to a notion of temporal change and a sense of place."[61] While I have struggled with whether to use the terms *play* or *performance* in discussing Ajchowen's work, the women use the term *k'ai* to describe what I am calling a play (or theater). And yet I sensed from the discussion that in practice what they were pointing to as *k'ai* has more to do with song, and more with corporeal movement than drama. As they explained, *k'ai* connotes seeing and entertaining an audience. I use the term interchangeably with *play* and *theater* (*obra* and *teatro*), as the women performers do but acknowledge Taylor and Townsend's point that "because theater was so closely associated with the emergence of a Spanish and Portuguese imperial identity, it seems problematic to use the word in relation to Amerindian and Afro-American cultures."[62] Nonetheless, as I have already suggested, indigenous theater and performative acts need to be analyzed in ways that problematize the assumption of theater as having European origins.

Kab'awil patently manifests in *Ixkik* through the play's attempt to obviate common binaries attributed to the indigenous and Western worlds, such as oral/written, tradition/modern, and passive/active. In particular, it invokes the past and relates it to the present, thus overcoming any temporal discontinuities between the ancient Maya civilization and the women's contemporary identities. The longitudinal and lateral moves offer an important revision of the ways the nation-state has romanticized the classical Maya civilization while ignoring the present state of indigenous peoples. It contests the claim that the Maya had disappeared by the time the Spaniards arrived. The modern-state of Guatemala was constructed by establishing Mayanness as part of the past, and contemporary indigenous peoples as simply a vanquished Indian group. Kab'awil, then, allows contemporary Mayas to make claims of both an ancient and a present civilization.

Activists evoke kab'awil as an ancestral paradigm that becomes useful in thinking about gender relations as well. In this sense, the concept of kab'awil offers a critical lens in examining the play because it allows the audience to view Maya struggles in a historical continuum and functions as an analytic tool that allows indigenous women to speak to gender and ethnic relations. As I have mentioned in previous chapters, the K'iche' feminist Alma López, noting that not all aspects of traditional culture are compatible with indigenous feminism, asserts that she would recuperate kab'awil as a central philosophical concept, a vision that encompasses all aspects of consciousness, expanding on the temporal and spatial planes. López proposes that to apply a kab'awilian lens on women means owning and understanding all of the terrible conditions women endure and changing them, while owning and evaluating all of the positive things they do have to transform themselves. It also entails realizing that not everyone is the same and that diversity exists among women along ethnic and class lines.[63] López synthesizes how this analytic lens corresponds to contemporary social relations between men and women, and indigenous and nonindigenous women. Of course, a caveat is in order here: none of the members of this theater group considers herself a feminist. When I asked them about feminism, they replied that they did not see their struggle as separate from that of men. However, I interpret *Ixkik* as a feminist intervention against neoliberal capitalist ventures in Guatemala because the play repudiates extractivism, represented in its symbolic use of the womb as natural resource and the kab'awilian strategy of alluding to another story within the main storyline, as I discuss below.

Ixkik incarnates a kab'awilian philosophy in its connection of the sixteenth-century sacred text and neocolonial issues. The title strategically alludes to the sixteenth-century sacred text, but it is not simply a retelling of Ixkik's story. In the *Popol Vuh*, Ixkik's story is not the main one. By titling the play with the maiden's name, Ajchowen honors her rebellious spirit. In the play, Ixkik's role is far greater than in the sacred text. In the play she is pregnant with a girl. The midwife, Ixmukané, assists her by giving her a spiritual cleansing. This process enables Ixkik to see that the lord of Xibalbá, the underworld, is trying to kill her unborn daughter. The struggle against the lord culminates in Ixkik's own death, but her demise ensures her daughter's survival.

Ajchowen animates the sixteenth-century story by turning it into an allegory that directly alludes to current political struggles in Guatemala. Twentieth-century politics and pre-Columbian cosmogonist struggles coalesce in the performance. Maya women's resistance across temporal, geographic, mythic, and historic lines becomes real in the specific political events they allude to from the past to the present. The play becomes what Macarena Barris de Gómez, in a different context, terms "a decolonial gesture."[64] In the twenty-first century, Maya women struggle against a different underworld, which in the play is represented by neoliberal forces embodied by mining companies intent on extracting gold and silver from ancestral lands. Ajchowen's play deviates in important ways from the *Popol Vuh*. For one, in the traditional version, Ixkik gives birth to twins, Jun Ajpu and Ixbalamkej, who are represented as male in classical Maya iconography. In the play, Ixkik gives birth to a daughter, Ixbalamkej. Of course, it is noteworthy that the prefix *ix-* is always associated with femininity, as well as with the jaguar. In the sacred text, Ixbalamkej eventually transforms into the moon, a celestial body associated with women, but in the play her fate is to be a leader. Another striking difference between the sacred text and the play is the grandmother Ixmukané. In the sacred text, Ixmukané does not represent a nurturing and welcoming mother-in-law; instead, she questions her daughter in law's truthfulness in claiming to carry her grandchildren. The most compelling deviations from the sacred text are in its representation of the forces of the underworld. Xibalbá, in the play, dons a business suit, making this representation anachronistic but relevant to a contemporary audience familiar with indigenous issues in Guatemala.

The play mainly tells the story of Ixmukané and Ixkik. Unlike traditional plays, Ajchowen's performance does not neatly divide into different acts or scenes, and the story unfolds without any breaks in between. The characters do not enter and exit the stage. The unborn daughter, for example, is visible to the audience, and Xibalbá simply waits on the side. Ixbalamkej's actions are externalized, but her dance and flute playing are all supposedly taking place in the womb. The singing and drumming in the opening scene invoke the ancestors, particularly the female line represented in the play by Ixmukané. Allen J. Christenson notes that to the K'iche' elders reading the ancestors' names out loud is believed to bring them back to life.[65] The actresses do not translate the songs or most of the dialogue, but the audience understands them to invoke the grandmother. Her spirit, then, is summoned through the play. The main action takes place inside the Temezcal or a pre-Columbian sweat lodge where Ixmukané plays the healer and midwife.

The plot unravels when the grandmother realizes Ixkik's unborn daughter has to be repositioned as she is breeched, or set to exit the womb feet first. Ixkik lies near the fire for the ritual. The ritual consists of prayers near the fire; the grandmother lightly passes tree branches over Ixkik's body. During the ceremony, the mother has a vision that the dark forces of Xibalbá want to murder her unborn daughter. She awakes and requests to return to the underworld. Ixmukané refuses and admonishes Ixkik for her rebellious nature—a trait noticeable since she was a child. Ixkik convinces her by asking the grandmother to think of the generations to come. Ixmukané acquiesces and returns her to the underworld. The impetus driving the story is a stake in the future, as the daughter's death would endanger the imminent leadership of Maya women. Ixkik battles against the lord of Xibalbá to save her daughter. She manages to transfer her unborn child to another womb. Symbolically, the fight continues in the hands of other women. In her battle against Xibalbá, the heroine sacrifices her life. But by thus preserving Ixbalamkej's life, she defeats the underworld lord's plan to prevent her daughter's future leadership.

The most compelling kab'awilian strategy worked in the play is the way other Maya women's voices resonate in the struggle against Xibalbá. The dialogue between Ixkik and Ixmukané establishes an inherited feminine rebellion. In the sacred text, Ixkik defies her father's prohibition about approaching the calabash tree. In Ixkik's dialogue with her mother-in-law, she directly references the fight against mining companies trying to displace communities from ancestral lands to make room for the extraction machines. In the most intense and dramatic segments of Ixkik's monologue, she screams, "I had to cut the electricity cables so that the machines would stop working." She continues, "Those people are contaminating my hair, my bones, my womb, my seeds will not sprout. Those men are invading my womb." "Those men" in this context refers both to the dark forces of Xibalbá and the foreign mining companies.

In those first few lines, another other story within the story is introduced and becomes key element in the play. Ixkik transforms her body into a spatial and racial geography grounded in a struggle for an autonomy that speaks both to the legacy of colonial forces and the present violence of neocolonial capitalist ventures. These few lines may be obscure for an audience unfamiliar with contemporary Guatemala and the countless Maya women who fight every day against external forces encroaching in their lives. In these few lines, Ixkik alludes to the story of Crisanta Pérez, a Mam woman who, with the support of other women, obstructed a Canadian mining company's operations. Known as the Goldcorp 8, the women were arrested for obstructing the mining company's activities. According to Pérez, the mining company asked for permission to allow a cable to pass through her property but did not ask for her consent to install an electricity post in her backyard. In a short interview, Pérez recalled that with the help of other women, she caused a short circuit—stalling the mining company for days.⁶⁶ The machines stopped working and no one knew what had happened until they realized the power had been cut off. Following the company's discovery of her action, police arrested Pérez, but the entire town stepped in to defend her, and thus she was saved from prison. The women argued that the mining company had tricked them into selling their lands. This is the gaze toward the present established through Ajchowen's work. Ixkik from the sixteenth century simultaneously embodies Crisanta Pérez in the twentieth century.

In the play, the dark forces of Xibalbá are a constant pre-Columbian reference. The personification of Xibalbá as a male in a business suit, however, reminds us of the present—of modernity, the West, patriarchy, and more explicitly foreign mining companies. At the same time, the lord of Xibalbá signifies Spanish colonizers, as his mask is that of a conquistador and the weapon he wants to use to murder Ixbalamkej is a spade. The other actresses' attire is reminiscent of classic Maya clothing and textiles. The flute, drum, and whistles replicate pre-Columbian instruments. This narrative thread represents one gaze, toward the past. The gestural and corporal movements by Ixkik and Ixbalamkej evoke dance movements captured in pre-Columbian sources, thus embedding and embodying kab'awil in the performance.

Ajchowen's play represents a montage of the struggles of past and modern Maya women. Its performance illuminates a bilateral movement from past to present and present to past. The cosmolectics evoked by the "double gaze" allows Ajchowen to reference the sacred and the secular, the ancient and the contemporary Maya. In Guatemala the play is read as transmitting an anti-mining company message. After learning more about their work, I promised the women that I would help disseminate the play in the United States. After a successful performance and a robust question-and-answer session at UCSD, three distinct narratives emerged. Clearly, for many students who have ties to Guatemala and El Salvador, the performance connected them to an imagined cultural belonging. I say "imagined" because many of the students were not necessarily Maya but Ladinos-Latinos (to borrow a term from the K'iche' anthropologist Giovanni Batz), whose life experience positions them differently vis-à-vis the Maya in Guatemala, or any other Mesoamerican country for that matter.⁶⁷ The second narrative the play elicited had to do with affective feelings about feminism, motherhood, and sacrifice. Lastly, for many students, the Maya people they knew and understood as descendants of a civilization that disappeared centuries ago became real. Maya struggles became palpable through indigenous activism against mine exploitation represented in the play by Xibalbá, the only character donning identifiable modern, Western clothing, and arguably representing global capitalism. The women succeeded in making theory visible through the play, re-presenting a narrative that can be read and interpreted by many simultaneously.

Conclusion

Time and space are fundamental differences between these two women theater companies, making their comparison richer and multifaceted. FOMMA is a more established group with an extended network of support in Mexico and the United States. Ajchowen is just beginning its career and building an international profile. FOMMA has focused on the fraught and extreme oppressive conditions that women often face within their communities, whereas Ajchowen speaks more directly to the external forces of a virulent neoliberal capitalism in Guatemala. Nonetheless, both groups address the critical role women play in society at the current moment, and the urgent need for political and cultural transformation at the local and national levels. These plays represent a departure from the informant position indigenous people have occupied in the literary imagination, especially in relationship to indigenous women's representation. These women's theater troupes circumvent the lettered city and illustrate a different relation to writing and embodiment of the arts. The next chapter highlights the emergence of the indigenous novel as a genre that ultimately reflects a rejection of world-systems for indigenous peoples, who instead propose an autonomy that is gender-cognizant and outside the liberal, nation-state discourse of integration or Marxism as solutions to indigenous oppression.

CHAPTER FIVE

The Novel in Zapotec and Maya Lands

It is no coincidence that an indigenous culture has not
produced or does not produce novels—and yet [does produce]
narratives of great importance in other genres—and that
indigenismo, in apparent contradiction, prefers the novel
as a genre particularly suited to its [own] purposes.
—Antonio Cornejo Polar (1979)

When the Indians actually get to write [novels], I suspect
that these will have a mestizo sensibility.
—Luis Cardoza y Aragón (1991)

THE PRECEDING CHAPTERS have demonstrated that the majority of writers in the Native languages of Mesoamerica share a penchant and enthusiasm for writing poetry and short stories, published predominantly in bilingual editions.[1] This chapter proposes that the novel is becoming an important genre for autonomous political projects. Kab'awil's presence in this chapter is evident through the characters' political outlooks, the written and oral texts evoked, and social relations. I will examine some of the debates about the origins of the novel as a genre, as well as the polemical nature of the *indigenista* novel in Latin America. Finally, the discussion turns to an analysis ze the first Maya and first Zapotec novels and their implications for the pursuit of autonomy under coloniality.

Not a single novel was produced in Latin America during the first 300 years of colonial rule, "despite the rich epic poetry and historical prose that brought the region into the history of literature in the Spanish language."[2] Many Latin American literary critics have attributed this vacuum to the Spanish Crown's prohibitions on the importation of the novel to its colonies. In 1531, the Crown enacted its first royal decree banning the circulation of the novel in its newly acquired territories.³ Romances, frivolous stories, including the Spanish chivalry text *Amadís*, and other similar works of fiction were proscribed by the court under the pretense that they constituted "a bad exercise for the Indians."⁴ The Spanish authorities suspected that if "Indians" read works of fiction, they may find the *Bible*'s teaching dubious and perhaps just another idiosyncratic story. Over a decade later, in 1543, a second royal decree went even further, emphasizing that "Indians" must be prevented from learning about "the fictional character of novels, lest they come to believe that the holy scripture, books by doctors, and others were works of fantasy."⁵ The novel and print cultures intersect in most national literary studies. However, in Latin America, the function of the press in the colonies and the legal decrees enacted by the Crown adversely affected the creation of early print culture. Hortensia Calvo, in "The Politics of Print: The Historiography of the Book in Early Spanish America," argues that printing presses in Latin America were imported to serve the ideological, political, and administrative purpose of the colonial power.⁶ This is not to say that novels never made it across the ocean. Calvo, Fernando Alegría, and other critics point out that the transatlantic book trade in the Spanish colonies took place both legally and illegally.⁷ Bishop Juan de Zumárraga introduced the first press to New Spain as he was systematically destroying painted indigenous books in central Mexico — depriving the indigenous populations of an essential tool for artistic and literary expression and replacing it with another system of communication. The first two imported printing presses were destined for the cities we now identify as Mexico City and Lima. This technology played a vital role in the spread of Christianity. The missionaries instrumentalized it in their proselytization. They believed that true conversion of Native peoples could only be accomplished if the Catholic teachings were published in indigenous languages. Indeed, the first works printed and circulated in the colonies were translated grammars, catechisms, sermons, and other religious material in various indigenous languages.⁸ By the seventeenth century, printing in indigenous languages decreased to 3 percent.⁹ A fundamental shift in the function of the press occurred in the mid-seventeenth century to satisfy the reading needs of *peninsulares* (people from Spain) and urban criollos (Europeans born in the Americas). The approval of the novel in the colonial period influenced the literary and cultural consensus that the genre's development in Latin America resulted from the continent's linguistic and cultural connection to Spain (and, more broadly, Europe).¹⁰ Ironically, Antonio Cornejo Polar notes that in the twentieth century intellectuals used the novel, and particularly the *indigenista* novel, to announce the demise of indigenous peoples.¹¹

A Western Form?

In *The Novel*, Franco Moretti argues for a world literature method and postulates that in "cultures that belong to the periphery of the literary system (which means: almost all cultures, inside and outside Europe), the modern novel first emerges not as an autonomous development but as a compromise between a western formal influence (usually French or English) and local materials."[12] Other literary critics have identified the weaknesses and problems in Moretti's seemingly innocuous cultural profiling, countering that the origins of the novel may be traced to *Don Quixote*,[13] influenced by *The Thousand and One Nights*, or that the novel can best be described as having a polygenesis.[14] Jack Goody, who belongs to the school of thought engaged in the orality/literacy divide, notes that "in terms of cultural history, what is surprising about the novel, as distinct from narrative more generally, is not simply its absence from oral cultures, but its late and sporadic appearing long after writing was introduced, followed by its great popularity despite the continuing hostility it attracted up to the nineteenth century in Europe, later elsewhere. Today we live in a culture dominated by fiction, as none other has been."[15] The novel, according to Goody, is a cultural product produced outside indigenous communities, traditionally been perceived as lacking writing systems. He also intimates that a society's relationship to storytelling and its conception of truth and fiction may be factors in the development of the novel. In general terms, fiction became not the opposite of truth but rather a form of literary entertainment. Catherine Gallagher builds on this notion and writes that notions of truth and fiction have shifted and affected the popularity of the novel.[16] "The widespread acceptance of verisimilitude as a form of truth, rather than a form of lying, founded the novel as a genre. It also created the category of fiction."[17] These explanations may not always translate across other communities, however. In the Mesoamerican context, the notions of verisimilitude, entertainment, and lying (or fiction) have been integral to tales, myths, and legends, and it is not until very recently that these elements have found their way into the Maya and Zapotec novel. This said, oral stories can be lengthy and equally complex as novels.

The novel's scarce production in indigenous nations of Mesoamerica makes it notable, considering the conventional thinking — as illustrated by Cornejo Polar in this chapter's second epigraph — that indigenous people have not and do not produce novels, and that it is precisely this genre that nonindigenous intellectuals used to narrate the disintegration of indigenous cultures. Cornejo Polar refers to the literary trends influenced by *indigenismo*, categorized under the rubric of *indigenista* literature. Indeed, a discussion of the indigenous novel would be incomplete without any reference to *indigenismo*. In general terms, *indigenismo*'s genesis has been attributed to Friar Bartolomé de las Casas and his defense of indigenous peoples in the sixteenth century.[18] In other words, since its origins, *indigenismo* has attempted to elicit readers' sympathy for indigenous peoples, generally by portraying them as victims. Various strands of *indigenismo* have emerged, but it became institutionalized in the 1940s with the creation of the Inter-American Indian Institute, ironically funded by the United States.[19] That decade also marks the formation of *indigenista* institutes throughout the Americas, following the initial meeting of nation-state heads that sought to address the "Indian problem."[20]

In the 1920s, José Mariátegui first proposed the difference between indigenous and *indigenista* literatures.[21] Mariátegui explains that readers cannot expect *indigenista* literature to be indigenous, as an indigenous literature has yet to come.[22] Cornejo Polar, of course, questions this assertion, arguing that Mariátegui failed to take into account oral literature or other artistic forms like performance and songs. Guatemalan critic Luis Cardoza y Aragón dismisses the *indigenista* novel as incapable of fully penetrating the Indian's reality, representing only an exotic, superficial image. "All that stuff about magical Indians and other childishness conceals glib ideas about the arcane and essential. When Indians are exhibited, ridiculed as toy dolls, they dress them like piñatas; they dress them like postcards."[23] Cardoza y Aragón dismisses the *indigenista* narrative as a gaze from above and a tradition of paternalism. However, when referring to indigenous literature and specifically the novel, Cardoza y Aragón comments that "when the Indians actually get to write them [novels], I suspect that these will have a mestizo sensibility."[24] His use of the verb *acierten* (here, "get") in the Spanish connotes doubt, suggesting that indigenous writers may miss their target. Not only that but, according to Cardoza y Aragón, if they do manage to learn how to write novels, these may be tainted by a mestizo worldview. Mariátegui and Cardoza y Aragón assume a teleological position about literature. In the case of Mariátegui, as Cornejo Polar observes, this has to do with his conception of literature as strictly alphabetic. In the case of Cardoza y Aragón, teleology results from his assumption that the genre's challenging nature may require that indigenous writers adopt a mestizo sensibility in order to produce novels. These critics echo the bigoted notion of "indio leído, indio perdido" (a well-read Indian is a lost Indian). Embedded in this dictum is the idea that acquiring an education taints an individual and dilutes indigeneity into a mestizo identity. Marisol de la Cadena notes that in Peru, landowners used this maxim to describe literate Indians who refused peon labor, encapsulating the hegemonic assumption that "real" Indians exist at the opposite end of the literacy spectrum.[25] According to this view, education and literacy lead not only to assimilation but also the transformation of indigenous identity.

Indigenista authors like Ramón Rubín (Chiapas), Eraclio Zepeda (Chiapas), and Mario Monteforte Toledo (Guatemala), among others, offered stories saturated in pathos about "Indians" and their exploitation. Following in the tradition of Mariátegui, Monteforte Toledo and Eraclio Zepeda, among other *indigenista* writers, believed that indigenous peoples were an exploited group who needed to come to consciousness to articulate a class struggle and ultimately make the nation whole and egalitarian.[26] *Indigenista* literature produced mainly by nonindigenous writers in solidarity provided an imagined, symbolic indigenous world — one alien to the nonindigenous author's everyday experience.[27] These novelists created a powerful narrative about the genre itself — one that by definition was *about* Indians not *by* them. It excluded them precisely because the novel in Latin America has been historically tied to allegories of the nation, primarily a search for national identity.[28]

Nonetheless, the relationship between *indigenista* and indigenous literature has an entangled and complex history. Estelle Tarica sees *indigenismo* as a connecting of "individual aspirations to the mystique of nationalist thought[, a connection that] enables them to coalesce."[29] The Maya linguist and anthropologist Fidencio Briceño Chel writes that there is a point where *indigenista* traditional and indigenous literatures "intersect, intertwine and produce that mixture of history, fantasy, reality."[30] The Zapotec intellectual Víctor de la Cruz adds to the debate by arguing that the main difference between *indigenista* and indigenous literature lies in the transition of indigenous intellectuals from the oral tradition to the written [in the Latin alphabet]. Cruz, however, is highly critical of the notion of "oral literature," which he calls "a monstrous concept," because for him the term reveals a prejudiced and limited view of indigenous people that ties their literary practices to the written even though (according to him) the oral tradition has nothing to do with writing.[31] More important, for this chapter and the larger argument of this book, for most of the history of the modern nation-state the decision of who is given the privilege and responsibility to narrate has not been in the hands of indigenous peoples.

Interrogating *Indigenista* Literature

Contemporary indigenous writers critique canonical writers who, despite their solidarity with indigenous struggles, unwittingly participate in the pervasive racism that remains deeply entrenched in Latin American societies. Q'anjobal writer Gaspar Pedro González, in an interview by Robert Sitler conducted in the 1990s, charges that Miguel Ángel Asturias obtained the Nobel Prize for Literature precisely because his writings are about the Maya. A day will come, he says, when more indigenous writers emerge "to expand our own concepts that differ from those of Asturias."[32] In a severe critique of the *indigenista* literary tradition, González contends that the Maya were simply another resource the novelist used. He affirms that Asturias "[saw] in the situation of the 'Indian' an opportunity to surpass him. But he in no way valued the Indian as a person. Miguel Ángel Asturias, when traveling to Europe, especially France, began to mature and came to feel the importance of the Maya civilization in the presence of his hosts. His vision is that of a Ladino."[33] González is observing here that writers have traditionally used indigenous culture for their own ends, in most cases to construct national identity.

In Mexico, where *indigenismo* became more institutionalized, indigenous writers have consistently differentiated their work from the *indigenista* tradition. Zapotec novelist Javier Castellanos Martínez, for example, in "Los que hablamos Dila Xhon," takes Francisco Rojas González's work to task for the racism embedded in it. Castellanos Martínez discusses "La Tona," a short text in *El diosero*, and its problematic stereotypes, condemning Rojas González's representation of the young indigenous woman, "her feet — at times claws, at other times hooves — slipped on the flagstones, sunk in lichens or settled like the extremities of a quadruped in the plateau of the hills."[34] Not only does the *indigenista* author clearly not know the topography, Castellanos Martínez writes, but Rojas González's "comparison of the indigenous woman to animals is mocking, humiliating, and unnecessary."[35] Like other indigenous writers, the Zapotec author identifies and indicts the linguistic disfiguration of Indian characters that manifests in *indigenista* literature. The *indigenista* narrative tradition — at its core — runs parallel to the concerted effort by indigenous writers who create indigenous literature in the twenty-first century. Of course, the irruption of indigenous writers in the literary terrain does not necessarily equate to a dearth in *indigenista* literature.[36]

Precursors

No writer published novels in an indigenous language or bilingually during Mexico's nation-formation period in the nineteenth century, or at the beginning of the twentieth century. Cultural and linguistic marginalization not only precluded literary creation in an indigenous language but also reflected deep-seated, culturally sanctioned racist beliefs about who was authorized to produce literature. Ángel Rama and other foundational Latin American critics were limited by their Eurocentric understandings of literature and history as well as of the place of indigenous peoples in these fields. As I noted in chapter 1, Latin American writers traditionally exploited indigenous oral literatures as raw material for their own literary production.

If colonialism severed indigenous peoples from their means of artistic and intellectual work, the nation-formation period threatened their very existence. The well-known Mexican writer of the nineteenth century Ignacio Manuel Altamirano serves as a clear example of the way official history in the nineteenth century subsumed indigenous identity under a nationalist guise. Born in Guerrero, Mexico (1834), Altamirano published in Spanish, and his work is considered a cornerstone of Mexican literature, but he also spoke Nahuatl.[37] He faced the same predicament as many indigenous intellectuals in the nineteenth century, when being an intellectual was perceived as at odds with being indigenous.[38] Altamirano believed in the nation-state project, as exemplified in his novel *El Zarco*.[39] The Nahua poet and essayist Natalio Hernández reclaims Altamirano in his prologue to Yolanda Matías García's collection of poems *Tonalxochimej/Flores del sol*. Altamirano raises important questions about the politics of language and identity, as nations were consolidated under the umbrella of a single, official language. His belief in liberal ideals as well as his education and publications in Spanish secured his status as a national writer. Although he is an important precursor of indigenous literatures, I am only focusing on indigenous novelists who have published bilingually since the 1990s and who belong to the Maya and Zapotec communities.[40]

Guatemala, with the larger indigenous population as a percentage of total inhabitants, experiences a similar nation-building ambition and offers an interesting comparative contrast to Mexico with respect to publications in Native languages. Luis de Lión's *El tiempo principia en Xibalbá* (Time commences in Xibalbá), written exclusively in Spanish—probably in the 1970s—and published posthumously in 1985, was the first contemporary indigenous novel in Guatemala.[41] No novel written in both Spanish and an indigenous language was published, however, until *Sb'eyb'al jun naq maya q'anjob'al*, the Q'anjobal edition of Gaspar Pedro González's novel *La otra cara del maya* (The other face of the Maya), which appeared in 1992, following the Spanish-only version.[42] González's bilingual novel has not been without controversy. Gail Ament asserts—based on conversations with the writer—that this text was originally written in Spanish and subsequently translated into Q'anjobal. In other words, there was no original text in his native language. Arturo Arias and Robert Sitler, however, claim that Gaspar Pedro González wrote the book first in Q'anjobal and then translated it to Spanish.[43] In my conversation with González, he told me that although the novel was first published in Spanish, he conceived of it in his mother tongue, Q'anjobal. The bilingual writing process has led to an unresolved and heated debate among writers concerning what constitutes a text's authenticity and originality.

The Novels

Two "first novels" innovated indigenous literatures in Mesoamerica and beyond Latin America. Javier Castellanos Martínez published *Wila che be ze lhao/ Cantares de los vientos primerizos* (The songs of the first winds), the first novel in Zapotec, in 1994, while Marisol Ceh Moo published *X-Teya, U puksi'k'al ko'olel/ Teya, un corazón de mujer* (Teya, heart of a woman), the first novel by a Maya woman, in 2005. My analysis is based on the self-translated Spanish versions.[44] I read the first Zapotec and Maya novels as adding a layer of resistance to what can be characterized as a continental response to colonialism, assimilation, and universalism. As Cherokee literary critic Sean Kicummah Teuton writes in the context of the United States, indigenous writers have used the novel as a space to respond to colonialism since the nineteenth century.[45]

The stakes for "first novels" are high, due to both their production and their reception. In other words, "first novels" are akin to the discursive formation of the indigenous author I discussed in chapter 2; they are subject to similar questions and expectations about themes and language. "First novels" published by members of communities traditionally imagined as oral elicit historical, political, and cultural expectations from which other authors may be exempt. In some respects, this state of affairs relates to relegating indigenous peoples to the opposite end of the literature spectrum in Latin America's Western project, or what Quijano and Mignolo call the coloniality of power.[46] The production of the novel opens up a new space for Zapotec and Maya writers to share "coevalness" with nonindigenous writers in Latin America. Put differently, Johannes Fabian writes that anthropologists—and I would add, *indigenista* writers like Ramón Rubín in *El callado dolor de los tzotziles* or Mario Monteforte Toledo in *Entre la piedra y la cruz*—employed "conceptions of time quite different from those that inform reports on [the anthropologist's] findings to construct the other."[47] *Indigenista* writers denied what in another context Fabian terms "coevalness" to indigenous peoples in the contradictory way they reproduced a temporal difference between indigenous peoples and mestizos.⁴⁸ In the Mesoamerican context, this temporal difference translated into indigenous peoples' being sited at the outer limits of modernity, as uneducated, inarticulate, and superstitious.

Indigenous narratives refract the time-space difference manifested in the *indigenista* novel, where the Indian occupies a premodern temporality and the writer a modern, cosmopolitan one. That said, unlike other genres that have clear antecedents in pre-Hispanic practices, the novel — as far as we can glean from the historical record and theorists of the genre — is a contested form in Latin America precisely because of its historical approbation. Keeping in mind the theoretical interventions by Jace Weaver, Craig S. Womack, and Robert Warrior in *American Indian Literary Nationalism*, my point is not that indigenous people live outside of modernity or literary practice as recognized in the West. Rather, my position is that since writers are developing these genres as political projects in their Native languages, their production raises important theoretical questions about their recent use — even though, at least in the Zapotec case, the terms for *novel* were registered in the colonial period, pointing to and earlier genealogy of intellectual autonomy.

I propose that through the voices of the main characters, the Maya and Zapotec novelists state their opposition to assimilation into the society's mainstream and their rejection of dominant discourses articulated as solutions to the "Indian problem" in Latin America. Of course, this is not the first time indigenous peoples have criticized these dominant discourses, but it is the first time these critiques have been dramatized by indigenous novelists in Maya and Zapotec lands. The novels decry the instrumental deployment of education as an achievement leading to social integration and racial harmony within the nation-state, in Castellanos Martínez's novel, or the economic equality assumed by the Communist Party as the entity that will clear the path to the liberation of indigenous peoples, in Ceh Moo's. In striving for other alternatives and decolonial maneuvers, both novels ultimately refute what Samir Amin, Mignolo, and others term Eurocentrism.⁴⁹ According to Amin, Eurocentrism is antiuniversalist — although it masks itself as universal — and is a modern formation established through capitalism.⁵⁰ Eurocentrism underpins the official integrationist policies enacted by the nation-state and informs the Marxist discourses that emphasize class at the expense of indigenous people's raison d'être. In other words, this chapter argues that the most visible indigenous novelists in Mexico reject the overarching and progressive discourses popularized and hailed in Latin America as solutions to the so-conveniently termed "Indian problem." The form allows indigenous authors to unfold their local histories through multiple perspectives that advocate for political autonomy.

The novelists cast a double gaze through their protagonists who embody kab'awil. This gives the writers creative license to theorize autonomy in their communities. The novelists imagine a delinking of indigenous peoples from traditional venues of political participation or world-system — whether the official, nation-state process or Marxist discourses — to imagine other possibilities. By delinking from the world-system, I reference a refusal of incorporation via nation-state education or corrupt electoral processes. The novelists deploy kab'awilian strategies reflected in their very use of the genre (a convention traditionally presumed to be a Western form relatively new to Latin America) to fictionalize the demand for intellectual and political autonomy and, significantly, their conscious engagement with gender parity. In some respects the novels anticipate (*Cantares*) and endorse (*Teya*) the Zapatistas' 2000 and 2006 political stances in their repudiation of leftist or conservative political parties in Mexico — a delinking from national politics that cost them support from leftist circles around the world.[51] Most important, both novels intimate that indigenous autonomy requires articulation on indigenous terms — terms that each indigenous community must determine and define. The recent announcement by the Zapatistas and the Congreso Nacional Indígena (National Indigenous Congress) that they have joined forces in endorsing an indigenous woman for president in the 2018 elections as an alternative option brought criticism from leftist parties in Mexico.[52] The novels do not offer a panacea for the problems they present but instead point to the need to carve out new political spaces.

Castellanos Martínez's and Ceh Moo's appropriation of the novel's dialogic nature in the Maya and Zapotec languages allows them to grapple with the social, cultural, political, and linguistic complexity of their quotidian lives, an articulation that might not be achievable through prayer or fable — popular genres in the indigenous literary repertoire. Certainly, the form encourages writers to engage with social and linguistic conflicts on the Maya Peninsula and in Oaxaca. It broaches the intricacies of indigenous people's material realities, ones not easily reduced to simple integration or Marxist analysis. Mikhail Bakhtin's heteroglossia as "competing discourses" becomes useful in thinking about the ideological effects of both novels.[53] Heteroglossia allows the authors to represent the social and linguistic conflicts in their communities.

Castellanos Martínez's and Ceh Moo's novels resist and refuse the very "progressive" discourses aimed at solving the "Indian problem" in Mesoamerica and Latin America more broadly. Their books reject Moretti's premise that novels on the periphery of world literature manifest a compromise between Western form and local materials. In this context, the novels reject a literary world-system that would interpret them as marginal. Through these novels the authors demystify the two foundational pillars of modernity and liberal thought in Latin American nationalist discourses. More pointedly, Castellanos Martínez's and Ceh Moo's novels bring to the forefront the potential of indigenous autonomy carved out beyond the parameters established by the nation-state, or by the Marxist discourse that leads to the founding of the Communist Party (in Ceh Moo's novel). They point to the urgency of thinking beyond traditional paradigms. The Kichua critic Armando Muyulema, in the context of Ecuador, aptly names this turn as a movement from the "Indian question" in Latin America to "Indian questioning" in Abya Yala.[54]

According to the critic Víctor de la Cruz, the word for novel in Zapotec, *tichacánitichaci* or *tichacoquite*, was defined in a colonial dictionary, but he concedes that no examples written in Zapotec existed prior to Castellanos Martínez's 1994 publication of *Wila che be ze lhao / Cantares de los vientos primerizos*.[55] Furthermore, Castellanos Martínez, in a recent interview asserts, that the genre of the novel was a natural one for him, since there are oral stories in the Zapotec communities that are as long and complex as any novel, constituting what he terms "oral novels."[56] While writers have turned to neologisms to describe the form, there is currently no consensus on the terms to describe it in most indigenous languages. Jorge Cocom Pech states that *noj tsikbal t'aan*, literally a great or long conversation, could describe the form.[57] Other Maya novelists, like Javier Abelardo Gómez Navarrete, use the term *nen óol k'ajlay* to approximate what the historical novel means by uniting the idea of image, as in mirror, and history or memory.[58] According to Ceh Moo, the novel can be described as a long breath or *chowak iik'* because it requires great inspiration and respiration to tell or write a story of novel proportions.[59] In this debate, the novel elicits intriguing deliberations as writers indigenize the form.

Javier Castellanos Martínez and the Novel

Born in the Yojovi Valley of Oaxaca in 1951, Javier Castellanos Martínez grew up in a monolingual household of Zapotec speakers and learned Spanish during his teenage years. Castellanos Martínez initiated his career working for Culturas Populares, a government institution. Indigenous employees like Castellanos Martínez were considered cultural promoters. The Mexican government established Culturas Populares under the auspices of the SEP (Secretaría de Educación Pública) to oversee art and culture in different parts of Mexico. During his stint with Culturas Populares, Castellanos Martínez published his first books of tales, theater, and poetry. *Wila che be ze lhao / Cantares de los vientos primerizos* (The songs of the first winds) (1994) is his first novel, followed by *Da kebe nho Seke gon ben xhi'ne Guzio / Relación de hazañas del hijo del relámpago* (Account of the exploits of the son of lightning) (2005), *Laxdao yelazeralle / El corazón de los deseos* (The heart of desires) (2007), and *Dxiokze xha... bene walhall / Gente del mismo corazón* (People of the same heart) (2014). He is very vocal about the preservation of indigenous languages. Castellanos Martínez's voice emerges during a distinct and important literary and political moment for the revitalization of the Zapotec language.

Although he came of age in the Valley of Oaxaca, the political and cultural effervescence of Mexico City in the late 1960s and the militant activism on the Isthmus of Tehuantepec resonate in Castellanos Martínez's political development. In the late 1970s, the Coalición Obrera, Campesina, Estudiantil del Istmo (COCEI) made considerable progress on the political front. COCEI emerged as a viable and popular political alliance that swayed elections on the isthmus.[60] Oaxaca, like Chiapas, makes regular headlines around the world, especially during its teacher strikes.[61] The energy animating indigenous peoples in the political arena bolstered literary production in Oaxaca. Indigenous writers forced and disfigured the Latin alphabet to represent sounds that only exist in Zapotec. Víctor de la Cruz, one of the most established Zapotec intellectuals, writes that the task of establishing a Zapotec literary tradition was not an easy one for those writing in the 1930s.[62] This first generation launched the important literary magazine *Neza*.[63] The standardization of Zapotec by academics and activists coincides with the founding of the important Zapotec magazine *Guchachi' reza / Iguana rajada* (Split iguana).[64] Not surprisingly, this magazine was key in establishing orthographical uniformity for the Zapotec language. As the then-editor de la Cruz admits, no one contributor could publish without using the "official" alphabet.[65]

Castellanos Martínez published *Wila che be ze lhao / Cantares de los vientos primerizos* in 1994. The novel was part of Letras Indígenas Contemporáneas, a new series spearheaded by Culturas Populares.[66] The linguistic organization of the chapters stands out in the novel. The Zapotec language is visually privileged. It precedes the Spanish on alternating pages, thus forcing the reader to physically confront its linguistic difference.[67] This arrangement differs from Ceh Moo's organization, in which the novel can be read seamlessly in either language, even though the Maya version precedes the Spanish.

Wila che be ze lhao/Cantares de los vientos primerizos tells the story of a young man, Jaime, who is forced to leave his familiar milieu by his parents, who want him to learn Spanish and receive an education that conforms to the ideal of a liberal, modern, national subject. Jaime's parents send him to a boarding school in the city, removed from the community. Despite his initial resistance to school, he learns Spanish, graduates, and trains to become an educator. After teaching in various towns, Jaime is invited to work for the government in Mexico City with the promise of a double salary. A government representative (who may be an anthropologist or a linguist) teaches him to read and write in Zapotec. Javier returns to his hometown to collect information and write about his people. He visits family in an attempt to obtain an old Zapotec book his father kept in the house. In town, he meets Trohn Lhia (also spelled Trhon Lia and Trhonlia), who is married but whose husband is in the United States, and they begin a romantic affair. Through Tron's visions or "revelations" readers learn about her peculiar ancestry, the Zapotec's pre-Columbian struggles against other tribes, and the intrusion of Spaniards on their lands. She leads Jaime to stray from his mission of gathering Zapotec stories. Jaime is eventually summoned back to Mexico City, but since he cannot prove any progress to his supervisor, the government representative will only allow him to return accompanied by an anthropologist.

In resisting a narrative of social ascendancy through education, the author also de-demonizes alcohol consumption outside the paradigm of colonialism. Throughout the Americas, alcohol consumption in indigenous communities has been interpreted as a symptom of colonialism, marginalization, and poverty. Stereotypes about alcoholism and Indians come together in the popular imagination, and Castellanos Martínez plays with these beliefs but also reveals positive aspects of mescal and beer. Alcohol consumption serves different functions in the novel. In some instances, it has positive associations with communion, celebration, and trust in others. In other instances, it impairs Jaime's ability to make judicious decisions. Inebriation leads the characters to express their inner feelings freely and honestly. The most striking example of alcohol consumption is when it enables Trohn Lia to access the past via a trance. This is an important counterdiscourse to the idea that inebriation is strictly for lazy people without any work ethic.

The central critique in the novel is of course that of education. Jaime's boarding-school experience echoes the types of terror other indigenous people on the continent have endured. In his ironic fashion, Castellanos Martínez makes sure the reader knows that the boarding-school idea originated with his parents and not the state. "After being in that house for one year, no longer able to stand the way the ladies in charge abused us, and because at the time my parents were still alive, I dared to escape from that place to return to mine. When I returned to my town, my parents were not convinced of the judiciousness of my decision and again took me to the city. And again to another house where there were children and many more than in the last one."[68] This detail dissuades the reader's empathy and illustrates the Zapotec's complicity in their assimilation. In other words, the parents do not resist the Spanish language but rather force their son to learn it. Indeed, throughout the novel, Castellanos Martínez implicates the Zapotec in their social and cultural marginalization. Recognizing the role of the Zapotec in the state's scheme of assimilation has critical implications for a project of autonomy. In a public lecture, for example, Castellanos Martínez berates the Zapotec for not resisting this linguistic assimilation.[69]

The epistemological fissures caused through the processes of colonialism, nation-state building, and migration (to the United States) mark the text and appear allegorized by the failed romantic couplings in the novel. Jaime's teacher training takes place in an indigenous town far from home. However, his real learning takes place after he refuses responsibility for the young indigenous woman he has impregnated. The novel illustrates that Jaime's desire to adapt to the Western capitalist norms blinds him to Zapotec conventions about courting, intimacy, and family traditions. School has transformed him into a daft adult when relating to others in indigenous communities. Put differently, Jaime's education threatens the community's social conventions, harmony, and cohesion. Community police jail Jaime for his contempt of the local laws and disrespect of community customs, releasing him only after he agrees to accept responsibility for the unborn child and the child's mother. The first lesson Jaime learns after his return to the community is respect for others. Through the young woman's family, he acquires an appreciation for the land and farming, but after six years the couple separates due to his philandering. Jaime petitions for teaching jobs but soon realizes the communities are not always welcoming of educators.

Eventually Jaime lands a government position in the city, with which he becomes enamored after two years. He only grudgingly agrees to return to his community at the urging of a government official. Ironically, it is this government bureaucrat who teaches him to write in Zapotec. This is a critical detail, as it implies that the Zapotec are complicit in their social position since they do not express interest in learning to write their language. His superior is interested in using Jaime as a "cultural promoter" — a title indicating the historical collaboration between trained indigenous men and women and government institutions in the 1970s, and which more than likely reflects the participatory *indigenismo* of the times.

The novel's structure enacts kab'awil through a duality represented by the perspectives of the male and female protagonists. On the one hand, Jaime, the male character allows the author to narrate a contemporary indigenous identity. Through Jaime, the novel's themes raise central questions of modernity, assimilation, migration and education, thus an exterior gaze to the community. On the other hand, through the female character, Trohn Lia, the novel allows readers to wrestle with the weight of Zapotec memory, myth, and history before Spanish colonialism, hence offering an inner gaze on the community. The deployment of these two characters allows Castellanos Martínez to represent a kab'awilian ontology in and outside the community and across time to previous eras. The writer's use of song lyrics, trances that induce stories, and prayers privileges the oral tradition in the novel. Even though an ancient Zapotec text surfaces in the story as *the* cultural artifact government officials covet, no one in the community can read it, nor has anyone expressed interest in reading it before the government's intention to secure the text. The place of orality in the novel seems highly regarded because through the intradiegetic narrators various stories are retold. In the conclusion, the readers learn that Jaime is not the principal voice telling the story. Instead, the narrator is a man who heard the story from Jaime. The historical, political, and cultural threads woven through this short novel illustrate the historical connection that bonds language and nation. It explodes the image of Mexico as monolingual, while at the same time revealing that the Zapotec nation, too, is in crisis, as represented by Jaime who speaks Zapotec but is illiterate in his mother tongue. The linguistic dissonance speaks to the historical repression of indigenous languages.

Above all, the genealogical and historical interventions of Jaime's counterpart, Trohn Lia, through what the author organizes as "revelations," offer readers a counterhistorical narrative about the ancient Zapotec culture that has been occluded by official nation-state history. She represents not just Zapotec women's historical memory but the ancestor's—one of the *yibedaos* or guardians of the universe. Trohn tells Jaime that she is a direct descendant of the *yibedaos*, mythological entities who ensure the well-being of the Zapotec people. In this context, she functions as a bridge to the past. Her interjections in the novel represent the oral tradition, myth history, and refer us back to the role Zapotec women play in the community. In the first revelation, Trohn says to Jaime, "I still am one of those branches from the old tree from which we sprung; with me ends the breath of life that Berhjashirha planted, he who brought us when the ancestors decided to leave the valley where our knowledge and Zapotec identity emerged."[70] It is also via Trohn's revelations that Castellanos Martínez references a tale from the oral tradition in which the husband's mistrust of the *yibedaos* leads to the disarray of colonialism. In other words, the husband's mistrust left the Zapotec universe vulnerable to external, foreign forces because the *yibedaos* have been pushed out of balance. These imbalances make the Zapotec susceptible to the Spanish conquest.

Jaime's ideological underpinnings transform through a decolonization process that starts through his treatment of women. Recall that in his first romantic experience, Jaime does not assume responsibility for his pregnant girlfriend. As the narrative progresses, he begins to think differently, especially when he questions his sexual desire for the two women who can potentially change his life trajectory: the white anthropologist and Trohn. The white anthropologist remains without a name throughout the novel. She is contrasted with Trohn, the keeper of historical memory. Through Jaime's relationship with the women, Castellanos Martínez addresses unresolved issues related to conquest, desire, history, memory, and sexuality. His relationship with the anthropologist parodies the cultural-informant role Indians have historically played in this field of inquiry. It reminds us that colonization gave birth to the discipline and has served the political objectives of those in power. The parody is evident in the liberal discourse driving their dialogue:

> —Beautiful anthropologist, what decision would you make, considering that you are a city dweller and that I am of these places, I am Indian, as you people say, and now I want you dare to sleep with me, you as a woman and I as a man.
> . . . .
> —Look, Jaime . . . I have not seen a written law anywhere that differentiates among humans by stating, "This one is Mexican or this one is European," for me, from the moment we are all born, we have the same rights; it is only people's ambition that has divided humanity.[71]

The anthropologist's lack of interest in his advances illustrates the vexed relationship between scholars interested in indigenous communities only due to an overvalorization of the past, and their affective rejection of present indigenous peoples who seek horizontal relationships.

While the relationship can be read as structured by a virile sexism, the character's self-reflection and analysis of his sexual desire for whiteness as part and parcel of the ideological effects of colonization save the novelist from falling into a facile sexist chauvinism, making this moment of clarity a representative part of Jaime's epistemological decolonizing process.[72] Jaime's romantic advances toward the anthropologist patently illustrate Quijano's theorization of the coloniality of power, which in this context can be seen as structuring sexual desire for whiteness. Recognizing this dimension of the coloniality of power finally allows Jaime to appreciate and fall in love with his indigenous female counterpart, Trohn Lhia. In other words, he realizes that by rejecting the indigenous woman and opting for the white one, he was rejecting himself and naturalizing a racial order where whiteness is more desirable.

Jaime's decolonization begins with his realization that what he has learned in school is official history and not necessarily true. In one pointed scene, Jaime accuses Trohn Lia of ignorance because she cannot read and does not know that before 1810 (the beginning of Mexican independence from Spain) the Zapotec were slaves, and that they won their freedom fighting. Trohn replies, "It is true when you say that I cannot read, but even if there is a pile of books saying that, I cannot believe it. We have not been at war with anyone and we will never be at war with anyone, because what is happening to us now is not that someone took our wealth and does not want to return it to us . . . wealth is the opposite of what we like to be, that is why our ancestors never intended to be the sole owners of the land and that is why they tolerated the foreigners."[73] Jaime's experience of education has been a process of nationalization, but Trohn's history is not limited to this official version. She connects him to a past when the Spaniards had yet to arrive and points to the fact that national independence had little to do with the liberation of the Zapotec. Trohn Lia's perspective and consciousness reflects another kab'awilian gaze.

Jaime responds violently to Trohn's assertion that the Zapotec are destined to be poor. He blames that line of thinking for inhibiting the Zapotec's economic progress. However, for Trohn, poverty has its origins in a curse one of her female ancestors casts on the Zapotec. Yabenetsi, Trohn's little sister, who along with her partner fights Spanish intrusion, ends up cursing the Zapotec for conforming to Spanish rule. As a leader and *Donaxhe*, or woman with great power, she listens to her people. At that historical moment, they do not perceive land as private property and decide that the Spaniards can coexist with them. According to Trohn, from this point onward two types of Zapotecs emerge, those who want to be just like the Spaniards and those who maintain their way of life. Once the Spaniards and those Zapotecs who want to emulate them take political control, Yabenetsi's power wanes and she is humiliated. Her bitter wail and curse, "'You'll be famed for your poverty,' is heard by the Lords of land, river, and wind," making all Zapotec poor, according to the oral tradition.[74] Jaime and Trohn engage in a physical fight that leads him to burn down the house they rent, effectively denouncing the illusion that land can be owned. Trohn, of course, laughs at his action, calling him a petit intellectual who does not even own a home. After she mocks him Jaime realizes that he wants to be just like her.

Jaime and Trohn accept their peripatetic fate and reject the idea of ownership in order to maintain their identity, since as Trohn asserts being wealthy runs counter to being an authentic Zapotec. The characters decide that if fleeing poverty is the condition that pushes Zapotecs out of their community and makes them suffer, the solution is to reject consumption and excess. Based on the revelations she received, particularly when she is intoxicated with alcohol and gets in touch with her cultural genealogy, she comforts him, saying the Zapotec should not be afraid of being poor. However, this is not an easy task. Jaime's decision to be like Trohn leads to a series of challenges in which he is tempted to steal corn, faces prison, and ultimately is forced into exile.

Castellanos Martínez's novel hammers home that a Western education is not necessarily a liberating path. It represents integration into the dominant culture, an integration that started in the colonial period. Education, then, functions as simply another extension of the nation-state's program. Castellanos Martínez does not absolve the Zapotec for collaborating with the state. The novel's anticapitalist and antiassimilationist stances are allegorized through the characters' rejection of consumption and education. Their embrace of poverty as a condition, however, is not simply about creating abject subjects. Here the novel tries to offer us a different epistemological dimension to the historical origins of poverty.

In this sense, the novel refuses a narrative of ascendance through education; instead, the answer lies in trying other models of self-sufficiency. In the end, far from offering us a utopian alternative, Castellanos Martínez's novel illustrates the Zapotec's capacity to survive, adapt, and thrive. This said, Zapotec autonomy is left as an unrealized project. The road to autonomy must begin with a conceptual rethinking of materialism, land ownership, and epistemology. This is not an easy path. Jaime's initial view of education as a means to material access is not a viable option, and he ultimately accepts Trohn's knowledge as valid. However, the temptation of having more does not disappear, as the novel ends with their being expelled from the town because Jaime steals maize — even when he steals from someone who is selling maize for profit and is not indigenous. The novel illustrates that autonomy still has to be articulated and constructed, and that it must take the form of economic self-sufficiency. Above all else the novel shows that indigenous communities still must undertake a lot of conceptual undoing before this autonomy can be realized.

Ceh Moo makes a similar call to delink from traditional venues of political participation to which women are not considered integral. She accentuates the need for a resolution to power differentials in gender relations before significant social change can transpire. While these novels represent two distinct linguistic and cultural indigenous nations, the authors use the genre to further illustrate through fiction the importance of an indigenous autonomy beyond either the nation-state's program of integration or Marxism.

Marisol Ceh Moo and the Novel

Born in Calotmul, Yucatán, Marisol Ceh Moo studied at the Autonomous University of Yucatán in Mérida. She is the first indigenous woman to publish a bilingual novel in Maya and Spanish. Among her well-known publications, *Jats'uts'il loolo'ob / Jardines de Xibalbaj* (2010) is a provocative collection of short stories, based on the Yucatán Peninsula, that makes an important reference to the *Popol Vuh*. *X-Teya, U puksi'ik'al ko'olel / Teya, un corazón de mujer* made headlines precisely because its contents deviate from the generic rubrics established for the production of Maya literature. In her second novel, *T'ambilak men tunk'ulilo'ob / El llamado de los tunkules* (The call of the tunkules) (2010), Ceh Moo addresses a more traditional subject on the peninsula, the Caste War of the nineteenth century. Her third novel, *Chen tumeen chú'upen / Sólo por ser mujer* (Just for being a woman), tackles another controversial theme: women, violence, and alcoholism in Maya communities.

Similar to Castellanos Martínez, Ceh Moo emerged as a writer in the context of a very vocal political literary movement on the peninsula whose focus has been on rescuing, recovering, and preserving traditional literature. Ceh Moo vehemently rejects criticism that her novel was inauthentic because it lacked traditional themes. In an interview in Mexico City, she expresses her concerns:

> They [the critics] also have to understand that what I am looking for is an opening. The Native languages of Mexico have lagged behind because there are groups within the same ethnic or cultural group that, one can say, decide which way one has to work. In other words, the nice thing is poetry, song in the native tongue, or in the Maya language, in my case; the legend is pretty, the writing down of the oral tradition is nice, and it is nice to say, "We will

represent the X-Tabay." [But] you can put the X-Tabay in 50,000 versions and that is not creation, it is not re-creation, not transcription, it is simply to change the context — right? — and reprint.[75]

She emphasizes that writing down the oral tradition does not necessarily lead to creativity, originality, or innovation in indigenous literatures. The conversations at different indigenous writers' meetings range from a type of strategic essentialism to some concession around creative autonomy, particularly in the production of poetry. Many contemporary indigenous writers initiated their careers by publishing in the series Letras Mayas Contemporáneas established by the socially committed writer Carlos Montemayor. The series made indigenous writers visible. Montemayor also offered many writing workshops for emerging writers in indigenous languages. Other key groups of writers emerged simultaneously on the peninsula, including Maya'on, Indemaya, and various independent writers. Ceh Moo, however, did not participate in any of Montemayor's workshops and represents what I periodize as a second generation of Maya writers who do not subscribe to the highly venerated dictum, set forth by the previous generation, that the oral tradition must be written down.

As a novelist, it is not surprising that her life experience contributes to the topics she fictionalizes. In a recent interview, responding to subjects in her novels and her concern with women, she states, "Fortunately, one day I had a conflict with my father due to his abuse of my mother; at the time he said I could never compare myself with him because I am a woman and he is a man; with that comment, he argued that men could do whatever they wanted, unlike women, for being what they are: women as well as Indians."[76] She uses "fortunately" in this instance because the experience allowed her to recognize the sexism that women face in indigenous families and communities and made her assume a political position as an indigenous woman. She asserts a critical posture as an indigenous woman who demands an analysis that moves beyond a one-dimensional concern with class or ethnicity to an intersectional analysis in the way Kimberle Crenshaw scrutinizes the ways that "race and gender intersect in shaping structural, political, and representational aspects of violence against women of color."[77] Through the character Teya and her domestic work, Ceh Moo maintains a double gaze on the interior of Maya communities that allows her to see the limitations of Marxism when dealing with women's domestic labor. Noteworthy is the fact that the name *Teya* may be a historical reference to a hacienda, founded in the seventeenth century in Yucatán, that was a highly profitable cattle ranch and, in the nineteenth century, a producer of henequen. During the

Lázaro Cárdenas administration's agrarian reform, Teya was divided into *ejidos* or communal lands. It is now a hotel.[78]

Teya, un corazón de mujer relates the story of a young mestizo lawyer named Emeterio Rivas who champions the cause of the poor and the indigenous people who are victimized by local powermongers (in the tradition of the cacique).[79] Marxist in his political orientation and a reprehensible womanizer, Emeterio is the favorite son of his mother, Teya. Similar in technique to Gabriel García Márquez's novel *Crónica de una muerte anunciada* (*Chronicle of a Death Foretold*), we know in the first pages that Rivas was murdered. The intellectual masterminds behind his murder are the governor and a local henchman who see him as standing in the way of their expropriation of indigenous and peasant lands. The henchman or cacique, Tiburcio, orders two men to murder Emeterio. Narrated from Teya's point of view, the first part of the novel reveals that she does not agree with her son's involvement in politics, and in particular his socialist leanings. In fact, she admonishes him that revolutionary men end up dead with their photographs adorning office walls. The list of this male genealogy is long: Canek, Che, Chi, Carrillo Puerto (she does not differentiate between Maya and mestizo heroes).[80] Structurally, the novel divides easily into three main parts. The first one relates Teya's relationship with her son. In the second part, we learn about Emeterio's upbringing and the critical mentorship of his communist father, his university training, and finally his work in the courts as a lawyer who defends the rights of indigenous and peasant peoples. The third main section relates the story of those who murdered him and the crime's political consequences. Readers enter the story through the first person and an omniscient narrator.

Since its publication, two notable critics in the North American academy have written about the novel. Arturo Arias argues that Ceh Moo's novel "traces the trajectory of Emeterio, Teya's son, to show how her offspring is a victim of the connections between racism and capitalism that were crucial to Teya's intellectual development."[81] Emilio del Valle Escalante, in contrast, proposes that the novel represents an end to *indigenismo*. He argues that "Ceh Moo attempts to disarticulate *indigenismo* by appropriating the Ladino or Mestizo world in order to establish her own authority as a Maya writer, and in turn, the authority of indigenous rights movements."[82] I build on both these insightful interpretations of the novel. In my critical reading of *Teya*, I focus on the ways Ceh Moo weaves gender, indigeneity, and a politics of autonomy to fictionalize the shortcomings of the Communist Party on the peninsula. In the early twentieth century, local politics on the peninsula was infused with progressive thought.

These progressive ideals aimed to better the conditions of Maya peasants and women in general. The universal feminism established by middle-class women did not lessen the racial discrimination Indian women faced, however. The novel illustrates that universalism and Eurocentrism haunt Marxism.

The legacy of the Maya rebellion during the Caste War on the peninsula became an important historical referent for indigenous novelists like Javier Gómez Navarrete in *Cecilio Chi'*. Ceh Moo continues and breaks away from this theme by focusing on the fictionalized story of a mother, her son, and a Maya communist leader. She uses multiple perspectives to narrate this story. Arias and del Valle Escalante discuss the significance of Maxim Gorky's *Mother* in Ceh Moo's text.[83] For Arias, it represents a future possibility of Teya's radicalization, while for del Valle Escalante, it represents a "resignification of 'revolutionary action.'"[84] I read it as reference that contrasts with Teya's apathy toward the class struggle. It represents the failure of the socialist ethos on the peninsula to engage Maya women in a political project that acknowledges the unique issues they face. In contrast to Pavel's mother in Gorky's novel, Teya does not join the revolution after her son is murdered; rather, she becomes even more skeptical of its potential for change. Ceh Moo invokes the merely cosmetic potential of revolution by allegorizing it through Emeterio's scaring off of recalcitrant classmates with a deactivated grenade given him by a comrade from El Salvador's Frente Farabundo Martí para la Liberación Nacional (Farabundo Martí National Liberation Front, or FMLN).[85] When his classmates ask him about the grenade, Emeterio replies, "That grenade was given to me by some comrades from the FMLN . . . it is in reality a nice toy . . . truly a nice toy, but useless."[86]

The failure of the socialist sector on the Maya Peninsula has to do precisely with the fact that for most indigenous women their labor remains hidden and unaccounted for in the private, domestic sphere. The relationship between the socialist groups (whether Maya or Ladino or white women) and Maya women remains contentious, especially in this context. One must recall that it was on the Yucatán Peninsula where women first won the right to vote in 1922, and that it would take more than two decades, until 1946, for the rest of Mexican women to enjoy the same right. Women's suffrage became law on the peninsula due to the support of the Socialist Party of the Southeast for women's rights.[87] Historian Emma Pérez, for instance, points out that during the Mexican Revolution (1910–20) various progressive revolutionary congresses were held in Yucatán to discuss women's contribution to the movement, but these were mainly for and about middle-class women. In Pérez's research, she found that these leftist government officials failed Maya and working-class women. She identifies the legal case of Casimira Palma as symbolic of this failure. When Palma, a Maya woman from Tekax, filed a case against a Ladina woman for stealing her jewels, not only did the court not rule in her favor but she was linguistically ostracized by a leftist official.[88] Pérez writes, "For a government official to reprimand an Indian for not speaking Spanish reveals the injustices suffered by the Maya in Yucatán even at a time when the revolution was supposed to alleviate differences."[89] In other words, even when courts were overseen by officials affiliated with socialist policy, this did not guarantee Maya women a fair trial, or justice.

Several examples in the novel powerfully indict sexism within the ranks of the Communist Party. The first critique relates to the lack of recognition of how women's work at home contributes to socialist organizing. The second has to do with the connection between the sexual manipulation of women and class exploitation. When Emeterio leaves the house on the day he is murdered, he yells at the mother, "See you later, Teya, prepare something good to eat for me, take care and don't work too much!"[90] She is not a salaried worker, thus her domestic effort is not seen as real labor. Teya's response offers a more sophisticated understanding of domestic work: "'Mmm . . . ! What do you mean don't work! Who do you think is going to prepare the food, you nitwit?' she responded slowly, when she knew no one could hear her."[91] Teya knows that if she stops cleaning, cooking, and so on, the household will fall apart and the work of both her husband and son would suffer. I think this is the most radical point Teya makes in the novel. Tellingly, no one can hear her rebuttal, but this becomes a strategy that entices readers to sympathize with her point of view.

While the members of the Communist Party in the novel do not consider women's household work as integral to socialist organizing, the novel illustrates that everything depends on Teya's labor.[92] We know, for example, that Teya regrets that she fell asleep on the day that the criminals-for-hire murder Emeterio. In Foucauldian terms, her mishap alters the order of things.[93] In other words, if she had begun work at the same time as usual, she may not have lived to regret the day. It is from this vantage point that we must analyze the novel's importance. She clearly suggests that her husband's and son's militant work is made possible by her indiscernible and unrecognized domestic toil, as del Valle Escalante also notes. Teya meditates on this predicament. She recalls that when women and men seek her husband's help, her husband orders her to make food for them. He chastises her begrudging attitude: "'Teya Martín, they have nothing but the clothes they are wearing,' he indicated to me, when he noticed my discomfort with sitting strangers at my table. They had me cooking, but it did not really matter, my Emeterio was growing and growing."[94]

The author's coupling of Emeterio and Tiburcio, the cacique, allows her to insert a mordant critique of patriarchy. She illustrates that men's sexist attitudes toward women — whether these men subscribe to socialist ideals or capitalist ones — inevitably negatively affect the larger social fabric. Significantly, Ceh Moo offers a sentimental explanation for Tiburcio's avarice. Tiburcio, whose wealth was accumulated by exploiting the labor of others, does not come from an elite bourgeoisie or criollo landowning class. The narrator, instead, painstakingly recounts his origins in a very poor and large family. Indeed, the subtext here is that Tiburcio became an oppressive man because he lacked his mother's love. He had too many brothers who took most of her time and affection. In the style of the nineteenth-century sentimental novel, the writer inserts her voice into the narrative, commenting that these characters did not necessarily represent good and evil and may even be similar but with two distinct visions of the world. What is striking about her description of both characters is Emeterio's selfish, insatiable sexual appetite, which brings misery to both rich and humble young women: "Emeterio also had his supporters and his detractors. His life, peppered with sex scandals, was known throughout the region. A player of humble females who fell for his verbiage of unfettered free love; who undressed to the verses of Neruda; a deflowerer of young girls of the middle class who would fall for the indoctrination that the hymen is a relic of capitalist moralist society; exposed as a sex addict who did not fuck himself because he could not reach. Despite their [Tiburcio and Emeterio's] similarities, two different worldviews."[95] The description of Emeterio is clearly a feminist critique of the leftist politics of a man who cannot see the connection between class and sexual exploitation. On the one hand, if Tiburcio (the man who orders his murder) grows up to be a bad man, it is because he lacked his mother's tenderness. On the other, Emeterio, who did not lack his mother's love but who, from the age of eight, was trained by his father to be a progressive Marxist intellectual, exploits women because his father taught him that the only real inequity is of class, leaving Emeterio unable to perceive the intersection between it, gender, and indigeneity.

The second-most important theme relates to the fact that at the end of the narrative, Uitzil, who had been mentored by Emeterio, becomes the first Maya communist representative. But, as the novel intimates, his election will not change Maya women's social status. The novel considers different political possibilities. Emeterio represents a mestizo, since he doesn't speak Maya and his father was a leftist mestizo in solidarity with the Maya. In some sense, then, Emeterio's demise is necessary in order for the first Maya community representative to be elected. But, as the novelist depicts, Uitzil is also blind to indigenous women's struggles. The movement of Maya peasants to workers within orthodox Marxism does not translate into autonomy for all members of indigenous communities. The specific way indigenous women experience inequality is incompatible with the ways the Communist Party in the novel operates. Society holds women accountable for things like honor and virginity — issues not addressed or taken into consideration in Emeterio's Communist Party. Ceh Moo's critique is clear: women, whether they are married to progressive men who read Marxist theory or criminals, are at a disadvantage. The author cleverly illustrates this through Telma Chel, a Maya woman who is married to the mastermind behind Emeterio's murder. Readers learn that in order to ensure the marriage, Tiburcio kidnaps her one morning and returns her to her parent's home in the evening — a conniving move because he knows Telma Chel's parents will suspect that her honor has been compromised and would agree to an expedited wedding.[96] Through Telma Chel's story, Ceh Moo illustrates that an intersectional analysis is integral to an autonomous project.

Ceh Moo's novel innovated Maya letters because she dared to deviate from the popular expectation that she write about Maya traditions. Its innovation also lies in the modicum of ethnic references and the lack of the lyricism one finds in the historical novels of Javier Navarrete or Isaac Carrillo (both Maya). Ethnic references are presented through the kitchen and interestingly through the very famous regional Maya expression *Pel'ana*, which literally translates as "your mother's vagina" and is considered the ultimate insult to a Maya speaker on the peninsula. In other words, Maya identity is rendered visible through Teya's unacknowledged labor in the kitchen and through her body. The meals she cooks all are traditional Maya cuisine. And it is the Maya term for vagina that forces readers back to its gendered indigenous referent.

The novel rejects class struggle as the antidote to the inequality indigenous peoples suffer. Instead, Ceh Moo advocates for an intersectional analysis that centralizes gender. Emeterio's murder by corrupt government representatives and the criminals they hire paves the way for his Maya protégé Uitzil Peba to become the first Maya representing the Communist Party. As we have seen, however, Uitzil Peba's ascension is hardly a game changer. After Emeterio's assassination, Uitzil comes to offer Teya his condolences, and she questions him: "What do people fight for, if in the end they end up doing the same [thing] they fought against. . . . evil is not in the system, evil is in the heart of men."[97] The novelist describes how Uitzil identifies conformism in her gaze, for him a disease that allows injustice and poverty. "There is too much conformism in the world," he retorts. "That's why poverty grows, injustice is rampant everywhere without anyone to denounce it, without anyone to rebel."[98] Her gaze is an internal one that allows her to see beyond class differences. However, Uitzil does not seem to understand that there is a power differential in the relationships between indigenous men and women. The desire for a politicized Teya to join the class struggle in a parallel to Gorky's mother is not satisfied. Social transformation cannot begin until the basic power and affective relations between men and women change to horizontal ones. Ceh Moo uses the novel to dramatize the legacy of socialism on the peninsula, of indigenous peoples, and of the potential for autonomy.

These novels refuse the grand narratives of integration through nation-state education and traditional political electoral participation. Of course, this is not to say that in real life, indigenous peoples should abstain from traditional politics. The novels reject Eurocentrism as a world-system propelled by capitalism and the modernity on which Moretti's literary world-system formulation is based. Emeterio Rivas succeeds as a lawyer and a Marxist militant, but as a mestizo he must disappear in order for Uitzil Peba to become the first Maya Marxist leader. Teya's kab'awilian gaze toward Uitzil Peba makes clear, however, that while his rise may be read as progress within socialist movements, he is as dismissive of women as his predecessor. In that respect, Teya's double gaze represents the irreconcilable difference she sees between her experience as an indigenous woman and a Communist Party narrative that does not recognize her condition as either a mother or a woman. It is not arbitrary that Ceh Moo feminizes the story's denouement, describing the protests of peasants and workers and the death of Emeterio Rivas as a protracted gestation, a long and painful birth. In Castellanos Martínez's novel, the main protagonist sees education as a laborious process that only leads to self-loathing, hence his choice to opt out of the system and reject assimilation into capitalism. Jaime and his partner, Trohn Lhia, have the capacity to generate a new way of being, but the tempting excesses of a consumer society must be ceaselessly resisted. Both novels postulate that real autonomy will have to come from indigenous communities and not as dictates from political and economic models of either the first or second worlds. And yet, these novels can only point to the absence of alternatives, since autonomy is still in the making.

Conclusion

The publication of bilingual novels by indigenous authors is a recent cultural phenomenon. The genre — more than any other literary form — provides the writer with a unique and necessary lens to imagine an intellectual and geopolitical autonomy outside a universalist (read, Eurocentric) discourse. Kab'awil, or the "double gaze," manifests through the male and female characters the authors create; through them, the authors challenge the nation-state stance about education as a way out of the social marginalization experienced in indigenous communities and the limitations of traditional venues of political participation. For the indigenous writer, the form of the novel acts as a powerful tool to reject the tenets of assimilation and absorption. The project of autonomy is proposed and represented as labor that lies ahead in order for indigenous nations to realize self-sufficiency.

EPILOGUE

Inverting the Gaze from California

In any case, to talk about an indigenous civilization project itself is thus the result of the intervention of activists and intellectuals who are gradually helping to reimagine, rethink, and regain the world. We still have to generate and deepen the dialogue between indigenous scholars from the north and south, and to think more carefully about the implications of these talks.—Emilio del Valle Escalante (K'iche', 2015)

If we take the Spanish book burnings of the Mayan códices in the 1540s as an example, we might describe this act of cultural genocide as one culture finding itself threatened by the profundity of the other's literacy. These were illiteracy campaigns, sponsored by the group claiming to be the most literate. Symbolically, and literally, this campaign still continues.—Craig S. Womack (Cree, 1999)

I CONCLUDE MY WRITING of this book from Luiseño land, a string of hills and mountains undulating between the coast and inland. I acknowledge my debt to Native American literary scholars whose works have been instrumental in my thinking about the rise of indigenous literatures in Mesoamerica and their connection to autonomy. Their theorizations influence my own subject position as an immigrant in the United States with indigenous and campesino roots. Nonetheless, I am fully cognizant that growing up and living in the United States makes my experience different from that of the Maya and Zapotec writers I discuss. While my background does not necessarily authorize this book's undertaking, my personal disclosure represents an acknowledgment that in many ways I am more of an outsider.

My family is from an area called *El Trifinio*, a biosphere protected by the governments of Honduras, El Salvador, and Guatemala. In terms of nation-state citizenship, my father had roots in the *aldea* (or communal land) called Pie del Cerro, a border area shared by Guatemala and Honduras, whereas my mother has roots in La Palma, a border area between El Salvador and Honduras.[1] I lived part of my childhood at the margins of Ocotepeque, Honduras; Chalatenango, El Salvador; and Esquipulas, Guatemala. I point out the border status of this area because it represents both confluence and conflict, guided by nation-state nationalisms on all sides. Many people maintain double citizenship. Historically and culturally, this area is Maya Ch'orti'. According to archeologists and epigraphers, the Ch'orti' language currently spoken in Guatemala and by only a handful of people in Honduras is, with Yukatek Maya, one of the languages related to the classical writing. It was brought by the Maya who migrated from the Chiapas region thousands of years ago to what is now the Trifinio area. Today, the Ch'orti' people are recognized by both the nation-states of Honduras and Guatemala. However, in the Trifinio part of El Salvador the remaining handful of indigenous peoples have historically identified as campesinos with Maya identity as historical memory. The few that identify as indigenous do not use external cultural markers or speak Ch'orti', although some areas share cultural practices and stories with their brethren in Guatemala and Honduras. The indigenous peoples movement in El Salvador has been criticized for stressing a Maya identity when in fact the overwhelming majority of indigenous people (about 10 percent or less of the population) is Nahuat, followed by Lenca and Kakawira (or Cacaopera).[2] Not to mention that it was not until 2014 that the nation-state of El Salvador officially acknowledged three indigenous nations in its constitution. In Honduras, the Maya Ch'orti' are a very small community and culturally mixed, but due to the tourism industry's promotion of the classical Maya ceremonial center of Copán (considered the first Mayan university), their presence overshadows larger, non-Maya indigenous nations in Honduras like the Pech, Lenca, and Miskito, among others. And yet they are the only indigenous nation in Mesoamerica that I know of to have occupied the archeological site to get the Honduran government to negotiate land rights. In Guatemala, compared to other Maya nations, the Ch'orti' have undergone quite a bit of acculturation and have suffered more language loss than other indigenous nations and thus have had less impact in the country's Pan-Maya Movement. Brent E. Metz claims that the Maya Ch'orti' of the Trifinio area have the potential for political unity across nation-states, as they enjoyed in pre-Columbian times, but I find that more of a romantic notion for now, especially given nation-state differences.[3]

    I live in Luiseño territory. Its people and sacred grounds have their own stories. In 2004, before this hilly farm area was leveled and built into a bedroom community, the San Luis Rey Band of Indians and the City of Oceanside inaugurated Luiseño Park, showcasing the tribe's heritage. According to newspaper sources, in 1984 the idea of the park came in a dream to Louise Munoa Foussat, a Luiseño elder. The park itself is a living memory of the Luiseño people's culture, welcoming and reminding us that we live on their land. Artists meticulously interpreted and reproduced a traditional garden, a dwelling ring, a shaman rock, and a number of boulders with various writings in the form of carvings and inscriptions. Many original petroglyphs found in the area have been reproduced in the large boulders arranged throughout the grounds. One of these stones resembles a Maya stelae—often used in Mesoamerica to record the history of kings. Writing is everywhere.

In many respects so is the oral tradition that is native to this land. While the process of colonialism brutally attempted to sever indigenous people from their means of knowledge production and strove to repress how the aesthetics and the sublime manifest, many of the stories continue to thrive. Indigenous nations' relationship to writing and literature may manifest differently across time and space, but there is no doubt as to their existence. In the city east of Oceanside according to local lore, a Luiseño man walked into what is now the City of Fallbrook and was turned into stone; hence, they call the place Sleeping Indian. Luiseños interpreted this topographical formation as a boundary marker. This account reminds me of other oral tradition stories I heard from my mother's side of the family about a place called Cihuatán (an archeological site whose name means "place of women"), where the mountain silhouette takes the shape of a sleeping Indian princess who will one day rise and avenge her subjugation. Cihuatán physically marks the boundary that separates three historical indigenous communities in El Salvador: the Nahuat, Maya, and Lenca. It resonates with countless stories I also heard in my childhood about people who can morph into other beings, the *nahuales* (or *nawales*). Family stories of nahuales abound in my family. Indigenous experiences are not identical, but parallels exist in how these communication practices, the written and the oral, endure, even under the pressure of marginalization. The stories authenticate the importance of land as a reservoir of memories, one that serves as a textual archive. This triumvirate of land, story, and language continues to be a foundational building block on which indigenous civilizations safeguard and ensure their survival and continuity. This relationship is an enduring indigenous cosmolectics.

Nonetheless, the oral tradition has not been the principal concern of this book. Instead, I have attempted to assiduously relate the story of a group of mostly bilingual indigenous writers who through their pioneering creative prose and poetry represent the endless possibilities to imagine and construct autonomous intellectual and political spaces in Mesoamerica that defy the social norm and unsettle national borders. This politically conscious and articulate indigenous literary movement represents one of the most significant cultural developments in Latin America. Akin to Native literature in the United States, this textual body hinges, not by its own volition, at the margins of literary studies. Since the nation-formation period, indigenous stories in Mesoamerica have served to supplement the formation of national literary canons. In other words, the contributions of indigenous literatures to national canons have been summarily submerged by form and content by *letrados* who have traditionally given them "legibility." The propensity to separate oral and written systems occludes the importance of indigenous productions to the very foundation of the field. Analyzing conventional literary forms historicizes indigenous writers' insertion into national and international literary circuits and involves a struggle for representation. The project of autonomy signifies differently in the literature, as it intersects with questions of gender and patriarchy.

I have traced the contours of Mesoamerican literary projects that reject a literary world-system that is assumed as originating outside indigenous lands. Indigenous literature emerges in the throes of a hemispheric movement, but nation-states influence their output or curtail others. Many indigenous nations have yet to produce writers in the conventional sense, which is the predicament of indigenous groups in the Mesoamerican region such as the nation-states of El Salvador and Honduras and to a lesser degree Belize, Costa Rica, and Nicaragua—although this is certainly starting to change. In some respects, this vacuum results from the fact that the indigenous communities in these countries are smaller, poorer, have less infrastructure and have suffered more cultural and linguistic loss.

As more indigenous writers reconfigure the traditional relationship of the Latin American *letrado* as the main interlocutor, for indigenous communities, more work must be done to think about autonomous spaces. I have accented kab'awil as a critical indigenous cosmolectics that originates in glyphic writing, expressed in the literature as a way to theorize indigenous intellectual autonomy. I stress that Maya and Zapotec writers deploy kab'awilian strategies that force readers to rethink the binaristic discourse of dominant societies in their separation of tradition and modernity, orality and literacy, and the racial construction of the other—discourses that have been fundamental to situating indigenous literary expressions as oral. Kab'awil, or the double gaze, is a constant presence in the production and interpretation of these texts. Indigenous contributions to philosophy and epistemology remain largely marginal, even though indigenous peoples have been central to philosophical debates in Western countries since the sixteenth century.[4]

Neoliberal political ideologies and globalizing forces continue to breed poverty, forcing displacement and maintaining illiteracy in innumerable indigenous communities, adversely affecting language preservation. It is estimated that half of the 7,000 languages in the world will be extinct by the end of the century. Humanity loses one language every two weeks. The future of indigenous languages in Mesoamerica may be uncertain, but Maya and Zapotec writers valiantly lead the fight to revive and preserve their respective languages by establishing this body of literature.[5] Nonetheless, Spanish does function as the lingua franca in many of today's literary gatherings, and writers self-translate either from Spanish to an indigenous language or vice versa. The question of what gets lost in translation poses an enigmatic dilemma for the critic, but as I have stated throughout, translation for indigenous writers can function as yet another kab'awilian device, offering them power over what terms they translate or not for readers.

I have shown throughout this book how Mesoamerican literature produced mainly in the late twentieth and early twenty-first centuries makes connections to a millenarian literary tradition. This corpus still faces the stigma and the prejudices attached to it by the publishing industry and reflected in its limited circulation and distribution. This said, many texts are gradually being translated and taught in higher education curriculums. My study of form and a periodization of indigenous literatures illustrate the resiliency of indigenous peoples in Mesoamerica. They also demonstrate that literary forms are not and do not have to be contained by disciplines. In the future, literature classes may incorporate readings of glyphs or other nonalphabetic texts along with novels or poetry.

Contemporary indigenous literature participates in a discourse of resistance to the nation-state's goals of assimilation and integration, therefore resisting a narrative of disappearance. But, what to make of literature that does not seek to function as political opposition or does not see itself as insurgent? This debate is relevant because many writers see themselves and their practice as simply part of a universal experience. And what of those texts where the violence of the state is less a concern than the viciousness of patriarchy? If indigenous writers cater to market demands and outsiders' notions of authorship, will they still be able to fruitfully contribute to an indigenous intellectual autonomy? The question of who is reading whom in this context continues to be fluid, as indigenous intellectuals are well aware of the uncertainty of appealing to the taste of certain audiences. Can literary criticism, even if it comes from outside indigenous communities, support or complement the work of indigenous writers? I do not have answers to these questions. Maybe the answers reside outside the realm of literature. The issues these questions raise make me acutely attuned to the various sites my work also misses. I am particularly referencing the emergence of various hip-hop, rock, and heavy metal groups in multiple indigenous languages as well as in Spanish that, in effect, circumvent the lettered city.[6] In the visual arts, the number of films and documentaries has grown exponentially, and some of them have deservedly reached international audiences.[7] Photography, digital projects, and other electronic media are increasingly used as tools for preservation and means of personal expression and represent significant sites of cultural production.[8] These modern and diverse creative sites share the same areas of interest as more traditional ones, such as weaving or storytelling.

Despite the recurrent genocidal tendencies by authoritarian regimes and the constant repression of personal expression in Mesoamerica, indigenous intellectuals have won key spaces from which to articulate their intellectual projects. In effect, indigenous literature forces readers to confront the elided condition of Latin America as a *plurilingual* and *pluricultural* site. It destabilizes the unitary conception of Latin America as well as challenges the subordinated status of indigenous languages and cultural practices. This body of work does not necessarily need to be studied only in relation to its difference from Latin American literature; these works can also be read in relation to each other. My study of contemporary indigenous literature shows it to be a practice that contributes and forges new and autonomous indigenous imaginaries. This said, more than ever, I am aware that nation-states structure indigenous identity even as we contest their impositions and limitations. Nation-states are gradually nationalizing indigenous languages and communities in their public discourse, which may jeopardize political autonomy in the future. This book stemmed from a need to frame an indigenous literary history beyond traditional nation-state nationalisms in Mesoamerica because indigeneity transcends the nation-state and could have critical implications for the political future of the region. This is my offering to future dialogues.

ACKNOWLEDGMENTS

THE PRODUCTION AND PUBLICATION of this book could not have been realized without the support and encouragement of mentors, colleagues, students, friends, and family. I am extremely grateful to J. Kēhaulani Kauanui and Jean O'Brien, the coeditors of the Critical Indigeneities Series, for believing in the promise of my work, and their insights and encouragement. I want to thank UNC Press editorial director, Mark Simpson-Vos, for his vote of confidence on the publication of this book, and Alex Martin and Mary Carley Caviness for their assistance in the final preparation of the book. I am indebted to the Literature Department at the University of California, San Diego (UCSD), for considering my research relevant in the configuration of the department, and in particular, for the welcoming reception of my work. I am especially grateful to my colleagues Rosaura Sánchez and Beatrice Pita for their critical feedback on various chapters of this work. I also want to thank Max Parra, Stephanie Jed, and Jin-Kyung Lee for their support and engagement. Outside my institution, I am extremely fortunate to have received important feedback on previous iterations of the manuscript from the sharp minds of Arturo Arias, Emilio del Valle Escalante, Carolina Jennifer Gómez, Claudia Milian Arias, and Juan Sánchez. I express my deep appreciation to Inés Hernández-Ávila, Elizabeth Martinez, Miguel Rocha Vivas, Maylei Blackwell, Josie Saldaña-Portillo, Robert Warrior, Mónica Albizúrez Gil and Alexandra Ortiz Wallner, Norma Klahn, Kirsten S. Gruesz, Rob Wilson, Carter Wilson, Sharon Farb, Norman Holland, Nancy Saporta Sternback, Alberto Sandoval, Rita Palacio, and Eduardo Contreras for their encouragement and support of my work. Special thanks to my family and friends who have supported me throughout the years. An immense debt of gratitude goes to the anonymous readers for UNC Press, whose perceptive comments, suggestions, and questions challenged me to make this a better book. I cannot thank them enough for their generous engagement and their time. I want to thank all of my wonderful students at UCSD, who have inspired me to push forward and who inspire me to be a better professor each year. I am grateful to Paulina González, Paulina Severiano-Pineda, Jackie Munguía, and Norell Martínez for their research assistance.

I want to recognize the following institutions and organizations for supporting and making this book possible. The Foreign and Language Area Studies Fellowship (FLAS) and a Foreign Language Fellowship from the Literature Department at the University of California, Santa Cruz, allowed me to immerse myself in the study of Maya K'iche' at the Francisco Marroquín Linguistics Project / Proyecto Lingüístico Marroquín (PLFM), located in Antigua, Guatemala. My stay there facilitated interactions with other cultural institutions such as the Center for Regional Research on Mesoamerica / Centro de Investigaciones Regionales de Mesoamerica (CIRMA), Oxlajuuj Keej Mayab' Ajtz'iib' / Thirteen Deer Maya Writers (OKMA), and the Ministry of Culture and Sports / Ministerio de Cultura y Deportes, which at the time was headed by the Q'anjobal critic, poet, and novelist Gaspar Pedro González. A year-long UC Mexus Research Fellowship facilitated my research in Mexico in 2003–4. It allowed me to directly establish relationships with ELIAC, Sna Jtz'ibajom / The House of the Writer, Fortaleza de la Mujer Maya (FOMMA), and the Centro Estatal de Literaturas y Artes en Lenguas Indígenas (CELALI). It also made my travel to Yucatán possible and helped me establish dialogue with many Maya writers. It also facilitated my conversations with academics at the Autonomous University of Yucatán (UADY) like Miguel Güemez-Pineda and Silvia Cristina Leirana Alcocer. The Ford Foundation, the UC President's Postdoctoral Fellowship, and the Council on Library and Information Resources Fellowship (CLIR) bolstered my research and writing endeavors between 2005 and 2010. The support of the Hellman Foundation, a Faculty Senate Grant, and UC San Diego's Center for the Humanities Fellowship have also helped me move forward with the completion of this book (2014–16).

I acknowledge and thank all the writers for their incredible efforts in establishing the field and for works that have had an impact on me in more ways than they will ever know. I want to particularly thank Jorge Cocom Pech, Feliciano Sánchez Chan, Pedro Martínez, Enrique Pérez López, Nicolás Huet Bautista, Diego Méndez Guzmán, Javier Castellanos Martínez, Marisol Ceh Moo, Ana Patricia Martínez Huchim, Enriqueta Lunez Pérez, Ruperta Bautista Vásquez, Natalia Toledo Paz, Irma Pineda Santiago, Yásnaya Aguilar, Humberto Ak'abal, Gaspar Pedro González, Maya Cú, Rosa María Chávez, Calixta Gabriel Xiquín, Isabel Juárez Espinosa, Clara Alicia Sens, and Mercedes García for their friendship and conversations throughout the years. I thank my colleagues Jessica Graham and Jillian Hernández for all the writing dates between Oceanside and North Park. Last but never least, I am forever indebted to my best friend and life partner, Abderrahim Jarane, for everything.

NOTES

Preface

1. Uruguay Cortazzo explains that *indigenous textualities* was the term agreed upon in 1991 to get away from the alphabetic emphasis haunting the term *literature*, and to move away from equating the term to established genres. Cortazzo, *Indios y latinos*, 50. I maintain the use of formal genres because as I explain in the book, their use by contemporary indigenous writers articulates political projects through recognizable genres, thus upending their elite connotations.
2. Benjamin, "The Task of the Translator," 70.
3. Ibid., 71.
4. "Hay que defender lo genuino de nuestras lenguas." Noh Tzec, *Workshop*, 2005. All translations from the Spanish to the English are mine unless noted otherwise.
5. I use the spelling that indigenous writers affiliated with CELALI utilize when describing their languages and identities. I am also aware that in most academic literature the standard spellings have been *Tzotzil* and *Tzeltal*, respectively.
6. "Fue un problema de rigurosidad en la traducción: eso si como en otros idiomas mayas las cualidades de la poesía apenas abren el campo de su acción." Reyes Matamoros, introduction to *Memoria del viento / Sbel sjol yo'onton ik'*, vi.
7. He read from the essay titled "El verdadero problema de la traducción en la literatura indígena" ("The True Problem of Translation in Indigenous Literature"), which has been published in two separate venues, but I will discuss the version he shared at the Primer Encuentro Literario Maya Zapoteca, November 11–14, 2010, in the offices of Escritores en Lenguas Indígenas, Asociación Civil (ELIAC), Mexico City.
8. "Tampoco basta con traducir, porque cualquier cosa se puede traducir, se puede buscar darle un sentido parecido en la otra lengua, pero inmediatamente se nota que algo anda mal, por ejemplo la frase: *Volcán de pétalos*." Castellanos Martínez, "El verdadero problema de la traducción."
9. "Esta frase (volcán de pétalos) nos remite a un volcán haciendo erupción y en lugar de arrojar lava, humo y ceniza; lanza, no flores, sólo sus pétalos, indudablemente que es una hermosísima imagen. En mi región no hay volcanes y son conocidos por los libros de texto o por la tele, y cuando hablan en zapoteco dicen 'volcan' sin el acento y para referirse a lo que expulsan dicen *dxichen*, o sea que caga que son desechos, además en esa región no se ha desglosado lingüísticamente la flor en todos sus componentes, como en español, por lo que la traducción vendría siendo *to volcan dxichen yej* (un volcán que caga flores) pero el escritor indígena logra hacer esta traducción *Ya' byalhje xtak yejé* que quiere decir 'el cerro de donde salieron pencas de flor,' que aunque es una bonita expresión pero ya no es lo que decía en español o lo que dice en zapoteco no es lo que está traducido al español." Ibid.

10. "Un escritor en lengua indígena, o en cualquier otra lengua, si se autotraduce, debe tener cuatro competencias: competencia lingüística en su lengua materna, competencia lingüística en la lengua a la que traduce el texto original, lengua terminal, competencia en la metodología de la traducción y, derivada de ésta, competencia literaria en la escritura de textos líricos, narrativos o de teatro; caso aparte lo es el ensayo. No más." Cocom Pech presented this paper at the Primer Encuentro Literario Maya Zapoteca.

11. I use "organic intellectuals," "cultural agents," and "organizers of culture"—in the Gramscian sense—interchangeably with "authors," "arts practitioners," and "situated intellectuals" throughout the manuscript.

12. "Escribir novelas, poemas, noticias, o carteles en un idioma maya contribuye a su mantenimiento." OKMA, *Maya' Chii'*, 120.

13. Venuti, *The Translation Studies Reader*, 3.

Introduction

1. This was the first time I met Adrián Esquino Lizco, from the Asociación Nacional Indígena Salvadoreña (ANIS). "Don't let them say we don't exist," Lizco pleaded, in reference to the staunch insistence of the Salvadoran nation-state on its mestizo identity. These are also the years when I met Crystos, Donna Good Leaf from the Mohawk nation, and many others.

2. PEN is an international writers association founded in 1902. The Sixty-Ninth PEN congress was held for the first time since its founding in Mexico City. At the time of the incident with Aridjis in 2003, I volunteered at ELIAC, which I will henceforth refer to in this book as the Indigenous Writers Association. Among the prominent writers attending the conference was Edith Gordimer. SOGEM is headquartered in Mexico City.

3. Casanova, *The World Republic of Letters*, xii.

4. Asturias's work received the highest honor, the "Mariano Gálvez" prize, for the best senior thesis of the year and the "Salvador Falla" award offered to the best thesis in the school of law. See Cardoza y Aragón, *Miguel Ángel Asturias*, 54.

5. Arturo Arias defines *Ladino* as a term originating in colonial times to designate someone who spoke Latin and who was at the service of the local priest, hence functioning as an intermediary. See Arias, "The Mayan Movement," 253. Today, *Ladino* refers to someone who does not identify as indigenous. In some instances it is used for someone who leaves his or her community and identifies with the existing dominant culture.

6. "A mí me produce incomodidad la introducción o preámbulo de las historias literarias consagradas a las literaturas indígenas. Siempre me pareció un poco mítica esa forma de organización porque es una entelequia; y me he preguntado si no obedecemos a una especie de dominante cronología: como evidentemente estaban antes y habían hecho su literatura, situémoslos antes para comenzar y terminar con el problema. Históricamente lo que ha ocurrido fue una cosa completamente diferente: es que las literaturas indígenas son un producto de la cultura europea sobre los materiales existentes." Qtd. in Pizarro, introduction to *La literatura latinoamericana*, 26–27.

7. I reclaim and repurpose the term *Mesoamerica* from archeology and anthropology for its explicit blurring of nation-state borders and its regional emphasis.

8. For indigenous literatures from the colonial period, see Brotherston, *La América indígena*; Garibay Kintana, *Historia de la literatura*; León-Portilla and Kemp, *The Broken Spears*; Bierhorst, *Latin American Folktales*; and Adorno, *Guáman Poma*, works that have developed the field of colonial indigenous literary studies.

9. Among the most salient with a Mesoamerican focus are Gutiérrez Chong, *National Myths and Ethnic Identities*; Perramon Ligorred, *U mahathanoob ti dzib / Las voces de la escritura*; Leirana Alcocer, "La literatura maya actual"; Tedlock, *2000 Years of Mayan Literature*; Máynez, *Lenguas y literaturas*; Montemayor and Frischmann, *Words of the True Peoples*, vols. 1–3; Lepe Lira, *Lluvia y viento*; Arias, "¿Tradición versus modernidad?"; Worley, *Telling and Being Told*; McDonough, *The Learned Ones*; and del Valle Escalante, *Teorizando las literaturas*.

10. I use *Maya* to describe writers in both Guatemala and Mexico because it expresses a cultural affinity that all the writers agree unites them despite modern-day borders. Government estimates report twenty indigenous languages in Guatemala and sixty in Mexico with some wide dialectic range, but Maya languages are spoken by 6 or 7 million people. Between Mexico and Guatemala, Maya languages outnumber the rest. The varieties of Zapotec spoken in Oaxaca, Mexico, are so different that they are not mutually intelligible to the writers.

11. Chacón, "Kabawil."

12. González Echevarría and Pupo-Walker consider the *Antología de poetas hispano-americanos* by Menéndez y Pelayo to be the first history of Spanish American literature. They do not mention that Menéndez y Pelayo states that he sees no merit in indigenous poetry and assumes Spanish to be a civilizing language. See Menéndez y Pelayo, *Antología*, 10. In their introduction to *The Cambridge History*, González Echevarría and Pupo-Walker write, "The burden of Latin American culture is a Western culture that extends back to the Middle Ages, when the foundations of the Spanish empire in the New World were set" (xvi).

13. "Los indios no tienen nada de común: ni lengua, ni tradición, ni tipo físico, ni costumbres, ni folklore, ni absolutamente nada. Si de Argentina a México y de Chile a Guatemala hay unidad, esta unidad es hispánica. Si no se admite lo hispano, no hay unidad." Salvador de Madariaga, qtd. in the prologue to Díaz-Plaja, *Antología mayor de la literatura hispanoamericana*, v.

14. See Arias, *Taking Their Word*, 66.

15. *Hispanic* and *Spanish America* as well as *Latin America* evoke the Latin aspects of French, Portuguese, and Spanish heritage. *Hispanic* emphasizes Spanish ancestry and language, leaving out the French/British Caribbean and Portuguese-speaking Brazil. *Spanish America* emerges with independence from Spain, accentuating a common language and culture.

16. Mignolo, *The Idea of Latin America*, 61–70.

17. McGuinness, "Searching for 'Latin America,'" 88–89.

18. Ibid.

19. Carlos González Peña's work on the history of Mexican literature declares that "Mexican literature is a branch of the Spanish, where part of the work that had to be done in New Spain was to incorporate indigenous peoples into 'Hispanic civilization'" ("La literatura mexicana es una rama de la española donde parte del trabajo que se tuvo

que hacer en la nueva España fue incorporar a los indios a la 'civilización hispánica'"). See González Peña, *Historia de la literatura mexicana*, 3–4. Major Latin American and national literature anthologies included a great number of Spanish texts and none or an insignificant number of indigenous works. For example, Stimson and Navas-Ruiz, *Literatura de la América hispánica*, includes texts by Cortés, Colón, Bartolomé de las Casas, and Díaz del Castillo, and only one indigenous/mestizo writer, El Inca Garcilaso de la Vega. See also Albareda and Garfias, *Antología de la poesía hispanoamericana*, which includes poems by peninsular and criollo writers, as well as numerous poems and odes to Cortés, with not the slightest mention of indigenous works.

20. Paul Kirchhoff coined the term *Mesoamerica* in the 1940s to define central Mexico and Central America. His definition was based on "geographic limits, ethnic composition, and cultural characteristics at the time of the conquest." Qtd. in Creamer, "Mesoamerica as a Concept," 35.

21. Víctor de la Cruz distinguishes two phases for Zapotec writing. The first tended toward phonetic representation, while the second consolidated an iconographic one. He postulates that this shift occurred in the classical period to facilitate communication among different linguistic groups living in Oaxaca. De la Cruz, "Reflexiones sobre la escritura," 487–501.

22. See Zapata, *Intelectuales indígenas*, 67–80.

23. See Mignolo and Walsh, *On Decoloniality*; Quijano, "Coloniality of Power"; and Maldonado-Torres, "Outline of Ten Theses on Coloniality and Decoloniality." Maldonado-Torres clarifies that "coloniality and decoloniality refer to the logic, metaphysics, ontology, and matrix of power created by the massive processes of colonization and decolonization" (10).

24. *Abya Yala* means land in maturation or land of eternal spring in the Guna language. The proposal to name the continent "Abya Yala" came from the Aymara leader Takir Mamani. Mamani argued that "placing foreign names on our towns, cities and continents is tantamount to subjecting our identity to the will of our invaders and their heirs." Cited in Albó, "Our Identity," 33. Also see del Valle Escalante, "Self-Determination: A Perspective from Abya Yala," for the renaming as an intellectual project.

25. Of course, this assumption is changing in great part due to the work being done in other disciplines. See Rappaport and Cummins, *Beyond the Lettered City*.

26. He notes that deciphering of Maya writing is guided by linguistic rather than literary goals. See Tedlock, *2000 Years of Mayan Literature*, 1–4.

27. "En realidad, desde la perspectiva indígena no hay una clara demarcación entre lo que es un cuento literario y la información médica, religiosa o histórica." Montemayor, *La literatura actual*, 46. By pointing out this limitation, I do not mean to take away from his solidarity with indigenous nations or diminish the important space he created for the dissemination of indigenous literatures.

28. Alegría, *Historia de la novela*, 9.

29. See Máynez, *Lenguas y literaturas*; and Leirana Alcocer, "La literatura maya actual" and *Conjurando el silencio*.

30. Genres are structures chosen by writers to ideally represent literary works. See Frye, *The Anatomy of Criticism*, 247.

31. Levine delinks forms from literary genres and argues that even social experience is organized by forms. My point is that that we must pay attention to forms in the

Mesoamerican context precisely because their use points to a politics around the autonomy of intellectual projects. See Levine, *Forms*, 2–3.

32. The genres of *lienzo* or land titles, for instance, were popular postcontact as the authors sought to prove land claims or royal genealogies. See Romero Frizz and Oudijk, "Los títulos primordiales."

33. See Alegría, *Historia de la novela*; and Moretti, *The Novel*.

34. For a fuller discussion of this idea, see Legrás, *Literature and Subjection*, 4.

35. See Gómez Grijalva, "Mi cuerpo es un territorio político," 263–76.

36. Paredes, "Hilando fino," 6–7.

37. Nez Perce and Tejana scholar Inés Hernández-Ávila differentiates between these models and U.S. multiculturalism. Hernández-Ávila remarks that interculturalism underscores "the actual dynamic nature and possibility of (inter)cultural exchange . . . [the concept is] tied to plurilingualism . . . [and therefore in] support of native languages." Hernández-Ávila, "The Power of Native Languages," 68. The strategic shift by Latin American nation-states to promote diversity has been linked to aggressive neoliberal policy and the necessity to calm any resistance by promoting multiculturalism, giving birth to what Charles Hale and Rosamel Millamán term—drawing from Silvia Rivera Cusicanqui—term *el indio permitido* loosely translated as "the tolerated Indian." Hale and Millamán argue that nation-states make certain types of concessions to indigenous peoples as long as the latter do not threaten to dominant state institutions. The neoliberal model, however, does not result in the cooptation of indigenous cultural productions by nation-states. See Hale and Millamán, "Cultural Agency."

38. De la Cruz, "Reflexiones sobre la escritura," 488.

39. De la Cruz, *La flor de la palabra / Guie' sti' diidxazá*, 18.

40. Marcus, *Monte Albán*, 189.

41. See May May, "La formación de escritores," 113–27. Silvia Cristina Leirana Alcocer, in "La literatura maya actual," identifies Maya'on as a group that published in newspapers and cultural magazines.

42. The workshops conducted by Carlos Montemayor through Culturas Populares aimed to link contemporary work with the ancient Maya tradition. The literary workshops conducted in Calkiní, Campeche, focused on the linguistic possibilities of the Maya language to produce poetry. Maya'on, an organization constituted mainly by public schoolteachers, aimed to foment Maya writing through didactic materials. See Leirana Alcocer, "La literatura maya actual."

43. ELIAC, "Declaración San Cristóbal," 15.

44. See Grandin, *The Last Colonial Massacre*.

45. Salazar Tetzagüic, *Rupach'uxik kina'oj qati't qamama' / Características de la literatura maya kaqchikel*, 30–31.

46. See del Valle Escalante, "El viaje a los orígenes."

47. Sam Colop, *Versos sin refugio* and *La copa y la raíz*.

48. See Warren, *Indigenous Movements*; and Konefal, *For Every Indio*.

49. There may be an earlier edition, but I have not seen it.

50. *Chatwalijoq*, year 5, no. 9.

51. The Accord on Identity and Rights of Indigenous Peoples was signed in 1995. Otilia Lux de Coti (Maya K'iche') was appointed minister of culture (2000–2004).

52. *Mestizo* refers to the paradigmatic national subject who has inherited both

Spanish and indigenous cultures but conforms to the mixed ideology of the state. While *mestizo* and *ladino* are sometimes used interchangeably, *ladino* is mainly used in Guatemala (and other Central American countries) as well as Chiapas to designate a nonindigenous person or an indigenous person who does not want to identify as indigenous.

53. See the discussion of Kamau Brathwaite's work in Reckin, "Tidalectic Lectures."
54. Recollet, "Gesturing Indigenous Futurities," 91–105.
55. Montemayor and Frischmann, *Words of the True Peoples*, 2:21.
56. de la Cruz, *El Pensamiento de los binningula'sa'*, 16–19. He differentiates between Binnigula'sa' as the ancestors or pre-Columbian peoples and Binnizá as the peoples after the Spanish invasion.
57. "A través de lápiz y papel comenzamos a defender nuestras lenguas, nuestras raíces, nuestra sabiduría, jp'ijiltik, jch'uleltik decían nuestros abuelos, guiados por el resplandor del Padre Sol y la Madre Luna, caminamos en las cuatros esquinas del Osil Balamil 'Universo.'" Statement from the Board of Directors of UNEMAZ, http://www.diariodechiapas.com/landing/huellas-artisticas-y-literarias-de-la-asociacion-de-escritores-mayas-zoques-a-c/ (accessed August 11, 2017).
58. Carlos López, in his discussion of the *Popol Vuh*, asserts that "Mayan cosmogonies might allow us to enrich our own epistemological perspectives." López inadvertently reproduces the idea that Mayas simply add to (Western) epistemology. López, "The *Popol Wuj*," 68.
59. Monasterios, "Uncertain Modernities," 556.
60. The spelling of this element varies in both glyphic and alphabetic representations. When citing other people's references to this term, I will adhere to their spellings.
61. Milbrath, "The Maya Lord of the Smoking Mirror."
62. Mendizábal, *El kab'wil en nuestra historia*, 5–13.
63. Canters and Jantzen, *Forever Fluid*, 10.
64. Ibid., 11.
65. Ibid., 13.
66. Lenkersdorf clarifies that every statement includes the speaker and the receptor. In Spanish or English, one utters a phrase such as "I told you" without thinking about the receptor, but in Maya Tojolabal, the statement is not just about the speaker but also about the receptor, so one would say in the same statement, "I speak, you listen." One can't state "I say" without including the other. He offers other examples where the singular and plural pronouns are not linguistically separated by speakers. See Lenkersdorf, "Lenguas y diálogo intercultural."
67. The anthropologist Sergio Mendizábal focuses on chemb'il, a strategic Maya Mam concept that articulates a periodization against hegemonic notions of history, a woven Mesoamerican matrix represented by four pillars, but he also recognizes kab'awil as a Mesoamerican civilization concept in *El Kaba'awil en muestra historia*, 5–13. In other initiatives, such as the one proposed by the Sotsil Jay Cultural Center's publication, the members propose *patän samaj*, in the Maya Kaqchikel language, to describe an art practice that is not divorced from other social realms. In their theorization, the Maya artist labors for the generation and rebirth of life, ethical and aesthetic values par excellence. See Movimiento de Artistas Mayas Ruk'u'x y Centro Cultural

Sotz'il Jay, *Algunas palabras sobre el trabajo del artista maya*, 209. All of these concepts represent a Mesoamerican cosmolectics.

68. See Milbrath, "The Maya Lord of the Smoking Mirror."
69. Ibid.
70. See thirteenth ruler of Copán, Honduras: Waxaklahun Ubah K'awil.
71. De la Garza Camino and Cuevas García, "El dios K'awiil," 99.
72. Colas, in "Monumentos mayas," discusses the Maya monuments in the Rufino Tamayo de Oaxaca. Of interest here is monument 2, which describes an important political ascension where the translated glyphs *ch'amaw K'awiil* read as a transitive verb, "es tomado el k'awiil," or *k'awill* is taken; that is, taking possession of power. See Doesburg, *Pictografía y escritura*, 80.
73. See López, "The *Popol Wuj*," 68–84.
74. The vigorous debate about the spelling of the title of the sacred text deserves more space, but I should at least note that since Chávez's translation, others have surfaced. The K'iche' linguist and poet Luis Enrique Sam Colop contests Chávez's argument for changing the *Popol* to *Pop*. I will not address the difference between *Pop* and *Popol* other than to note that Pop means "mat" and also "month," whereas Popol means "council." I do acknowledge that *Popol* is the most widely accepted translation, but in everyday speech most K'iche' speakers prefer *Pop Wuj*. Vuh and Wuj differ in my analysis due to the instability of orthography, but the K'iche pronunciation is "wooh," meaning "book." Falla, *El Popol Wuj: Una interpretación para el día de hoy*, discusses the difference in detail. I use Adrián Inés Chávez's version, because he is the first modern Maya-K'iche intellectual to explain the term as a Maya-K'iche' concept. Adrián Inés Chávez, *Pop Wuj*. I use *Popol Vuh* because it is the spelling most English speakers recognize.
75. W. E. B. Dubois theorizes a similar ontology for African Americans as "double consciousness," but, given kab'awil's glyphic origin, the similarities appear coincidental. *Kab'awil*'s use in the twenty-first century as a social ontology has a strong echo in Du Bois's thought; see *The Souls of Black Folks*.
76. See Sam Colop, "The Discourse of Concealment in 1992," 89–113.
77. See Columbus's "First letter" in *Four Voyages to the New World*.
78. Schevill, *Evolution in Textile Design*, 20.
79. Ibid.
80. Ibid., 7.
81. Ibid.
82. Ibid., 22.
83. Ibid.
84. López Coti et al., "La interculturalidad."
85. Huipiles are typically handwoven blouses, though nowadays women also wear manufactured ones.
86. "Kab'awil es todo, es el tiempo, el espacio, el movimiento." Upún Sipac, *Maya' Ajilab'äl Q'ij / La cuenta maya de los días*, 21.
87. Morales Sic, "Religión y espiritualidad maya," 250.
88. "Para la filosofía maya, el kab'awil es el constructor de una teoría de conocimiento que se reconoce como la lógica inclusiva, porque el kab'awil es un símbolo desarrollado

por los antepasados mayas para lograr una mejor valorización y comprensión del contexto múltiple y a la vez unitario en el que se habita." Ibid.

89. Matul Morales and Cabrera, *La cosmovisión maya*, 1:105–7.

90. "'Kawilo saqil hab'e' eso quiere decir . . . no solo mira tu camino, sino que debes mirar en trasparencia los pasos y la dirección . . . no solo el camino físico . . . sino también el camino del destino." Menchú, "Importancia del Congreso de literatura indígena de América," 10.

91. Batzibal Tujal, "Mujer maya: Rectora de nuestra cultura," 25.

92. "Podríamos decir que en casi todos los trajes de nuestro pueblo aparece nuestra filosofía representada en el Kab'awil, el Doble Mirada, el que ve de día y ve de noche, el que ve el pasado y ve el porvenir." Ibid., 30.

93. "Estos tejidos equivalen a una especie de alfabeto maya, por lo que se dice que nos vestimos con libros que han sido escritos hace miles de años." Ibid., 34.

94. "Nos han enseñado a escribir nuestra lógica de una manera estética." Ibid., 30.

95. Hostnig and Vásquez Vicente, *Nab'ab'l qtanam*.

96. "The system known as *usos y costumbres* represents what critics consider to be a cultural feature of indigenous societies with a Mesoamerican style of political organization and representation." See Sorroza Polo and Danielson, "Political Subsystems," 169.

97. I am relying here on Walter Mignolo's definition of the decolonization process as "epistemological reconstitution." See Mignolo, introduction to *Cultural Studies*, 164.

98. "A España le regreso la cruz porque con esa subyugaron a nuestros pueblos; la espada porque con esa destruyeron nuestros pueblos. Pero hay algo que yo no le regreso a España: *El Quijote*. Gracias a *El Quijote* y al español, puedo escribir mi lengua materna." Miguel Jorge Cocom Pech, personal communication, July 2014.

99. Even Marisol Ceh Moo, who in my mind represents the younger generation, avers that to understand contemporary Maya writing one must understand the Maya's literary past. Ceh Moo, "Situación de la literatura actual."

100. "Yo aprendí la sabiduría del libro. Después . . . el libro ya no aparecía porque su contenido ya lo guardaba en mi memoria." Regino, "Na Sabi a María Sabina," 3.

101. Feliciano Sánchez Chan, interview, Mérida, Mexico, March 2004.

102. Past, *Incantations*, 29.

103. Ibid.

104. Ibid., 31.

105. See Burns, *An Epoch of Miracles*, 21, 72–73; and Carmack, *Evolución del reino k'iche'*, 110.

106. González, *La otra cara*, 106. "Este había sido el punto de partida—según recordaría él más adelante—para comenzar una doble personalidad, doble actitud, doble nombre, doble comportamiento: una forma ante su gente y la otra ante los ladinos."

107. "Aquellos eran dos mundos, dos vivencias y dos conceptos de uno mismo: el de la escuela y el de la familia. Cuando los fines de semana comenzaba a habituarme a la alegría del hogar, debía despojarme de ella y dejarla colgada el día lunes e irme con una personalidad postiza y unas costumbres artificiales a la escuela." González, *La otra cara*, 109.

108. Qtd. in Hernández Castillo, "The Emergence of Indigenous Feminism," 226.

109. See Gruzinski, *La colonización del imaginario*, 104–48.

110. See Moretti, *The Novel*; González Echevarría, *Myth and Archive*; and Kundera, *The Art of the Novel*.

Chapter One

1. See King, "Inventing the Indian," 1–51.
2. See de las Casas, *The Devastation of the Indies*. El Inca Garcilaso de la Vega's work, however, was not disseminated until the nineteenth century.
3. López de Gómara's *crónica* was controversial at the time of its publication because he had never set foot in the Americas but instead took the information from the conquistadores who returned to Spain, prompting Bernal Díaz del Castillo to write the *Historia verdadera de la conquista de la Nueva España*.
4. For a visual timeline of the letter's printing and translation history, see "The Columbus Letter."
5. My idea of literature in this context obviously extends to verbal arts as well as other mechanisms used to relate stories.
6. Of course, this may not necessarily be historically accurate as glyphic writing may have already been in decline by the time the Spaniards arrived in the Maya area.
7. Coe, *Breaking the Maya Code*, 117–18.
8. De Landa, *An Account of the Things of Yucatán*, 169.
9. Ibid.
10. Although expelled from Yucatán at the written request of the Maya and other missionaries for his cruelty and infamous *actos de fé*, Franciscan Bishop Diego de Landa's *relación* offered scholars like Charles Étienne Brasseur de Bourbourg and Ernest Forstemann in the late nineteenth century concrete insights into the calendar days as well as the phonetic component of Mayan glyphs.
11. See de la Cruz, *La flor de la palabra / Guie' sti' diidxazá*, 9.
12. "Son tantos los desatinos de sus historias y pinturas que el demonio les persuadía, que es indecente referirlas . . . como su lenguaje era tan metafórico, como el de los palestinos, lo que querían persuadir, hablaban siempre con parábolas, y sus historiadores formaban caracteres, de lo que decían." See de la Cruz, *La flor de la palabra / Guie' sti' diidxazá*, 33.
13. The 1880s mark the beginning of academic inquiries into Mayan writing. Many European aficionados of antiquities moved forward in understanding calendrical notations. Monuments began to be accepted as historical and political structures after 1958 due to Linda Schele's work on the subject. The phonetic dimension of Mayan writing was discussed by Yuri Knorozov in 1952 and expanded upon in writings from the 1970s. See Coe, *Breaking the Maya Code*; and Colas, "Monumentos mayas."
14. Restall, "Heirs to the Hieroglyphs," 247.
15. See Restall, "Heirs to the Hieroglyphs"; Boone and Mignolo, *Writing without Words*; Coe, *Breaking the Maya Code*; and Tedlock, *2000 Years of Mayan Literature*.
16. Marcus's "La escritura zapoteca" argues it is the most ancient writing system in Mesoamerica, whereas Urcid's "Zapotec Writing" argues Mesoamerican writing systems emerged simultaneously.
17. Urcid, "Zapotec Writing," 15.

18. For specific readings, see Tedlock, *2000 Years of Mayan Literature*; Freidel, Schele, and Parker, *Maya Cosmos*; and Stuart and Stuart, *Palenque*.

19. See Coe, *Breaking the Maya Code*, 227–29.

20. Sten, *Codices of Mexico*, 7–8.

21. See Boone and Mignolo, *Writing without Words*, 4.

22. For example, Gelb, in 1963, stated, "I find myself thus in complete accord with the opinions of two eminent Americanists as expressed in the following: 'No native race in America possessed a complete writing.'" Gelb, *A Study of Writing*, 59. Bloomfield, in his book published in 1933, identified the Aztec and Maya systems of writing as largely hieroglyphic, at the early stages of development in writing systems, when thinking about the transition from picture to real writing. Bloomfield, *Language*, 73, 284–85.

23. See Marcus, *Mesoamerican Writing Systems*, 17.

24. Ibid., 28.

25. Ibid., 17.

26. "No podemos olvidar que, en el caso del español por ejemplo, las normas escriturarias todavía son vacilantes a lo largo de todo el siglo XVI y que se fijarán apenas en el primer tercio del siglo XVIII." ALMG, *La planificación lingüística en países multilingües de Abya Yala / Cholb'al ub'antajik ri kitzijob'aal ri amaq'-tinamit Abya Yala*, 15.

27. Schroeder, *The Conquest All over Again*, 4–7.

28. "Es posible pensar que el empleo de la nueva forma de escritura por los indígenas se debió a una razón práctica, aquella de defender lo suyo ante la nueva autoridad. . . . Si escritura y poder habían estado asociados y uno apoyaba al otro, es probable que esta misma manera de actuar los influyera para que utilizaran la nueva forma de registro." Romero Frizzi, "Los zapotecos," 39.

29. David Murray, in reference to North American tribes but relevant to the discussion at hand, argues that "the assumption that [alphabetic] literacy necessarily moved the Indians across the great divide into abstract thought, and that their failure to learn it was because of intellectual deficiency in this respect are thrown into doubt by the rapid spread of writing in situations where it was fulfilling a culturally conserving role." See Murray, *Forked Tongues*, 26.

30. See Bricker, "The Last Gasp," 39–50.

31. See Romero Frizzi and Oudijk, "Los títulos primordiales," 18–48.

32. Tedlock, *Popol Vuh*, 63.

33. Ibid., 198.

34. Ibid., 63.

35. Havelock, *Origins of Western Literacy*, 58.

36. "Aún no terminaba de contarse 11 Ahau [11.17.0.0.0: 1539–1559], cuando llegaron los españoles, hombres arrojados. Del oriente vinieron cuando llegaron por primera vez aquí hasta esta tierra de nosotros los hombres mayas, en el año *domini* 1513. 9 Ahau [11.18.0.0.0: 1559–1579], comenzó el cristianismo; se verificó el Bautismo. Dentro de este mismo katún llegó el primer Obispo de nombre Toral. También cesó el Colgamiento." See Barrera Vásquez and Rendón, *El libro de los libros de Chilam Balam*, 42.

37. All English citations in this section are from the translation by Ruth Gabler reproduced in León-Portilla and Shorris, *In the Language of Kings*, 531–35.

38. Ibid., 531.
39. Ibid.
40. "Constituyendo el único ejemplo conocido hasta hoy de un códice de este tipo de literatura en toda el área maya." Barrera Vázquez, "Los cantares de Dzitbalché," 350.
41. These scenes can be found in Bonampak, Toniná, and Palenque, as well as other important sites.
42. "En medio de la plaza / está un hombre / atado al fuste de la columna / pétrea, bien pintado / con el bello / añil. Puéstole han muchas / flores de Balché para que se perfume; / así en las palmas de sus manos, en / sus pies, como en su cuerpo también." "X-Colom-Che," 357.
43. Morales Damián, , 144.
44. "Endulza tu ánimo, bello / hombre; tú vas / a ver el rostro de tu Padre / en lo alto. No habrá de / regresarte aquí sobre / la tierra bajo el plumaje / del pequeño Colibrí o / bajo la piel / . . . del bello Ciervo. / del Jaguar, de la pequeña / Mérula o del pequeño Paují. / Date ánimo y piensa / solamente en tu Padre; no / tomes miedo; no es / malo lo que se te hará." Ibid., 357–58.
45. Calvo, "The Politics of Print."
46. De Acosta, *Natural and Moral History*, 340.
47. González Echevarría and Pupo-Walker, *The Cambridge History*, 197.
48. See González Echevarría, *Myth and Archive*.
49. See Cornejo Polar, *Escribir en el aire*.
50. "Mientras no podamos leer sus códices e inscripciones, éstas forman parte del acervo arqueológico y no del acervo literario." De la Garza, *Literatura maya*, ix.
51. See Mignolo, *The Darker Side of the Renaissance*, 125–29.
52. Mignolo, "Preamble," 16.
53. Goody, *The Power of the Written Tradition*; Rousseau, *The First and Second Discourses*.
54. Collins and Blot, "Literacy and Literacies," 3. For other discussions in Spanish, consult Olson and Torrance, *Cultura escrita y oralidad*.
55. Ong, *Orality and Literacy*; Goody, *The Domestication of the Savage Mind*; Goody and Watt, "The Consequences of Literacy."
56. Finnegan, *Literacy and Orality*, 11.
57. Said, *Culture and Imperialism*; Watt, *The Rise of the Novel*.
58. Jacques Derrida's seminal work points to the logocentrism of writing (in its alphabetic script) as well as the epistemological contradictions of writing and speech in philosophy. As Derrida observes, logocentrism privileges writing and reason over mythos and orality. He further underlines that the significance of writing in the West has not been uncontested, and that even in Western antiquity, writing was not trusted because it was mediated and incapable of representing truth in the same way that speech did. He writes that "writing cannot be thought of outside the horizon of intersubjective violence." Derrida, *Of Grammatology*, 120–21. His circuitous argument that speech could not exist without writing closely echoes the project that Maya and Zapotec intellectuals and other indigenous writers undertake by writing down the oral tradition in the modern Latin alphabet and acknowledging glyphic writing.

59. Senner, *The Origins of Writing*, 9.

60. A shift in the way orality, writing, and literature were understood in the United States and Europe serves as an important contrast to the way *letrados* established the genealogies of Latin American literature in the nineteenth century. The historical expansion of the concept of literature as "culture preserved in letters ... to the imaginative and affective utterance, spoken or written," espoused mainly by literary critics in the United States and Europe, swayed understandings of indigenous literature from Mesoamerica. Critics were generally influenced by the Romantic movement in the nineteenth century and its new interest in oral literature. It was not until then, argues Arnold Krupat in *The Turn to the Native: Studies in Criticism and Culture* (1996), that the illiterate Indians of the New World were granted a literary sensibility. In effect, this new conception of the literary directly corresponds to the ways texts like the *Popol Vuh* and *The Books of Chilam Balam*, which were written postcontact but evoke a pre-Columbian past, were received for the first time in Europe and the United States in the late nineteenth and early twentieth centuries. But the European and U.S. American fascination with orality in these texts contrasted with Latin America's emphasis on written literature during the same period.

61. Mignolo, *The Darker Side of the Renaissance*, 29–67; Seed, "Taking Possession," 112–33; Lienhard, *La voz y su huella*; Cornejo Polar, *Escribir en el aire*.

62. See Lienhard, *La voz y su huella*, esp. chap. 1; and Mignolo, *The Darker Side of the Renaissance*.

63. See the introduction in Rappaport and Cummins, *Beyond the Lettered City*.

64. Rama, *The Lettered City*, 71–75.

65. Ibid.

66. For background on this debate, see the critical edition of Arguedas, *El zorro de arriba*.

67. See Cornejo Polar, *Escribir en el aire*, 7.

68. Of course, these have been criticized for their hegemonic use, but my point is that these discourses have not disappeared in the twenty-first century. See Beverley, *Subalternity*; de la Campa, *Latin Americanism*; and Moreiras, *The Exhaustion of Difference*.

69. See Cornejo Polar, "Mestizaje"; Beverley, *Subalternity*; Beverley, "The Im/possibility"; and Taylor, *Indigeneity*.

70. Vasconcelos, *La raza cósmica*; Gamio, *Forjando patria*.

71. Rama takes the concept of *transculturación* from the Cuban anthropologist Fernando Ortiz, who coined it to counter the notion of acculturation. Rama's *Transculturación narrativa en América Latina* was not published until 1982, but his main theoretical armature can be traced to his article "Los procesos de transculturacion en América Latina."

72. Cornejo Polar, "Mestizaje"; Cornejo Polar, "Indigenismo"; García Canclini, *Hybrid Cultures*.

73. See Arroyo, "Transculturation, Syncretism, and Hybridity."

74. See Arias, "¿Tradición versus modernidad"; del Valle Escalante, *Teorizando las literaturas*; Worley, *Telling and Being Told*; Lepe Lira, *Lluvia y viento*; and McDonough, *The Learned Ones*.

75. "Las fuentes de la tradición oral de los pueblos indígenas no son 'primitivas': son

al menos la tradición escrita y oral española y la tradición escrita y oral de la civilización prehispánica." Montemayor, *Arte y trama*, 22.

76. "El concepto de la oralidad es un constructo elaborado desde la cultura escrita." Morales López, *Raíces de la ceiba*, 65–66.

77. "No puede hablarse de la oralidad sino desde una posición grafocentríca." Ibid., 66.

78. Del Valle Escalante, *Teorizando las literaturas*; Arias, Cárcamo-Huechante, and del Valle Escalante, "Literaturas de Abya Yala"; Worley, *Telling and Being Told*.

79. "En el nivel cultural (García Canclini, 1989) y en el ámbito de la literatura latinoamericana (Rama, 1980 y Cornejo Polar, 1978), se plantea como una fórmula que dé salida a la heterogeneidad cultural y lingüística del continente, un 'hibridismo' como la síntesis deseada en la constitución de la cultura y la literatura." Muyulema, "Una óptica quichua," 21.

80. "No obstante, aun en esta perspectiva, se percibe el anhelo de unidad, anhelo que lleva implícita la asimilación del uno por el otro; de la cultura criolla europeizante como paradigma a cuya constitución las culturas indígenas aportarían con la cosmética, en el mejor de los casos." Ibid.

81. Spivak, "Can the Subaltern Speak?"

82. "Extinguir el idioma de los primeros indígenas." Sam Colop, *La planificación lingüística en países de Abya Yala / Cholb'al ub'antajik ri kitzijob'aal ri amaq'-tinamit Abya Yala*, 3.

83. "Cuando los pueblos indígenas quedaron bajo el dominio de la cultura y lengua que vino de Europa, perdieron el arte propio de escribir y fueron sometidos a otro tipo de arte que ya no tenían que ver nada con su cosmovisión propia." López Gómez, "Una propuesta," 16.

84. "Perdidas nuestras formas de escrituras, necesariamente debemos adoptar el alfabeto castellano y forzarlo para darle forma escrita a nuestras lenguas." Ak'abal, "Literatura maya," 9.

85. Aguilar Gil, "(Is There) an Indigenous Literature?," 59.

86. See Sam Colop, "Maya Poetics," 11.

87. Ibid., 12.

88. Montejo, "The Power of Language," 47.

89. Ibid.

90. "En la época prehispánica los binnigula'sa' crearon un sistema de escritura para representar su lengua ... algunas en lápidas o esculturas integradas a los edificios y otras sueltas, estelas elaboradas por los escribas de aquella época." De la Cruz, "Reflexiones sobre la escritura," 490.

91. De la Cruz, *La flor de la palabra / Guie' sti' diidxazá*, 8.

92. "La palabra que esculpieron nuestros abuelos / sobre las piedras, / la que cantaron en la noche, / cuando hicieron su danza, / la que usaron para decorar sus casas, dentro de sus santuarios, / en sus palacios reales? / Quien trajo la segunda lengua / vino a matarnos junto a nuestra palabra, / vino a pisotear a la gente del pueblo como si fuéramos gusanos / caídos del árbol, tirados en la tierra. "¿Quiénes somos, cuál es nuestro nombre?" De la Cruz, *La flor de la palabra / Guie' sti' diidxazá*, 105.

93. "Toda oscuridad era / cuando nacieron los zapotecas. / Brotaron de los viejos

árboles, / como la ceiba, / del vientre de las fieras nacieron, / como el tigre, el lagarto.// Al caer la gran luz / que lanzó el sol alto, / nuestro padre grande, / entrelazaron sus manos / con las nutrias, / también madres nuestras. / Se salvaron los zapotecas / al flotar sobre el agua / como tortugas grandes. / Se inundaron de agua / como sierpes celentéreos, / cargando sus hijos en los pezones." (Nacáahui dóo biráa guéela / dxíi gúule cáa Binni Záa. / Bindáani cáa lúu xcúu yáaga / nandxóo síica yáaga bióongo, / biáale cáa ndáani máani dúuxhu / síica béedxe, síica máni béeñee.// Ráa biéete biáani dóo / bizáani gubíidxa zóo, / Iáani bixhóoze dóo dúu / bidxáaga náa cáa bée / cáa dxáa bíicu níisa, / Iáaca mée ucáa jñáa dúu. / Raquée biláa cáa binni záa / ráa biníidxi cáa bée / síica bíigu ngóola, / biláahua cáa bée Iúu níisa / síica béenda gáali / nuáa xhíiñi íique xhíidxi.) Matus, "Los zapotecas / Binni Záa," blog entry in *400 elefantes: Revista nicaraguense de arte y cultura*, August 12, 2009, https://400elefantes.wordpress.com/2009/08/12/binni-zaa-los-zapotecas-poemas-de-macario-matus/.

94. Pineda Santiago, "Laanu." The original in Zapotec and Spanish reads: "Zadundarunu xtiidxanu / xhiiñi yaga nga laanu / laaca' gudiica' bandá' neza ziuunu / xhiiñi guié nga laanu / laaca' gunica' qui gusiaandanu / "Nosotros" / Nuestra palabra seguirá siendo canto / somos hijos de los árboles / que darán sombra a nuestro camino / somos hijos de las piedras / que no permitirán el olvido."

95. "Y sobre la piedra, aparecen las huellas de sus manos." González, *Kotz'ib'*, 7.

96. "Un enjambre de signos / brotaron entre reguero de glifos: / Incrustados en los amplios frontispicios, / enraizados en los silenciosos monumentos. / Rodaron sobre las escalinatas / cayeron de las bóvedas / surgieron de los altos y bajos relieves, / estallaron como rugidos de jaguares / entre la espesura de los verdes jades; / como sinfonía de tambores y atabales / enrollados entre pentagramas de amate." Ibid., 141.

97. "Nuestros padres y madres de la antigüedad sabían leer y escribir. Se olvidaron cuando les quitaron sus escritos los españoles. Por eso solo sabemos escribir nuestra lengua como si nuestros ojos estuvieran cerrados." Qtd. in Morales López, *Raíces de la ceiba*, 66.

98. See the discussion of hieroglyphic literacy in Sturm, "Old Writing," 114; and Warren, *Indigenous Movements*, 148–62.

99. Jorge Cocom Pech, Ana Patricia Martínez Huchim, and Luis Enrique Sam Colop, among others, have participated in workshops to learn glyphs.

Chapter Two

1. Morales López follows the work of other scholars like Enrique Ballon, who view indigenous literary production in opposition to writing and modernity. She notes that "for Ballon (1995), oral production—stories and Native poetry— which circulate among ancestral ethnic groups where neither the technology of writing nor modernity have penetrated, constitutes what he terms ethno-literature." This posture leaves out the city dwellers, creative writers who seek to imagine alternatives to mainstream literature. ("Para Enrique Ballon [1995], la producción oral—relatos y poesía nativa—que circula entre los grupos étnicos ancestrales, donde aún no ha penetrado la tecnología de la escritura, ni la modernidad constituye la llamada etnoliteratura.") Morales López, *Raíces de la ceiba*, 86.

2. "De ahí la pertinencia de realizar un análisis vinculado con la mitocrítica y con la antropología para vislumbrar si los textos desempeñan una función en la cotidianidad de las diversas comunidades estudiadas, de ser afirmativa la hipótesis comprender, entonces, cómo se manufacturan en el imaginario indígena." Ibid., 94.

3. Braz, "Collaborative Authorship and Indigenous Literatures."

4. In response to the anthropologist David Stoll's accusation that the events narrated in Rigoberta Menchú's testimonio did not all take place, Menchú distanced herself from the testimonio, arguing that Elizabeth Burgos-Debray was the author. See Arias, *The Rigoberta Menchú Controversy*.

5. See Faudree, "What Is an Indigenous Author?," 5–35.

6. "La tensión [entre la] oralidad y escritura se produce en grado extremo porque las estrategias básicas de composición literaria son producto, por un lado, de las formas tradicionales de la oralidad que los autores viven cotidianamente en sus comunidades; y por otro, de un tipo de racionalidad diferente que otorga un lugar primordial a la palabra y su sonido." Lepe Lira, *Lluvia y viento*, 127.

7. "Desde lo primitivo subvierte lo culto.... La escritura se convirtió en un artefacto de los indios para revivir su lengua y su cultura." Ibid., 129.

8. Quijano, "Coloniality of Power, Eurocentrism, and Latin America."

9. See, for example, Alvarado, *Don't Be Afraid, Gringo*; and Reuque Paillalef, *When a Flower Is Reborn*. For more background on the testimonio, see the critical essays compiled in Gugelberger, *The Real Thing*.

10. While some early literary productions may include testimonial-like characteristics, the fundamental difference lies in the fact that they are free from any form of intervention or mediation. My argument does not seek to relegate testimonio to the fringes of literature; instead, it is an interrogation about the ownership of the intellectual means of production.

11. "En este contexto, la irrupción autoral indígena en el sistema literario canónico—sea poesía escrita, novela o cuento—posee hitos tempraneros en dicha contemporaneidad, los que paulatinamente se hacen visibles con la autoridad alcanzada por el testimonio." ("In this context, the indigenous authorial irruption in the canonical literary system—whether it be written poetry, a novel or short story—possesses early milestones in its contemporaneity, which gradually become visible with the authority reached by the testimonio.") Arias, Cárcamo-Huechante, and del Valle Escalante, "Literaturas de Abya Yala," 7.

12. Needless to say, I am not dismissing the important political work those testimonies did for various communities. See, for example, Menchú, *I, Rigoberta Menchú*; Alvarado, *Don't Be Afraid, Gringo*; Dalton, *Miguel Mármol*; and Barrios de Chungara, *Let Me Speak!*

13. Figueroa Saavedra, "Palabras olvidadas," 74.

14. Critical anthropology has supported indigenous movements. Many anthropologists have explicitly supported indigenous projects of cultural autonomy, sometimes directly helping by securing funds for organizations.

15. The theorization of the figure of the author by Michel Foucault, Walter Benjamin, and Roland Barthes informs my analysis of indigenous authorship, but I filter this through an indigenous cosmolectics.

16. The Maya Kaqchikel writer Luis de Lión emerged as an independent voice with the publication of his short story collection *Los zopilotes*. Government forces kidnapped and disappeared him as he left the university in Guatemala City on May 15, 1984, during the most violent decade in Guatemala. See Arias, "Asomos de la narrativa indígena maya"; Palacios, "Luis de Lión's *El tiempo principia en Xibalbá*"; and del Valle Escalante, "El viaje a los orígenes."

17. See Ramírez Castañeda, *La educación indígena en México*.
18. Earle, *The Return of the Native*, 190.
19. See Dawson, "Histories and Memories," 83.
20. Ibid.
21. Ibid.
22. Ibid., 83–84.
23. Ibid.
24. Fischer and Brown, *Maya Cultural Activism in Guatemala*, 209.
25. Earle, *The Return of the Native*, 190.
26. Perera, *Unfinished Conquest*, 9, 65.
27. See Herranz et al., *Educación bilingüe e intercultural en Centroamérica y México*.
28. Yanes, "Guatemalan Spanish as Act of Identity," 5.
29. Emma Delifina Chirix García (Maya Kaqhikel) discusses the ways this school disciplined Mayan women's bodies. See Chirix García, *Cuerpos, poderes y políticas*, 124–38.
30. See Casey, "Indigenismo."
31. Chirix García, *Cuerpos, poderes y políticas*, 124–38.
32. Iwańska, *The Truth of Others*, 47.
33. Ibid.
34. "Tanto la corriente liberal como la marxista favorecieron la pérdida de la identidad étnica de los grupos indígenas." Waldman, "El florecimiento de la literatura indígena actual en México," 64.
35. Bastos and Camus, *Quebrando el silencio*, 17–18.
36. "Que los idiomas Mayas han existido solo en el plano oral muestra que en lo escrito se han desarrollado muy poco por la misma condición política a la que han sido sujetos." Jiménez Sánchez, "Tensión entre idiomas," 13–14.
37. López Hernández distinguishes among the oral tradition, *recopilación*, and creation. See López Hernández, "Géneros literarios."
38. Nefi Fernández Acosta, personal communication, Mexico City, 2004.
39. Barthes, "The Death of the Author," 147.
40. Foucault, "What Is an Author?," 107.
41. The "spiritual" sensibility evoked here does not necessarily have a direct relationship to "magic realism," although it has informed a style of writing popularized as "magic realism." By the spiritual I simply refer to the everyday material realities perceived by indigenous peoples, along with its sacred aspects.
42. See Izquierdo y de la Cueva, "Reseña de *Secretos del abuelo*"; and del Valle Escalante, "Ambivalence and Contradiction."
43. Sommer, "Rigoberta's Secrets."
44. "Procedente de la ciudad de Campeche, donde trabajaba como checador de boletos en la compañía de Ferrocarriles Unidos de Yucatán, llegaba vestido con un pantalón

y chamarra color beige; la chamarra siempre abierta le permitía lucir una camiseta blanca—marca Pirata—, hecha en China; traía también un sombreo de fieltro café oscuro.... En la mano derecha traía aferrada una radio portátil, que emitía canciones norteñas al compás del acordeón." Cocom Pech, *Secretos del abuelo / Muk'ult'an in nool*, 86–87.

45. "Nunca faltaron ejemplares del *Diario de Yucatán* y de la revista *Alarma* que, a punto de caer, traía en cualquiera de las bolsas traseras de su pantalón." Ibid., 87.

46. "En esos días, y a falta de libros y revistas ilustradas, hacíamos esfuerzos por llevar a nuestras cabecitas duras la imagen de todas esas maravillas descritas en las narraciones." Ibid., 49.

47. "Long Live Christ the King!." Ibid., 97.

48. "Yo ya no escuché más sus palabras. Sólo evocaba al coro en el pórtico de la iglesia confundiéndose con el incesante repique de campanas." Ibid.

49. "Siempre he pensado que los cohetes o voladores, serpientes de humo, estallan luminosos al surcar la inmensidad de los cielos en los días de fiesta en mi pueblo.... Pueblo inundado de ruidos, como el de la llegada de los trenes." Ibid.

50. "El coraje de escribir nace del conocimiento de las culturas y lenguas indígenas anteriormente saqueado por los investigadores extranjeros." Instituto Nacional de Comunicación Social del Estado de Chiapas, "UNICH difunde literatura indígena."

51. Huet Bautista, personal communication, Chiapas, Mexico, May 21, 2004.

52. "Florido j-abtel jpatan / Florido señor / Sean consagradas / Sean veneradas / Tus trece flores / Tus trece palabras." Huet Bautista, *La última muerte / Ti slajebalxa lajele*, 25.

53. "Somos una hoja / somos una hierba / somos un bejuco / somos un árbol, solo respiramos un rato solo ensuciamos / a la sagrada madre tierra." Ibid., 1.

54. "Me he topado con él en las montañas, en lo alto del cielo; hemos probado nuestros poderes pero siempre me vence, puede convertirse en viento y rayo, conoce mucho el camino del espacio, siempre viaja a la tercera capa de las nubes." Ibid., 12.

55. "Otra vez el Viejo Pedro alcanzó de un machetazo a mi madre, cayó boca abajo con su pequeño hijo, cubriéndolo con su cuerpo como una gallina cubre sus polluelos contra el frio.... Miré como destrozaban el cuerpo de mi madre sin compasión, por diferentes partes volaban pedazos de carne, el filoso metal regaba sangre por todos lados." Ibid., 19.

56. Ibid., 23. The Spanish reads, "tiempo que me ha devuelto ... la sabiduría de mis padres."

57. "Durante veinte años he robado el aire en este espacio, he ensuciado la madre tierra, el esplendor de la palabra me ha fortalecido, aprendí del rugir del viento y del canto de las aves que el respeto a los pequeños dioses de la tierra es más poderoso que la venganza." Ibid., 23.

58. Ibid., 24.

59. The spelling of this word varies. A *nahual* or *nawal* is a Mesoamerican concept found in central Mexico all the way to Nicaragua. It is defined as an animal double, sometimes a form assumed by people who can transform themselves and sometimes the energy we are all born with and that corresponds to the sacred 260-day calendar.

60. "Lo que llamo casa, era una pequeña construcción de adobes sin escalar, techo

de tejas de barro, y un solo cuarto que servía de cocina y dormitorio." Ak'abal, *Grito en la sombra*, 2.

61. "Mi madre sembró en mi la inquietud por la palabra. Sea éste, un intento por continuar con la tradición de mis mayores." Ibid., 3.

62. "El tiempo ya no es como antes. Ya no tiene sentido contar esas cosas con luz eléctrica. Antes sí daba gusto, porque la luz de ocote era otra luz. Ya ves, hasta los espantos se han ido. Ahora te toca crear tus propios cuentos para contárselos a tus hijos." Ibid.

63. "Di dos o tres vueltas arrastrando mi desesperación. Parecía como si todos los del pueblo se hubieran ido quien sabe a dónde." Ibid., 6.

64. "Miré hacia atrás y vi que el pueblo estaba desapareciendo, las casas chocaban unas contra otras y se hundían." Ibid.

65. "Tal vez me dormí." Ibid., 7.

66. "Cuando recobré la razón ya era un hombre." Ibid., 8.

67. "'Qué le dijistes?' 'Le conté de tu viaje.'" Ibid.

68. Marisol Ceh Moo's short story collection *Jats'uts'il loolo'ob Xibalabaj / Jardines de Xibalbaj* points to a new direction. The title of Ceh Moo's anthology references the sacred *Popol Wuj*, but it does not deal with a creation story. Lack of space does not allow me to comment on this anthology.

69. "La palabra 'contrayerba' aplica como antídoto de picada de víboras, pero también [aplica] para todas las plantas que curan. Yo había escuchado la palabra 'contracultura' para las culturas no occidentales—para los pueblos indígenas, pues. Y me pareció titular el libro con una palabra que existía en el habla popular, que no es medicina occidental, sino que es medicina tradicional; 'contrayerba' es todo lo que no es occidental. Después hice la traducción al maya. La planta se llama 'xkaambal jaw,' y cura mordida de víbora. El título del libro se traduce literalmente como 'su energía de la hierba xkaambal jaw,' pero me gusta más la palabra sola 'contrayerba.' Es fácil de decir y recordar, pero tiene un significado profundo." Martínez Huchim, personal communication, Facebook, October 25, 2015.

70. Martínez Huchim, *U yóol xkaambal jaw xíiw / Contrayerba*, 59. The author also describes Cahum as someone from a small town and the name can also mean something like "noise," thus Soledad's last names together mean "to write with noise or force." Martínez Huchim, personal communication, Facebook, October 12, 2016.

71. In chapter 3 I discuss the use of *lienzo* in Rosa María Chávez's poem "Cíclica." I explain the multilayer denotation and connotation of the term both as a sixteenth-century cloth/textile used to establish genealogies and, today, as a name for a sanitary napkin.

72. This literary trope manifests in much of the poetry by indigenous women. Writing is also on the body.

73. "Mi señor, / te pido / me concedes capacidad para escribir / las cosas que pasan ante mi vista, / mi Señor." Martínez Huchim, *U yóol xkaambal jaw xíiw / Contrayerba*, 76.

74. "Vamos a quemarlo, si no van a pensar que es hechizo y el padre y la gente no van a permitir que la entierren en el cementerio, sino en el monte, como si fuera animal." Martínez Huchim, *U yóol xkaambal jaw xíiw / Contrayerba*, 119.

Chapter Three

1. See Brumfiel, "Methods in Feminist."
2. See Lugones, "Colonialidad y género."
3. López Mejía, "Aciertos y desaciertos," 30.
4. In her essay "Mi cuerpo es un territorio político," Gómez Grijalva, a K'iche' poet and feminist, draws on the politics of the body and territory in disclosing how the intensification of the war manifested in inexplicable rashes (263-75).
5. Marcos, *Taken from the Lips*, 64.
6. See León-Portilla and Shorris, *In the Language of Kings*.
7. Qtd. in Marcos, *Taken from the Lips*, 70.
8. "Las contradicciones del nacionalismo, modernidad y atraso, urbano y rural, tradición y cultura, reaparecen y se intensifican al abordar la situación de las mujeres [indígenas]." Gutiérrez Chong, "Nacionalismos y etnocentrismos," 184.
9. Nelson, "Stumped Identities," 314-53.
10. Ibid., 315.
11. Eber, "Seeking Our Own Food," 8.
12. Hernández Castillo, "Entre el etnocentrismo feminista," 214.
13. See Pu Tzunux, *Representaciones sociales*.
14. "A pesar de que las mujeres indígenas comenzamos a ser protagonistas de nuestras historias, nos exigen, ya sea desde la comunidad o de la sociedad no indígena, ser las portadoras de la 'autenticidad' indígena, dada a través del uso del traje, de la transmisión de las lenguas indígenas y del manejo de cuerpo, elementos que actúan como marcadores de identidad que reproducen, en ciertos contextos, relaciones de poder entre los géneros y nos plantean la disyuntiva de cómo vivir los cambios en nuestras identidades sin que por ello se cuestione nuestra palabra." Méndez Torres, "Identidades cambiantes," 27.
15. "Esta naturalización de los roles sociales y culturales adjudicados a las mujeres indígenas son la síntesis del proyecto nacional para consolidar el Estado mexicano. Por lo tanto, el ser mujer indígena fue y sigue siendo un recurso fundamental para la formación y el mantenimiento del Estado mexicano, la consolidación de nuestra subordinación es uno de los diversos factores que posibilita la reproducción del sistema capitalista, patriarcal y blanco." Bautista Pérez, "El racismo," 15.
16. See DeMott, *Into the Hearts of the Amazons*; Stephen, *Zapotec Women*; and the documentary by Gosling and Osborne, *Blossoms of Fire*.
17. See Cruz Velázquez, "Los dilemas."
18. "En Juchitán, por conducto de las mujeres se desgasta ese argumento [la idea de la mujer indígena sumisa], demostrando que la filosofía de la comunidad tiene vida y no depende de la sumisión de los individuos entre sí. Más bien, es una vida en colectivo, en donde la colaboración de cada uno de los miembros de la familia cuenta para la armonía comunitaria. De esta forma y rompiendo con la idea de que los hombres en Juchitán no trabajan y, de que la mujer es el único sostén económico, la contribución económica de ambos le da un nivel de vida diferente a una familia y a todo un pueblo, sin descuidar la tradición ni el sistema de organización comunitaria." Ibid., 62-63.

19. Góngora Pacheco, "La mujer maya," 6.

20. Indigenous women tend to be monolingual in greater numbers than men. They also have the highest rates of illiteracy. See Sieder, "Sexual Violence," 110–11.

21. Ibid.

22. Ésta no es una lucha de competencia, no debemos permitir que se convierta en una lucha de géneros." Jiménez Pérez, "El futuro de la palabra," 7.

23. Juárez Espinoza, "La mujer maya," 13.

24. Ibid.

25. See Gutierrez Chong, *Mujeres y nacionalismos*.

26. See Mignolo, *Local Histories / Global Designs*.

27. For example, throughout the Mayan peninsula no male poet occupies privileged status equal to that of Briceida Cuevas Cob. In Chiapas, despite the number of poets in Tsotsil, no one is more recognized than Enriqueta Lunez Pérez. Among the Zapotecs Natalia Toledo and Irma Pineda Santiago's verses are best-known despite the long tradition of poetry writing by men in Juchitán. We can make similar observations for other indigenous nations and languages. However, the situation is radically different in Guatemala, where no indigenous woman poet has reached Humberto Ak'abal's national and international stature.

28. Natalia Toledo, for example, was the first Zapotec poet to publish (not necessarily to write, since that order is not always followed, especially in the production of women's poetry) a complete bilingual book, *Mujeres de sol, mujeres de oro* (January 2002), in Zapotec and Spanish.

29. Among the poets who have begun to achieve importance we find Elizabeth Pérez (P'urhépecha), Ruperta Bautista (Tsotsil), Alicia Mateo (P'urhépecha), Emilia Buitimea (Mayo), Flora Hernández (Nahua), Leonarda Contreras (Hñahñu), Irma Martínez (Nahua), Josefa Leonarda Ventura (Mixteca), Fenicia Trinidad (Téenek), Jaquelina Fernández (Maya), Socorro Gómez (Tsotsil), Leticia Pérez (Chichimeca Jonaz), Evangelina Pérez (Chichimeca Jonaz), Diana Maribel García (Chichimeca Jonaz), María Patricia García (Chichimeca Jonaz), Angélica Ortíz (Wishárika), and Yolanda Matías García (Nahua).

30. Weaving and writing are closely related practices and represent a valuable contribution to the maintenance of culture, symbolically and materially. In my work on Maya women I note that petitions for weaving and writing appear in religious solicitations to Chul jme'vixtik, the Great Mother associated with the moon. Chacón, "Kabawil," 165.

31. See, for example, the compact discs of Yolanda Matías García (Nahua), *Xochitlajtol ika moyojlo / Palabra florida para tu corazón*, and Dolores Batista (Raramuri), *Anayáwari Ra'icháara*. Conaculta y Culturas Populares have played an important role in the recording and distribution of the three CDs called *Lluvia de sueños: Poetas y cantantes indígenas* with Roselia Jiménez, Angélica Ortiz, Elizabeth Pérez, Juana Inés Reza, Delfina Albáñez, Enriqueta Lunez, and Martha Toledo.

32. See de la Cruz, "Reflexiones sobre la escritura"; Pineda Santiago, "Las mujeres"; and Sullivan, "The State of Zapotec Poetry."

33. "Pero apenas cruzaba el corredor, la vida estallaba en zapoteco." Pineda Santiago, "Mis dos lenguas," 161.

34. See Pineda Santiago, "No hay perdón ni olvido a 33 años." COCEI was an important political movement on the Isthmus of Oaxaca. It was a coalition of workers, peasants, and students.
35. López Chiñas, "El zapoteco." "¡Ay! Zapoteco, zapoteco, / lengua que me das la vida, / yo sé que morirás, / el día que muera el sol."
36. *Binnizá* translates as "people of the cloud" in Zapotec but can also simply mean "language."
37. "No me verás morir / Habrá una semilla / escondida entre los matorrales del camino / que a esta tierra ha de volver / y sembrará el futuro / y será alimento de nuestras almas / y renacerá nuestra palabra / y no me verás morir / porque seremos fuertes / porque seremos siempre vivos / porque nuestro canto será eterno / porque seremos nosotros y tú / y los hijos de nuestros hijos / y el temblor de la tierra / que sacudirá el mar / y seremos muchos corazones / aferrados a la esencia de los binnizá / y no me verás morir / no me verás morir / no me verás morir." Pineda Santiago, "No me verás morir," 73. For a different translation of this poem, see Pineda Santiago, "You Will Not See Me Die."
38. Henestrosa, "The Forms of Sexual Life in Juchitán," 129–31.
39. Underiner, *Contemporary Theatre in Mayan Mexico*, 47.
40. See Ruiz Campbell, "Representations of Isthmus Women," 137–41.
41. "Beeu riaba lu gueela' laga ca bigarí huaxha ruunda' ra nuu yu guiigu' guídxica / zisa'ca cadi cugabaca xpiní ne pabia' guendaranaxhi' huaxhinni. / Zitu'pe ri huinni ti yoo beñe rinda'yu gaxhape laa ti bacuzaguii biaani gati sti' ruzuí' ne rudí tiidi guand aranaxhi sti' gueela.' / Ti jñiaa ribidxi ca binni lidxi nisa dxu'ni' ri nase ca xpia ca guere bele biaani rucuani telayú na laca la ruluí guenda binnidxapa sti' siadó' guie.'" (La luna cae sobre la noche / mientras los grillos cantan / en la arcilla del río, / entrelazados caminan / sin medir horas y espacios / el amor nocturno. // A lo lejos se mira / la choza con olor a tierra, una luciérnaga junto a ella / apaga su luz intermitente / y deja pasar los amores de la noche. // Una madre llama a las vecinas, el mezcal asalta las costumbres, los cohetes despiertan la madrugada / para dar testimonio / de la virginidad del alba.) López Pérez, "El rapto / Guendaruxhoñenee gunaa," 5.
42. Qtd. in Mejía Amador, "Representaciones del cuerpo,"117.
43. Ibid.
44. Pineda Santiago, *Doo yoo ne ga' bia' / De la casa del ombligo a las nueve cuartas*, 45.
45. "Prenden cohetes en casa del varón / la noche del rapto / la gente sabe entonces que una flor sangró / y sobre el dolor celebran con música y guirnaldas. / Pero la vergüenza es una piedra grande / si en lugar de cohetes en la boca de una casa / una olla de barro colocan con una herida / que cuenta la historia de una mujer que no supo esperar." Pineda Santiago, "Untitled," 45. See Mejía Amador, "Representaciones del cuerpo," 45.
46. Ruiz Campbell, "Representations of Isthmus Women," 139.
47. "Una abuela de vientre ancho / diez hijos alumbró / para cultivar la tierra. / Con una guirnalda en la cabeza / se embriagó de alegría / cuando la boda de sus hijas / pues la mancha de sangre en un paño blanco / le gritó al pueblo que se guardaron bien." See Pineda Santiago, "La abuela," 43.

48. "Yo creo que la poesía contemporánea indígena no tiene porqué renunciar a absolutamente nada, todo participa en tu vida, todo te influye. Como alguien dijo, 'nada me es ajeno': ni la cultura griega ni ninguna otra, además de que las hemos leído, afortunadamente. Como poeta he tratado de leer a los clásicos y lo que se escribe ahora.... Tenemos que buscar un más allá, es la única manera de hacer que sobrevivan nuestras lenguas, hay que crear nuevas tradiciones, nuevos mitos. No podemos estar recreando permanentemente los mismos mitos, que si bien son una maravilla, también tenemos que buscar lo que dice el hombre de ahora, somos seres de este tiempo; lo que está pasando, socialmente, políticamente, culturalmente te influye, uno no está con los ojos cerrados." Castañeda Barrera, "Entrevista con Natalia Toledo."

49. "Me masturbo frente al espejo / como Egon Schiele. / Un muelle en mis ojos, me separa de mi imagen. / En el sudor el rostro de la muerte es una gota. / Exhalo la sonrisa final de la locura / Mi autorretrato no existe." Toledo Paz, "Mutilación," in *Del silencio*.

50. Egon Schiele was known for his self-portraits and visceral sexuality.

51. "Hubo quien probó el mosto de tu piel, / te caminó de la cabeza a los pies sin abrir los ojos / para no descubrir el resplandor del sol. / Hubo quien sólo pellizcó la comida / y no quiso beber el chocolate de los compadres / y el pozol de semilla de mamey. // Hubo quien colgó en la puerta de tu casa una olla rota / y no quiso pagar la fiesta. / No supieron los tontos que una flor caída al suelo / sigue siendo flor hasta su muerte." Toledo Paz, "Tradición," in *Flor de pantano*, 123.

52. See Ruiz Campbell, "Representations of Isthmus Women," 139.

53. Diego Rivera painted women from Oaxaca. Graciela Iturbide made Zapotec women famous in her photography, and the journalist Jocasta Shakespeare wrote of the women's healthy sexuality in the Isthmus of Tehuantepec. For a lively discussion of the outsider's fascination with Zapotec women, see DeMott, *Into the Hearts of the Amazons*, 19.

54. I foresee this changing in the future given El Salvador's recent recognition of three indigenous nations in its constitution. Historically, the repression of indigenous peoples in both countries has made the emergence of organic intellectuals impossible.

55. *Najt* is a Maya concept that does not separate space and time.

56. Moya, "Interculturalidad y reforma," 22–24; Bastos and Camus, "Mayanización y vida cotidiana," introduction.

57. Jorge Cocom Pech (Maya Yukatek, Mexico) and Pedro Gaspar González (Maya Q'anjobal, Guatemala), in the first international conference on indigenous literatures and globalization, held in Pasto, Colombia, evoked this Maya collectivity as one that transgresses nation-state borders (2006). Rosa María Chávez (Maya K'iche and Kaqchikel, Guatemala) and Jorge Cocom Pech also identified as belonging to one Maya nation at the Medellín Poetry Festival 2006.

58. See Harvey, *The Chiapas Rebellion*; Hayden, *The Zapatista Reader*; Collier and Quaratiello, *Basta!*, to name a few U.S. authors who focused on the Zapatista uprising.

59. See Speed, Hernández Castillo, and Stephen, *Dissident Women*.

60. The act of writing in indigenous languages dispels the old hegemonic notion that they are dialects. They also counter the social stigma attached to indigenous languages as lacking the ability express literary language.

61. Certain groups like Sna Jtz'ibajom were established in the early 1980s, but my point is that after the Zapatista uprising these organizations gained more international prominence.

62. I am using the preferred spelling by Tsotsil and Tseltal speakers to describe their language.

63. CONECULTA (at the state level) and CONACULTA (at the national level) also finance many writing fellowships. The novelist, Carlos Montemayor, spearheaded a series of contemporary Maya literature. He included in the series many members from the Sna Jtz'ibajom as well as Fortaleza de la Mujer Maya (FOMMA) theater groups. Montemayor galvanized support for indigenous literature across Mexico and other Latin American countries. José Antonio Reyes Matamoros, the late director of the Jaime Sabines Cultural Center, along with CELALI organized writing workshops and edited many anthologies as well.

64. See, for example, CELALI's narrative contest, Y el Bolom Dice. Funding, of course, depends on state politics. This is one of the most difficult issues the center has been dealing with in the last few years.

65. The statistics available about indigenous women's lack of access to education are staggering. According to Mercedes Olivera Bustamante, 60 percent of indigenous women lack literacy. Only 9 percent have had access to postelementary education. See Olivera Bustamante, *De sumisiones*, 87. It is important to note that despite the statistics, indigenous women poets are highly regarded and occupy a prominent space in national and international literary gatherings.

66. As I note in the next chapter, the two female founding members of the theater group Sna Jtz'ibajom left because of the sexism they encountered in the group. Isabel Juárez Espinoza and Petrona de la Cruz Cruz went on to form an all-women's Maya group, Fortaleza de la Mujer Maya (FOMMA).

67. As I have made evident throughout the book, translation remains a highly contested issue among the poets. In the case of most poems, an indigenous language original and a Spanish translation is de rigueur. In López Díaz, Díaz Ruiz, and López Díaz, *Sbel sjol yo'onton ik' / Memoria del viento*, for example, poems were first created in Spanish and then translated into the Tsotsil language. The objective in translating from the Spanish to Maya Tsotsil was to explore the indigenous language's poetic structure. My contact with some of the writers cannot be underestimated, as they graciously responded to questions about cultural and linguistic references I was not familiar with or did not understand in the context of the poem. My elementary knowledge of the K'iche', Yukatek, and Tsotsil languages is helpful in this analysis. I do see how the translations lose beauty, or miss a deliberate play on words, but ultimately, my position is that the writers have control over the translation and thus have in their hands an important mechanism of cultural, linguistic, and political resistance.

68. Gosner, *Soldiers of the Virgin*.

69. Of course the Catholic Church's turn to liberation theology in the 1960s had critical implications for indigenous movements in both Mexico and Guatemala. The conflicts in Chiapas and Yucatán were articulated as racial conflicts. This simplifies other social dimensions heightened in the 1980s and 1990s in Chiapas and Guatemala.

70. See, for example, the representation of indigenous people in Castellanos, *Balún-Canán*; and Rubín, *El callado dolor de los tzotziles*.

71. See Dawson, "One from the Heart," 25.

72. "[La imagen de la mujer indígena] está en una vitrina donde no hay una mujer capaz de luchar por sí misma, se le trata como inválida." See Molina, "Los autores indígenas escribimos de un nosotros."

73. Gosner discusses moral economy as a useful framework to interpret the 1776 Tzeltal rebellion in Chiapas. His analysis builds on Thompson, "The Moral Economy of the English Peasant"; and Scott, *The Moral Economy of the Peasant*. Thompson and Scott analyze the motivations driving peasant rebellions in Burma and Vietnam, respectively. They argue that when certain communities perceive a threat to their moral economy, ethical outrage leads to political action. Moral economy represents a community's "shared moral universe, a common notion of what is just." See Gosner, *Soldiers of the Virgin*, 7. According to Gosner, a violation of the main moral principles identified as "the norm of reciprocity and the right to subsistence" inspires social discontent. I extend this idea of a moral economy in my analysis of the force driving the poets' verses, as the norm of reciprocity in Maya religion saturates Enriqueta Lunez Pérez's stanzas, and the idea of a right to subsistence influences Angelina Díaz Ruiz's poem.

74. This translation was done from both the Spanish and Mayan versions in consultation with the author. The Tsotsil version reads:

> La jti jbé svayel kajvaltik
> jutun sk'an o'lol ak'obal
> sjelobil svayel
> la jkakbe'
> vukub nichimal k'op
> vukub a vokol
> la jchapbe' jmul,
> skotol jmul,
> la jbuts'be' sti ba.
>
> La jti jbe svayel kajvaltik
> jutun sk'an o'lol ak'obal
> li o'ra mux ech' no'ox yaluk
> tilanuk vuk tos kantilaetik,
> li banomil la yuch' ch'ul pox,
> k'unk'un li yav ak'al la stu'm sba
> li ts'ebal alak la sjoybi'nsba ta jbektal.
> la jti jbe' svayel kajvaltik
> jutun sk'an o'lol ak'obal
> k'unk'un li o'ra
> la sjoybin jk'op ta kambail
> (Lunez Pérez, "La jti jbe' svayel kajvaltik/ Desperté a Dios," 44)

75. A homemade alcoholic drink consumed during carnival or fiestas.

76. "Desperté a Dios / cerca de la media noche / y el tiempo interminable / consumió

los siete colores / la tierra bebió del aguardiente sagrado / lentamente se apagó el incensario / paloma se convirtió en mi carne." It is interesting to note that in the Tsotsil version, she uses the word *Ak'obal*. The term is far more poetic in Tsotsil going from darkness to light and probably closer to the English word *dawn* as opposed to simply "an hour" or "midnight." Also *Ak'abal* represents one of the twenty-day signs in the sacred calendar, which has important implications in the poem. The linguistic nuance here, however, gets lost in the translation. Notable, too, is the spelling of the term, which is different in Tsotsil than in K'iche', for example. However, I have translated *Ak'obal* as "midnight" to follow Lunez Pérez's own Spanish translation. Lunez Pérez, "La jti jbe' svayel kajvaltik / Desperté a Dios," 45.

77. Enriqueta Lunez Pérez, personal communication, Facebook, 2013.

78. "Desperté a dios / cerca de la medianoche / y poco a poco el tiempo / convirtió mi oración en sublime deseo." Lunez Pérez, "La jti jbe' svayel kajvaltik / Desperté a Dios," 45.

79. Lunez Pérez, *Tajimol ch'ulelaletik / Juego de nahuales*.

80. Spelling of the term varies; in Guatemala it has been standardized as *Nawal*. See Lunez Pérez, "Enriqueta Lunez (poeta) mov."

81. López Díaz, Díaz Ruiz, and López Díaz, *Sbel sjol yo'onton ik' / Memoria del viento*.

82. According to oral tradition, the Virgin Suyul lives in the lake of the same name. Many believers come to this area to offer flowers, candles, and prayers.

83. "Angelina Suyul."

84. Convened by Azalera Organization, the University of the Americas in Puebla, and the Rigoberta Menchú Tum Foundation, the contest helps indigenous youth attend universities.

85. Díaz Ruiz, "Riqueza/K'ulejal," 18–19.

86. Ibid., 18.

87. See Llorente, "Marxism," 170–84.

88. This is the Tsotsil translation of "Riqueza" (the poem was first written in Spanish): "Ta jk'an chka'i k'u schi'il la milombae, / ta jnop ta jmilot / k'ucha'al volje, / li ta nekebe ta jmalka'i avik'al ch'ich'el, / ta yamak'il sna ajvalile ta jk'el / kurusetik jech ch'abal j-o / tey, ta jk'el pixil ta ik'obal ak'ob jok'olot. / Ta jk'an jtsal ka'i ta tuil k'ulejale, / Ta jnop yaxal chakxik' li vaknabale, / Skoj ip ti jme'e xti'et ko'nton avu'un, / Skoj chyakub li / jtote ta jchopol k'optaot, / Skoj namajem ti jbankile ko'nton ka'i jtik'ot ta chukel, / Akuchojbe yik' ti vokolil la viktabune. / Ta jtunes tubem k'analetik, / Ta jk'oopon li vitsetik joybijem ta jch'ultotiketik, / Ta spelet jme'ta jnau kuxlejal, / Li ch'a svale'al tsajal askale ta xka'i k'u yelan; / Tajimol xa no'ox ta joyibajel kuxlejal . . . / Ok'ome chisutal, / Noj ta tak'in chkil ti asate, / K'ik stanal ave ta lekil ve'lil, / Xchi'uk nojem spukujil bolom ta jol." ("Quiero saber cómo es tu dulce suicidio, / pensar como ayer, matarte / deseo derramar tu sangre negra en tus hombros, / mirar cruces en el patio del palacio sin llantos, / ahí, verte colgado con tus manos cubiertas de mugre. // Quiero derrotar tu apestable riqueza / imaginar el arco iris en gris azul para ti / odiarte por mi madre enferma, / maldecirte por mi padre ebrio, / encarcelarte por mi hermano emigrado, / hueles a la desgracia que me has dejado . . . // Volveré mañana, / veré tus ojos repletos de monedas, / tus dientes sucios de finos almuerzos, / tu mente llena de barbaries.") Díaz Ruiz, "Riqueza/K'ulejal," 18.

89. "Las mujeres indígenas nos encontramos en una situación de doble o hasta triple discriminación, por condición de género, por pertenencia étnica y en algunas ocasiones, también por edad en el caso de las niñas." Gómez Gutiérrez, "Mujeres indígenas," 49.

90. Olivera Bustamante, *De sumisiones*, 87.

91. "¿Por qué no llaman prostituta a la luna? Ella acostumbra apostar su cuerpo, / acostumbra ocultar su vergüenza." Cuevas Cob, "In káabá / Mi nombre."

92. "Mi madre guarda en las redes de su vientre un balón / En este juego no cuentan los goles sino el tiempo / prolongado que tiembla en su piel. / De sus senos escurre la luna cuerpo venerado de x-balamque / Ella cuenta ya con nueve amonestaciones / Es momento que estalle la lluvia preciosa de sus entrañas y / expulse ya el balón hacia el ombligo de la cancha morena." Cuevas Cob, "Orígenes II."

93. Grupo de Mujeres Mayas Kaqla, *La palabra y el sentir*.

94. Alaimo and Hekman, *Material Feminisms*, 4–5.

95. Chirix García, "Los cuerpos."

96. Acevedo and Toledo, *Para conjurar el sueño*, 9.

97. Beverley and Zimmerman, argue that in Guatemala, María Josefa Granados (or "Pepita") in the nineteenth century already referred to these issues. Granados along with José Batres Montufar wrote a sermon for José María Castillo that scandalized society and was described as pornographic. See Beverley and Zimmerman, *Literature and Politics*.

98. The poetry of Adela Pop Delgado and Rosa María Chávez graces several chapters of Grupo de Mujeres Mayas Kaqla, *Tramas y trascendencias*.

99. Refer to Delgado Pop, Macleod, and Pérez-Armiñán, in *Identidad: Rostros sin máscara*, to which Emma Delfina Chirix García, Amanda Pop Bol, and other women contributed. Also see the work of Aura Estela Cumes in Pequeño Bueno, *Participación y políticas de mujeres indígenas*. See Cumes and Monzón, *La encrucijada*.

100. Chirix García, "Los cuerpos," 150.

101. Douglas, *Natural Symbols*, 78.

102. See García Domingo, *Chemomiltoj tzoti' / Artesano de palabras* and *Tzetet b'ay xhkawxi ko k'ul / Raíces de esperanza*.

103. See López Austin, *Cuerpo humano e ideología*, 7; and Aguado Vázquez, *Cuerpo humano*, 46.

104. Calixta Gabriel Xiquín first published in newspapers; her poems were also anthologized in Anglesey, *Ixok Amar-Go*.

105. Cú Choc, "Poemaya."

106. Chávez, *Casa solitaria*.

107. Some poets have been writing since the 1960s but have not published a complete book. Most of them have been anthologized by del Valle Escalante in *Uk'u'x kaj, uk'u'x ulew: Antología de poesía maya*.

108. Gabriel Xiquín, *Hueso de la tierra*.

109. Cú Choc, *Novísimos*.

110. "Una de las formas para comprender al ser humano es mediante una trilogía que interrelaciona cuerpo, mente y espíritu. Estos tres elementos forman una unicidad y si se fragmentan provocan un desequilibrio en la vida de la persona. Esta cosmovisión indígena percibe al cuerpo como un ser viviente, con energías y sentimientos, y con

necesidades . . . y muy poco se habla sobre los deseos del cuerpo." Chirix García, "Los cuerpos," 150.

111. "Escribo con rojo / como roja es mi condición; / bendición o infortunio / ese color pinta mi lienzo / y se plasma en cada luna, / . . . / femenina y clandestina / desborda placer." Chávez, "Cíclica," 83.

112. Here I refer to the indigenous Quichua figure Domitila Barrios de Chúngura and the Maya hero Canek.

113. "En las manos de la mujer, / brilla, brilla poesía, / y su alma crea esperanza / con sus manos los colores, / rojo, amarillo, azul, verde y negro. / Con estos colores teje las poesías de angustia, / de dolor, de agonía y / de esperanza." Gabriel Xiquín, "Poema," 88–89.

114. Calixta Gabriel Xiquín, personal communication, Guatemala City, 2005.

115. "Mujer, / tu profesión mujer / tu misión madre . . . // Mujer, / Buena que trabaja / Mental, / Física y espiritual / Violada su dignidad. [/ . . . /] Mujer / no vas a la escuela porque tienes muchos hijos." Gabriel Xiquín, "Mujer," originally published under the pseudonym Caly Domitila Kanek. See Asociación Cultural B'eyb'al, *Literatura indgena de América: Segundo congreso*, 155.

116. "Toscas por el trabajo duro en las fincas y en el campo." Gabriel Xiquín, "Mujer campesina," 157.

117. Chirix García, "Los cuerpos," 151.

118. "Existe una gran riqueza de significados al hablar en kaqchikel sobre el cuerpo vinculado a la sexualidad, lo cual prueba el interés que este tema despierta." Ibid.

119. Ibid., 152.

120. Cú Choc, "¡Pobrecita yo!"

121. "Pobre vagina mía / que conociste tan solo un parto / en tu vida // condenada vagina / también conociste el gozo / La ternura y la ricura / de unas manos ardientes / Y por ellos / Serás condenada // ay, mis pechos / pobrecitos / porque únicamente / amamantaron una cría / / éstos, también serán condenados / por no resistirse al placer / de manos / y lenguas / llenas de locura." Ibid., 42.

122. Arias, "Asomos de la narrativa indígena maya," v.

123. Acevedo and Toledo, *Para conjurar el sueño*.

124. Chávez, *Casa solitaria*.

125. "Mujer solitaria / de visiones selladas / cicatrizada en el alma / y en el vientre / aprietas los dientes / y la vulva / encerrando en tus puños / melancolías silvestres / orgullosamente fémina // celebrando tu libertad / gritando al mundo esa caótica alegría / oculta y resguardada / en tu protagonismo maternal / ancestral cautiverio del silencio." Ibid., 14.

126. Chávez, *Piedra/Ab'aj*.

127. "A los nueve días / de mi nacimiento / el abuelo se fue al monte / en su morral mi ombligo / seco como la tusa / lo colgó en un árbol de aguacate / de allí proviene / la fuerza de mi espíritu / y la seguridad de mis pasos." Ibid., 54.

128. "Arde vagina seca / clítoris vencido / saliva espumosa / gemidos calculados por minuto / lubricando las culpas / raspa el cuerpo ausente / arde clítoris hinchado / pedacito de nadie / arde, lástima, esta soledad tan seca." "Rosa Chávez, poesía palpitante."

129. "La poesía creada por mujeres durante el siglo XX no abandonará el tratamiento

de lo erótico y el reconocimiento del cuerpo, la necesidad de buscar una manera de manifestar sus voces dentro de un espacio poético que les pertenezca, para abandonar de alguna forma, el o los espacios cedidos por el sistema patriarcal, que las orillaba a tratar temas asexuados, hablar de denuncia política en la cual no tenían ninguna participación, o tratar temas cortesanos y amatorios, sin enfrentarse en la escritura, con un lenguaje despojado de lo femenino." Acevedo and Toledo, *Para conjurar el sueño*, 11.

130. "El cuerpo humano que hoy se menciona en los idiomas mayas está interrelacionado con la naturaleza y el cosmos, pero no ha sido asociado al territorio, porque el hacerlo implica ver al cuerpo como cuerpo político y al territorio como cuerpo de mujer." Chirix García, "Los cuerpos," 160.

131. "Se basa en la defensa del territorio cuerpo-tierra. Los cuerpos de las mujeres forman parte del territorio que habitan y la violencia que sufre la mujer en su cuerpo se transmite de generación en generación como un legado a través de la memoria del pensamiento y de la memoria corporal de las mujeres." Blanco, "Mujer, maya-xinca y feminista."

Chapter Four

1. Macleod, *Nietas del fuego*, 123–47.
2. The system known as *usos y costumbres* is "a feature of indigenous societies with a Mesoamerican style of political organization and representation." Sorroza Polo and Danielson, "Political Subsystems," 169.
3. Taylor and Townsend, *Stages of Conflict*, 2.
4. Graham-Jones, "Editorial Comment: Theorizing Globalization through Theater," i–viii.
5. See Boal, *Theater of the Oppressed*.
6. See Vince, "Theater History," 1.
7. Ibid.
8. Roach, "Theatre History and Historiography," 293.
9. Vince, "Theater History," 2.
10. Roach, "Theatre History and Historiography," 293.
11. León-Portilla mentions Bernal Díaz del Castillo, Motolinía (Toribio de Benavente), Bernardino de Sahagún, Diego Durán, Jerónimo de Mendieta, Juan de Torquemada, and Fernando de Alva Ixtlilxóchitl among the best-known chroniclers and historians who refer to theater and performance in their observation of pre-Columbian cultural practices. See León-Portilla, "Teatro náhuatl prehispánico," 39–61.
12. Diego de Landa was a Franciscan monk sent to the Yucatán, where he arrived in 1549. When he returned to Spain, while awaiting trial for his cruelty, he wrote the manuscript to justify his acts, recording the Mayan religion, language, and writing system. See de Landa, *An Account of the Things of Yucatán*, 144.
13. León-Portilla, "Teatro náhuatl prehispánico," 41.
14. See Montemayor and Frischmann, *Words of the True Peoples*, vol. 3; Tedlock, *Rabinal Achí*; and Underiner, *Contemporary Theater in Mayan Mexico*.
15. See Sten, *Vida y muerte*.
16. See Sten and Viveros, *Teatro náhuatl II*.

17. "Y se puede decir, sin exageración, que el teatro fue en la conquista espiritual de México lo que los caballos y la pólvora fueron en la conquista militar." Sten, *Vida y muerte*, 8.

18. *Macho Ratón*, also known as *El Güegüense*, is considered the first written literary work produced in post-Columbian Nicaragua. It is a satirical drama that combines music, dance, and theater. See Field, *The Grimace of Macho Ratón*.

19. A bilingual play in Quechua (sometimes performed in both Quechua and Spanish) dramatizes the tragic fall of the Inca ruler Atahualpa to Francisco Pizarro.

20. Tedlock, *Rabinal Achí*, 6.

21. Ibid., 1.

22. Ibid. Tedlock reminds us that Bourbourg was an aficionado of indigenous antiquities and the person responsible for securing a copy of the sacred text *Popol Vuh*. Tedlock, *Rabinal Achí*, 6.

23. Ibid., 199.

24. Ibid., 199–200.

25. Ibid., 200.

26. Qtd. in Underiner, *Contemporary Theatre in Mayan Mexico*, 22.

27. See de Landa, *An Account of the Things of Yucatán*; Bricker, *The Indian Christ, the Indian King*; and Carmack, Gasco, and Gossen, *The Legacy of Mesoamerica*.

28. Frischmann, "A Question of Balance," 19.

29. See Underiner, *Contemporary Theatre in Mayan Mexico*, 31.

30. Lewis, "Mexico's National Indigenist Institute," 609–32.

31. Ibid.

32. Underiner, "Transculturation in the Work of Laboratorio de Teatro Campesino e Indígena," 78–100.

33. See Hernández Gerónimo et al., *La tragedia del jaguar*, 1.

34. Salazar Tetzagüic, *Rupach'uxik kina'oj qati't qamama' / Características de la literatura maya kaqchikel*, 33.

35. See de la Cadena, "Las mujeres son más indias," 279–352.

36. See Weiss, *Latin American Popular Theatre*.

37. "Ladino hegemony" here refers to a society that is not indigenous and tends to look down on indigenous peoples.

38. Shillington, *Grappling with Atrocity*, 25.

39. Frischmann, "Contemporary Mayan Theatre," 71.

40. Underiner, *Contemporary Theatre in Mayan Mexico*, 5.

41. Robert M. Laughlin recalls, in a chapter of his *Monkey Business Theater* titled "Looking Back, Looking Forward," that he originally met some of Sna Jtz'ibajom's founders during his early days as an anthropologist in Chiapas in the late 1950s. Three men who had participated in the Harvard Project sought his help in 1982 to establish a Tsotsil-Tseltal cultural association. Laughlin, *Monkey Business*, 1–8.

42. Ibid., 49.

43. Pérez Hernández's recollections of Sna Jtz'ibajom and the members' forays into acting offer more detail as to how the theater troupe emerges. See Montemayor and Frischmann, *Words of the True Peoples*, 3:13.

44. Marrero, "Eso Sí Pasa Aquí," 312.

45. Ibid.
46. Ibid.
47. Ibid., 313.
48. Juárez Espinosa, "Migration," in *Words of the True Peoples*, 3:221-29.
49. Taylor and Constantino, *Holy Terrors*, 293-310.
50. See Turner, *The Anthropology of Performance*.
51. See Ceh Moo, *X-Teya, U puksi'ik'al ko'olel / Teya, un corazón de mujer*.
52. See Lovera and Palomo, *Las alzadas*. On Patricio Martínez's candidacy, see Reuters, "Indigenous Woman Registers to Run for Mexican Presidency."
53. Loucky and Moors, *The Maya Diaspora*.
54. Paredes, "Hilando fino."
55. See Underiner, *Contemporary Theater in Mayan Mexico*.
56. Banham, *The Cambridge Guide to Theatre*, 459.
57. Shillington, *Grappling with Atrocity*, 37.
58. Ibid., 34.
59. Alicia Clara Sen, personal communication, August 2014.
60. The Dresden Codex is a pre-Columbian Maya book of the Yukatek Maya in Chichén Itzá from the eleventh or twelfth century. The Madrid Codex dates back to the postclassic period of Mesoamerican chronology and is one of three surviving pre-Columbian Maya books.
61. Taylor and Townsend, introduction to *Stages of Conflict*, 1.
62. Ibid., 2.
63. See Hernández Castillo, "The Emergence of Indigenous Feminism," 226.
64. See Lane, Godoy-Anatvia, and Gómez-Barris, "Gesto decolonial."
65. Christenson, *Popol Wuj*, 6-7.
66. Gregoria Crisanta Pérez, "Hermanas en resistencia," https://www.youtube.com/watch?v=UFPsUBmKscs.
67. Batz used this term in his presentation at the "Critical Indigeneities" symposium, University of Texas at Austin, April 2015. Batz, "Ixil Migration to the United States."

Chapter Five

1. While indigenous languages have been written down since the sixteenth century by both indigenous and nonindigenous peoples, it was not until the 1980s and 1990s that writers began to agree on standardized alphabets.
2. Alegría, *Historia de la novela*, 9.
3. Ibid.
4. Ibid.
5. Ibid.
6. Calvo, "La política de la impresión," 278.
7. Ibid., 281.
8. Ibid., 279.
9. Ibid.
10. See Moretti, "Conjectures on World Literature"; Sommer, *Foundational Fictions*; and Jameson, "Third World Literature."

11. See Cornejo Polar, "La novela indigenista."
12. Moretti, *The Novel*, 58.
13. Kundera, *The Art of the Novel*.
14. Plaks, "The Novel in Premodern China."
15. Goody, "From Oral to Written," 18.
16. Gallagher, "The Rise of Fictionality," 341.
17. Ibid.
18. See Villoro, *Los grandes momentos del indigenismo en México*. Critics differentiate between *indianismo* and *indigenismo* in their overall aesthetic and political goals. *Indianismo* idealized a pre-Hispanic past, focusing on Indians as noble savages. While *indigenista* literature shares some of this idealization, its main political goal was to illustrate the oppressive conditions indigenous peoples endure. Rodríguez-Luis, "El indigenismo." *Indianismo* in Bolivia also differs from its definition by the Quechua/Aymara intellectual Fausto Reinaga as a political process that contests and resists Western order. See Rocabado, "Bolivia frente a su espejo."
19. See Giraudo and Lewis, "Re-thinking Indigenismo."
20. Ibid.
21. "*Indigenista* literature cannot offer us a rigorous, factual version of the Indian. The writer has to idealize and stylize him. Neither can the writer offer us his soul. It is still a literature of mestizos. That is why it is called *indigenista* and not indigenous. An indigenous literature, if it is to come, will come at its own time. When the Indians themselves are able to produce it." ("La literatura indigenista no puede darnos una versión rigurosamente verista del indio. Tiene que idealizarlo y estilizarlo. Tampoco puede darnos su propia ánima. Es todavía una literatura de mestizos. Por eso se llama indigenista y no indígena. Una literatura indígena, si debe venir, vendrá a su tiempo. Cuando los propios indios estén en grado de producirla.") Mariátegui, *Siete ensayos de interpretación de la realidad peruana*, 209. Later in his life Mariátegui advocated for adapting Marxism to national problems in Latin America and founded the Socialist Party. See Becker, *Mariátegui*.
22. Ibid.
23. "Todo eso de indios mágicos y otras puerilidades suele ser ocultamiento impensado de lo recóndito y esencial. Cuando se muestra a los indios, burlados como muñecos, los visten de piñatas, los visten de tarjeta postal." See Cardoza y Aragón, *Miguel Ángel Asturias*, 88.
24. "Cuando los indios acierten a escribirlas [las novelas] intuyo que tendrán coloración mestiza." Ibid.
25. In this text, de la Cadena writes that in Peru, this adage was used by landowners to describe literate Indians who refused peon labor, arguing that it is a generalized cultural idea that once Indians acquire an education, they become culturally mestizos. See de la Cadena, *Indigenous Mestizos*, 314.
26. Bollinger and Lund explain that class struggles in the 1920s undermined minority oppression in the U.S. context especially in relation to the black population and in Latin America in relation to indigenous groups. Bollinger and Lund, "Minority Oppression," 10–11.
27. See Rubín, *El callado dolor de los tzotziles*; Castellanos, *Balún-Canán*; and Monteforte, *Entre la piedra y la cruz*.

28. See López y Fuentes, *El indio*; Gallegos, *Doña Barbara*; and Martin, *Journeys through the Labyrinth*. The latter sees Latin American literature as the search for national identity.

29. Tarica, *The Inner Life of Mestizo Nationalism*, xxi.

30. "Se entrecruzan, se entretejen y sale esa mezcla de historia, fantasía, realidad." See Briceño Chel, "¿Literatura indigenista o literatura?," 26.

31. De la Cruz, "Reflexiones sobre la escritura," 331.

32. "El día en que haya más escritores maya vamos a ampliar nuestros conceptos diferentes que Asturias." Sitler, "Entrevista con Gaspar Pedro González."

33. "El ve en la situación del 'indio' una oportunidad para poder sobresalir él. Pero de ninguna manera valora aquella persona humana. Cuando viaja Miguel Ángel Asturias a Europa, especialmente Francia, comienza a madurar y aprende a sentir la importancia de la civilización maya ante sus anfitriones. Su visión es una visión ladina sobre los mayas." Ibid.

34. "Sus pies—garra a ratos, pezuñas por momentos—resbalan sobre las lajas, se hundían en los líquenes o se asentaban como extremidades de plantígrado en las planadas del serillo." Rojas González, "La Tona," 7.

35. "Para el que se siente y es parte de la gente como la que menciona Francisco Rojas González, la comparación con animales es burlesca, denigrante e innecesaria." Castellanos Martínez, "La narrativa de los que hablamos Dila Xhon," 45.

36. See Gollnick, "El ciclón de Chiapas"; and Steele, "Indigenismo y posmodernidad" and *Narrativa indigenista*.

37. Lund clarifies that Altamirano was not the poor, monolingual Indian that critics make him out to be. See Lund, "Altamirano's Burden," 34–37.

38. Ignacio Manuel Altamirano, born in 1834, spoke Nahuatl and did not learn Spanish until he was fourteen. See "Altamirano, Ignacio Manuel," 12–13.

39. Altamirano, *El Zarco*.

40. In Chiapas, Diego Méndez Guzmán published the first novel in Maya Tseltal and Spanish, *Kajkanantik Jch'ulta tiketik te leke sok te chopole / El Kajkanantik: Los dioses del bien y el mal* (Kajkanantik: The gods of good and evil). *Kajkanantik* was published in the now-canonical Letras Mayas Contemporáneas series spearheaded by the committed mestizo writer Carlos Montemayor. *Kajkanantik* indigenizes colonial history as it narrates the founding of Tenejapa, a Tseltal town in Chiapas. *Kajkanantik*, however, reads more like a *crónica* and is not as aesthetically developed as other indigenous novels. Josias López K'ana from the Tseltal community published *Sakubel k'inal jachwinik / La aurora lacandona* (The Lacandon dawn). This text, however, is best characterized as a collection of short stories. Javier Gómez Navarrete's *Cecilio Chi'* is another important novel published in Mexico. Since these publications, other important novelists have emerged in Maya-Yukatek, including Isaac Carrillo Can (*U yóok'otilo'ob áak'ab / Danzas de la noche* [Dances of the night]), as well as in other indigenous languages, particularly Nahuatl and Zapotec. South America has seen the publication of the first Mapuche novel, *Cherrufe* by Ruth Mariela Fuentealba Milaguir, and the first Quechua novel, *Apu Kolki Hirka / Dios Montaña de plata* (Silver mountain god) by Macedonio Villafán Broncano.

41. As I noted in chapter 2, Luis de Lión was a politically committed teacher who was "disappeared" by military forces in Guatemala City in 1984.

42. González's publisher, the Yax Te' Foundation, is a U.S.-based entity that has supported the publication of other indigenous writers in Guatemala.

43. See Arias, "Kotz'ib"; and Sitler, "Entrevista con Gaspar Pedro González."

44. As I mentioned in the introduction, authors usually self-translate, which raises another set of questions about the text. My position is that the translation is also an original artifact. This said, some knowledge of the Mayan language helps. For instance, the term *pelaná* is left untranslated in the Spanish version of *Teya*, but having informally taken Maya Yukatek classes I knew that it literally refers to a mother's vagina and is considered by Mayas and mestizos to be the worst of insults.

45. Teuton, "The Indigenous Novel," 318–32.

46. A reference to the structural, economic, and epistemological changes, brought about by the Spanish colonization of the Americas, that instituted a racial hierarchy associated with the distribution of labor as well. See Quijano, "Coloniality of Power, Eurocentrism, and Social Classification," 181–224.

47. Fabian, *Time and the Other*, 21.

48. "It is not the dispersal of human cultures in space that leads anthropology to 'temporalize' . . . it is naturalized-spatialized Time which gives meaning . . . to the distribution of humanity in space." Ibid., 25.

49. See Amin, *Eurocentrism*; and Mignolo, *The Darker Side of the Renaissance*. For Amin, Eurocentrism unfolds at the same time as capitalism; both are part of the same development and thus cannot be separated. Similarly, Mignolo identifies modernity as the other side of coloniality.

50. See Amin, *Eurocentrism*.

51. The EZLN communiqué that circulated in June 2000 clearly stated that the Zapatistas would not vote for the Partido de la Revolución Democrática, considered the leftist party in Mexico, or any other party, as they did not feel represented. See "EZLN Communique Regarding Elections," http://www.csuchico.edu/zapatist/HTML/Archive/Communiques/ccri_elections_june.html . In 2006, the EZLN began the "Otra campaña," arguing for a new politics from below that neither the Left nor the Right have achieved in Mexico. See Ross, "The Zapatista Challenge."

52. See Henríquez, "Lanzarán EZLN y CNI candidata indígena."

53. See Bakhtin, "Discourse in the Novel."

54. Many indigenous intellectuals propose to rename the continent Abya Yala. See Albó, "Our Identity," 33, and Muyulema, "De la 'cuestión indígena,'" 327–64.

55. See de la Cruz, "Reflexiones sobre la escritura."

56. Brígido-Corachán, "Una aproximación a la obra de Javier Castellanos Martínez."

57. Cocom Pech, personal communication, July 2014.

58. Gómez Navarrete, *Cecilio Chi'*.

59. Ceh Moo, personal communication, July 2014.

60. See Campbell et al., *Zapotec Struggles*.

61. See Stephen, *We Are the Face of Oaxaca*.

62. De la Cruz, "Reflexiones sobre la escritura."

63. *Neza* translates as "el camino" (or "the path" in English). The magazine was published from June 1935 to January 1937.

64. The magazine was published regularly from 1970 to 2000.

65. De la Cruz, "Reflexiones sobre la escritura," 492–95.

66. See CDI, "Serie Letras Indígenas," 59.

67. A reprint of this novel in the twenty-first century has changed the order.

68. "Un año estuve en esa casa, ya no pude soportar más el maltrato que nos daban las señoras que mandaban ahí y, gracias a que en ese tiempo aún vivían mis padres, me atreví a escapar de ese lugar para regresar a lo mío. Cuando regresé al pueblo, mis padres no se convencieron de mi decisión, y otra vez, me llevaron a la ciudad. Y de nuevo, a otra casa en donde había niños y muchos más que en la anterior." Castellanos Martínez, *Wila che be ze lhao / Cantares de los vientos primerizos*, 20.

69. See Castellanos Martínez, "La lengua zapoteca hoy."

70. "Yo soy todavía una de las ramas de aquel Viejo tronco de donde nosotros surgimos, conmigo termina el aliento de vida que sembró Berhjashirha, aquel que nos trajo cuando los viejos se decidieron salir del valle de donde surgió nuestra sabiduría y nuestra zapoteikedad." Castellanos Martínez, *Wila che be ze lhao / Cantares de los vientos primerizos*, 71.

71. "Linda antropóloga, qué decisión podrías tomar, teniendo en cuenta que tú eres gente de ciudad y que yo soy de estos lugares, soy indígena, como ustedes dicen y ahora quiero que te atrevas a dormir conmigo, tú como mujer y yo como hombre.

"Mira, Jaime . . . yo no he visto dónde esté escrita la ley que hace a los seres humanos diferentes como para que digamos, 'este es mexicano o este otro es europeo'; para mí, desde el momento que nacimos tenemos los mismos derechos, sólo que la ambición humana es la que ha dividido a la humanidad." Ibid., 126.

72. Maldonado-Torres, "On the Coloniality of Being."

73. "Es verdad cuando dices que yo no sé leer, pero aunque así esté el montón de libros, diciendo eso; yo no lo puedo creer. Nosotros no hemos estado en guerra con nadie y no vamos a estar en guerra con nadie, porque lo que ahora nos sucede no es que alguien nos haya arrebatado nuestra riqueza y que ahora no nos la quiera entregar . . . la riqueza es lo contrario de lo que a nosotros nos gusta ser, por eso nuestros antepasados nunca se propusieron ser dueños únicos de la tierra y por eso toleraron al extranjero." Castellanos Martínez, *Wila che be ze lhao / Cantares de los vientos primerizos*, 139.

74. The Spanish reads, "fama van a tener por su pobreza." Ibid., 134.

75. "Ellos también tienen que entender que yo lo que estoy buscando es la apertura. Ha habido mucho rezago dentro de las lenguas originarias de México porque hay grupos dentro de las mismas etnias o los grupos culturales que podría decirse que deciden de qué manera uno tiene que trabajar. O sea, lo bonito es la poesía, es la canción en la lengua originaria o en el idioma maya, en mi caso; es bonita la leyenda, es bonita la recopilación, es bonito hacer o decir, 'vamos a ejemplificar a la X-tabay.' Pones la X-tabay en cincuenta mil versiones y eso no es creación, no es recreación, no es transcripción, no, es simplemente modificar contextos—¿sí?—y volver a imprimir." Ceh Moo, "Primera novela en maya."

76. "Afortunadamente, un día tuve un conflicto con mi padre por razones de maltrato a mi madre, él, en ese entonces dijo que yo nunca podría compararme con él

porque yo soy mujer y el hombre; con ese comentario aducía que los hombres podían hacer lo que quisieran, muy al contrario las mujeres, por ser lo que son; mujeres además de indias." Ceh Moo, "Conversación con Sol Ceh Moo."

77. See Crenshaw, "Mapping the Margins," 1244.

78. Machuca Gallegos, "En los márgenes de Mérida."

79. The term *cacique* comes from the Arawak language and means "chief." During the colonial period in Mexico, caciques were indigenous leaders, or what Alan Knight calls vital cogs, in the colonial administration. During the nineteenth century, *cacique* came to mean a political boss. See Knight and Pansters, *Caciquismo*, 9–47.

80. Jacinto Canek (born Jacinto Santos Uc) was a Mayan leader who valiantly fought the Spanish in 1761. Cecilio Chi' was a Maya commander in the Caste War. Felipe Carrillo Puerto was a socialist governor in Yucatán from 1922 to 1924.

81. "Traza la trayectoria de Emeterio, el hijo de Teya, por tratarse del vástago víctima de los vínculos entre el racismo y el capitalismo que fueron cruciales para el desarrollo intelectual de Teya." Arias, "¿Tradición versus modernidad?," 217.

82. Del Valle Escalante, "The Maya World," 27–50.

83. *Mother* narrates Pavel's political activism and his eventual arrest. His mother becomes part of the revolution. See Gorky, *Mother*.

84. Del Valle Escalante, "The Maya World," 42.

85. Although I am not assuming that Marisol Ceh Moo tries to make this point, the Left in El Salvador since 1932 has co-opted indigenous struggles by marking 1932 as a class struggle, not an indigenous one.

86. "Esa Granada me la dieron unos camaradas del FMLN . . . es en realidad un juguete. . . . Es en verdad un bonito juguete pero, inservible." Ceh Moo, *X-Teya, U puksi'ik'al ko'olel / Teya, un corazón de mujer*, 313.

87. Villagómez Valdés, "Mujeres de Yucatán," 3–19.

88. Pérez, *The Decolonial Imaginary*, 50.

89. Ibid., 50.

90. "¡Nos vemos, Teya, prepárame algo rico para comer, cuídate y no trabajes mucho!," Ceh Moo, *X-Teya, U puksi'ik'al ko'olel / Teya, un corazón de mujer*, 199.

91. "Mmm . . . ! ¡Cómo que no voy a trabajar! ¿Entonces quien crees que va a preparar la comida, zopenco?—respondía muy despacio, cuando sabía que nadie la oía." Ibid., 200.

92. Although various Marxist ideologies coexist, the original conception proposed by Karl Marx did not engage with a number of other social sectors. As López de Lara Marín explains, "We now know that [this early Marxist paradigm] forgets—and when it obtains power represses—other differences and oppositions: farmers, women, oppressed nationalities, Dostoyevsky's subterranean man: the other in each one of us, sexuality and its contradictory complement: our aspiration to the divine, our beliefs that are called irrational, poetry . . . anyway, every one of these reasons governed by exception and difference, the world of the other and the other. This multiple other that Marx could not recognize." ("Ahora sabemos que este esquema olvida—y cuando toma el poder las reprime—otras diferencias y oposiciones: Los campesinos, la mujer, las nacionalidades oprimidas, el hombre subterráneo de Dostoyevsky: el otro que es cada uno de nosotros, la sexualidad y su complemento contradictorio: la aspiración hacia lo

divino, las creencias que llamamos irracionales, la poesía ... en fin, todas esas razones regidas por la excepción y la diferencia, el mundo de los Otros y del Otro. Ese otro múltiple que Marx no pudo reconocer.") López de Lara Marín, "Marxismo y cuestión indígena," 4.

93. See Foucault, *The Order of Things.*

94. "Teya Martín, ellos vienen sólo con lo que tienen puesto— me indicaba cuando notaba mi molestia por sentar en mi mesa a gente desconocida. Ahí me tienen cocinando, pero que importaba, mi Emeterio crecía y crecía." Ceh Moo, *X-Teya, U puksi'ik'al ko'olel / Teya, un corazón de mujer,* 232.

95. "Emeterio también tenía sus seguidores y sus detractores. Su vida, salpicada de escándalos sexuales, era conocida en toda la región. Embaucador de féminas humildes que caían ante su verborrea del amor libre y sin ataduras; que se desvestían con los versos de Neruda; desvirginador de muchachitas de la clase media que caían redonditas bajo el adoctrinamiento de que el himen es un resabio de la sociedad capitalista moralista; exhibido como un enfermo sexual que no se jode él mismo porque no se alcanza. Aun así, con sus semejanzas, dos visiones distintas del mundo." Ibid., 273.

96. Ibid., 263.

97. "Para qué luchan si todos al final terminarán haciendo lo mismo por lo que pelearon ... el mal no está en el sistema, el mal está en el corazón del hombre." Ibid., 330.

98. "Hay demasiado conformismo en el mundo, por eso la pobreza crece, la injusticia campea por doquier sin que nadie la denuncie, sin que nadie se rebele." Ibid., 331.

Epilogue

1. Many Ch'orti' in Honduras had Guatemalan grandparents because of the redrawing of borders in 1932, which the nation-state of Honduras uses to dismiss indigenous claims in Honduras. See Mena Cabezas, "Los chortis."

2. Tilley, *Seeing Indians,* 2005.

3. Metz, "An Ambivalent Nation."

4. I am referring here to the famous debate between Bartolomé de las Casas and Juan Ginés de Sepúlveda, who, basing his arguments on Aristotle, advocated that the subjugation of Indians was lawful.

5. Arturo Arias points out that the emergence of multiple linguistic registers limits the critic's ability to analyze indigenous literature. See Arias, "¿Tradición versus modernidad?," 12.

6. See, for example, Sak Tzevul (Tsotsil), Gonzalo Candia ("Rapero de Tlalpa") (Mixteco), Pat Maya ("Rap in Maya"), Tzutu Baktun Kan (Tz'utujil), Luzmila Carpio (Quechua), among many others.

7. See the essays in Wilson and Stewart, *Global Indigenous Media.*

8. See, for example, the Chiapas Photography Project, founded by Mexican American Carlota Duarte in 1992.

BIBLIOGRAPHY

Abel, Elizabeth, ed. *Writing and Sexual Difference*. Chicago: University of Chicago Press, 1982.
Acevedo, Anabella, and Aída Toledo, eds. *Para conjurar el sueño: Poetas guatemaltecas del siglo XX*. Guatemala City: Papiro, 1998.
Adorno, Rolena, ed. *From Oral to Written Expression: Native Andean Chronicles of the Early Colonial Period*. Foreign and Comparative Studies. Latin American Series, no. 4. Syracuse, N.Y.: Maxwell School of Citizenship and Public Affairs, Syracuse University, 1982.
———. *Guaman Poma: Writing and Resistance in Colonial Peru*. Austin: University of Texas Press, 1986.
Aguado Vázquez, José Carlos. *Cuerpo humano e imagen corporal: Notas para una antropología de la corporeidad*. Mexico City: UNAM, Instituto de Investigaciones Antropológicas, 2004.
Aguilar Gil, Yasnaya Elena. "(Is There) an Indigenous Literature?" Translated by Gloria E. Chacón. *Diálogo* 19, no. 1 (2016): 157–59. https://muse.jhu.edu/.
Aguirre Beltrán, Gonzálo. "Teoría y práctica de la educación indígena." *Revista Mexicana de Sociología* 16, no. 2 (May–August 1954): 225–34.
Ajchowen. *Ixkik*. Unpublished m.s., n.d.
Ak'abal, Humberto. *Ajkem tzij / Tejedor de palabras*. 2nd ed. Guatemala City: UNESCO, 1998.
———. *El animalero: Poemas*. Guatemala City: Ministerio de Cultura y Deportes, 1990.
———. *Aqajtzij / Palabramiel*. Guatemala City: Nawal Wuj, 2001.
———. *Corazón de toro*. Guatemala City: Artemis Edinter, 2002.
———. *Grito en la sombra*. Guatemala City: Artemis Edinter, 2001.
———. "Literatura maya contemporánea." *Blanco Movil*, no. 70 (1996): 8–9. http://www.blancomovil.com.mx/pdf/BlancoMovil_70.pdf.
Akkeren, Ruud van. *La visión indígena de la conquista*. Guatemala City: Serviprensa, 2007.
Alaimo, Stacy, and Susan J. Hekman, eds. *Material Feminisms*. Bloomington: Indiana University Press, 2008.
Alarcón. Norma. "Traddutora, traditora: Una figura paradigmática del feminismo de las chicanas." Translated by Cecilia Olivares. *Debate Feminista* 4, no. 8 (September 1993): 19–48.
Albareda, Ginés de, and Francisco Garfias, eds. *Antología de la poesía hispanoamericana: México*. Madrid: Biblioteca Nueva, 1958.
Albó, Xavier. "Our Identity Starting from Pluralism in the Base." In *The Postmodern-*

ism Debate in Latin America, edited by John Beverley, José Oviedo, and Michael Aronna, 18–33. Durham, N.C.: Duke University Press, 1995.

Albó, Xavier, ed. *Raíces de América: El mundo aymara*. Madrid: Alianza, 1988.

Alcina Franch, José, ed. *Floresta literaria de la América indígena: Antología de la literatura de los pueblos indígenas de América*. Madrid: Aguilar, 1957.

———. *Indianismo e indigenismo en América*. Madrid: Alianza, 1990.

Alegría, Fernando. *Historia de la novela hispanoamericana*. Mexico City: Andrea, 1966.

Allen, Chadwick. *Blood Narrative*. Durham, N.C.: Duke University Press, 2002.

———. *Trans-Indigenous: Methodologies for Global Native Literary Studies*. Minneapolis: University of Minnesota Press, 2012.

ALMG (Academia de las Lenguas Mayas de Guatemala). *La planificación lingüística en países multilingües de Abya Yala / Cholb'al ub'antajik ri kitzijob'aal ri amaq'-tinamit Abya Yala*. Guatemala City: ALMG, 1996.

Altamirano, Ignacio Manuel. *El Zarco*. Buenos Aires: Espasa-Calpe, 1945.

"Altamirano, Ignacio Manuel." In *Diccionario de escritores hispanoamericanos: Del siglo XVI al siglo XX*, edited by Aarón Alboukrek and Esther Herrer, 12–13. Mexico City: Larousse, 1998.

Alvarado, Elvia. *Don't Be Afraid, Gringo: A Honduran Woman Speaks from the Heart—The Story of Elvia Alvarado*. Translated by Medea Benjamin. New York: Harper and Row, 1989.

Álvarez, Sonia E., Evelina Dagnino, and Arturo Escobar, eds. *Cultures of Politics / Politics of Cultures: Re-Visioning Latin American Social Movements*. Boulder, Colo.: Westview, 1998.

Ament, Gail R. "The Postcolonial Mayan Scribe: Contemporary Indigenous Writers of Guatemala." PhD diss., University of Washington, 1998.

Amin, Samir. *Eurocentrism*. New York: Monthly Review Press, 1989.

Anderson, Benedict R. *Imagined Communities: Reflections on the Origin and Spread of Nationalism*. London: Verso, 1991.

"Angélica Ortiz en el IV festival de poesía en las lenguas de América." Video. Posted by PUIC-UNAM, September 17, 2012. http://vimeo.com/49636771.

"Angelina Suyul." YouTube video. Posted by "vayijel," October 20, 2010.

Anglesey, Zoë. *Ixok Amar-Go: Central American Women's Poetry for Peace / Poesía de mujeres centroamericanas por la paz*. Penobscot, Me.: Granite, 1987.

Arguedas, José María. *El zorro de arriba y el zorro de abajo*. Edited by Eve-Marie Fell. Nanterre, France: ALLCA XX, 1990.

Arias, Arturo. "Asomos de la narrativa indígena maya." Introduction to *El tiempo principia en Xibalbá*, by Luis de Lión, i–vii. Guatemala City: Artemis Edinter, 1997.

———. *Gestos ceremoniales: Narrativa centroamericana, 1960–1990*. Guatemala City: Artemis Edinter, 1998.

———. *La identidad de la palabra: Narrativa guatemalteca del siglo veinte*. Guatemala City: Artemis Edinter, 1987.

———. *Ideologías, literatura y sociedad durante la Revolución Guatemalteca, 1944–1954*. Havana: Casa de las Américas, 1979.

———. "Kotz'ib: The Emergence of a New Maya Literature." *Latin American Indian Literatures Journal* 24 (2008): 7–28.
———. "The Mayan Movement, Postcolonialism, and Cultural Agency." *Journal of Latin American Cultural Studies* 15, no. 2 (August 2006): 251–62.
———. "Racialized Subalternity as Emancipatory Decolonial Project: *Time Commences in Xibalba* by Luis de Lión." In *Time Commences in Xibalbá*. Translated by Nathan C. Henne, 85–115. Tucson: University of Arizona Press, 2012.
———. *Taking Their Word: Literature and the Signs of Central America*. Minneapolis: University of Minnesota Press, 2007.
———. "¿Tradición versus modernidad en las novelas yukatekas contemporáneas? Yuxtaponiendo X-Teya, u puksi'ik'al ko'olel y U yóok'otilo'ob áak'ab." *Cuadernos de Literatura* 32 (July–December 2012): 208–35.
Arias, Arturo, ed. *The Rigoberta Menchú Controversy*. Minneapolis: University of Minnesota Press, 2001.
Arias, Arturo, Luis E. Cárcamo-Huechante, and Emilio del Valle Escalante. "Literaturas de Abya Yala." *LASA Forum* 43, no.1 (Winter 2012): 7–10.
Arias, Jacinto. "Reconstitución de la intelectualidad Maya-Zoque." *Nuestra Palabra*, supplement to *El Nacional* 3, no. 12 (December 1992): 1.
Armstrong, Jeannette C., ed. *Looking at the Words of Our People: First Nations Analysis of Literature*. Penticton, B.C.: Theytus, 1993.
Arriaza, Gilberto, and Arturo Arias. "Claiming Collective Memory: Maya Languages and Civil Rights." *Social Justice* 25, no. 3 (Fall 1998): 70–79.
Arroyo, Jossianna. "Transculturation, Syncretism, and Hybridity." In *Critical Terms in Caribbean and Latin American Thought*, 133–44. New York: Palgrave Macmillan, 2016.
Arzápalo Marín, Ramón. *El ritual de los bacabes*. Mexico City: Instituto de Investigaciones Filológicas, Centro de Estudios Mayas, Universidad Nacional Autónoma de México, 1987.
Asociación Cultural B'eyb'al. *Literatura indígena de América: Primer congreso*. Guatemala City: Asociación Cultural B'eyb'al, 1999.
———. *Literatura indígena de América: Segundo congreso*. Guatemala City: Asociación Cultural B'eyb'al, 2001.
Asociación de Escritores Mayenses de Guatemala. *Chatwalijoq* 5, no. 9 (January–March 1990). Quetzaltenango, Guatemala.
Asturias, Miguel Ángel. *Hombres de maíz*. Guatemala City: Editorial Universitaria, Universidad de San Carlos de Guatemala, 2008.
Báez-Ronquillo, Carlos. "Retorno a la novela indigenista del cardenismo: Derechos humanos, antropología y literatura como instrumentos del Estado." PhD diss., University of Minnesota Conservancy, 2011.
Bakhtin, M. M. *The Dialogic Imagination: Four Essays*. Edited by Michael Holquist. Austin: University of Texas Press, 1981.
———. "Discourse in the Novel." *Literary Theory: An Anthology* 2 (1934): 674–85.
Ballesteros Gaibrois, Manuel, and Julia Ulloa Suárez. *Indigenismo americano*. Madrid: Cultura Hispánica, 1961.

Ballón Aguirre, Enrique. "La literatura oral en Latinoamérica: Una hipótesis semiolingüística." *Escritos* 11, no. 12 (1995): 17–34.

Banham, Martin. *The Cambridge Guide to Theater.* Cambridge: Cambridge University Press, 1998.

Barre, Marie-Chantal. *Ideologías indigenistas y movimientos Indios.* Mexico City: Siglo Veintiuno, 1983.

Barrera Vásquez, Alfredo. *El libro de los cantares de Dzitbalché: Una traducción con notas y una introducción.* Mexico City: Instituto Nacional de Antropología e Historia, 1965.

———. "Los cantares de Dzitbalché." In *Literatura maya,* edited by Mercedes de la Garza, 350–53. Barcelona: Biblioteca Ayacucho, 1980.

Barrera Vásquez, Alfredo, and Silvia Rendón, eds. *El libro de los libros de Chilam Balam.* 3rd ed. Mexico City: Fondo de Cultura Economica, 1965.

Barrios de Chungara, Domitila. *Let Me Speak! Testimony of Domitila, a Woman of the Bolivian Mines.* Edited by Moema Viezzer. New York: Monthly Review Press, 1978.

Barthes, Roland. *Análisis estructural del relato.* Translated by Beatriz Dorriots. Mexico City: Coyoacán, 1998.

———. "The Death of the Author." In *Image, Music, Text,* 142–48. New York: Hill and Wang, 1977.

Bastos, Santiago, and Manuela Camus. *Abriendo caminos: Las organizaciones mayas desde el Nobel hasta el Acuerdo de derechos indígenas.* Guatemala City: FLACSO, 1995.

———. *Mayanización y vida cotidiana: La ideología multicultural en la sociedad guatemalteca.* Vol. 1. Guatemala City: FLACSO, CIRMA, CHOLSAMAJ, 2007.

———. *Quebrando el silencio: Organizaciones del pueblo maya y sus demandas (1986–1992).* Guatemala City: FLACSO, 1993.

Basso, Ellen B., ed. *Native Latin American Cultures through Their Discourse.* Bloomington: Folklore Institute, Indiana University, 1990.

Batista, Dolores. *Anayáwari Ra'icháara.* CD. Instituto Chihuahuense de la Cultura; Conaculta. 1999.

Batz, Giovanni. "Ixil Migration to the United States." Paper presented at Critical Indigeneities Symposium, Austin, April 2015.

Batzibal Tujal, Juana. "Mujer maya: Rectora de nuestra cultura." In *Identidad: Rostros sin máscara,* edited by A. Pop Delgado, Morna Macleod, and María Luisa Cabrera Pérez-Armiñán, 25–43. Guatemala City: Oxfam-Australia, 2000.

Bautista Pérez, Judith. "El racismo en el desarrollo profesional y académico de las mujeres indígenas." *Aquí Estamos* 5, no. 9 (July–December 2008): 11–26.

Bautista Vázquez, Ruperta. *Ch'iel K'opojelal / Vivencias.* Tuxtla Gutiérrez, Mexico: CELALI, 2003.

Becker, Marc. *Mariátegui and Latin American Marxist Theory.* Ohio: Ohio University Center for International Studies, 1993.

Benjamin, Walter. "The Storyteller." In *Illuminations: Essays and Reflections,* edited by Hannah Arendt, 83–109. New York: Schocken, 1969.

———. "The Task of the Translator." In *Illuminations: Essays and Reflections,* edited by Hannah Arendt, 69–82. New York: Schocken, 1969.

Bethell, Leslie. *A Cultural History of Latin America: Literature, Music, and the Visual Arts in the 19th and 20th Centuries*. Cambridge History of Latin America. New York: Cambridge University Press, 1998.

Beverley, John. *Against Literature*. Minneapolis: University of Minnesota Press, 1993.

———. "The Im/possibility of Politics?' Subalternity, Modernity, Hegemony." In *The Latin American Subaltern Studies Reader: Latin America Otherwise*, edited by Ileana Rodríguez and María Milagros López, 47–63. Durham, N.C.: Duke University Press, 2001.

———. *Subalternity and Representation: Arguments in Cultural Theory—Postcontemporary Interventions*. Durham, N.C.: Duke University Press, 1999.

Beverley, John, Michael Aronna, and José Oviedo, eds. *The Postmodernism Debate in Latin America*. Durham, N.C.: Duke University Press, 1995.

Beverley, John, and Marc Zimmerman. *Literature and Politics in Central American Revolutions*. Austin: University of Texas Press, 1990.

Bierhorst, John. *Latin American Folktales: Stories from Hispanic and Indian Traditions*. New York: Pantheon, 2002.

"Binni Záa / Los zapotecas—Poemas de Macario Matus." *400 elefantes: Revista nicaragüense de arte y cultura*. August 12, 2009. https://400elefantes.wordpress.com/2009/08/12/binni-zaa-los-zapotecas-poemas-de-macario-matus/.

Black, Chad Thomas. *The Making of an Indigenous Movement: Culture, Ethnicity, and Post-Marxist Social Praxis in Ecuador*. Albuquerque: University of New Mexico Latin American Institute, 1999.

Blanco, Txus [Lorena Cabnal]. "Mujer, maya-xinca y feminista." *La Independent*, November 30, 2011. http://www.laindependent.cat/index.php?option=com_content&view=article&id=1634%3Adona-maia-xinca-i-feminista-el-25n-a-barcelona&catid=78%3Aviolencia-masclista&Itemid=178&lang=es.

Bloomfield, Leonard. *Language*. New York: Holt, Rinehart and Winston, 1933.

Boal, Augusto. *Theatre of the Oppressed*. Translated by Charles A. and Maria-Odilia Leal McBride. New York: Urizen, 1979.

Bollinger, William, and Daniel Manny Lund. "Minority Oppression: Toward Analyses That Clarify and Strategies That Liberate." "Minorities in the Americas," special issue, *Latin American Perspectives* 9, no. 2 (Spring 1982): 2–28.

Bonfil Batalla, Guillermo. "El concepto de indio en América: Una categoría de la situación colonial." *Anales de Antropología* (1972): 105–24.

———. *Identidad y pluralismo cultural en América Latina*. Buenos Aires: Fondo Editorial del CEHASS; San Juan: Editorial de la Universidad de Puerto Rico, 1992.

———. *México profundo: Una civilización negada*. 2nd ed. Mexico City: Grijalbo: Consejo Nacional para la Cultura y las Artes, 1990.

———. *Pensar nuestra cultura: Ensayos*. Mexico City: Alianza, 1991.

———. *Utopía y revolución: El pensamiento político contemporáneo de los indios en América Latina*. Serie Interétnica. 2nd ed. Mexico City: Nueva Imagen, 1988.

Boone, Elizabeth, and Walter D. Mignolo, eds. *Writing without Words: Alternative Literacies in Mesoamerica and the Andes*. Durham, N.C.: Duke University Press, 1999.

Boot, Erik. "The Life and Times of B'alah Chan K'awil of Mutal (Dos Pilas), According to Dos Pilas Hieroglyphic Stairway 2." *Mesoweb* (2002). http://www.mesoweb.com/features/boot/DPLHS2.pdf.

Bracamonte y Sosa, Pedro. *La memoria enclaustrada: Historia indígena de Yucatán, 1750–1915.* Historia de los Pueblos Indígenas de México. Mexico City: Ciesas, INI, 1994.

Braz, Albert. "Collaborative Authorship and Indigenous Literatures." *Comparative Literature and Culture* 13, no. 2 (2011). http://docs.lib.purdue.edu/clcweb/vol3/iss2/3.

Briceño Chel, Fidencio. "¿Literatura indigenista o literatura? ¿Renacimiento o apertura? El caso de los mayas." In *Arguedas: Entre la antropología y la literatura*, edited by Francisco Amezcua Pérez, 25–31. Mexico City: Taller Abierto, 2000.

Bricker, Victoria. *The Indian Christ, the Indian King: The Historical Substrate of Maya Myth and Ritual.* Austin: University of Texas Press, 1981.

———. "The Last Gasp of Maya Hieroglyphic Writing in the Books of Chilam Balam of Chumayel and Chan Kan." In *Word and Image in Maya Culture: Explorations in Language, Writing, and Representation*, edited by William Hanks and Don S. Rice, 39–50. Salt Lake City: University of Utah Press, 1989.

Brígido-Corachán, Anna M. "Una aproximación a la obra de Javier Castellanos Martínez en el marco de la literatura zapoteca contemporánea: Reflexiones, inquietudes y pláticas." *Diálogo* 19, no.1 (Spring 2016): 175–83.

Brotherston, Gordon. *La América indígena en su literatura: Los libros del cuarto mundo.* Sección de Obras de Historia. Mexico City: Fondo de Cultura Económica, 1997.

Brown, Cecil L. *Hieroglyphic Literacy in Ancient Mayaland: Inferences from Linguistic Data. Current Anthropology* 32 (1991): 489–96.

Brumfiel, Elizabeth. "Methods in Feminist and Gender Archeology: A Feeling for Difference—and Likeness." In *Handbook of Gender in Archaeology*, edited by Sarah M. Nelson, 31–58. Oxford, Calif.: AltaMira, 2006.

Burns, Allan, ed. *An Epoch of Miracles: Oral Literature of the Yucatec Maya.* Austin: University of Texas Press, 1983.

C., Cesar. "'Poesía es sinónimo de libertad': Entrevista a Mikeas Sánchez, poeta y narradora zoque de Chiapas." *Zapateando 2*, January 13, 2008. https://zapateando2.wordpress.com/2008/01/13/%E2%80%9Cpoesia-es-sinonimo-de-libertad%E2%80%9D-entrevista-a-mikeas-sanchez-poeta-y-narradora-zoque-de-chiapas/. September 4, 2015.

Call, Wendy. "The Light of Translation." *Many Words for Welcome: Words That Fascinate, Agitate, or Simply Stop Me in My Tracks*, February 25, 2011. http://wendycall.blogspot.com/2011/02/light-of-translation.html.

Calvo, Hortensia. "The Politics of Print: The Historiography of the Book in Early Spanish America." *Book History* 6 (2003): 277–305.

Cammett, John. *Antonio Gramsci and the Origins of Italian Communism.* Stanford, Calif.: Stanford University Press, 1969.

Campbell, Howard, et al. *Zapotec Struggles: Histories, Politics, and Representations from Juchitán, Oaxaca.* Washington, D.C.: Smithsonian Institution Press, 1993.

Canché Canul, Vicente. *U tsikbalil juntul chak nuxiib wíinik / La leyenda del hombre colorado.* Mexico City: Aldina, 1998.

Canché Móo, Vicente. *U Tzikbalilo'ob Mayab / Relatos del Mayab*. Mexico City: Instituto para el Desarollo de la Cultura Maya de Yucatán, 2002.
Can Pat, Gerardo. "Kin dzu'udziko'ob / Las beso." *Navegaciones Zur* 20 (1998): 16.
Canters, Hanneke, and Grace M. Jantzen. *Forever Fluid*. Manchester, U.K.: Manchester University Press, 2005.
Cardoza y Aragón, Luis. *Miguel Ángel Asturias: Casi novela*. Mexico City: Era, 1991.
Carey, David. *Engendering Mayan History: Kaqchikel Women as Agents and Conduits of the Past, 1875–1970*. New York: Routledge, 2006.
Carmack, Robert M. *Evolución del reino k'iche' / Kik'ulmatajem le k'iche'aab'*. Guatemala City: Cholsamaj, 2001.
———. *Guatemala: Cosecha de violencias*. San José, Costa Rica: FLACSO, 1991.
———. *Harvest of Violence: The Maya Indians and the Guatemalan Crisis*. Norman: University of Oklahoma Press, 1988.
———. *Rebels of Highland Guatemala: The Quiché-Mayas of Momostenango*. Civilization of the American Indian, vol. 215. Norman: University of Oklahoma Press, 1995.
Carmack, Robert M., Janine L. Gasco, and Gary H. Gossen, eds. *The Legacy of Mesoamerica: History and Culture of a Native American Civilization*, 2nd ed. Upper Saddle River, N.J.: Pearson, 2007.
Carmack, Robert M., and James L. Mondloch. *El título de Totonicapán: Texto, traducción y comentario*. Fuentes para el Estudio de la Cultura Maya, no. 3. Mexico City: Universidad Nacional Autónoma de México, 1983.
Carrillo Can, Isaac. *U yóok'otilo'ob áak'ab / Danzas de la noche*. Mexico City: Consejo Nacional para la Cultura y las Artes, Dirección General de Culturas Populares, 2011.
Casanova, Pascale. *The World Republic of Letters*. Translated by M. B. DeBevoise. Cambridge, Mass.: Harvard University Press, 2004.
Casey, Dennis F. "Indigenismo: The Guatemalan Experience." PhD diss, University of Kansas, 1979.
Castaneda, Carlos. *The Teachings of Don Juan: A Yaqui Way of Knowledge*. Berkeley: University of California Press, 1968.
Castañeda Barrera, Eva. "Entrevista con Natalia Toledo." *Periódico de Poesía*, October 2012. http://www.periodicodepoesia.unam.mx/index.php?option=com_content&view=article&id=1540:entrevista-con-natalia-toledo&catid=563:-no-34&Itemid=154.
Castellanos, Rosario. *Balún-Canán*. Mexico City: Fondo de Cultura Económica, 1957.
———. *El rescate del mundo: Poemario de Rosario Castellanos*. CD. Puertavor, 2013.
Castellanos Martínez, Javier. *Da kebe nho Seke gon ben xhi'ne Guzio / Relación de hazañas del hijo del relámpago*. Oaxaca City: Instituto Oaxaqueño de las Culturas, 2002.
———. *Dxiokze xha . . . bene walhall / Gente del mismo corazón*. Mexico City: Conaculta, 2014.
———. "La lengua zapoteca hoy." YouTube vídeo, November 25, 2010. https://www.youtube.com/watch?v=N8R-K_5TDBE.
———. "La narrativa de los que hablamos el Dilla Xhon." In *Los escritores indígenas actuales*, vol. 2, edited by Carlos Montemayor, 39–50. Mexico City: Tierra Adentro, 1992.

———. *Laxdao yelazeralle / El corazón de los deseos*. Oaxaca City: Secretaría de Cultura del Gobierno del Estado de Oaxaca, 2007.
———. "El verdadero problema de la traducción en la literatura indígena." Paper presented at Primer Encuentro Maya-Zapoteca, Mexico City, November 11–14, 2010.
———. *Wila che be ze lhao / Cantares de los vientos primerizos*. Mexico City: Diana, 1994.
Cata, Víctor. "Untitled." Paper presented at Primer Encuentro Literario Maya-Zapoteca, Mexico City, 2010.
Cavarero, Adriana. *In Spite of Plato: A Feminist Rewriting of Ancient Philosophy*. New York: Routledge, 1995.
Cayuqui Estage, N. "El teatro indígena viviente. Una reseña." México: El Centavo, n. 176, marzo, Morelia, Michoacán, 1994, 29.
CDI (Comisión para el Desarrollo de los Pueblos Indígenas). "Serie Letras Indígenas Contemporáneas de los pueblos originarios." March 22, 2009. http://www.cdi.gob.mx/index.php?option=com_content&view=article&id=308&Itemid=5.
Ceballos, Rita, ed. *Antropología y políticas culturales: Patrimonio e identidad*. Buenos Aires: Rita Ceballos, 1989.
Ceh Moo, Marisol. "Conversación con Sol Ceh Moo." Interview by Código Mujer, 2014. http://codigomujer.com/interview/sol-ceh-moo/#.
———. *Jats'uts'il loolo'ob Xibalbaj / Jardines de Xibalbaj*. Mérida, México: Instituto de Cultura de Yucatán, Dirección de Patrimonio Cultural, 2010.
———. "Primera novela en maya: Literatura indígena." YouTube video. Posted by "Ojocosmogónico," June 30, 2009. https://www.youtube.com/watch?v=OcyYa5-YltM.
———. "Situación de la literatura actual." Paper presented at Primer Encuentro Literario Maya Zapoteca, Mexico City, 2010.
———. *T'ambilak men tunk'ulilo'ob / El llamado de los tunkules*. Mexico City: Conaculta, 2010.
———. *X-Teya, U puksi'ik'al ko'olel / Teya, un corazón de mujer*. Mexico City: Consejo Nacional para la Cultura y las Artes, 2008.
Centro Estatal de Lenguas, Arte y Literatura Indígenas (CELALI), Gobierno de Chiapas. March 12, 2014. http://www.celali.gob.mx.
Cerda García, Alejandro. "Multiculturalidad y educación intercultural entre el neoindigenismo y la autonomía." *Andamios* 3, no. 6 (June 2007): 97–135.
Cevallos, Diego. "Indígenas-México: Esterilizados esperan justicia y sufren rechazo." *IPS Inter Press Service Agencia de Noticias*, January 17, 2008. http://www.ipsnoticias.net/2008/01/indigenas-mexico-esterilizados-esperan-justicia-y-sufren-rechazo/.
Chacón, Gloria E. "Cultivating Nichimal K'op (Poetry) from the Heart: Indigenous Women of Chiapas." *Revista Canadiense de Estudios Hispánicos* 39, no. 1 (Autumn 2014): 165–80.
———. "Cuerpo y poesía: Transgresiones culturales en el trabajo de mujeres mayas." *Poéticas y políticas de género: Ensayos sobre imaginanos, literaturas y medios en Centroamérica*, edited by Monica Albizúrez Gil and Alexandra Ortiz Wallner, 269–83. Berlin: Tranvia, 2013.
———. "Escritores mayas contemporáneos: Redefiniendo nociones de tradición y

autoría." In *Diversidad y diálogo intercultural a través de las literaturas en lenguas mexicanas: Memoria del Encuentro Nacional de Literatura en Lenguas Indígenas, octubre de 2007*, 55–61. Mexico City: Secretaria de Cultura, 2007.

———."Kabawil: Contemporary Maya Writers and the Making of a Millenarian Literary Tradition." PhD diss., University of California, 2006.

———. "Poetizas mayas: Subjetividades contra la corriente." *Cuadernos de Literatura* 11, no. 22 (January–June 2007): 94–106.

Chacón Pineda, Nazario. *Estatua y danza*. Mexico City: Imprenta Escuela Nacional de Maestros, 1939.

Chanady, Amaryll Beatrice. *Latin American Identity and Constructions of Difference*. Minneapolis: University of Minnesota Press, 1994.

Chatterjee, Partha. *The Nation and Its Fragments: Colonial and Postcolonial Histories*. Princeton Studies in Culture/Power/History. Princeton, N.J.: Princeton University Press, 1993.

Chávez, Adrián Inés. *Pop Wuj*. Guatemala City: Timach, 2001.

Chávez, Rosa María. *Casa solitaria*. Guatemala City: Oscar de León, 2005.

———. "Cíclica." In *Rosa palpitante: Poesía femenina del siglo XX*, edited by Juan Fernando Cifuentes and Aida Toledo, 83. Guatemala City: Guatemala Palo de Hormigos, 2005.

———. *Piedra/Ab'aj*. Guatemala City: Cultura, 2009.

Chirix García, Emma Delfina. *Alas y raíces: Afectividad de las mujeres mayas / Rik'in ruxik' y ruxe'il: ronojel kajoqab'al ri mayab' taq ixoqi'*. Guatemala City: Grupo de Mujeres Mayas Kaqla, 2003.

———. "Los cuerpos y las mujeres kaqchikeles." *Desacatos* 36, no. 30 (2009): 149–60.

———. *Cuerpos, poderes y políticas: Mujeres mayas en un internado Católico / Ch'akulal, chuqʼaib'il chuqa b'anobäl: Mayab' ixoqi' chi ru pam jun kaxlan tz'apatäl tijonïk*. Guatemala City: Maya' Na'oj, 2013.

———. *Ru rayb'äl ri qach'akul / Los deseos de nuestro cuerpo*. Antigua Guatemala: Pensativo, 2010.

Christenson, Allen J. *Popol Wuj: The Sacred Book of the Maya*. Norman: University of Oklahoma Press, 2007.

Clifford, James. *The Predicament of Culture: Twentieth-Century Ethnography, Literature, and Art*. Cambridge, Mass.: Harvard University Press, 1988.

———. *Returns: Becoming Indigenous in the Twenty-First Century*. Cambridge, Mass.: Harvard University Press, 2013.

Cocom Pech, Jorge Miguel. *El cazador de auroras y otros relatos*. Bacalar, Mexico: Nave de Papel, 1997.

———. *Secretos del abuelo / Muk'ult'an in nool*. Mexico City: Universidad Nacional Autónoma de México, 2001.

———. "El secreto de los pájaros II." In *Secretos del abuelo / Muk'ult'an in nool*, 85–98. Mexico City: Universidad Nacional Autónoma de México, 2001.

———. "Testimonio de una iniciación: La prueba del aire, la prueba del sueño." In *Secretos del abuelo / Muk'ult'an in nool*, 35–41. Mexico City: Universidad Nacional Autónoma de México, 2001.

Coe, Michael D. *Breaking the Maya Code*. 3rd ed. New York: Thames and Hudson, 2012.

———. *The Maya Scribe and His World*. New York: Grolier Club, 1973.
Cojtí Cuxil, Demetrio. *Runa'oj ri maya' amaq / Configuración del pensamiento político del pueblo maya*. [Primera part]. Guatemala City: Asociación de Escritores Mayances de Guatemala, 1991.
———. *Políticas para la reivindicación de los mayas de hoy: Fundamento de los derechos específicos del pueblo maya*. Guatemala City: Cholsamaj, 1994.
———. *Ri Maya' moloj pa Iximulew / El movimiento maya (en Guatemala)*. Guatemala City: Cholsamaj, 1997.
Colas, Pierre Robert, and Sebastián Van Doesburg. "Monumentos mayas en el museo de arte prehispánico." In *Pictografía y escritura alfabética en Oaxaca*, edited by Sebastián van Doesburg, 73–88. Oaxaca City, Mexico: Fondo Editorial del IEEPO, 2008.
Collier, George Allen, and Elizabeth Lowery Quaratiello. *Basta! Land and the Zapatista Rebellion in Chiapas*. Oakland, Calif.: Food First Book, Institute for Food and Development Policy, 1994.
Collins, James, and Richard K. Blot. *Literacy and Literacies: Texts, Power, and Identity*. Cambridge: Cambridge University Press, 2003.
Colombres, Adolfo. *Sobre la cultura y el arte popular*. Mexico City: Del Sol, 1987.
Columbus, Christopher. *Four Voyages to the New World: Letters and Selected Documents*. Edited and translated by R. H. Major. New York: Citadel, 1992.
"The Columbus Letter: The Diffusion of Columbus's Letter through Europe, 1493–1497." Online at the University of Southern Maine. http://oshermaps.org/special-map-exhibits/columbus-letter/iv-diffusion-columbuss-letter-through-europe-1493-1497. Accessed June 20, 2016.
Comas, Juan. *Ensayos sobre indigenismo*. Mexico City: Instituto Indigenista Interamericano, 1953.
Cornejo Polar, Antonio. *Escribir en el aire: Ensayo sobre la heterogeneidad sociocultural en las literaturas andinas*. Lima: Horizonte, 1994.
———. "Indigenismo and Heterogeneous Literatures: Their Double Sociocultural Statute." In *The Latin American Cultural Studies Reader*, edited by Ana del Sarto, Alicia Ríos, and Abril Trigo, 100–115. Durham, N.C.: Duke University Press, 2004.
———. "Mestizaje, Transculturation, Heterogeneity." In *The Latin American Cultural Studies Reader*, edited by Ana del Sarto, Alicia Ríos, and Abril Trigo, 116–19. Durham, N.C.: Duke University Press, 2004.
———. *Mestizaje e hibridez: Los riesgos de las metáforas*. La Paz: Carrera de Literatura Facultad de Humanidades y Ciencias de la Educación UMSA, 1997.
———. *The Multiple Voices of Latin American Literature*. Morrison Library Inaugural Address Series, no. 1. Berkeley: Doe Library University of California, 1994.
———. "La novela indigenista: Un género contradictorio." *Texto Crítico* 14 (1979): 58–70.
Coronado, Jorge. *The Andes Imagined: Indigenismo, Society and Modernity*. Pittsburgh: University of Pittsburgh Press, 2009.
Cortazzo, Uruguay. *Indios y latinos*. Montevideo: Vinter, 2001.
Creamer, Winifred. "Mesoamerica as a Concept: An Archaeological View from

Central America." *Latin American Research Review* 22, no. 1 (1987): 35–62. http://www.jstor.org/stable/2503542.

Crenshaw, Kimberle. "Mapping the Margins: Intersectionality, Identity Politics, and Violence against Women of Color." *Stanford Law Review* 43, no. 6 (July 1991): 1241–99.

Cruz Velázquez, Bettina. "Los dilemas de la educación para las mujeres indígenas: ¿Instrumento para la marginalización o herramienta de emancipación?" *Aquí Estamos* 5, no. 9 (July–December 2008): 52–67.

Cú Choc, Maya Rossana. "¡Pobrecita yo!" In *Recorrido*, 41–42. Guatemala City: Saquil Tzij, 2005.

———. "Poemaya." In *Novísimos*, edited by Marco Anotino Flores et al., 69–102. Guatemala City: Cultura, 1996.

———. *Recorrido*. Guatemala City: Saquil Tzij, 2005.

———. *La rueda*. Guatemala City: Cultura, 2001.

Cuevas Cob, Briceida. "In k'aaba' / Mi nombre." September 18, 2005. http://www.jornada.unam.mx/2005/09/18/index.php?section=cultura&article=a06a1cu.

———. "Orígenes II (Briceida Cuevas, Nación Maya, Mexico)." YouTube video. Posted by "Revista Prometeo," June 27, 2007. https://www.youtube.com/watch?v=wMbGycJTyoI.

———. *Ti' u billil in nook' / Del dobladillo de mi ropa*. Mexico City: Comisión Nacional para el Desarrollo de los Pueblos Indígenas, 2008.

———. *U yok'ol auat pek'ti u kuxtal pek': ik'tanil ich maya t'an / El quejido del perro en su existencia: Poesía en lengua maya*. Bacalar, Mexico: Nave de Papel, 1998.

Cumes, Aura Estela, and Ana Silvia Monzón. *La encrucijada de las identidades: Mujeres, feminismos y mayanismos en dialogo*. Guatemala City: Instituto Universitario de la Mujer, 2006.

Cupil López, Saq No'jAlfredo. "Los derechos indígenas y la literatura maya." In *Literatura indígena de América: Segundo congreso*, 167–68. Guatemala City: Asociación Cultural B'eyb'al, 1999.

Dalton, Roque. *Miguel Mármol: Los sucesos de 1932 en El Salvador*. San José, Costa Rica: Editorial Universitaria Centroamericana, 1972.

Dary, Claudia, Guillermo de la Pena, and FLACSO. *La construcción de la nación y la representación ciudadana en México, Guatemala, Perú, Ecuador y Bolivia*. Guatemala City: FLACSO, 1998.

Dawson, Alexander S. "Histories and Memories of the Indian Boarding Schools in Mexico, Canada, and the United States." *Latin American Perspectives* 39, no. 5 (September 2009): 80–99.

———. *Indian and Nation in Revolutionary Mexico*. Tucson: University of Arizona Press, 2004.

Dawson, Victoria. "One from the Heart." *Smithsonian* 33, no. 11 (February 2003): 25.

de Acosta, José. *Natural and Moral History of the Indies*. Durham, N.C.: Duke University Press, 2002.

"Deadly Goddess." In *In the Language of Kings: An Anthology of Mesoamerican*

Literature—Pre-Columbian to the Present, edited by Miguel León-Portilla and Earl Shorris, 531–35. New York: W. W. Norton, 2001.

DeFrancis, John. *Visible Speech: The Diverse Oneness of Writing Systems*. Honolulu: University of Hawai'i Press, 1989.

de la Cadena, Marisol. *Indigenous Mestizos: The Politics of Race and Culture in Cuzco, Peru, 1919–1991*. Durham, N.C.: Duke University Press, 2000.

———. "Las mujeres son más indias." *Espejos y travesías* 16 (1992): 25–46.

de la Campa, Román. *Latin Americanism*. Cultural Studies of the Americas, vol. 3. Minneapolis: University of Minnesota Press, 1999.

de la Cruz, Víctor. "Indigenous Peoples' History (by Whom and for Whom?)." In *Zapotec Struggles: History, Politics, and Representations from Juchitán, Oaxaca*, edited by Howard Campbell et al., 29–37. Washington, D.C.: Smithsonian Institution Press, 1993.

———. Introduction to *El pensamiento de los binnigula'sa'*. Mexico City: Instituto Nacional de Antropología e Historia, 2007.

———. *Jardín de cactus*. Mexico City: Ocelote Servicios, 1991.

———. *La flor de la palabra / Guie' sti' diidxazá*. Mexico City: Premia Editora de Libros, 1983.

———. "Reflexiones sobre la escritura y el futuro de la literatura indígena." In *Escritura zapoteca: 2500 años de historia*, edited by Maria de los Ángeles Romero Frizzi, 487–501. Mexico City: Porrúa, Conaculta, Instituto Nacional de Antropología e Historia, 2003.

de la Cruz Cruz, Petrona. *A Desperate Woman: A Play in Two Acts*. Translated by Shanna Lorenz. In *Holy Terrors*, edited by Diana Taylor and Roselyn Costantino, 293–310. Durham, N.C.: Duke University Press, 2003.

de la Garza, Mercedes, ed. *Literatura maya*. Barcelona: Biblioteca Ayacucho, 1980.

de la Garza Camino, Mercedes, and Martha Cuevas García. "El dios K'awiil en los incensarios del Grupo de las Cruces de Palenque." *Mayab* 18 (2005): 99–112.

de Landa, Diego. *An Account of the Things of Yucatán*. Translated by David Castledine. Mexico City: Monclem, 2000.

de las Casas, Bartolomé. *The Devastation of the Indies: A Brief Account*. New York: Seabury, 1974.

Delgado Pop, Adela, Morna Macleod, and María Luisa Cabrera Pérez-Armiñán. *Identidad: Rostros sin máscara—Reflexiones sobre cosmovisión, género y etnicidad*. Guatemala City: Oxfam Australia, 2000.

de Lión, Luis. *Su segunda muerte*. Guatemala City: Nuevo Siglo, 1970.

———. *El tiempo principia en Xibalbá*. Guatemala City: Artemis Edinter, 1997.

———. *Los zopilotes*. Guatemala City: Landivar, 1968.

del Valle Escalante, Emilio. "Ambivalence and Contradiction in Contemporary Maya Literature from Yucatán: Jorge Cocom Pech's Muk'ult'an in Nool (Gradfather's Secrets)." In *Oxford Handbook of Indigenous American Literature*, edited by James H. Cox and Daniel Health Justice, 50–64. New York: Oxford University Press, 2014.

———. "The Maya World through Its Literature." In *The World of Indigenous North America*, edited by Robert Warrior, 27–50. New York: Routledge, 2015.

---. "Nacionalismo maya y descolonización política: Luis de Lión y *El tiempo principia en Xibalbá.*" *Cuadernos de Literatura* 19, no. 38 (July–December 2015): 318–37.

---. *Nacionalismos mayas y desafíos postcoloniales en Guatemala: Colonialidad, modernidad y políticas de la identidad cultural.* Guatemala City: FLACSO Guatemala, 2008.

---. "Self-Determination: A Perspective from Abya Yala." In *Restoring Indigenous Self-Determination: Theoretical and Practical Approaches*, edited by Marc Woons. Ku Leuven, 114–23. Belgium: E-International Relations Edited Collections, 2014.

---. "El viaje a los orígenes y la poética 'decolonial' maya en 'Madre, nosotros también somos historia' de Francisco Morales Santos." *Revista de Crítica Literaria Latinoamericano* 37, no. 74 (2011): 351–72.

del Valle Escalante, Emilio, ed. *Teorizando las literaturas indígenas contemporáneas.* Raleigh, N.C.: A Contracorriente, 2015.

---. *Uk'u'x kaj, uk'u'x ulew: Antología de poesía maya guatemalteca contemporánea.* Pittsburgh: Instituto Internacional de Literatura Iberoamericana, 2010.

DeMott, Tom. *Into the Hearts of the Amazons: In Search of a Modern Matriarchy.* Madison, Wisc.: Terrace, 2006.

Derrida, Jacques. *Of Grammatology.* Translated by Gayatri Chakravorty Spivak. Baltimore: Johns Hopkins University Press, 1976.

Díaz del Castillo, Bernal. *Historia verdadera de la conquista de la Nueva España.* No. 5. Linkgua Digital, 2010.

Díaz-Plaja, Guillermo, ed. *Antología mayor de la literatura hispanoamericana.* Vol. 1. Barcelona: Labor, 1969.

Díaz Polanco, Héctor. *Indigenous Peoples in Latin America: The Quest for Self-Determination.* Translated by Lucia Reyes. Boulder, Colo.: Westview, 1997.

Díaz Ruiz, Angelina. "Mujeres de mi presente" / "Ta jk'ak'al tana antsetik." In *Sbel sjol yo'onton ik' / Memoria del viento*, edited by Andrés López Díaz, Angelina Díaz Ruiz, and Luis López Díaz, 8–20. San Cristóbal de las Casas, Mexico: Unidad de Escritores Mayas-Zoques, 2006.

---. "Riqueza" /"K'ulejal." In *Sbel sjol yo'onton ik' / Memoria del viento*, edited by Andrés López Díaz, Angelina Díaz Ruiz, and Luis López Díaz, 18. San Cristóbal de las Casas, Mexico: Unidad de Escritores Mayas-Zoques, 2006.

Doesburg, Sebastián van. *Pictografía y escritura alfabética en Oaxaca.* Oaxaca City, Mexico: Instituto Estatal de Educación Pública de Oaxaca, 2008.

Douglas, Mary. *Natural Symbols: Explorations in Cosmology.* New York: Pantheon, 1970.

Du Bois, W. E. B. *The Souls of Black Folk.* New York: Penguin Classics, 1996.

Durán-Cogan, Mercedes F., and Antonio Gómez-Moriana, eds. *National Identities and Sociopolitical Changes in Latin America.* New York: Routledge, 2001.

Dzul Chablé, Irene, et al. *Cuentos mayas tradicionales.* Mexico City: Aldina, 1998.

Earle, Rebecca. *The Return of the Native: Indians and Myth-Making in Spanish America, 1810–1930.* Durham, N.C.: Duke University Press, 2007.

Eber, Christine E. "Seeking Our Own Food: Indigenous Women's Power and

Autonomy in San Pedro Chenalho, Chiapas (1980–1998)." *Latin American Perspectives* 26, no. 3 (May 1999): 6–36.

Echeverría, Esteban. *El matadero*. Buenos Aires: Cina-Cina, 1963.

Edmonson, Munro S. *The Book of Counsel: The Popol Vuh of the Quiche Maya of Guatemala*. New Orleans: Middle American Research Institute, Tulane University, 1971.

ELIAC (Escritores en Lenguas Indígenas, Asociación Civil). "Declaración San Cristóbal." *Nuestra Palabra*, supplement to *El Nacional* 11, no. 12 (December 1991): 15.

Eliot, T. S. *Selected Prose of T. S. Eliot*. Orlando, Fla.: Harcourt, 1975.

Emery, Amy Fass. *The Anthropological Imagination in Latin American Literature*. Columbia: University of Missouri Press, 1996.

Escobar, Arturo, and Sonia E. Alvarez, eds. *The Making of Social Movements in Latin America: Identity, Strategy, and Democracy*. Political Economy and Economic Development in Latin America. Boulder, Colo.: Westview, 1992.

Escritores en Lenguas Indígenas.. 2 vols. Mexico City: Escritores en Lenguas Indígenas, 2008.

Espinosa Miñoso, Yuderkys, Diana Gómez Correal, and Karina Ochoa Muñoz. *Tejiendo de otro modo: Feminismo, epistemología y apuestas descoloniales en Abya Yala*. Popayán, Colombia: Universidad del Cauca, 2014.

Estrada, Álvaro. *Vida de María Sabina: La sabia de los hongos*. Mexico City: Siglo Veintiuno, 1989.

"EZLN Communiqué Regarding Elections." Trans. Irlandesa. http://www.csuchico.edu/zapatist/HTML/Archive/Communiques/ccri_elections_june.html. Accessed January 22, 2018.

Fabian, Johannes. *Time and the Other: How Anthropology Makes Its Object*. New York: Columbia University Press, 1983.

Falla, Ricardo. *Masacres de la selva: Ixcán, Guatemala (1975–1982)*. Guatemala City: Editorial Universitaria Universidad de San Carlos de Guatemala, 1992.

———. *El Popol Wuj: Una interpretación para el día de hoy*. Guatemala City: Avancso, 2013.

———. *Quiché Rebelde: Religious Conversion, Politics, and Ethnic Identity in Guatemala*. Translations from Latin America. Austin: University of Texas Press, 2001.

Faudree, Paja. "What Is an Indigenous Author? Minority Authorship and the Politics of Voice in Mexico." *Anthropological Quarterly* 87, no. 4 (Winter 2015): 5–35.

Fernández de Lizardi, José Joaquín. *El Periquillo Sarniento*. Mexico City: Porrúa, 1963.

Fernández de Lizardi, José Joaquín, and David L. Frye. *The Mangy Parrot: The Life and Times of Periquillo Sarniento, Written by Himself for His Children*. Indianapolis: Hackett, 2004.

Field, Les W. *The Grimace of Macho Ratón: Artisans, Identity, and Nation in Late Twentieth-Century Western Nicaragua*. Durham, N.C.: Duke University Press, 1999.

Figueroa Saavedra, Miguel. "Palabras olvidadas, letras borradas: La literatura de los pueblos indígenas de México." *Cuadernos del Minotauro* 1 (2005): 67–78.

Finnegan, Ruth. *Literacy and Orality: Studies in the Technology of Communication*. New York: Blackwell, 1988.

Fischer, Edward F. *Cultural Logics and Global Economies: Maya Identity in Thought and Practice*. Austin: University of Texas Press, 2001.
Fischer, Edward F., and R. McKenna Brown, eds. *Maya Cultural Activism in Guatemala*. Austin: University of Texas Press, 1996.
Florescano, Enrique. *Memoria indígena*. Mexico City: Taurus, 1999.
Foucault, Michel. *Aesthetics, Method, and Epistemology*. Translated by Robert Hurley et al. New York: New Press, 1998.
———. *The Order of Things: An Archaeology of the Human Sciences*. New York: Routledge, 1989.
———. "What Is an Author?" In *The Foucault Reader*, edited by Paul Rabinow, 101–20. New York: Pantheon, 1984.
Freidel, David A., Linda Schele, and Joy Parker. *Maya Cosmos: Three Thousand Years on the Shaman's Path*. New York: W. Morrow, 1993.
Frischmann, Donald. "Contemporary Mayan Theatre and Ethnic Conflict: The Recovery and (Re)Interpretation of History." In *Imperialism and Theatre: Essays on World Theatre, Drama, and Performance*, edited by J. Ellen Gainor, 71–84. New York: Routledge, 1995.
———. *El nuevo teatro popular en México: Posturas ideológicas y estáticas*. Investigación y Documentación de las Artes. Segunda Época. Teatro. Mexico City: INBA, 1990.
———. "A Question of Balance: Indigenous Theater at the Conjunction of Millennia." In *Words of the True Peoples*, vol. 3, edited by Carlos Montemayor and Donald Frischmann, 19–47. Austin: University of Texas Press, 2007.
Frye, Northrop. *The Anatomy of Criticism: Four Essays*. Princeton, N.J.: Princeton University Press, 1957.
Fuentealba Milaguir, Ruth Mariela. *Cherrufe: La bola del fuego*. Santiago de Chile: CONADI, 2008.
Gabriel Xiquín, Calixta. *Hueso de la tierra*. Antigua Guatemala: San Cristóbal, 1996.
——— (Caly Domitila Canek). "Mujer." In *Literatura indígena de América: Segundo congreso*, 155. Guatemala City: Asociación Cultural B'eyb'al, 2001.
———. (Caly Domitila Canek). "Mujer campesina." In *Literatura indígena de América: Segundo congreso*, 157. Guatemala City: Asociación Cultural B'eyb'al, 2001.
———. "Poema." In *Tejiendo los sucesos en el tiempo / Weaving Events in Time*. Translated by Susan G. Rascón and Suzanne M. Strugalla, 88–89. Rancho Palos Verdes, Calif.: Yax Te' Foundation, 2002.
———. "Raíces escribiendo." In *Tejiendo los sucesos en el tiempo / Weaving Events in Time*. Translated by Susan G. Rascón and Suzanne M. Strugalla, 1–2. Rancho Palos Verdes, Calif.: Yax Te' Foundation, 2002.
Gallagher, Catherine. "The Rise of Fictionality." In *The Novel*, vol. 1, *History, Geography, and Culture*, edited by Franco Moretti, 336–63. Princeton, N.J.: Princeton University Press. 2006.
Gallegos, Rómulo. *Doña Barbara*. Translated by Robert Malloy. New York: Peter Smith, 1948.
Gamio, Manuel. *Forjando patria*. Mexico City: Porrúa, 1982.

García, Pablo. *B'ixonik tzij kech juk'ulaj kaminaqib' / Canto palabra de una pareja de muertos*. Guatemala City: F&G, 2009.
García Canclini, Néstor. *Hybrid Cultures: Strategies for Entering and Leaving Modernity*. Translated by Christopher L. Chiappari and Silvia L. López. Minneapolis: University of Minnesota Press, 1995.
———. *Transforming Modernity: Popular Culture in Mexico*. Translations from Latin America. Translated by Linda Lozano. Austin: University of Texas Press, 1993.
García Domingo, Santos Alfredo. *Chemomiltoj tzoti' / Artesano de palabras*. Guatemala City: Tipografía Nacional, 2006.
———. *Tzetet b'ay xhkawxi ko k'ul / Raíces de esperanza*. Rancho Palos Verdes, Calif.: Yax Te' Foundation, 2000.
García Márquez, Gabriel. *Crónica de una muerte anunciada*. Bogotá: Oveja Negra, 1981.
García-Moreno, Laura, and Peter C. Pfeiffer, eds. *Text and Nation: Cross-Disciplinary Essays on Cultural and National Identities*. Quiason Lecture Series. Columbia, S.C.: Camden House, 1996.
Gargallo, Francesca. *Feminismo desde Abya Yala: Ideas y proposiciones de las mujeres de 607 pueblos en nuestra América*. Mexico City: Corte y Confección, 2013.
Garibay Kintana, Ángel María. *Historia de la literatura n*. Mexico City: Porrúa, 2000.
Gelb, Ignace J. *A Study of Writing*. Chicago: University of Chicago Press, 1963.
Giraudo, Laura. "Neither 'Scientific' nor 'Colonialist': The Ambiguous Course of Inter-American *Indigenismo* in the 1940s." *Latin American Perspectives* 39, no. 5 (2012): 33–44.
Giraudo, Laura, and Stephen E. Lewis. "Pan American *Indigenismo* (1940–1970): New Approaches to an Ongoing Debate." *Latin American Perspectives* 39, no. 5 (2012): 3–11.
———. "Re-thinking Indigenismo on the American Continent." *Latin American Perspectives* 39, no. 5 (September 2012): 100–110.
Gollnick, Brian. "El ciclón de Chiapas: El desarrollo reciente del indigenismo mexicano." *Revista de crítica literaria latinoamericana* 25, no. 49 (1999): 199–216.
Gómez Grijalva, Dorotea. "Mi cuerpo es un territorio político." In *Tejiendo de otro modo: Feminismo, epistemología y apuestas descoloniales en Abya Yala*, edited by Yuderkys Espinosa Miñoso, Diana Gómez Correal, and Karina Ochoa Muñoz, 263–75. Popayán, Colombia: Universidad del Cauca, 2014.
Gómez Gutiérrez, Rosalba. "Mujeres indígenas, tres niveles de desigualdad y discriminación." *Aquí Estamos* 5, no. 9 (July–December 2008): 27–40.
Gómez Navarrete, Javier Abelardo. *Cecilio Chi': Nen óol k'ajlay / Cecilio Chi': Novela histórica*. Mexico City: Secretaría de Educación Pública, 2006.
Góngora Pacheco, María Luisa. *Cuentos de Oxkutzcab y Maní*. Mexico City: Aldina, 1998.
———. "La mujer maya: Pensamiento y voz del corazón." *Nuestra Palabra*, supplement to *El Nacional* 2, no. 2 (December 1991): 6.
González, Gaspar Pedro. *Kotz'ib,' Nuestra literatura maya*. Rancho Palos Verdes, Calif.: Yax Te' Foundation, 1997.

———. *La otra cara*. Guatemala City: Editorial Cultura, Ministerio de Cultura y Deportes, 1992.
———. *El retorno de los mayas*. Guatemala City: Fundación Myrna Mack, 1998.
———. *Sb'eyb'al jun naq maya q'anjob'al / La otra cara*. Rancho Palos Verdes, Calif.: Yax Te' Foundation, 1996.
———. *Sq'anej maya' / Palabras mayas: Poemas en maya q'anjob'al y español*. Rancho Palos Verdes, Calif.: Yax Te' Foundation, 1998.
González Echevarría, Roberto. *Myth and Archive: A Theory of Latin American Narrative*. Cambridge Studies in Latin American and Iberian Literature, no. 3. Cambridge: Cambridge University Press, 1990.
———. *The Voice of the Masters: Writing and Authority in Modern Latin American Literature*. Austin: University of Texas Press, 1985.
González Peña, Carlos. *Historia de la literatura mexicana: Desde los orígenes hasta nuestros días*. 8th ed. Mexico City: Porrúa, 1963.
Goody, Jack. *The Domestication of the Savage Mind*. Cambridge: Cambridge University Press, 1977.
———. "From Oral to Written: An Anthropological Breakthrough in Storytelling." In *The Novel*, vol. 1, *History, Geography, and Culture*, edited by Franco Moretti, 3–36. Princeton, N.J.: Princeton University Press, 2006.
———. *The Power of the Written Tradition*. Washington, D.C.: Smithsonian Institution Press, 2000.
Goody, Jack, and Ian Watt. "The Consequences of Literacy." *Comparative Studies in Society and History* 5, no. 3 (April 1963): 304–45.
Gordon, Lewis R. *Existentia Africana: Understanding Africana Existential Thought*. New York: Routledge, 2000.
Gordon, Lewis R., ed. *Existence in Black: An Anthology of Black Existential Philosophy*. New York: Routledge, 1996.
Gorky, Maxim. *Mother*. New York: D. Appleton, 1907.
Gosling, Maureen, and Ellen Osborne, dirs. *Blossoms of Fire*. DVD. 2000.
Gosner, Kevin. *Soldiers of the Virgin: The Moral Economy of a Colonial Maya Rebellion*. Tucson: University of Arizona Press, 1992.
Goubaud Carrera, Antonio. *Indigenismo en Guatemala*. Guatemala City: Centro Editorial José de Pineda Ibarra, Ministerio de Educación Pública, 1964.
Gracia, Jorge J. E., and Mireya Camurati, eds. *Philosophy and Literature in Latin America: A Critical Assessment of the Current Situation*. SUNY Series in Latin American and Iberian Thought and Culture. Albany: State University of New York Press, 1989.
Graham, Laura R., and H. Glenn Penny, eds. *Performing Indigeneity: Global Histories and Contemporary Experiences*. Lincoln: University of Nebraska Press, 2014.
Graham-Jones, Jean. "Editorial Comment: Theorizing Globalization through Theatre." *Theatre Journal* 57, no. 3 (2005): i–viii.
Gramsci, Antonio. *Letters from Prison*. Edited by Frank Rosengarten. Translated by Raymond Rosenthal. New York: Columbia University Press, 1994.

Grandin, Greg. *The Blood of Guatemala: A History of Race and Nation.* Latin America Otherwise. Durham, N.C.: Duke University Press, 2000.
———. *The Last Colonial Massacre: Latin America in the Cold War.* Chicago: University of Chicago Press, 2004.
Grandis, Rita de, and Zilà Bernd, eds. *Unforeseeable Americas: Questioning Cultural Hybridity in the Americas.* Critical Studies, vol. 13. Amsterdam: Rodopi, 2000.
Grupo de Mujeres Mayas Kaqla. *Mujeres mayas, universo y vida / Kinojib'al qati't.* Iximulew, Guatemala: Mujeres Mayas Kaqla, 2009.
———. *La palabra y el sentir de las mujeres mayas de Kaqla.* Guatemala City: Grupo de Mujeres Mayas Kaqla, 2004.
———. *Tramas y trascendecias: reconstruyendo historias con nuestras abuelas y madres.* Guatemala City: Magna Tierra, 2011.
Gruzinski, Serge. *La colonización del imaginario: Sociedades indígenas y occidentalización en el México español, siglos XVI–XVIII.* Mexico City: Fundo de Cultura Económica, 1991.
———. *La guerra de las imágenes: De Cristóbal Colón a "Blade Runner" (1492–2019).* New York: Fondo de Cultura Económica, 1994.
———. *The Mestizo Mind: The Intellectual Dynamics of Colonization and Globalization.* New York: Routledge, 2002.
Guamán Poma de Ayala, Felipe. *Nueva crónica y buen gobierno.* Crónicas de América 29. Madrid: Historia 16, 1987.
Gugelberger, Georg M. *The Real Thing: Testimonial Discourse and Latin America.* Durham, N.C.: Duke University Press, 1996.
Guinea Diez, Gerardo. "El poeta de la brevedad H. Ak'abal." Interview. *Crónica*, October 13, 1995.
Gutiérrez Chong, Natividad. "Nacionalismos y etnocentrismos: La escritura maya de Briceida Cuevas Cob y Flor Marlene Herrera." *La Ventana* 18 (2003): 169–209.
———. *National Myths and Ethnic Identities: Indigenous Intellectuals and the Mexican State.* Lincoln: University of Nebraska Press, 1999.
Gutiérrez Chong, Natividad, ed. *Mujeres y nacionalismos en América Latina: De la independencia a la nación del nuevo milenio.* Mexico City: Universidad Nacional Autónoma de México, 2004.
Hale, Charles, and Rosamel Millamán. "Cultural Agency and Political Struggle in the Era of the Indio Permitido." In *Cultural Agency in the Americas*, edited by Doris Sommer, 281–304. Durham, N.C.: Duke University Press, 2006.
Harvey, Neil. *The Chiapas Rebellion: The Struggle for Land and Democracy.* Durham, N.C.: Duke University Press, 1998.
Havelock, Eric Alfred. *Origins of Western Literacy.* Toronto: Ontario Institute for Studies in Education, 1976.
Hayden, Tom, ed. *The Zapatista Reader.* New York: Thunder's Mouth/Nation Books, 2002.
Hendrickson, Carol. "Women, Weaving, and Education in Maya Revitalization." In *Maya Cultural Activism in Guatemala*, edited by Edward F. Fischer, 156–64. Austin: University of Texas, 1996.

Henestrosa, Andrés. "The Forms of Sexual Life in Juchitán." In *Zapotec Struggles: Histories, Politics, and Representations from Juchitán, Oaxaca*, edited by Howard Campbell et al., 129–31. Washington, D.C.: Smithsonian Institution Press, 1993.

———. *Los hombres que dispersó la danza*. Mexico City: Porrúa, 1997.

Henríquez, Elio. "Lanzarán EZLN y CNI candidata indígena independiente para 2018." *La Jornada*, October 15, 2016. http://www.jornada.unam.mx/2016/10/15/politica/003n1pol.

Hernández, Natalio. *In tlahtoli, in ohtli / Palabra, el camino: Memoria y destino de los pueblos indígenas*. Mexico City: Plaza y Valdés, 1998.

———. "Prólogo: Tisentica cuicaseh / Invitación al canto." In *Flores del sol / Tonalxochim*, 23–27. Chilpancingo, Mexico: Fundación Académica Guerrerense, 2013.

Hernández-Ávila, Inés. "The Power of Native Languages and the Performance of Indigenous Autonomy: The Case of Mexico." In *Native Voices: American Indian Identity and Resistance*, edited by Richard A. Grounds, George E. Tinker, and David E. Wilkins, 35–74. Lawrence: University Press of Kansas, 2003.

Hernández Bringas, Héctor Hiram. *Los indios de México en el siglo XXI*. Mexico City: Universidad Nacional Autónoma de México, 2007.

Hernández Castillo, Rosalva Aída. "The Emergence of Indigenous Feminism in Latin America." *Signs* 35, no. 3 (Spring 2010): 539–45.

———. "Entre el etnocentrismo feminista y el esencialismo étnico: Las mujeres indígenas y sus demandas de género." *Debate Feminista* 24 (October 2001): 206–29.

Hernández Gerónimo, Auldárico, et al. *La tragedia del jaguar*. Xalapa, Mexico: Universidad Veracruzana, 1992.

Herranz, Atanasio, et al. *Educación bilingüe e intercultural en Centroamérica y México: Ponencias del Primer Simposium de Educación Bilingüe Intercultural en Honduras, Tegucigalpa, 27, 28 y 29 de julio de 1995*. Tegucigalpa: Guaymuras; Servicio Holandés de Cooperación al Desarrollo, 1998.

Hobsbawm, Eric, and Terence Ranger, eds. *The Invention of Tradition*. New York: Cambridge University Press, 2012.

Hoil, Juan José, and Bolio Antonio Mediz. *Libro de Chilam Balam de Chumayel*. Mexico City: Universidad Nacional Autónoma de México, 1941.

Horcasitas, Fernando. "Los principios del drama náhuatl en México." In *El teatro franciscano en la Nueva España: Fuentes y ensayos para el estudio del teatro de evangelización en el siglo XVI*, edited by María Sten, 131–40. Mexico City: Universidad Nacional Autónoma de México, 2000.

Hornberger, Nancy H., ed., *Indigenous Literacies in the Americas: Language Planning from the Bottom Up*. New York: Mouton de Gruyter, 1997.

Hostnig, Rainer, and Luis Vásquez Vicente. *Nab'ab'l qtanam: La memoria colectiva del pueblo mam de Quetzaltenango*. Quetzaltenango, Guatemala: Centro de Capacitación e Investigación Campesina, 1994.

Huanosto Cerano, Dagoberto. "Residuos de identidad." *Nuestra Palabra*, supplement to *El Nacional* 3, no. 12 (December 1992): 3.

Huet Bautista, Nicolás. "Reflexiones en torno a la problemática indígena de Chiapas."

Paper presented at the Tercer Encuentro Nacional de Escritores en Lenguas Indígenas, Ixmiquilpan, Mexico, November 11–14, 1992.

———. *La última muerte / Ti slajebalxa lajele*. Mexico City: El Animal, 2001.

———. "La última muerte: Cuento / Ti slajebalxa lajele: Lo'il a' yej." In *La última muerte / Ti slajebalxa lajel*, 1–24. Mexico City: El Animal, 2001.

Hunt, Kevin T. "Beyond Indigenismo: Contemporary Mexican Literature of Indigenous Theme." PhD diss., University of North Carolina, 2007.

Instituto Nacional de Comunicación Social del Estado de Chiapas. "UNICH difunde literatura indígena." May 14, 2013. http://www.icosochiapas.gob.mx/2013/05/14/unich-difunde-literatura-indigena/.

Iwańska, Alicja. *The Truth of Others: An Essay on Nativistic Intellectuals in Mexico*. Cambridge, Mass.: Schenkman, 1977.

Izquierdo y de la Cueva, Ana Luisa. "Reseña de *Secretos del abuelo: Muk'ult'an in nool* de Jorge Cocom Pech." *Estudios de Cultura Maya* 23 (2006): 175–77.

Jameson, Fredric. "Third World Literature in the Era of Multinational Capitalism." *Social Text*, no. 15 (Autumn 1986): 65–88.

Jiménez Pérez, María Roselia. "El futuro de la palabra." *La Palabra Florida* 1, no. 1 (Winter 1996): 7–9.

Jiménez Sánchez, Ajb'ee Odilio. "Tensión entre idiomas: Situación actual de los idiomas mayas y español en Guatemala." Paper presented at the Latin American Studies Association, Guadalajara, Mexico, 1997.

Juárez Espinosa, Isabel. "Migración." In *Words of the True Peoples*, 3:211–31. Austin: University of Texas Press, 2007.

———. "Migración." In *Cuentos y teatro tzeltales*, 143–63. Mexico City: Diana, 1994.

———. "La mujer maya como fuente de cultura." *Nuestra Palabra*, supplement to *El Nacional* 2, no. 12 (1992): 13.

Junqueira, Carmen, and Edgar de Assis Carvalho, eds. *Los indios y la antropología en América Latina*. Desde Sudamérica. Buenos Aires: Búsqueda-Yuchán, 1984.

Kaplan, Caren, Norma Alarcón, and Minoo Moallem, eds. *Between Woman and Nation: Nationalisms, Transnational Feminisms, and the State*. Durham, N.C.: Duke University Press, 1999.

Kellogg, Susan. *Weaving the Past: A History of Latin America's Indigenous Women from the Pre-Hispanic Period to the Present*. New York: Oxford University Press, 2005.

King, Linda. *Roots of Identity: Language and Literacy in Mexico*. Stanford, Calif.: Stanford University Press, 1994.

King, Thomas Hunt. "Inventing the Indian: White Images, Native Oral Literature, and Contemporary Native Writers." PhD diss., University of Utah, 1986.

Klahn, Norma. "El indigenismo desde la indigeneidad." *Nuevo Texto Crítico* 24/25, no. 47–48 (2011–12): 165–86.

Klor de Alva, Jorge. "Colonialism and Postcolonialism as (Latin) American Mirages." *Colonial Latin American Review* 1, no. 1–2 (January 1992): 3–23.

Knight, Alan. "Racism, Revolution, and *Indigenismo*: Mexico, 1910–1940." In *The Idea of Race in Latin America, 1870–1940*, edited by Richard Graham, 71–113. Austin: University of Texas Press, 1990.

Knight, Alan, and W. G. Pansters. *Caciquismo in Twentieth-Century Mexico*. London: Institute for the Study of the Americas, 2005.
Konefal, Betsy. *For Every Indio Who Falls: A History of Maya Activism in Guatemala, 1960–1990*. Albuquerque: University of New Mexico Press, 2010.
Kowalewski, Stephen A., and Jacqueline J. Saindon. "The Spread of Literacy in a Latin American Peasant Society: Oaxaca, Mexico, 1890–1980." *Comparative Studies in Society and History* 34, no. 1 (January 1992): 110–40.
Krupat, Arnold. *The Turn to the Native: Studies in Criticism and Culture*. Lincoln: University of Nebraska Press, 1996.
Kumu, Umúsin Panlõn, and Tolamãn Kenhíri. *Antes o mundo não existia: A mitologia heróica dos índios desâna*. São Paulo: Livraria Cultura, 1980.
Kundera, Milan. *The Art of the Novel*. New York: Grove, 1988.
Lane, Jill, Marcial Godoy-Anativia, and Macarena Gómez-Barris. "Gesto decolonial." *E-Misférica* 11, no. 1 (2014). http://hemisphericinstitute.org/hemi/es/e-misferica-111-gesto-decolonial/e111-editorial-remarks.
Larraín, Jorge. *Identity and Modernity in Latin America*. Hoboken, N.J.: Wiley, 2013.
Larsen, Neil. *Reading North by South: On Latin American Literature, Culture, and Politics*. Minneapolis: University of Minnesota Press, 1995.
Laughlin, Robert M. *Monkey Business Theatre*. Austin: University of Texas Press, 2008.
Legrás, Horacio. *Literature and Subjection: The Economy of Writing and Marginality in Latin American Literature*. Pittsburgh: University of Pittsburgh Press, 2008.
Lehmann, Walter, and Jorge Eduardo Arellano, eds. *El Güegüence, o, macho ratón: Bailete dialogado de la época colonial*. Managua: Americanas, 1984.
Leirana Alcocer, Silvia Cristina. *Conjurando el silencio: Algunos aspectos de la diversidad literaria*. Mexico City: Instituto de Cultura de Yucatán, 2005.
———. "La literatura maya actual vista por sus autores (Un acercamiento a la literatura maya-peninsular contemporánea." MA thesis, Universidad Autónoma de Yucatán, 1996.
Lenkersdorf, Carlos. *Indios somos con orgullo: Poesía maya-tojobal*. Mexico City: Centro de Estudios Mayas, Instituto de Investigaciones Filológicas, Universidad Nacional Autónoma de México, 1996.
———. "Lenguas y diálogo intercultural." *Revista Electrónica de Estudios Filológicos* 6 (2003). https://www.um.es/tonosdigital/znum6/estudios/Lenkersdorf.htm. Accessed December 20, 2017.
León-Portilla, Miguel. *El destino de la palabra: De la oralidad y los glifos mesoamericanos a la escritura alfabética*. Mexico City: Fondo de la Cultura Económica; Colegio Nacional, 1996.
———. "Teatro náhuatl prehispánico." In *El teatro franciscano en la nueva España: Fuentes y ensayos para el estudio del teatro de evangelización en el siglo XVI*, edited by María Sten, 39–61. Mexico City: Facultad de Filosofía y Letras, UNAM, 2000.
———. *Visión de los vencidos*. Madrid: Historia 16, 1985.
León-Portilla, Miguel, ed. *Yancuic Tlahtolli: La nueva palabra*. Estudios de Cultura Nahua, nos. 18 and 19. Mexico City: Universidad Nacional Autónoma de México, 1986.

León-Portilla, Miguel, and Lysander Kemp. *The Broken Spears: The Aztec Account of the Conquest of Mexico*. Boston: Beacon, 1962.

León-Portilla, Miguel, and Earl Shorris, eds. *In the Language of Kings: An Anthology of Mesoamerican Literature, Pre-Columbian to the Present*. New York: W. W. Norton, 2001.

Lepe Lira, Luz María. *Lluvia y viento, puentes de sonido: Literatura indígena y crítica literaria*. Monterrey, Mexico: Consejo para la Cultura y las Artes de Nuevo León, 2010.

Levine, Caroline. *Forms: Whole, Rhythm, Hierarchy, Network*. Princeton, N.J.: Princeton University Press, 2015.

Lévi-Strauss, Claude. *Antropología estructural: Mito, sociedad, humanidades*. Translated by J. Almela. Mexico City: Siglo Veintiuno, 1979.

———. *Tristes Tropiques*. Paris: Plon, 1955.

Lewis, David L., ed. *W. E. B. DuBois: A Reader*. New York: H. Holt, 1995.

Lewis, Stephen E. "'Indigenista' Dreams Meet Sober Realities: The Slow Demise of Federal Indian Policy in Chiapas, Mexico, 1951–1970." *Latin American Perspectives* 39, no. 5 (2012): 63–79.

———. "Mexico's National Indigenist Institute and the Negotiations of Applied Anthropology in Highland Chiapas, 1951–1954." *Ethnohistory* 55, no. 4 (Fall 2008): 609–32.

Lienhard, Martin. "La noche de los Mayas: Representaciones de los indígenas mesoamericanos en el cine y literatura, 1917–1943." *Mesoamérica* 44 (2002): 82–117.

———. *La voz y su huella: Escritura y conflicto étnico-social en América Latina, 1492–1988*. Mexico City: Casa Juan Pablos, 2003.

Ligorred Perramón, Francisco de Asís. *U Mayathanoob ti dzib / Las voces de la escritura: Ensayos y textos de literatura maya*. Mérida, Mexico: Ediciones de la Universidad Autónoma de Yucatán, 1997.

"Literatura Maya-Yukateka contemporánea (tradición y futuro)." *Mesoamérica* 39 (June 2000): 333–57.

Llorente, Renzo. "Marxism." In *A Companion to Latin American Philosophy*, edited by Susana Nuccetelli, Ofelia Schutte, and Otavio Bueno, 170–84. Hoboken, N.J.: Wiley-Blackwell, 2009.

Lluvia de sueños: Poetas y cantantes indígenas. With Roselia Jiménez, Angélica Ortiz, Elizabeth Pérez, Juana Inés Reza, Delfina Albáñez, Enriqueta Lunez, and Martha Toledo. 3 CDs. DGCP, CNCA-DGCPI, 2005.

López, Carlos M. "The *Popol Wuj*: The Repositioning and Survival of Mayan Culture." In *A Companion to Latin American Literature and Culture*, edited by Sara Castro-Klaren, 68–85. Malden, Mass.: Blackwell, 2008.

López Austin, Alfredo. *Cuerpo humano e ideología: Las concepciones de los antiguos nahuas*. Mexico City: Universidad Nacional Autónoma de México, Instituto de Investigaciones Antropológicas, 1984.

López Chiñas, Gabriel. "El zapoteco." In *Guendaxheela / El casamiento*, 64. Mexico City: Complejo Editorial Mexicano, 1975.

———. *Vinnigulasa: Cuentos de Juchitán*. Mexico City: Universidad Nacional Autónoma de México, 1960.

———. *El zapoteco y la literatura zapoteca del istmo de Tehuantepec*. Mexico City: Edición del Autor, 1982.

López Chiñas, Gabriel, Jeremías López Chiñas, and José Vázquez Amaral. *Conejo y coyote*. Mexico City: Vinnigulasa, 1943.

López Coti, René Humberto, Daniel Matu, José de Sousa Silva, and Rony Alvarado. "La interculturalidad como plenitud de vida, el paradigma de la vida en plenitud/buen vivir/vivir bien educación intercultural." Chap. 6 in *Retos actuales de educación y salud transcultural*. Vol. 1, edited by Encarnación Soriano Ayala, Antonio Gonzales Jiménez, and Verónica C. Cala. Almeria, Spain: Editorial Universidad de Almería, 2014.

López Díaz, Andrés, Angelina Díaz Ruiz, and Luis López Díaz, eds. *Sbel sjol yo'onton ik' / Memoria del viento*. San Cristóbal de las Casas, Mexico: Unidad de Escritores Mayas-Zoques, 2006.

López y Fuentes, Gregorio. *El indio*. New York: F. Ungar, 1961.

López de Lara Marín, Alejandro. "Marxismo y cuestión indígena: El indigenismo marxista latinoamericano de Vicente Lombardo Toledano y José Carlos Mariátegui." Santiago de Chile: Centro Estudios Miguel Enríquez (CEME), Archivo Chile, 2005. http://www.archivochile.com/Ideas_Autores/mariategui_jc/s/mariategui_s0061.pdf.

López de Gómara, Francisco. *Historia general de las Indias y todo acaescido en ellas, dende que se ganaron hasta agora: y la conquista de Mexico y de la nueva España*. Antwerp, Belgium: Nuvio, 1554.

López Gómez, Josías "Una propuesta para la unificación de la escritura de la lengua tseltal bats'il k'op'." *Nuestra Sabiduría*, época 3, year 7, no. 11. San Cristóbal de las Casas, Mexico: CELALI, Unidad de Escritores Mayas-Zoques (January–June 1997): 16–27.

López Gómez, Josías, Juana Karen Peñate Montejo, Ruperta Bautista Vásquez, Nicolás Huet Bautista et al. *Palabra conjurada: Cinco voces, cinco cantos*. San Cristóbal de las Casas, Mexico: Fray Bartolomé de las Casas, 1999.

López Hernández, Antonio. "Géneros literarios indígenas en el Estado de Chiapas." October 12, 2001. http://www/laneta.apc.org/menriquez/12oct2001/html.

López, Josías. "Elek'k'op / El ladrón de palabras." In *Palabra conjurada: Cinco voces, cinco cantos*, edited by Josías López-K'ana et al., 1–18. San Cristóbal de las Casas, Mexico: Fray Bartolomé de las Casas, 1999.

———. *Sakubel k'inal jachwinik / La aurora lacandona*. San Cristóbal de las Casas, Mexico: Fray Bartolomé de las Casas, 2005.

López Mejía, Alma Gilda. "Aciertos y desaciertos de la participación política de las mujeres maya kichés: Un reto histórico de nosotras." In *La doble mirada: Voces e historias de mujeres indígenas latinoamericanas*, edited by Marta Sánchez Nestor, 23–32. Mexico City: Instituto de Liderazgo de Simone de Beauvoir/UNIFEM, 2005.

López Pérez, Antonio. "El rapto / Guendaruxhoñenee gunaa." "Ojarasca," special supplement, *La Jornada*, edited by Hermann Bellinghausen, no. 180 (April 2012): 5. http://www.jornada.unam.mx/2012/04/14/ojarasca180.pdf.

Loucky, James, and Marilyn M. Moors, eds. *The Maya Diaspora: Guatemalan Roots, New American Lives*. Philadelphia: Temple University Press, 2000.

Lovera, Sara, and Nellys Palomo, eds. *Las alzadas*. Mexico City: Comunicación e Información de la Mujer, 1997.
Lugones, María. "Colonialidad y género." *Tabula Rasa*, no. 9 (July–December 2008): 73–101.
Luis, William, and Julio Rodríguez-Luis, eds. *Translating Latin America: Culture as Text*. Binghamton: State University of New York, 1991.
Lund, Joshua. "Altamirano's Burden." In *The Mestizo State: Reading Race in Modern Mexico*, 29–70. Minneapolis: University of Minnesota Press, 2012.
———. *The Impure Imagination: Toward a Critical Hybridity in Latin American Writing*. Minneapolis: University of Minnesota Press, 2006.
Lunez Pérez, Enriqueta. "Enriqueta Lunez (poeta) mov." YouTube video. Posted by "vayijel," June 12, 2011. https://www.youtube.com/watch?v=OimOaXeKLoo.
———. "La jti jbe' svayel kajvaltik / Desperté a Dios." In *Yi'beltak ch'ulelaletik / Raíces del alma: Poesía*, 44–45. Hermosillo, Mexico: Instituto Sonorense de Cultura, 2007.
———. *Tajimol ch'ulelaletik / Juego de nahuales*. Mexico City: Programa Nacional de Lectura de la Secretaría de Educación Pública, 2008.
———. *Yi'beltak ch'ulelaletik / Raíces del alma: Poesía*. Hermosillo, Mexico: Instituto Sonorense de Cultura, 2007.
Machuca Gallegos, Laura. "En los márgenes de Mérida, de la época colonial a 1917: Apuntes sobre la historia olvidada de Cholul, Kanasín, San José Tzal y Umán." Península, Mérida, vol. 6, no. 1, pp. 159–84, January 2011. http://www.scielo.org.mx/scielo.php?script=sci_arttext&pid=S1870-57662011000100007&lng=es&nrm=iso.
Macleod, Morna. *Nietas del fuego, creadoras del alba: Luchas político-culturales de mujeres Mayas*. Guatemala City:FLACSO, 2011.
Maiguashca, Bice. "The Role of Ideas in a Changing World Order: The International Indigenous Movement, 1975–1990." CERLAC Working Paper. Center for Research on Latin America and the Caribbean, York University, 1994.
Maldonado-Torres, Nelson. "On the Coloniality of Being (Contributions to the Development of a Concept)." "Globalization and De-colonial Opinion," special issue, *Cultural Studies* 21, nos. 2–3 (April 2007): 240–70.
———. "Outline of Ten Theses on Coloniality and Decoloniality." Franz Fanon Foundation. http://franzfanonfoundation. Accessed August 27, 2017.
Mallon, Florencia E. *Peasant and Nation: The Making of Postcolonial Mexico and Peru*. Berkeley: University of California Press, 1995.
Manguel, Alberto, and Marcelo Cohen. *En el bosque del espejo: Ensayos sobre las palabras y el mundo*. Madrid: Alianza, 2001.
Manrique, Nelson. *La piel y la pluma: Escritos sobre literatura, etnicidad y racismo*. Lima: CiDiAG, Sur Casa de Estudios del Socialismo, 1999.
Marcos, Sylvia. "The Borders Within: The Indigenous Women's Movement and Feminism in Mexico." In *Dialogue and Difference: Feminisms Challenge Globalization*, edited by Marguerite Waller and Sylvia Marcos, 81–112. New York: Palgrave Macmillan, 2005.
———. *Taken from the Lips: Gender and Eros in Mesoamerican Religions*. Leiden, the Netherlands: Brill, 2006.

Marcus, Joyce. "La escritura zapoteca." *Investigación y Ciencia*, no. 43 (April 1980): 28–30.
———. *Mesoamerican Writing Systems: Propaganda, Myth, and History in Four Ancient Civilizations*. Princeton, N.J.: Princeton University Press, 1992.
———. *Monte Albán*. Mexico City: Fideicomiso Historia de las Américas, Colegio de México, 2008.
Mariátegui, José Carlos. "El problema agrario y el problema del indio." In *Siete ensayos de interpretación de la realidad peruana*, 26–38. http://www.lahaine.org/amauta/b2-img/Mariategui%20Siete%20Ensayos.pdf. Accessed January 22, 2018.
Marrero, Teresa. "Eso Sí Pasa Aquí: Indigenous Women Performing Revolutions in Mayan Chiapas." In *Holy Terrors: Latin American Women Perform*, edited by Diana Taylor and Roselyn Costantino, 311–30. Durham, N.C.: Duke University Press, 2003.
Martin, Gerald. *Journeys through the Labyrinth: Latin American Fiction in the Twentieth Century*. Critical Studies in Latin American Culture. London: Verso, 1989.
———. "The Novel of a Continent: Latin America." In *The Novel*, vol. 1, edited by Franco Moretti, 632–66. Princeton, N.J.: Princeton University Press, 2006.
Martín-Barbero, Jesús. *De los medios a las mediaciones: Comunicación, cultura y hegemonía*. Barcelona:: Editorial GustavoGili, 1987.
Martínez, Luis Mauricio. Interview at the FIL 2013. http://periodismoatoctli.blogspot.com/2014/03/isaac-esau-carrillo-can_28.html. Accessed August 11, 2017.
Martínez Huchim, Ana Patricia. *Chen konel / Es por demás*. Mérida, Mexico: Universidad Autónoma de Yucatán, 2006.
———. *U k'a'ajsajil u ts'u'noj k'áax / Recuerdos del corazón de la montaña*. Mérida, Mexico: Secretaría de la Cultura y las Artes de Yucatán; Consejo Nacional para la Cultura y las Artes, 2013.
———. *U tsikbalo'ob mejen paalal / Cuentos de Niños*. Mérida, Mexico: Gobierno del Estado de Yucatán: Instituto de Cultura de Yucatán: Consejo Nacional para la Cultura y las Artes: Dirección General de Culturas Populares: Dirección de Culturas Populares de Yucatán: Programa de Apoyo a las Culturas Municipales y Comunitarias, PACMYC, 1997.
———. *U yóol xkaambal jaw xíiw / Contrayerba*. Mexico City: Comisión Nacional para el Desarrollo de los Pueblos Indígenas, 2013.
Martínez Peláez, Severo. *Motines de indios: La violencia colonial en Centroamérica y Chiapas*. Puebla, Mexico: Centro de Investigaciones Históricas y Sociales Instituto de Ciencias Universidad Autónoma de Puebla, 1985.
———. *La patria del criollo: Ensayo de interpretación de la realidad colonial guatemalteca*. Mexico City: Fondo de Cultura Económica, 1998.
Marzal, Manuel María. *Antropología indigenista*. Quito: Abya Yala. 1998.
Matías García, Yolanda. "Azul." http://poesianahuatlyolandamatiasgarcia.blogspot.com. Accessed November 17, 2015.
———. *Tonalxochimej / Flores del sol*. Chilpancingo, Mexico: Fundación Académica Guerrerense, 2013.
———. *Xochitlajtol ika moyojlo / Palabra florida para tu corazón*. CD. 2005.
Matto de Turner, Clorinda. *Aves sin nido*. Charleston, S.C.: BiblioBazaar, 2007.

Matul Morales, Daniel, and Edgar Cabrera. *La cosmovisión maya.* Vols. 1 and 2. Guatemala City: Liga Maya de Guatemala, 2007.
Matus, Macario. *Palabra desnuda.* Mexico City: Diana, 1991.
──. *Los zapotecas / Binni Záa.* Mexico City: Diana, 1998.
May May, Miguel Angel. "La formación de escritores en lengua maya." In *Los escritores indígenas actuales,* vol. 1, edited by Carlos Montemayor, 113–27. San Angel, Mexico: Tierra Adentro, Consejo Nacional para la Cultura y las Artes, 1992.
Máynez, Pilar. *Lenguas y literaturas indígenas en el México contemporáneo.* Mexico City: Universidad Nacional Autónoma de México, 2003.
Mazzotti, José Antonio, and U. Juan Zevallos Aguilar, eds. *Asedios a la heterogeneidad cultural: Libro de homenaje a Antonio Cornejo Polar.* Philadelphia: Asociación Internacional de Peruanistas, 1996.
McCaughan, Edward J. "Of Zapotecs, Zapatistas and Xicanistas: Ethnic and Feminist Challenges to Mexican/Chicano Nationalism." In *Las nuevas fronteras del siglo XXI / New Frontiers of the 21st Century,* edited by Alejandro Álvarez Béjar, Norma Klahn, Federico Manchon, and Pedro Castillo, 167–93. La Democracia en México. Mexico City: La Jornada Ediciones; Centro de Investigaciones, 2000.
McClintock, Anne, Aamir Mufti, and Ella Shohat, eds. *Dangerous Liaisons: Gender, Nation, and Postcolonial Perspectives.* Minneapolis: University of Minnesota Press, 1997.
McDonough, Kelly S. *The Learned Ones: Nahua Intellectuals in Postconquest Mexico.* Tucson: University of Arizona Press, 2014.
McGuinness, Aims. "Searching for 'Latin America': Race and Sovereignty in the Americas in the 1850s." In *Race and Nation in Modern Latin America,* edited by Nancy P. Appelbaum, Anne S. Macpherson, and Karin Alejandra Rosemblatt, 87–107. Chapel Hill: University of North Carolina Press, 2003.
McKeon, Michael. *Theory of the Novel: A Historical Approach.* Baltimore: Johns Hopkins University Press, 2000.
Mejía Amador, Georgina. "La escritura bilingüe en un país multilingüe y multicultural." Unpublished ms., n.d.
──. "Representaciones del cuerpo femenino en la poesía maya de Briceida Cuevas Cob y en la poesía binnizá de Irma Pineda." MA thesis, UNAM, 2012.
Mena Cabezas, Ignacio R. "Los chortis de Honduras en la encrucijada: Tradición, identidad y globalización." *Yaxkin* 25, no. 2 (2009): 211–35.
Menchú, Rigoberta. "Importancia del Congreso de literatura indígena de América." In *Literatura indígena de América: Primer congreso,* 10. Guatemala City: Asociación Cultural B'eyb'al, 1999.
──. *I, Rigoberta Menchú: An Indian Woman in Guatemala.* Edited by Elisabeth Burgos-Debray. Translated by Ann Wright. London: Verso, 1984.
Mendizábal, Sergio. *El Kab'awil en nuestra historia.* Cuadernos Winaq, no 3. Guatemala City: Universidad Rafael Landívar, Instituto de Estudios Humanísticos, 2010.
Méndez Guzmán, Diego. *Kajkanantik: Jch'ulta tiketik te leke sok te chopole: La yak' jipik ta spojel te jun lum tseltal ja' la sts'ibuj Tsiak Tsa'pat Ts'it / El Kajkanantik: Los dioses del bien y el mal: Luchas de liberación de un pueblo tzeltal.* Mexico City: Instituto Nacional Indigenista, 1998.

Méndez Torres, Georgina. "Identidades cambiantes e imaginarios sociales de las mujeres indígenas: Reflexionando desde la experiencia." *Aquí Estamos* 5, no. 9 (July–December 2008): 27–40.

Menéndez y Pelayo, Marcelino. *Antología de poetas hispano-americanos publicada por la Real Academia Española*. Madrid: Sucesores de Rivadeneyra, 1893.

Meneses, Teodoro L., ed. *Teatro quechua colonial: Antología*. Lima: Edubanco, 1983.

Metz, Brent E. "An Ambivalent Nation: Chortís in Eastern Guatemala and Western Honduras." Presentation, LASA, Puerto Rico, 2015.

Metz, Brent E., Cameron L. McNeil, and Kerry M. Hull. *The Ch'orti' Maya Area: Past and Present*. Gainesville: University Press of Florida, 2009.

Mignolo, Walter. *The Darker Side of the Renaissance: Literacy, Territoriality, and Colonization*. Ann Arbor: University of Michigan Press, 1995.

———. *The Darker Side of Western Modernity: Global Futures, Decolonial Options*. Durham, N.C.: Duke University Press, 2011.

———. *Globalization and the Decolonial Option*. London: Routledge, 2010.

———. *The Idea of Latin America*. Malden, Mass.: Blackwell, 2005.

———. Introduction to *Cultural Studies* 21, nos. 2–3 (March/May 2007): 155–67.

———. *Local Histories / Global Designs: Coloniality, Subaltern Knowledges, and Border Thinking*. Princeton, N.J.: Princeton University Press, 2000.

———. "Preamble." In *A Companion to Latin American Literature and Culture*. Edited by Sara Castro-Klaren, 553–70. Malden, Mass.: Blackwell, 2008.

Mignolo, Walter, and Catherine E. Walsh. *On Decoloniality: Concepts, Analytics, and Praxis*. Durham, N.C.: Duke University Press, 2018.

Milbrath, Susan. "The Maya Lord of the Smoking Mirror." In *Tezcatlipoca: Trickster and Supreme Deity*, edited by Elizabeth Baquedano, 163–96. Boulder: University Press of Colorado, 2014.

Miller, Mary Ellen, and Karl Taube. *The Gods and Symbols of Ancient Mexico and the Maya: An Illustrated Dictionary of Mesoamerican Religion*. London: Thames and Hudson, 1993.

Miller, Marilyn Grace. *Rise and Fall of the Cosmic Race: The Cult of Mestizaje in Latin America*. Austin: University of Texas Press, 2004.

Miranda, Boris. "Así fueron las esterilizaciones forzadas que ahora son asunto de interés nacional en Perú." *BBC Mundo*, November 9, 2015. http://www.bbc.com/mundo/noticias/2015/11/151108_esterilizaciones_forzadas_historias_interes_nacional_peru_bm.

Molina-Cruz, Mario. *Volcán de pétalos / Ya 'byalhje xtak yejé*. Mexico City: Diana, 1996.

Molina, Javier. "Los autores indígenas escribimos de un nosotros: Enriqueta Lunez." *La Jornada*, February 3, 2014. http://www.jornada.unam.mx/2014/02/03/cultura/a11n2cul.

Monasterios P., Elizabeth. "Uncertain Modernities: Amerindian Epistemologies and the Reorienting of Culture." In *A Companion to Latin American Literature and Culture*, edited by Sara Castro-Klaren, 553–70. Malden, Mass.: Blackwell, 2008.

Monteforte Toledo, Mario. *Entre la piedra y la cruz*. Guatemala City: Piedra Santa, 2013.

Montejo, Víctor Dionicio. *Las aventuras de Mister Puttison entre los mayas.* Rancho Palos Verdes, Calif.: Yax Te' Foundation, 1998.

———. *The Bird Who Cleans the World and Other Mayan Fables.* Willimantic, Conn.: Curbstone, 1991.

———. "The Dynamics of Cultural Resistance and Transformations: The Case of Guatemalan-Mayan Refugees in Mexico." PhD diss., University of Connecticut, 1993.

———. *Maya Intellectual Renaissance: Identity, Representation, and Leadership.* Austin: University of Texas Press, 2005.

———. *Oxlanh B'aqtun: Recordando al sacerdote Jaguar (Chileam Balam) en el portón del nuevo milenio.* Guatemala City: Cultura, 2003.

———. "The Power of Language: The Mayan Writer (Ahtz'ib')." *Review: Literature and Arts of the Americas* 36, no. 67 (Fall 2003): 7–50.

———. *Q'anil, el hombre rayo: Una leyenda de jacaltenango / Komam Q'anil, ya' k'uh Winaj.* Rancho Palos Verdes, Calif.: Yax Te' Foundation, 1999.

———. *Testimonio: Muerte de una comunidad indígena en Guatemala.* Guatemala City: Universitaria, 1993.

Montejo, Víctor Dionicio, and Luis Garay, eds. *Popol Vuj: Libro sagrado de los mayas.* Mexico City: Artes de México, 1999.

Montejo, Víctor Dionicio, and Victor Perera. *Sculpted Stones / Piedras labradas.* Willimantic, Conn.: Curbstone, 1995.

Montemayor, Carlos. *Arte y plegaria en las lenguas indígenas de México.* Mexico City: Fondo de Cultura Económica, 1999.

———. *Arte y trama en el cuento indígena.* Mexico City: Fondo de Cultura Económica, 1998.

———. *El cuento indígena de tradición oral: Notas sobre sus fuentes y clasificaciones.* Oaxaca City: Centro de Investigaciones y Estudios Superiores en Antropología Social (CIESAS) Instituto Oaxaqueño de las Culturas (IOC), 1996.

———. *Los escritores indígenas actuales.* Vols. 1 and 2. San Angel, Mexico: Tierra Adentro, Consejo Nacional para la Cultura y las Artes, 1992.

———. Introduction to *Tejedor de palabras.* 2nd ed. Guatemala City: UNESCO, 1998.

———. *Letras mayas contemporáneas.* Mérida, Mexico: Instituto Nacional Indigenista. 1996.

———. *La literatura actual en las lenguas indígenas de México.* Mexico City: Universidad Iberoamericana, 2001.

———. *Situación actual y perspectivas de la literatura en lenguas indígenas.* Mexico City: Consejo Nacional para Cultura y las artes, Dirección General de Publicaciones, 1993.

———. *La voz profunda: Antología mexicana contemporánea en lenguas indígenas.* Mexico City: Joaquín Mortíz, 2004.

Montemayor, Carlos, and Donald H. Frischmann, eds. *U túumben k'aayilo'ob x-ya'axche': u meyaj bejlabeno'ob maaya aj ts'íibo'ob ti' u petenil Yúucataane' / Los nuevos cantos de la ceiba: Antología de escritores mayas contemporáneos de la Península de Yucatán.* Mérida, Mexico: Instituto de Cultura de Yucatán, 2009.

———. *Words of the True Peoples*. Vol. 1. Austin: University of Texas Press, 2004.
———. *Words of the True Peoples*. Vol. 3. Austin: University of Texas Press, 2007.
Montemayor, Carlos, Donald H. Frischmann, and George O. Jackson, eds. *Words of the True Peoples*. Vol. 2. Austin: University of Texas Press, 2005.
Morales, Mario Roberto. *La articulación de las diferencias, o, el síndrome de Maximón: Los discursos literarios y políticos del debate interétnico en Guatemala*. Guatemala City: FLACSO Guatemala, 1998.
Morales Damián, Manuel Alberto. *Árbol sagrado: Origen y estructura del universo en el pensamiento maya*. Pachuca, Mexico: Universidad Autónoma del Estado de Hidalgo, 2006.
Morales López, Micaela. *Raíces de la ceiba: Literatura indígena de Chiapas*. Mexico City: Miguel Ángel Porrúa, 2004.
Morales Sic, José Roberto. "Religión y espiritualidad maya." In *Mayanización y vida cotidiana: La ideología multicultural en la sociedad guatemalteca*, edited by Santiago Bastos and Aura Cumes, 3:247–81. Guatemala City: Cholsamaj, 2007.
Moraña, Mabel. *Indigenismo hacia el fin del milenio: Homenaje a Antonio Cornejo-Polar*. Biblioteca de América. Pittsburgh: Instituto Internacional de Literatura Iberoamericana, University of Pittsburgh, 1998.
Moraña, Mabel, Enrique D. Dussel, and Carlos A Jáuregui, eds. *Coloniality at Large: Latin America and the Postcolonial Debate*. Durham, N.C.: Duke University Press, 2008.
Moreiras, Alberto. *The Exhaustion of Difference: The Politics of Latin American Cultural Studies*. Durham, N.C.: Duke University Press, 2011.
Moretti, Franco, ed. "Conjectures on World Literature." *New Left Review*, no. 1 (January–February 2000). http://newleftreview.org/II/1/franco-moretti-conjectures-on-world-literature.
———. *The Novel*. Vol. 1. Princeton, N.J.: Princeton University Press, 2006.
Movimiento de Artistas Mayas Ruk'u'x y Centro Cultural Sotz'il Jay. *Algunas palabras sobre el trabajo del artista maya*. Sololá, Guatemala: Movimiento de Artistas Mayas Ruk'u'x, 2014.
Moya, Ruth, Luis Enrique López, and Teresa Valiente Catter. "Interculturalidad y reforma educativa en Guate." In *Interculturalidad y educación: Diálogo para la democracia en América Latina—La interculturalidad en la educación bilingüe para poblaciones indígenas de América Latina*, 19–50. 49 ICA, Quito, July 7–11, 1997, SIMPOSIO LIN 06. Iberoamericana de Educación 13. Quito, Ecuador: Abya Yala, 1999.
Murray, David. *Forked Tongues: Speech, Writing, and Representation in North American Indian Texts*. Bloomington: Indiana University Press, 1991.
Muyulema, Armando. "De la 'cuestión indígena' a 'lo indígena' como cuestionamiento: Hacia una crítica del latinoamericanismo, el indigenismo y el mestiz(o)aje." In *Convergencia de tiempos: Estudios subalternos / contextos latinoamericanos estado, cultura, subalternidad*, edited by Ileana Rodríguez, 327–63. Amsterdam: Rodopi, 2001.
———. "Una óptica quichua sobre el debate tradición-modernidad ¿Reflexiones en la modernidad desde la tradición?" *Cuadernos de Literatura*, no. 31 (2000): 5–23.

Nelson, Diane. *A Finger in the Wound: Body Politics in Quincentennial Guatemala*. Berkeley: University of California Press, 1999.

———. "Stumped Identities: Body Image, Bodies Politic, and the Mujer Maya as Prosthetic." *Cultural Anthropology* 16, no. 3 (2001): 314–53.

Noh Tzec, Waldmar. *Workshop*. San Cristóbal de las Casas: CELALI, 2005.

O'Gorman, Edmundo. *La invención de América*. Mexico City: Fondo de Cultura Económica, 1977.

OKMA. *Maya' Chii': Los idiomas maya de Guatemala*. Edited by Nora England. Guatemala City: Cholsamej, 1993.

Olivera Bustamante, Mercedes. *De sumisiones, cambios y rebeldías: Mujeres indígenas de Chiapas*. Vol. 1. Tuxtla, Mexico: Universidad de Ciencias y Artes de Chiapas, 2004.

Olson, David R., and Nancy Torrance, eds. *Cultura escrita y oralidad*. Barcelona: Gedisa, 1995.

Ong, Walter. *Orality and Literacy: The Technologizing of the Word*. New York: Routledge, 2002.

Ortega, Aquino de la Cruz. *Los abuelos cantan*. Oaxaca City: Coordinación de Comunicación Visual de la Casa de la Cultura Oaxaqueña, 1986.

Ortiz, Fernando. *Cuban Counterpoint: Tobacco and Sugar*. Translated by Harriet de Onis. Durham, N.C.: Duke University Press, 1995.

Oxlaj Cúmez, Miguel Ángel. *Ru taqikil ri Sarima' = La misión del Sarima'*. Guatemala City: F&G, 2009.

Pacheco, Gabriel. *Tatei Yurienaka y otros cuentos huicholes*. Mexico City: Diana, 1994.

Palacios, Rita M. "Luis de Lión's *El tiempo principia en Xibalbá* and the Foundation of a Contemporary Indigenous Literature in Guatemala." *Revista Canadiense de Estudios Hispánicos* 35, no. 3 (2011): 577–95. http://www.jstor.org/stable/41636559.

Paredes, Julieta. "Hilando fino: Desde el feminismo comunitario." Comunidad Mujeres Creando Comunidad, 2008. http://mujeresdelmundobabel.org/files/2013/11/Julieta-Paredes-Hilando-Fino-desde-el-Fem-Comunitario.pdf.

Parry, Milman. *The Making of Homeric Verse: The Collected Papers of Milman Parry*. Edited by Adam Parry. Oxford, U.K.: Clarendon, 1971.

Partnoy, Alicia, ed. *You Can't Drown the Fire: Latin American Women Writing in Exile*. Pittsburgh: Cleis, 1988.

Past, Ámbar, ed. *Incantations: Song, Spells and Images by Mayan Women*. El Paso, Tex.: Cinco Puntos, 2008.

Payeras, Mario. *Los días de la selva: Relatos sobre la implantación de las guerrillas populares en el norte del quiché, 1972–1976*. Guatemala City, 1980.

———. *Los pueblos indígenas y la revolución guatemalteca: Ensayos étnicos, 1982–1992*. Guatemala City: Magna Terra, Luna y Sol, 1997.

Peñalosa, Fernando. *The Mayan Folktale: An Introduction*. Rancho Palos Verdes, Calif.: Yax Te' Foundation, 1996.

Peñate, Juana. *Mi nombre ya no es silencio*. Tuxtla Gutiérrez, Chiapas: Gobierno del Estado de Chiapas, 2002.

Pequeño Bueno, Andrea, ed. *Participación y políticas de mujeres indígenas en América Latina*. Quito: FLACSO, 2009.

Perera, Victor. *Unfinished Conquest: The Guatemalan Tragedy.* Berkeley: University of California Press, 1993.

Pérez, Emma. *The Decolonial Imaginary: Writing Chicanas into History.* Bloomington: Indiana University Press, 1999.

Pérez Brignoli, Héctor. *A Brief History of Central America.* Berkeley: University of California Press, 1989.

Piazza, Michael, and Marc Zimmerman. *New World (Dis)Orders and Peripheral Strains: Specifying Cultural Dimensions in Latin American and Latino Studies.* Chicago: MARCH/Abrazo Press, 1998.

Pineda Santiago, Irma. *Doo yoo ne ga' bia' / De la casa del ombligo a las nueve cuartas.* Mexico City: Comisión Nacional para el Desarrollo de los Pueblos Indígenas, 2008.

———. "La abuela." In *Doo yoo ne ga' bia' / De la casa del ombligo a las nueve cuartas,* 43. Mexico City: Comisión Nacional para el Desarrollo de los Pueblos Indígenas, 2008.

———. "Laanu." In *Xilase qui rié di' sicasi rié nisa guiigu' / La nostalgia no se marcha como el agua de los ríos,* 47–48. Mexico City: Escritores en Lenguas Indígenas, 2007.

———. "La literatura de los Binnizá, zapotecas del Istmo." In *De la oralidad a la palabra escrita: Estudios sobre el rescate de las voces originarias en el sur de México,* edited by Floriberto González González and Humberto Santos Bautista, 293–310. Chilpancingo, Mexico: Colegio de Guerrero, 2012.

———. "Mis dos lenguas." *Debate Feminista* 16, no. 32 (October 2005): 161–75. http://www.debatefeminista.pueg.unam.mx/wp-content/uploads/2016/03/articulos/032_10.pdf.

———. "Las mujeres indígenas y la literatura." *Revista médica de arte y cultura,* December 2008, 31. https://xa.yimg.com/kq/groups/18167712/1515459363/name/Literatura+Indigena+en+Mexico,+2008.pdf.

———. "No hay perdón ni olvido a 33 años." *Periódico de Poesía.* http://www.periodicodepoesia.unam.mx/index.php/4568. Accessed January 22, 2018.

———. "No me verá morir." *Xilase qui rié di' sicasi rié nisa guiigu': La nostalgia no se marcha como el agua de los ríos,* 72–75. Mexico City: Escritores en Lenguas Indígenas, 2007.

———. "You Will Not See Me Die." Translated by Wendy Call. *The Translation Issue: Within and beyond the Metropole* 52, no. 2 (Spring 2013). http://hdl.handle.net/2027/spo.act2080.0052.211.

———. "Untitled." In *Doo yoo ne ga' bia' / De la casa del ombligo a las nueve cuartas,* 45. Mexico City: Comisión Nacional para el Desarrollo de los Pueblos Indígenas, 2008.

Pizarro, Ana. Introduction to *La literatura latinoamericana como proceso,* ed. Ana Pizarro, 13–33. Buenos Aires: Bibliotecas Universitarias, Centro Editorial de América Latina, 1985.

Plaks, Andrew H. "The Novel in Premodern China." In *The Novel,* vol. 1, edited by Franco Moretti, 181–216. Princeton, N.J.: Princeton University Press, 2006.

Pratt, Mary Louise. "Arts of the Contact Zone." *Profession* (1991): 33–40.

Preuss, Mary H. *Beyond Indigenous Voices.* Lancaster, Calif.: Labyrinthos, 1996.

Pu Tzunux, Rosa. *Representaciones sociales mayas y teoría feminista: Crítica de la* aplicación literal de modelos teóricos en la interpretación de la realidad de las mujeres mayas. Guatemala: Iximulew, 2007.

Quijano, Anibal. "Coloniality of Power, Eurocentrism, and Latin America." *Nepantla: Views from South* 1, no. 3 (2000): 533–80.

———. "Coloniality of Power, Eurocentrism, and Social Classification." In *Coloniality at Large: Latin America and the Postcolonial Debate*, edited by Mabel Moraña, Enrique D. Dussel, and Carlos A. Jáuregui, 181–224. Durham, N.C.: Duke University Press, 2008.

Rama, Ángel. *The Lettered City*. Translated by John Charles Chasteen. Durham, N.C.: Duke University Press, 1996.

———. "Los procesos de transculturación en América Latina." *Revista de literatura hispanoaméricana*, April 1974, 9–38.

———. *Transculturación narrativa en América Latina*. 3rd ed. Mexico City: Siglo Veintiuno, 1987.

Ramírez, Sergio. *Antología del cuento centroamericano (La narrativa centroamericana)*. San José, Costa Rica: Universitaria, 1970.

Ramírez Calvo, Rosa. *Ba kal k'u x-elan sp'ejel yu'un slomlejal totik ch'ul bale / Flor y pensamiento de los totikes, San Bartolomé de Los Llanos*. Mexico City: Letras Mayas Contemporáneas, 1995.

Ramírez Castañeda, Elisa. *La educación indígena en México*. Pluralidad Cultural en México, no. 10. Mexico City: Universidad Nacional Autónoma de México, 2006.

Ramos, Julio. *Desencuentros de la modernidad en América Latina: Literatura y política en el siglo XIX*. Mexico City: Fondo de Cultura Económica, 1989.

Rappaport, Joanne, and Tom Cummins. *Beyond the Lettered City: Indigenous Literacies in the Andes*. Durham, N.C.: Duke University Press, 2012.

Reckin, Anna. "Tidalectic Lectures: Kamau Brathwaite's Prose and Poetry as Sound-Space." *Anthurium: A Caribbean Studies Journal* 1, no. 1 (December 2003): 1–16.

Recollet, Karyn. "Gesturing Indigenous Futurities through the Remix." *Dance Research Journal* 48, no. 1 (2016): 91–105.

———. "Glyphing Decolonial Love through Urban Flash Mobbing and Walking with Our Sisters." *Curriculum Inquiry* 45, no. 1 (2015): 129–45.

Regino, Juan Gregorio. "Na Sabi a María Sabina." *Nuestra Palabra*, supplement to *El Nacional*. Mexico City: Consejo Nacional para la Cultura y las Artes (Conaculta), May 1993, 3.

Rehaag, Irmgard. "La perspectiva intercultural en la educación." *El Cotidiano* 160 (March–April 2010): 75–83.

Restall, Matthew. "Heirs to the Hieroglyphs: Indigenous Writing in Colonial Mesoamerica." *Americas* 54, no. 2 (October 1997): 239–68.

Reuque Paillalef, Rosa Isolde. *When a Flower Is Reborn: The Life and Times of a Mapuche Feminist*. Durham, N.C.: Duke University Press, 2002.

Reuters. "Indigenous Woman Registers to Run for Mexican Presidency in 2018." Reuters.com, October 7, 2017. https://www.reuters.com/article/us-mexico-politics/indigenous-woman-registers-to-run-for-mexican-presidency-in-2018-idUSKBN1CCoT6.

Reyes Matamoros, José Antonio. Introduction to *Memoria del viento / Sbel sjol yo'onton ik'*, Edited by Andrés López Díaz, Angelina Díaz Ruiz, and Luis López Díaz. San Cristóbal de las Casas, Mexico: Unidad de Escritores Mayas-Zoques, 2006.

"Ritual of the Bacabs." In *In the Language of Kings: An Anthology of Mesoamerican Literature—Pre-Columbian to the Present*, edited by Miguel León-Portilla and Earl Shorris, 528–50. Translated by Ruth Gabler and Ralph L. Roys. New York: W. W. Norton, 2001.

Roach, Joseph R. "Theatre History and Historiography." In *Critical Theory and Performance*, edited by Janelle G. Reinelt and Joseph R. Roach, 293–98. Ann Arbor: University of Michigan Press, 2007.

Rocabado, Franco Gamboa. "Bolivia frente a su espejo: El indianismo, sus orígenes y limitaciones en el siglo XXI." *Estudios Sociológicos* 28, no. 83 (2010): 529–60. http://www.jstor.org/stable/20749181.

Rodríguez, Ileana. *Women, Guerrillas, and Love: Understanding War in Central America*. Minneapolis: University of Minnesota Press, 1996.

Rodríguez, Ileana, and María Milagros López, eds. *The Latin American Subaltern Studies Reader: Latin America Otherwise*. Durham, N.C.: Duke University Press, 2001.

Rodríguez-Luis, Julio. "El indigenismo como proyecto literario: Revalorización y nuevas perspectivas." *Hispamérica* 19, no. 55 (April 1990): 41–50.

———. *Hermenéutica y praxis del indigenismo: La novela indigenista, de Clorinda Matto a José María Arguedas*. Mexico City: Fondo de Cultura Económica, 1980.

Rojas González, Francisco. "La Tona." *El diosero*. 1952. Xalapa, Veracruz: Al Fin Liebre Ediciones Digitales, 2009.

Román-Lagunas, Jorge, ed. *La literatura centroamericana: Visiones y revisiones*. Lewiston, N.Y.: E. Mellen, 1994.

Román-Lagunas, Jorge, and Richard McCallister. *La literatura centroamericana como arma cultural*. Colección Centro Internacional de Literatura Centroamericana. Guatemala City: Oscar de León Palacios, 1999.

Romero Frizzi, María de los Ángeles, ed. *Escritura zapoteca: 2500 años de historia*. Mexico City: INAH, 2003.

———. "Los zapotecos a través de su historia y sus escritores: La escritura prehispánica." In *Escritura zapoteca: 2500 años de historia*, 13–67 Mexico City: INAH, 2003.

Romero Frizzi, María de los Ángeles, and Michael Oudijk. "Los títulos primordiales: Un género de tradición mesoamericana del mundo prehispánico al siglo XXI." *Relaciones 95* 24 (Summer 2003): 18–48.

"Rosa Chávez, poesía palpitante." *El Aquelarre Taller*, April 9, 2012. http://elaquelarretaller.blogspot.com/2012/04/rosa-chavez-poesia-palpitante.html.

Rosado Avilés, Celia Esperanza, and Óscar Ortega Arango. "Los labios del silencio: La literatura femenina maya actual." In *Mujer maya: Siglos tejiendo una identidad*, edited by Sergio Quezada and Georgina Rosado Rosado, 111–86. Mérida, Mexico: Conaculta, 2001.

Ross, John. "The Zapatista Challenge in Mexico's Presidential Elections." *Counterpunch*, November 5, 2005. http://www.counterpunch.org/2005/11/05/the-zapatista-challenge-in-mexico-s-presidential-elections/.
Rousseau, Jean-Jacques. *The First and Second Discourses, Together with the Replies to Critics and the Essay on the Origin Languages*. Translated by Victor Gourevitch. New York: Harper, 1986.
Rovira Sancho, Guiomar. "Ahora es nuestra hora, la hora de las mujeres indígenas." *Debate Feminista* 12, no. 24 (October 2001): 191–205.
———. *Mujeres de maíz: La voz de las indígenas de Chiapas y la rebelión Zapatista*. Mexico City: Era, 1996.
Rowe, William, and Vivian Schelling. *Memory and Modernity: Popular Culture in Latin America*. New York: Verso, 1991.
Rubín, Ramón. *El callado dolor de los tzotziles*. Mexico City: Libro México, 1957.
Ruiz Campbell, Obdulia. "Representations of Isthmus Women: A Zapotec Woman's Point of View." In *Zapotec Struggles: Histories, Politics, and Representations from Juchitán, Oaxaca*, edited by Howard Campbell et al., 137–41. Washington, D.C.: Smithsonian Institution Press, 1993.
Sacoto, Antonio. *El indio en el ensayo de la América Española*. New York: Las Américas, 1971.
Saer, Juan José. *The Witness*. Translated by Margaret Jull Costa Acosta. London: Serpent's Tail, 1990.
Said, Edward W. *Culture and Imperialism*. London: Vintage, 1993.
Salazar Tetzagüic, Manuel de Jesús. *Rupach'uxik kina'oj qati't qamama' / Características de la literatura maya kaqchikel*. 2nd ed. Guatemala City: Cholsamaj, 1995.
Sam Colop, Luis Enrique. *La copa y la raíz*. Guatemala City: Rin 78, 1980.
———. "The Discourse of Concealment in 1992." In *Maya Cultural Activism in Guatemala*, edited by Edward F. Fischer and R. McKenna Brown, 89–113. Austin: University of Texas Press, 1996.
———. "Maya Poetics." PhD diss., State University of New York at Buffalo, 1994.
———. *Versos sin refugio*. Guatemala City: San Antonio, 1978.
Sammons, Kay, and Joel Sherzer, eds. *Translating Native Latin American Verbal Art: Ethnopoetics and Ethnography of Speaking*. Washington, D.C.: Smithsonian Institution Press, 2000.
Sánchez, Celerina Patricia. "Palabra de lluvia." *Mundo Indígena*, no. 1 (May 12, 2008). http://www.redindigena.net/mundoindigena/n1/pag16.html.
Sánchez, Consuelo. *Los pueblos indígenas: Del indigenismo a la autonomía*. Mexico City: Siglo Veintiuno, 1999.
Sánchez, Mikeas. *Tumjama Maka Müjsi' / Y sabrás un día: Poemas*. Tuxtla Gutiérrez, Mexico: Centro Estatal de Lenguas, Arte y Literatura Indígenas, 2006.
Sánchez Chan, Feliciano. *Ba'alche'ob yéetel Ch'iich'o'ob / Animales y pájaros*. Mexico City: Instituto de Cultura de Yucatán Miatzil Maayáa, Ethnic A, UNESCO, 2002.
———. *Del sabucán del abuelo*. Mexico City: Instituto de Cultura de Yucatán del Gobierno del Estado de Yucatán, Dirección de Culturas Populares e Indígenas, Ethnic A, UNESCO, 2001.

Santopietro, Judith. *Palabras de agua*. Mexico City: Praxis, 2010.
Schevill, Margot Blum. *Evolution in Textile Design from the Highlands of Guatemala: Seventeen Male Tzutes, or Headdresses, from Chichicastenango in the Collections of the Lowie Museum of Anthropology, University of California, Berkeley*. Berkeley: Lowie Museum of Anthropology, University of California, 1985.
Schleiermacher, Friedrich. "On the Different Methods of Translating." In *The Translation Studies Reader*, 3rd ed., edited by Lawrence Venuti, 43–63. New York: Routledge, 2000.
Schlesinger, Stephen C., and Stephen Kinzer, eds., *Bitter Fruit: The Untold Story of the American Coup in Guatemala*. Garden City, N.Y.: Doubleday, 1982.
Schroeder, Susan, ed., *The Conquest All over Again: Nahuas and Zapotecs Thinking, Writing, and Painting Spanish Colonialism*. Eastbourne, U.K.: Sussex Academic, 2010.
Scott, James C. *The Moral Economy of the Peasant: Rebellion and Subsistence in Southeast Asia*. New Haven, Conn.: Yale University Press, 1976.
Seed, Patricia. "Taking Possession and Reading Texts: Establishing the Authority of Overseas Empires." In *Early Images of the Americas: Transfer and Invention*, edited by Jerry M. Willimas and Robert E. Lewis, 112–33. Tucson: University of Arizona Press, 1993.
Senner, Wayne, ed. *The Origins of Writing*. Lincoln: University of Nebraska Press, 1989.
Shillington, John Wesley. *Grappling with Atrocity: Guatemalan Theater in the 1990s*. Madison, N.J.: Fairleigh Dickinson University Press, 2002.
Sieder, Rachel. "Sexual Violence and Gendered Subjectivities: Indigenous Women's Search for Justice in Guatemala." In *Gender Justice and Legal Pluralities: Latin American and African Perspectives*, edited by Rachael Sieder and Edrew McNeish, 110–11. New York: Routledge, 2013.
Simpson, Audra, and Andrea Smith, eds. *Theorizing Native Studies*. Durham, N.C.: Duke University Press, 2014.
Sitler, Robert. "Entrevista con Gaspar Pedro González" (May 11, 1995). *San Pedro Soloma.com*, November 2005. http://blog.sanpedrosoloma.com/2005/11/entrevista-con-gaspar_113127121181104384.asp.
Smith, Carol A., and Marilyn M. Moors, eds. *Guatemalan Indians and the State, 1540–1988*. Austin: University of Texas Press, 1990.
Smith, Linda Tuhiwai. *Decolonizing Methodologies: Research and Indigenous Peoples*. 2nd ed. New York: Zed, 2012.
Sommer, Doris. *Foundational Fictions: The National Romances of Latin America*. Berkeley: University of California Press: 1991.
———. *Proceed with Caution, When Engaged by Minority Writing in the Americas*. Cambridge, Mass.: Harvard University Press, 1999.
———. "Rigoberta's Secrets." *Latin American Perspectives* 18, no. 3 (Summer 1991): 32–50.
———, ed. *Cultural Agency in the Americas*. Durham, N.C.: Duke University Press, 2005.

Sorroza Polo, Carlos, and Michael S. Danielson. "Political Subsystems in Oaxaca's Usos y Costumbre Municipalities." Translated by Andrew McKelvy. In *Latin America's Multicultural Movements: The Struggle between Communitarism, Autonomy and Human Rights*, edited by Todd A. Eisenstadt, Michael S. Danielson, Moises Jaime Bailon Corres, and Carlos Sorroza Polo, 169–91. Oxford: Oxford University Press, 2013.

Sotsil Jay Cultural Center. *Algunas palabras sobre el trabajo del artista maya*. Guatemala City: Centro Cultural Sotsil Jay, 2014.

Speed, Shannon, Rosalva Aída Hernández Castillo, and Lynn Stephen, eds. *Dissident Women: Gender and Cultural Politics in Chiapas*. Austin: University of Texas Press, 2006.

Spitta, Silvia. *Between Two Waters: Narratives of Transculturation in Latin America*. Houston: Rice University Press, 1995.

Spivak, Gayatri C. "Can the Subaltern Speak?" In *Marxism and the Interpretation of Culture*, edited by Cary Nelson and Lawrence Grossberg, 271–313. Urbana: University of Illinois Press, 1988.

Steele, Cynthia. "Indigenismo y posmodernidad: Narrativa indigenista, testimonio, teatro campesino y video en el Chiapas finisecular." *Revista de Crítica Literaria Latinoamericana* 19, no. 38 (1993): 249–60.

———. *Narrativa indigenista en los Estados Unidos y México*. Colección INI. Serie de Investigaciones Sociales, no. 15. Mexico City: Instituto Nacional Indigenista, 1985.

Sten, María, ed. *Codices of Mexico and Their Extraordinary History*. Mexico City: Panorama, 1979.

———. *El teatro franciscano: Fuentes y ensayos para el estudio del teatro de evangelización en el siglo XVI*. Mexico City: Universidad Nacional Autónoma de México, 2000.

———. *Vida y muerte del teatro náhuatl: El Olimpo sin Prometeo*. Mexico City: Secretaría de Educación Pública, 1974.

Sten, María, and Germán Viveros, eds. *Teatro náhuatl II: Selección y estudio crítico de los materiales inéditos de Fernando Horcasitas*. Mexico City: Universidad Nacional Autónoma de México, 2004.

Stephen, Lynn. *We Are the Face of Oaxaca: Testimony and Social Movements*. Durham, N.C.: Duke University Press, 2013.

———. *Zapotec Women: Gender, Class, and Ethnicity in Globalized Oaxaca*. Durham, N.C.: Duke University Press, 2005.

Stephenson, Marcia. *Gender and Modernity in Andean Bolivia*. Austin: University of Texas Press, 1999.

Stimson, Frederick S., and Ricardo Navas-Ruiz. *Literatura de la América hispánica: Antología e historia*. New York: Dodd, Mead: 1971.

Stuart, David, and George E. Stuart. *Palenque: Eternal City of the Maya*. New York: Thames & Hudson, 2008.

Sturm, Circe. "Old Writing and New Messages: The Role of Hieroglyphic Literacy in Maya Cultural Activism." In *Maya Cultural Activism in Guatemala*, edited by Edward F. Fischer and R. McKenna Brown, 114–30. Austin: University of Texas Press, 1996.

Sullivan, Clare. "The State of Zapotec Poetry: Can Poetry Save an Endangered Culture?" *World Literature Today* 86, no. 1 (January 2012): 43–45.
Suzack, Cheryl, Shari M. Huhndorf, Jean Barman, and Jeanne Perreault, eds. *Indigenous Women and Feminism: Politics, Activism, Culture.* Vancouver: University of British Columbia Press, 2010.
Tarica, Estelle. *The Inner Life of Mestizo Nationalism.* Minneapolis: University of Minnesota Press, 2008.
Taussig, Michael T. *Shamanism, Colonialism, and the Wild Man: A Study in Terror and Healing.* Chicago: University of Chicago Press, 1986.
Taylor, Analisa. *Indigeneity in the Mexican Cultural Imagination: Thresholds of Belonging.* Tucson: University of Arizona Press, 2009.
Taylor, Diana. *The Archive and the Repertoire: Performing Cultural Memory in the Americas.* Durham, N.C.: Duke University Press, 2003.
———. *Theatre of Crisis: Drama and Politics in Latin America.* Lexington: University of Kentucky Press, 1991.
Taylor, Diana, and Roselyn Costantino, eds. *Holy Terrors: Latin American Women Perform.* Durham, N.C.: Duke University Press, 2003.
Taylor, Diana, and Sarah J. Townsend, eds. *Stages of Conflict: A Critical Anthology of Latin American Theater and Performance.* Ann Arbor: University of Michigan Press, 2008.
Taylor, Diana, and Juan Villegas Morales, eds. *Negotiating Performance: Gender, Sexuality, and Theatricality in Latin/o America.* Durham, N.C.: Duke University Press, 1994.
Taylor, Isaac. *The History of the Alphabet: An Account of the Origin and Development of Letters.* Vols. 1 and 2. New York: C. Scribner's Sons, 1899.
Tec Chi, Andres, et al. *Cuentos sobre las apariciones en el mayab.* Mexico City: Aldina, 1998.
Tedlock, Dennis. *Rabinal Achí: A Mayan Drama of War and Sacrifice.* Oxford: Oxford University Press, 2003.
———. *The Spoken Word and the Work of Interpretation.* Philadelphia: University of Pennsylvania Press, 1983.
———. *2000 Years of Mayan Literature.* Berkeley: University of California Press, 2010.
———, ed. *Popol Vuh: The Definitive Edition of the Mayan Book of the Dawn of Life and the Glories of Gods and Kings.* Rev. ed. New York: Touchstone, 1996.
Teuton, Sean Kicummah. "The Indigenous Novel." In *The Oxford Handbook of Indigenous Literatures*, edited by James H. Cox and Daniel Heath Justice, 318–32. Oxford: Oxford University Press, 2014.
Thompson, E. P. "The Moral Economy of the English Crowd in the Eighteenth Century." *Past and Present*, no. 50 (February 1971): 76–136.
Thompson, J. Eric S. *Maya Hieroglyphic Writing: An Introduction.* 3rd ed. Norman: University of Oklahoma Press, 1971.
Tilley, Virginia Q. *Seeing Indians: A Study of Race, Nation, and Power in El Salvador.* Albuquerque: University of New Mexico Press, 2005.
Todorov, Tzvetan. *The Conquest of America: The Question of the Other.* New York: Harper & Row, 1984.

Toledo Paz, Natalia. *Flor de pantano: Antología, 1992–2002*. Oaxaca City: Instituto Oaxaqueño de las Culturas, 2004.

———. *Guie' yaase' / Olivo negro*. Mexico City: Consejo Nacional para la Cultura y las Artes, Dirección General de Culturas Populares e Indígenas, 2005.

———. "La realidad/Reality." A poem dedicated to the Zapatistas and read at the Poetry Festival in Medellin in 2002. YouTube video. Posted by "Revista Prometeo," April 19, 2007. https://www.youtube.com/watch?v=PcKlFJQ-q6g.

———. *Mujeres de sol, mujeres de oro*. Oaxaca City: Instituto Oaxaqueño de Cultura, 2002.

———. "Mutilación." In *Flor de pantano: Antología, 1992–2002*, 45. Oaxaca City: Instituto Oaxaqueño de las Culturas, 2004.

———. "Mutilación." In *Del silencio hacia la luz: Mapa poético de México*, edited by Adán Echeverría and Armando Pacheco, 1120. Mérida, Mexico: Navegaciones del Sur, 2008.

———. "Tradición." In *Guie' yaase' / Olivo negro*, 123. Mexico City: Consejo Nacional para la Cultura y las Artes, Dirección General de Culturas Populares e Indígenas, 2005.

Toledo Paz, Natalia, and Francisco Toledo. *Guendaguti Ñee Sisi: Diidxazá-diidxastiá / La muerte pies ligeros: Zapoteco-español*. Mexico City: Fondo de Cultura Económica, 2005.

Tozzer, Alfred Marston, ed. *Landa's "Relación de las cosas de Yucatán."* Papers of the Peabody Museum of American Archeology and Ethnology 18. Cambridge, Mass.: Harvard University Press, 1941.

Trigo, Abril. "General Introduction." In *The Latin American Cultural Studies Reader*, edited by Ana del Sarto, Alicia Ríos, and Abril Trigo, 1–14. Durham, N.C.: Duke University Press, 2004.

Trujillo Carrasco, Taína. "Palabra de lluvia." *Mundo indígena*, no. 1 (May 12, 2008). http://www.redindigena.net/mundoindigena/n1/pag16.html.

Tula, María Teresa. *Hear My Testimony: Maria Teresa Tula, Human Rights Activist of El Salvador*. Translated by Lynn Stephen. Boston: South End, 1994.

Turner, Victor. *The Anthropology of Performance*. New York: PAJ, 1988.

Tutino, John. "Ethnic Resistance: Juchitán in Mexican History." In *Zapotec Struggles: Histories, Politics, and Representations from Juchitán, Oaxaca*, edited by Howard Campbell et al., 41–61. Washington, D.C.: Smithsonian Institution Press, 1993.

Ugalde, Keefe Sharon. "Hilos y palabras: Diseños de una ginotradición." *INTI: Revista de Literatura Hispánica* 51 no. 4 (2000): 54–67.

Underiner, Tamara L. *Contemporary Theatre in Mayan Mexico: Death-Defying Acts*. Austin: University of Texas Press, 2004.

———. "Transculturation in the Work of Laboratorio de Teatro Campesino e Indígena." In *Contemporary Theatre in Mayan Mexico: Death-Defying Acts*, 78–100. Austin: University of Texas Press, 2004.

Upún Sipac, Damián. *Maya' ajilab'äl / La cuenta maya de los días*. Guatemala City: Cholsamaj, 1999.

Urban, Greg, and Joel Sherzer. *Nation-States and Indians in Latin America*. Austin: University of Texas Press, 1991.

Urcid, Javier. "Zapotec Writing: Knowledge, Power and Memory in Ancient Oaxaca." Foundation for the Advancement of Mesoamerican Studies, 2005. http://www.famsi.org/zapotecwriting/.
Valenzuela Arce, José Manuel, ed. *Decadencia y auge de las identidades: Cultura nacional, identidad cultural y modernización.* Tijuana, Mexico: Colegio de la Frontera Norte, Programa Cultural de las Fronteras, 1992.
Varese, Stefano. *Pueblos indios, soberanía y globalismo.* Quito: Abya Yala, 1996.
Vargas Llosa, Mario. *El hablador.* Barcelona: Seix Barral, 1995.
———. "Questions of Conquest." *Harper's Magazine,* December 1990, 45–53.
Vasconcelos, José. *La raza cósmica: Misión de la raza iberoamericana, Argentina y Brasil.* Mexico City: Espasa-Calpe Mexicana, 1992.
Vázquez, Juan Adolfo. *The Field of Latin American Indian Literatures.* Latin American Reprint Series, no. 14. Pittsburgh: Center for Latin American Studies, University of Pittsburgh, 1978.
Velásquez Nimatuj, Irma Alicia. "Flight 795: A Tale of Structural Racism." *ReVista: Harvard Review of Latin America* 10, no.1 (Fall 2010/Winter 2011): 27–29. http://revista.drclas.harvard.edu/files/revista/files/guatemala.pdf.
Venuti, Lawrence, ed. *The Translation Studies Reader.* New York: Routledge, 2000.
Villafán Broncano, Macedonio. *Apu Kolki Hirka / Dios Montaña de plata.* Perú: Universidad Nacional Santiago Antúnez de Mayolo, 2014.
Villagómez Valdés, Gina. "Mujeres de Yucatán: Precursoras del voto femenino." *Revista de la Universidad Autónoma de Yucatán,* no. 225 (2003): 3–19.
Villagutierre-Soto-Mayor, Juan de. *History of the Conquest of the Province of the Itza.* Culver City, Calif.: Labyrinthos, 1983.
Villoro, Luis. *Los grandes momentos del indigenismo en México.* Mexico City: Colegio de México, 1950.
Vince, R.W. "Theater History as an Academic Discipline." In *Interpreting the Theatrical Past,* edited by Thomas Postlewait and Bruce A. McConachie, 1–18. Iowa City: University of Iowa Press, 1989.
Waldman, Gilda. "El florecimiento de la literatura indígena actual en México: Contexto social, significado e importancia." https://xa.yimg.com/kq/groups/18167712/1012536742/name/El+florecimiento+de+la+literatura+indigena+mexico.pdf. Accessed January 22, 2018.
Warren, Kay B. *Indigenous Movements and Their Critics: Pan-Maya Activism in Guatemala.* Princeton, N.J.: Princeton University Press, 1998.
———. *The Symbolism of Subordination: Indian Identity in a Guatemalan Town.* Texas Pan American Series. Austin: University of Texas Press, 1978.
Warren, Kay B., ed. *The Violence Within: Cultural and Political Opposition in Divided Nations.* Boulder, Colo.: Westview, 1993.
Warren Kay, B., and Jean E. Jackson. *Indigenous Movements, Self-Representation, and the State in Latin America.* Austin: University of Texas Press, 2002.
Watt, Ian. *The Rise of the Novel: Studies in Defoe, Richardson, and Fielding.* Berkeley: University of California Press, 1957.
Weaver, Jace, Craig S. Womack, and Robert Warrior. *American Indian Literary Nationalism.* Albuquerque: University of New Mexico Press, 2006.

Weiss, Judith. *Latin American Popular Theatre: The First Five Centuries*. Albuquerque: University of New Mexico Press, 1993.

Willis Paau, Lucía. "Reflexiones desde mi experiencia de mujer." In *Identidad: Rostros sin máscara—Reflexiones sobre cosmovisión, género y etnicidad*, edited by Pop A. Delgado, Morna Macleod, and M. Luisa Cabrera Pérez-Armiñan, 73–94. Guatemala City: Oxfam Australia, 2000.

Wilson, Carter. "Serving Two Mistresses: Maria Escandon's Life with Rosario Castellanos and Trudi Blom." *Southwest Review* 96, no.3 (2011): 414–18.

Wilson, Pamela, and Michelle Stewart. *Global Indigenous Media: Cultures, Poetics, and Politics*. Durham, N.C.: Duke University Press, 2008.

Womack, Craig S. *Red on Red: Native American Literary Separatism*. Minneapolis: University of Minnesota Press, 1999.

Worley, Paul. *Telling and Being Told: Storytelling and Cultural Control in Contemporary Yucatec Maya Literatures*. Tucson: University of Arizona Press, 2013.

"X-Colom-Che." In *Literatura maya*. Translated by Alfredo Barrera Vasquez. Edited by Mercedes de la Garza, 355–59. Barcelona: Ayacucho, 1980.

Yanes, Kenneth. "Guatemalan Spanish as Act of Identity: An Analysis of Language and Minor Literature within Modern Maya Literary Production." MA thesis, City University of New York, 2014.

Young, Robert. *Colonial Desire: Hybridity in Theory, Culture, and Race*. New York: Routledge, 1995.

Yuval-Davis, Nira, and Floya Anthias, eds. *Woman, Nation, State*. New York: St. Martin's, 1989.

Zapata, Claudia. *Intelectuales indígenas en Ecuador, Bolivia y Chile: Diferencia, colonialismo y anticolonialismo*. Quito: Abya Yala, 2013.

Zavala, Magda, ed. *La historiografía literaria en América Central, 1957–1987*. Heredia, Costa Rica: Editorial Fundación UNA, 1995.

Zimmerman, Marc. *Literature and Resistance in Guatemala: Textual Modes and Cultural Politics from "El Señor Presidente" to Rigoberta Menchú*. Athens: Ohio University Center for International Studies, 1995.

Zimmerman, Marc, and Raúl Rojas. *Guatemala: Voces desde el silencio—Un collage épico*. Guatemala City: Oscar de León Palacios; Palo de Hormiga, 1993.

INDEX

Abya Yala, 5, 7, 23, 28, 135, 164n24
Acevedo, Anabella, 94, 100–101
Adorno, Rolena, 25, 35
Aguilar Gil, Yásnaya Elena, 40
Ajchowen, 6, 22, 104, 105, 110, 11, 116–21, 123–24
Ak'abal, Humberto, 2, 6, 21, 40, 47, 48, 53, 61, 160, 180n27; *Grito en la sombra*, 48, 53, 61–63, 66
alphabetic script, 25, 29, 30, 33, 171n58
Altamirano, Ignacio Manuel, 131
Amerindians, 13, 119
amonestaciones, 92, 93
anthropology, 46, 63, 66, 72
Arévalo, Juan José, 50, 51
Arias, Arturo, 5, 11, 39, 47, 99, 132, 145
Aridjis, Homero, 2
Asociación de Escritores Mayances de Guatemala, 11
Asturias, Miguel Ángel, 2, 61, 130
Aztec, 15; past of, 83; people of, 106

Bakhtin, Mikhail, 134
Barbados meetings, 3
Barthes, Roland, "The Death of the Author," 53–54
Bautista Vásquez, Ruperta, 85, 160
Benjamin, Walter, "The Storyteller," 54
Binnigula'sa', 12, 41, 42
Binnizá, 12, 41, 42, 78
body-as-territory, 70, 93, 102
Books of Chilam Balam, 14, 30, 31, 40, 172n60
Brathwaite, Kamau, 12
Braz, Albert, 46

Canclini, Néstor García, 38–39
Canek, Caly Domitila, 97–98. *See also* Gabriel Xiquín, Calixta
Cantares de Dzitbalché, Los (The songs of Dzitbalché), 30–32
Canters, Hanneke, 13, 14
capitalism, 70, 85, 89, 91, 111, 124, 133, 145, 150
Carrillo Can, Isaac Esau, 1, 192n40
Casanova, Pascale, 2
Castellanos Martínez, Javier, 6, 8, 130, 132, 135–40, 142–43, 150, 160; *Da kebe nho seke gon ben xhi'ne guzio / Relación de hazañas del hijo del relámpago* (Account of the exploits of the son of lightning), 136; *Dxiokze xha . . . bene walhall / Gente del mismo corazón* (People of the same heart), 136; *Laxdao yelazeralle / El corazón de los deseos* (The heart of desires), 136; *Wila che be ze lhao / Los cantares de los vientos primerizos* (Song of the first winds), 22, 135, 136–37
Caste War, 143, 146
Catholicism, 57, 58, 86, 87, 89, 91, 99, 108, 126, 183n69
Ceh Moo, Marisol, 6, 113, 132–36, 143–50, 160; *Chen tumeen chúupen / Solo por ser mujer* (Just for being a woman), 143; *Jats'uts'il Loolo'ob / Jardines de xibalbaj*, 143; *T'ambilak men tunk'uli-lo'ob / El llamado de los tunkules* (The call of the tunkules), 143; *X-Teya, U puksi'k'al ko'olel / Teya, un corazón de mujer* (Teya, heart of a woman), 132

Centro Estatal de Literatura, Artes y Lenguas Indígenas (State Center for Literature, Arts, and Indigenous Languages, or CELALI), 10, 58, 84, 85, 160
Cerano, Dagoberto Huanosto, 1
Chakrabarty, Dipesh, 5
Chamula, Mexico, 19, 85, 91
Chávez, Adrián Inés, 15, 51, 167n74
Chávez, Rosa María, 6, 95, 96, 100, 117, 160; *Piedra/Ab'aj*, 100
Chiapas, Mexico, 4, 10, 21, 22, 28, 38, 58, 70–71, 72–73, 76, 83–86, 88, 91, 103, 109, 111–13, 129, 136, 154, 180n27, 183n69, 184n73, 189n41
Chirix García, Emma Delfina, 51, 71, 93, 94, 96, 98, 102
Ch'orti, 12, 154
Cloud People, 12, 41, 42, 181n36
Coalición Obrera, Campesina, Estudiantil del Istmo (Coalition of Workers, Peasants, and Students of the Isthmus, or COCEI), 10, 77, 136
Cocom Pech, Jorge, 2, 6, 18, 21, 48, 52–54, 135, 160; *El cazador de auroras* (The hunter of dawns), 55; *Secretos del abuelo / Mukult'an in nool* (Grandfather's secrets), 48, 53, 55, 66; *Testimonio de una iniciación: La prueba del aire, la prueba del sueño* (Testimonial of an initiation: The air challenge, the dream challenge), 55–56
colonialism, 25, 31, 36, 44, 115, 131–32, 137, 138, 140, 155
coloniality of power, 35, 37, 132, 141
colonial past, 86, 91
Columbus, Christopher: accounts of, 25; letters of, 34–35
Columbus Day, 11
Communist Party, 133, 135, 145, 147, 149, 150
Congreso Nacional Indígena (National Indigenous Congress), 134
Córdova, Juan de, 8, 26
Cornejo Polar, Antonio, 37–38, 39, 125, 126, 128

Cortés, Hernán, 28, 106
cosmolectics, 12–13, 15, 20, 39–41, 47, 48, 55, 58, 69, 70, 74, 76, 88, 92–93, 102, 123, 180
cosmovisión, 85
criollos, 12, 39, 126, 148, 164n19
crónicas, 30, 35, 192n40
Cú Choc, Maya, 6, 21, 52, 95, 98, 100; *Recorrido*, 98
Cuevas Cob, Briceida, 10, 21, 70, 91; *U yok'ol auat pek' ti u kuxtal pek' / El quejido del perro en su existencia*, 91
Culturas Populares, 10, 52, 135–36, 165n42
customary law. See *usos y costumbres*

de la Cadena, Marisol, 110, 128
de la Cruz, Víctor, 6, 8, 9, 21, 41, 129, 135, 136
de la Cruz Cruz, Petrona, 112, 113–14
de Landa, Diego (Friar), 26, 28, 66; *An Account of the Things of Yucatán*, 106; *Relación*, 15
de Lión, Luis, 11, 131; *El tiempo principia en Xibalbá* (Time commences in Xibalbá), 131
de los Ángeles, María, 29, 30
del Valle Escalante, Emilio, 11, 39, 47, 55, 145–47, 153
Díaz Ruiz, Angelina, 6, 21, 71, 84, 85, 86, 89–91, 184n73; "Riqueza/K'ulejal" (Wealth), 85, 89
doble mirada, 15, 18. See also double gaze.
double consciousness, 19–20
double gaze, 15–21, 26, 29–30, 40, 43, 44, 45, 49, 53, 54, 58, 69–102, 105, 112, 123, 134, 144, 150–51, 156; strategies of, 109
Dresden Codex, 13, 28, 118
Du Bois, W. E. B., 19

education, 16, 48–52, 74, 77, 84, 88, 89, 91, 109, 111, 117, 128–29, 131, 133–34, 137–39, 141–42, 150–51, 157; bilingual, 50, 51; higher, 1, 52, 84, 89, 157; Western, 142; nation-state, 134, 150; of boys, 94

epistemology, 1, 13, 18, 142, 156
Escuela Normal de Indígenas, 49, 50
Esquit, Edgar, 51
essentialism, 72, 144
ethnography, 46, 47, 53, 66, 67
Eurocentrism, 133, 146, 150

Faudree, Paja, 46
feminism, 72, 120, 123, 146
Fernández Acosta, Nefi, 53
Fernández de Lizardi, José Joaquín, 8; *El periquillo sarniento* (*The Mangy Parrot*), 8
Fortaleza de la Mujer Maya (Strength of the Maya Woman, or FOMMA), 6, 10, 22, 75, 104–5, 110–13, 115–16, 124, 160, 183n63
Foucault, Michel, 54
foundational fictions, 38
Frischmann, Donald, 106, 109, 111

Gabriel Xiquín, Calixta, 6, 22, 52, 95, 96, 97, 160; *Hueso de la tierra*, 95; *Tejiendo los sucesos en el tiempo / Weaving Events in Time*, 97; *X-Teya, U puksi'ik'al ko'olel / Teya, un corazón de mujer* (Teya, heart of a woman), 22, 132, 143
García Canclini, Néstor, 38–39
gender complementarity, 21, 62, 67, 70, 103
gender relations, 70, 105, 115–16, 120, 143
globalization, 9, 182n57
glyphs, 12, 16, 30, 36, 43–44, 45, 157; Maya, 11, 14, 26, 27; glyphic traditions, 45; Zapotec, 27, 34
Gómez Grijalva, Dorotea, 70
Gómez Navarrete, Javier Abelardo, 135, 146, 149
Góngora Pacheco, María Luisa, 74
González, Gaspar Pedro, 6, 19, 21, 42, 130, 132, 160; *La otra cara del maya* (The other face of the Maya), 19, 131; "Stz'ib'," 43
Goody, Jack, 35, 127
Guarcax González, Leonardo Lisandro, 117–18

Guatemala, 51, 95
Guchachi' reza / Iguana rajada (Split iguana) (magazine), 10, 136

Henestrosa, Andrés, 9, 78
Huet Bautista, Nicolás, 21, 48, 53, 58–59, 160; *La última muerte / Ti slajebalxa lajele* (The last death), 48, 53, 58, 63, 66
human sacrifice, 32, 108
hybridity, 38–39

"Indian problem," 22, 128, 133, 134
Indians, 4–5, 13, 39, 46, 106, 108, 128–29, 137, 140, 144, 170n29, 172n60; agraphic nature of, 40; and alcohol, 137; and fiction, 8, 125–26; assimilation of, 49–50; as "inferior race," 3; as literate, 128–29; as noble savage, 25, 191nn18, 21; and orality, 52
indigenista literature, 22, 67, 128–30, 191nn18, 21
indigenista novel, 125, 126, 128, 133
indigenous author, 2, 5, 21, 46–49, 53–54, 62, 66–67, 129, 132, 134, 150
indigenous cosmolectics, 45, 155, 156
indigenous languages, 4, 5, 10, 25, 34, 39, 49, 50, 52, 73–75, 107, 126, 135, 136, 139, 144, 157–58, 192n40
indigenous peoples, 1–3, 6–7, 11, 17, 22, 23, 39, 47, 50, 52, 70, 74, 76, 77, 85, 87–89, 91, 94, 95, 99, 106–8, 124, 128–29, 132–34, 140, 149–50, 154, 157, 165n37, 191n18; and Christianity, 85, 87, 106, 108, 126; and colonialism, 131; contemporary, 119–20; demise of, 126; and Marxism, 89; and migration, 116; and orality, 36, 48; and politics, 134, 136, 150
indigenous theater, 104–6, 109–11, 117, 119
indigenous women, 67, 71, 73, 74, 86, 89, 98, 113, 130, 134, 138, 141, 143, 144, 150, 180n27
Indigenous Writers Association (ELIAC), 11, 54, 160
indio permitido ("the tolerated Indian"), 165n37

intercultural education, 49, 51
intercultural spaces, 48, 103
intertexuality, 40, 59
itzamná, 14, 32
Ixchel, 92, 98
Ixkik (play), 22, 117, 119–23

Jantzen, Grace M., 13, 14
Jiménez Pérez, María Roselia, 74
Jiménez Sánchez, Ajb'ee, 52
Juárez Espinosa, Isabel, 75, 112, 115, 160
Juchitán, 6, 70, 73, 76–77, 80, 180n27

kab'awil, 4, 13–23, 26, 34, 39–40, 43, 45, 47, 48, 51, 52–53, 57–60, 63, 66, 69, 85, 105, 117, 119–20, 122–23, 125, 134, 139; and gender, 16; and poetry, 70–71, 75; as double gaze, 29–30, 40, 44, 105, 141, 150, 151, 156; as ontology, 23, 29, 71, 139, 167n75; as philosophy, 4, 13, 120; view of, 114
kab'awil cosmolectics, 11, 40, 55, 69, 74, 88, 93, 102, 156
kab'awilian strategies, 18, 20, 21, 29, 30, 51, 54, 109, 120, 122, 134, 156–57
Kaqchikel peoples, 11, 12, 17, 94, 96, 98, 117
Krichoff, Paul,
Kukulcán, 55, 57–58

Ladinos, 3, 19, 85, 96, 123, 130, 145, 146, 162n5, 166n52; society of, 100, elites of, 105; hegemony of, 111
Latin alphabet, 9, 10, 26–30, 34–36, 44, 129, 136, 171n58
Laughlin, Robert, 10, 86
Leirana Alcocer, Cristina, 10, 160
Lenkersdorf, Carlos, 14, 166n66
Lepe Lira, Luz María, 38, 46; *Lluvia y viento, puentes de sonido*, 46
letrados, 34, 35, 37, 67, 156, 172n60
Ley orgánica de educación (Organic Education Law), 51
libanas, 7, 30

literary forms, 8, 84, 94, 156, 157
López, Alma, 19–20, 70, 120
López Chiñas, Gabriel, 9, 45, 77–78
López de Gómara, Francisco: *Historia general de las Indias*, 25
López Hernández, Antonio, 52
López K'ana, Josías, 45, 192n40
Lunez Pérez, Enriqueta, 6, 21, 70, 84, 85–88, 91, 160; "La jti jbe' svayel kajvaltik/ Desperté a Dios," 85, 86; *Tajimol ch'ulelaletik/Juego de nahuales*, 87; *Yi'beltak ch'ulelaletik/Raíces del alma* (Roots of the soul), 86

Madrid Codex, 28, 118
Marcos, Sylvia, 69, 71
Marrero, Teresa, 112, 115
Martínez Arias, María Dolores, 88
Martínez Huchim, Ana Patricia, 6, 21, 160; *Chen kolel/Es por demás* (It is pointless), 64; *K'aaylay* (The song of memory), 64; *U k'a'ajasajil u ts'u 'noj K'aax/Recuerdos del corazón de la montaña* (Memories of the heart of the forest), 64; *U Tsikbalil Juntúul Tsíimin Tuunich/El caballo de piedra* (The story of the stone horse), 64; *U tsikbaloób mejen paalal/Cuentos de niños* (Children's stories), 64; ; *U yóol xkaambal jaw xíiw/Contrayerba* (Antidote) 48, 53, 63, 66
Marxism, 89, 124, 143, 144, 145, 146, 148–50, 191n21, 195n92; discourses of, 22, 133–35
Matías García, Yolanda, 76, 131
Matus, Macario, 6, 21, 41
Maya (as term), 83
Maya activism, 83, 84
Maya calendar, 11, 30
Maya civilization, 15, 83, 113, 119, 130; writing tradition of, 15
Maya cosmology, 91, 92, 96
Maya literature, 10, 35, 40, 143, 183n63
mayanidad, 83

Maya'on, 10, 52, 144, 165n42
Maya Peninsula, 10, 74, 76, 83, 91, 134, 146
Maya spirituality, 57, 86, 89
Maya Tsotsil, 52, 58, 59, 71, 86, 89; language of, 183n67
Maya women, 21–22, 52, 64, 66, 71, 74, 93, 95, 96, 100; theater of, 103–24
Maya world, 83, 100, 108
Maya writing, 4, 7, 27, 40, 43, 61
Menchú, Rigoberta, 4, 16, 46, 55
Méndez Torres, Georgina, 73
Mendizábal, Sergio, 13, 166n67
Menéndez y Pelayo, Marcelino, 4
Mesoamerica, 4–7, 12, 16, 18, 20, 25–39, 46, 48, 58, 88, 95, 102, 125, 127, 132, 134, 153–58, 164n20; cuisine of, 65; history of, 27; literature of, 4, 122, 157, 172n60; tradition of, 21, 65; writing system in, 32
Mesoamerican authors, 21, 45
Mesoamerican cosmolectics, 7, 11, 13, 17–18, 29, 44, 48, 53, 55, 58, 60, 66
mestizaje, 38, 50
mestizos, 166n52; identity of, 128, 162n1; literature of, 191n21; paradigm of, 11, 44; sensibility of, 125, 128; theater of, 117; worldview of, 128
Mexico, 4, 5, 6, 10, 14, 21, 22, 25, 28, 30, 34, 38, 39, 49, 52, 61, 74–76, 83, 88, 91, 95, 105, 108–11, 124, 126, 130, 133, 136, 139; cultural activism in, 83; indigenous literature in, 9, 46; Maya in, 40; poetry in, 21; political parties in, 134; social movements in, 51
Mexico City, 2, 6, 49, 50, 85, 126, 136–37, 143
Miano Borruso, Marinella, 79
Mignolo, Walter, 5, 35, 76
Migración (play), 22, 113, 115
migration, 44, 114, 116, 138, 139
Molina Cruz, Mario, 12
Monteforte Toledo, Mario, 129, 132
Montemayor, Carlos, 7, 10, 38, 92 106, 144, 165n42, 183n63, 192n40; *Arte y trama en el cuento indígena*, 38

Morales López, Micaela, 38, 46; *Raíces de la ceiba: Literatura indígena de Chiapas*, 38
Moretti, Franco, 127, 135, 150
Muyulema, Armando, 39, 135

nahuales, 42, 59, 61, 76, 86, 155
Nahuatl language, 25, 27, 75–76, 131
National Indigenista Institute (INI), 52, 109, 111
National Indigenous Writers Association (ELIAC), 2, 11, 54, 77, 160
New Spain, 26, 126, 163n19
Neza (literary journal), 10, 136
Neza Cubi (literary journal), 10
noble savage, 25, 191n18
Noh Tzec, Waldemar, 10

Oaxaca, 6, 10, 26, 27, 30, 70, 73–74, 76, 79, 80, 85, 134, 135, 136, 163n10, 164n21
Obrador, Manuel López, 2
Occidentalism, 76
Ong, Walter, 35
orality, 7, 8, 18, 20–21, 23, 29, 35–39, 44, 45–46, 48, 52, 67, 127, 139, 156
orality/literacy, 37, 39, 127
oral tradition, 8, 30, 37, 38, 39, 40, 42, 44, 45–48, 52–54, 56, 58, 59, 61–64, 67, 88, 113, 115, 129, 139–40, 142–44, 155; and authorship, 47, 53; in novel, 139; myths from, 62; preservation of, 10; and writing, 63, 143–44, 171n58
Ortiz, Angélica, 75

pan-Maya movement, 11, 51, 72, 154
Paris Codex, 28
Past, Ámbar, 18–19; *Incantations: Songs, Spells, and Images by Mayan Women*, 18
patriarchy, 9, 73, 89, 94, 115, 123, 148, 156, 157
Peñate, Juana Karen, 84–85
Pérez, Crisanta, 122–23
Pérez, Emma, 146–47

Pineda Santiago, Irma, 6, 21, 42, 69, 70, 75, 77, 79, 80, 82, 160; "Laanu/Nosotros," 42
politics, 6, 7, 16, 46, 52, 70, 103, 109, 112, 120–21, 134, 145, 150; leftist, 148; neoliberal, 11; of land, 78; of language, 106, 131
polygenesis, 106, 127
Ponce, Alonso, 26
Popol Vuh, 15, 22, 30, 31, 35, 46, 74–75, 93, 105, 120–21, 143, 172n60
preclassic Maya, 14–15
pre-Columbian era, 49, 97; activism and ancestors of Maya, 83; communism of, 89; civilizations of, 17, 31, 34; and double gaze, 20; forms of literature of, 7; history of, 108; images, 16; indigenous writing systems of, 45; literary tradition, 44; and Maya Ch'orti'; philosophy of, 20; references of, 123; as source of art, 30, 118, 123; spirituality of, 57; struggles of, 137; temporalities of, 93; theater of, 105–6, 108, 116; writing of, 13, 19, 26, 28, 29, 30–31, 33–34, 39, 52
pre-Columbian Mesoamerica, 28
print culture, 36, 56, 126
Pythagorean table, 13–14

Quiché, 30–31, 108
Quijano, Anibal, 132, 141
Quijote, El, 18
quincentenary, Columbian, 1, 3, 11

Rabinal Achí (play), 107–8
racism, 3, 73 84, 89, 93, 115, 129, 130, 145
Rama, Ángel, 3, 37, 104, 131; *La ciudad letrada*, 37
rapto, 78–82
Recollet, Karyn, "kinstallations," 12, 13
Republic of Letters, 2, 3, 44, 53, 75, 102
Rey Rosa, Rodrigo, 3
ritual de los bacabes, El, 15, 31, 64
Romero Frizzi, María de los Ángeles, 29

Rousseau, Jean-Jacques, 35
Rubín, Ramón, 129, 132
Ruiz Campbell, Obdulia, 79–80, 82

Salazar Tetzagüic, Manuel de Jesus, 11, 110
Sam Colop, Enrique Luis, 11, 15, 39, 40, 167n74
Sánchez, Mikeas, 75, 84
Sánchez Chan, Feliciano, 10, 18, 47, 160
San Cristóbal de las Casas, Mexico, 11, 85, 105, 111, 112, 114
San Luis Rey Band of Indians, 22, 154
Santopietro, Judith, 76; *Palabras de agua*, 76
Secretaría de Educación Pública (SEP), 49–50, 136
Sen, Clara Alicia, 118, 160
sexism, 20, 72, 74, 89, 140, 144
Sna Jtzibajom (House of the Writer), 10, 105, 111–13
Socialist Party, 146, 191n21
Sololá, Guatemala, 22, 105, 108, 118
Sommer, Doris, 38, 55
Sotz'il Jay Cultural Center, 117, 118
Spain, 18, 25, 28, 34, 126; independence from, 33, 44, 50, 141, 163n15
Spanish colonialism, 25, 83, 107, 115, 131, 132, 137–40, 155
Spanish Crown, 8, 125–26
Sten, María, 27, 107

Taylor, Diana, 104, 111, 119
Tedlock, Dennis, 7, 30, 106–8
testimonio, 44, 47, 55, 66
textiles, 16, 17, 35, 65, 123, 178n71
títulos primordiales, 30
Toledo Paz, Natalia, 1, 6, 12, 21, 70, 77, 79, 81–82, 160; *Mujeres de sol, mujeres de oro*, 81
Townsend, Sarah J., 104, 119
tradition, 5, 7, 17–23, 33, 48, 53–55, 58, 61–62, 81, 85, 88, 94, 95, 109, 112, 116; as ancestral, 119; as cultural, 76, 100; as

literary, 5, 34, 40, 53, 55; as misogynist, 82; as paternalistic, 128; as romantic, 78; and storytelling, 21, 65; and writing, 15, 29, 44, 65
transculturación narrativa, 38
Tsotsil culture, 85–86

Ubico, Jorge, 50, 117
Una mujer desesperada (play), 22, 112–13, 115
Underiner, Tamara, 103, 106, 110–11, 115
Unidad de Escritores Maya-Zoques, La (Unity of Maya-Zoque Writers, or UNEMAZ), 10, 13, 84
usos y costumbres (customary law), 17, 70, 104, 168n96

Vasconcelos, José, 13, 38
Virgin Suyul, 89, 90

Warrior, Robert, 9, 133
Weaver, Jace, 9, 133
weaving, 66, 76, 92, 97, 158, 180n30
Womack, Craig S., 9, 133, 153

Yucatán Peninsula, 10, 30, 31, 52, 54, 64, 70, 83, 85, 143, 146
Yukatek Maya, 39, 154

Zapatismo, 112–13
Zapatista Army for National Liberation, 84
Zapatistas, 112, 134, 193n51; communities of, 84; revolutionaries, 4; uprising of, 84
Zapotec languages, 5, 6, 45, 76, 77, 143, 136
Zapotec literature, 4–9, 12, 18, 20, 27, 39, 44
Zapotec peoples, 6, 41, 104

www.ingramcontent.com/pod-product-compliance
Lightning Source LLC
Chambersburg PA
CBHW021700230426
43668CB00008B/687